A Guide to t
Competition Ac

Peter Freeman, MA (Cantab), Lic Sp en Dr Eur (Brussels),
Solicitor, Partner, Simmons & Simmons

Richard Whish, BA, BCL (Oxon), Solicitor,
Professor of Law, King's College, London

Butterworths
London, Edinburgh, Dublin
1999

United Kingdom	Butterworths a Division of Reed Elsevier (UK) Ltd, Halsbury House, 35 Chancery Lane, LONDON WC2A 1EL and 4 Hill Street, EDINBURGH EH2 3JZ
Australia	Butterworths, a Division of Reed International Books Australia Pty Ltd, CHATSWOOD, New South Wales
Canada	Butterworths Canada Ltd, MARKHAM, Ontario
Hong Kong	Butterworths Asia (Hong Kong), HONG KONG
India	Butterworths India, NEW DELHI
Ireland	Butterworth (Ireland) Ltd, DUBLIN
Malaysia	Malayan Law Journal Sdn Bhd, KUALA LUMPUR
New Zealand	Butterworths of New Zealand Ltd, WELLINGTON
Singapore	Butterworths Asia, SINGAPORE
South Africa	Butterworths Publishers (Pty) Ltd, DURBAN
USA	Lexis Law Publishing, CHARLOTTESVILLE, Virginia

© Reed Elsevier (UK) Ltd 1999

All rights reserved. No part of this publication may be reproduced in any material form (including photocopying or storing it in any medium by electronic means and whether or not transiently or incidentally to some other use of this publication) without the written permission of the copyright owner except in accordance with the provisions of the Copyright, Designs and Patents Act 1988 or under the terms of a licence issued by the Copyright Licensing Agency Ltd, 90 Tottenham Court Road, London, England W1P 0LP. Applications for the copyright owner's written permission to reproduce any part of this publication should be addressed to the publisher.

Warning: The doing of an unauthorised act in relation to a copyright work may result in both a civil claim for damages and criminal prosecution.

Any Crown copyright material is reproduced with the permission of the Controller of Her Majesty's Stationery Office.

Peter Freeman and Richard Whish have asserted their rights under the Copyright, Designs and Patents Act 1988 to be identified as the authors of this work.

A CIP Catalogue record for this book is available from the British Library.

ISBN 0 406 90521 5

Printed and bound in Great Britain by Redwood Books, Trowbridge, Wiltshire

Visit us at our website: http//www.butterworths.co.uk

Preface

The Competition Act 1998 comes exactly fifty years after the first UK competition statute and twenty five years after the Fair Trading Act 1973. It may therefore have to last for a quarter of a century at least. The Act seeks to bring UK competition law into line with its European equivalent whilst preserving its national flavour. Although much elaboration of the meaning of the Act's provisions is still to come, and many of the procedural aspects have still to be worked out, there is, we believe, a value in producing an initial guide covering the Act's provisions and such interpretative material as has so far been produced.

This book is not a text book of EC competition law; and it does not pretend to describe UK competition law as a whole. It is intended instead to introduce the reader to the provisions of the new Act, to explain how they relate to EC competition law and to explore some of the complexities that are already apparent. It is our contribution to the task of understanding and explaining this landmark legislation.

We owe our thanks to our respective, and mutual, friends and colleagues, particularly those at Simmons & Simmons and King's College, who have been willing to discuss numerous points of interpretation. We wish to thank Derek Morris and others in the MMC for reading Chapter 5; also Margaret Bloom and Henry Emden of the OFT for answering our queries. In addition, thanks go to Richard's research assistant Manish Das for some assiduous research on Chapter 2; to Jenny Block of Simmons & Simmons for her comments on Chapter 9; to Peter's secretary Jean Corrie, who typed the manuscript; and to the editorial team at Butterworths for their meticulous work on the text and appendices and general support.

Responsibility for any opinions and errors is ours alone. In a situation where draft material is still emanating from the authorities and former drafts are re-appearing in final form, any cut-off date is necessarily arbitrary. Therefore, we have taken the position as it stands on 5 March 1999.

Peter Freeman
Partner
Simmons & Simmons
London and Brussels

Richard Whish
Solicitor
Professor of Law
King's College, London

March 1999

Contents

Contents

Table of Statutes

Table of Statutory Instruments

Table of EC Legislation, Treaties and Conventions

Table of Cases

**Decisions of the European Court of Justice are listed below numerically. These
decisions are also included in the preceding alphabetical list.**

Table of Cases

Table of DGFT's guidelines

The following is a list of guidelines issued by the DGFT in the first week of March 1999—

The guidelines can be found on the OFT website at—

http://www.oft.gov.uk/html/new/guide-ln.htm

1 History and background

1.1   The domestic competition law of the UK has developed in a piecemeal fashion over the last 50 years. The first legislation to be enacted was the Monopolies and Restrictive Practices (Inquiry and Control) Act 1948, which established the Monopolies and Restrictive Practices Commission, a direct ancestor of the Competition Commission established by the Competition Act 1998. After the 1948 Act, there followed numerous additions to the domestic legislation, in particular the Restrictive Trade Practices Acts 1956, 1968, 1976 and 1977, the Resale Prices Acts 1964 and 1976, the Fair Trading Act 1973 (FTA 1973), the Competition Act 1980, the Companies Act 1989 and the Deregulation and Contracting Out Act 1994.

THE MOVEMENT TOWARDS REFORM[1]

1.2   The system of domestic law that resulted from this legislation was complex, difficult to apply, and in numerous respects defective. As long ago as 1978–79 two Green Papers were published, entitled 'A Review of Monopolies and Mergers Policy'[2] and 'A Review of Restrictive Trade Practices Policy',[3] suggesting the need for certain modifications of the law. The latter of these two Green Papers led to the provisions for the control of anti-competitive practices contained in the Competition Act 1980, but the legislation on restrictive trade practices and on resale prices remained in place.

---

[1]   See generally Wilks 'The Prolonged Reform of UK Competition Policy' in *Comparative Competition Policy* eds Doern and Wilks (1996), Oxf UP.
[2]   Cmnd 7198 (May 1978).
[3]   Cmnd 7512 (March 1979).

The Green and White Papers of 1988–89

1.3   Dissatisfaction with the law on restrictive trade practices led to the publication in 1988 of the Green Paper 'Review of Restrictive Trade Practices Policy: a Consultative Document',[1] in which the Government suggested that the restrictive trade practices legislation should be fundamentally altered, and should be modelled upon the Treaty of Rome (the EC Treaty), Art 81.[2] After a period of consultation, the Government published the White Paper 'Opening Markets: New Policy on Restrictive Trade Practices',[3] in which it confirmed its intention to proceed along these lines. However no Bill was forthcoming, so the highly unsatisfactory Restrictive Trade Practices Act 1976 remained in place, notwithstanding the numerous weaknesses that had been set out so clearly in the Green and White Papers.

---

[1]   Cm 331 (March 1988).
[2]   In this book we will use the Treaty Articles as renumbered by the Treaty of Amsterdam, on the assumption that the latter will be ratified by all the Member States and enter into force in 1999. In the

new numbering, the former Art 85 becomes Art 81; Art 86 becomes Art 82; Art 90 becomes Art 86
and Art 177 becomes Art 234. See Appendix 2 for text of these Articles.
3   Cm 727 (July 1989).

The Green Paper of 1992

1.4   The next Green Paper on the reform of domestic competition law dealt not
with restrictive trade practices, but rather with the control of firms with significant
market power. In 'Abuse of Market Power: a Consultative Document on Possible
Legislative Options'[1] the Government examined the case for introducing stronger
provisions, modelled upon the EC Treaty, Art 82,[2] to deal with this problem. Views
were sought from the business community and other interested parties on a range of
options, including, most radically, the introduction of a prohibition system based on
Art 82. The responses to the Green Paper were varied and inconsistent, and the
Government announced that rather than taking the radical option, it would instead
seek to strengthen the existing legislation (FTA 1973 and the Competition Act 1980)
to deal with some of the criticisms. As in the case of the restrictive trade practices
proposals, however, no Bill was forthcoming, and the law remained unreformed.

1   Cm 2100 (November 1992).
2   See para 1.3, fn 2.

The Consultative Document and the draft Bill of 1996

1.5   During the debate on the Queen's Speech in the autumn of 1995, the President
of the Board of Trade, Ian Lang, announced to the House of Commons on
20 November that the Government would proceed with a consultation exercise for
fundamental reform of domestic competition law. In March 1996 the consultation
document 'Tackling Cartels and the Abuse of Market Power: Implementing the
Government's Policy for Competition Law Reform' was published.[1] This repeated the
proposals that had been suggested earlier, namely that legislation modelled upon
Art 81 should be introduced to deal with the problems of restrictive trade practices,
but that the issue of market power should be addressed by a strengthening of the
current law rather than by adopting a prohibition system based upon Art 82.
Following a period of consultation, the Government published, in August 1996, an
explanatory document 'Tackling Cartels and the Abuse of Market Power: a Draft Bill'.[2]
This set out not only the Government's proposals and a summary of the results of the
consultation procedure, but also a draft Bill running to 54 clauses and five schedules. It
seemed that, at last, reform of the law would become a reality. However, the Queen's
Speech of November 1996 did not contain any mention of a Competition Bill, and
the Conservative Government lost the general election on 1 May 1997. It was now
necessary to await the proposals of the new Labour Government.

1   DTI, March 1996 (URN 96/760).
2   DTI, August 1996 (URN 96/905).The Labour Government's proposals of 1997

The Labour Government's proposals of 1997

1.6   The Labour Party manifesto of 1997 set out plans to adopt a tough prohibition
approach for competition law. Upon election, the new Government announced in

the Queen's Speech on 14 May 1997 its intention to 'bring forward legislation to reform and strengthen competition law'. In relation to restrictive trade practices, the Government broadly agreed with its predecessor that a system modelled upon Art 81 should be introduced. However, in relation to the abuse of market power, the new Government announced that it would opt for the 'radical' solution of introducing a prohibition based upon Art 82, although it would also retain the scale and complex monopoly provisions in FTA 1973.

THE COMPETITION ACT 1998

Passage of the Competition Bill through Parliament

1.7   A Consultation Document[1] and a working draft Competition Bill were published in August 1997 and the Bill itself was published in October 1997—the DTI received over 150 responses to this round of consultation. The Competition Bill was introduced into the House of Lords and received its first reading on 15 October 1997. It received Royal Assent on 9 November 1998 and will fully enter into force on 1 March 2000. The full chronology of the Bill's passage through Parliament is set out in Appendix 1.

---

[1]   'A prohibition approach to anti-competitive agreements and abuse of dominant position' (URN 97/803).

1.8   The passage of the Competition Bill proved to be at times controversial, and numerous issues—for example the possible exclusion of pharmacies from the legislation, the issue of predatory pricing in the newspaper industry, the powers of the various sectoral regulators, the possibility of using this legislative opportunity to repeal the Patents Act 1977, ss 44 and 45, and the treatment of vertical agreements—were the subject of quite heated debate. These matters are recorded in detail in Hansard, and there will be many occasions, particularly in the light of the House of Lords' judgment in *Pepper v Hart,*[1] on which it will be helpful to refer to the debates in Parliament, and in particular to many of the statements of Lord Simon of Highbury in the House of Lords, in order to understand fully how the Act and some of its provisions are intended to operate.

---

[1]   [1993] AC 593.

OVERVIEW OF THE LEGISLATION

1.9   The Competition Act 1998 is a complex and technical piece of legislation. It is divided into four parts, as follows—
> Pt I—Competition;
> Pt II—Investigations in relation to Articles 81 and 82 (formerly Arts 85 and 86; see para 1.3, fn 2);
> Pt III—Monopolies;
> Pt IV—Supplemental and Transitional.

Part I—Competition

Introduction

1.10 The most important provisions in the Competition Act 1998 are contained in Pt I, and the major part of our text will be concerned with this Part. In particular it introduces offences that are modelled closely upon Art 81 (the 'Chapter I prohibition') and Art 82 (the 'Chapter II prohibition') of the EC Treaty, while repealing the Restrictive Trade Practices Acts 1976 and 1977, the Restrictive Practices Court Act 1976, the Resale Prices Act 1976 and most of the Competition Act 1980. It confers substantial powers of investigation and enforcement on the Director General of Fair Trading (the DGFT) and the other sectoral regulators such as the Director General of Telecommunications, and establishes a new Competition Commission with a variety of roles, including the hearing of appeals against decisions of the DGFT and of the relevant regulators.

1.11 Part I of the Competition Act 1998 is divided into five Chapters, as follows—
    Ch I—Agreements;
    Ch II—Abuse of dominant position;
    Ch III—Investigation and enforcement;
    Ch IV—The Competition Commission and appeals;
    Ch V—Miscellaneous.

Part II—Investigations in relation to Arts 81 and 82

1.12 Part II of the 1998 Act gives power to a judge of the High Court to issue a warrant for the DGFT to enter premises in connection with an investigation requested by the European Commission under EC law. Curiously, there has never been any legislation to deal with this situation, and the 1998 Act rectifies this omission.[1]

---

[1]   See paras 4.28–4.30.

Part III—Monopolies

1.13 Part III of the 1998 Act makes some changes to the monopoly provisions of FTA 1973, in particular by amending the powers of the DGFT to obtain information. As will be explained in Ch 8, the monopoly provisions contained in FTA 1973 have been retained, notwithstanding the introduction of the 'Chapter II prohibition' for the abuse of dominance. It is likely that the FTA 1973 system will be used less in the future, but the Act nevertheless makes a few improvements to the system for those cases in which it will continue to be used.

Part IV—Supplemental and transitional

1.14 Part IV of the 1998 Act contains various supplemental and transitional provisions, including the repeal of the Patents Act 1977, ss 44 and 45, and provisions on Crown application. These are explained in Ch 10.

Schedules

1.15 The 14 Schedules to the Act contain much important detail, for example on exclusions, notifications, regulators and transitional provisions.

Guidelines and procedural rules

1.16 The Competition Act 1998 requires the DGFT and the sectoral regulators to publish guidance as to how it will operate in practice, and already there are some guidelines published[1] while further draft guidelines are in existence in relation to which a consultation process is taking place. We have commented in the text on the guidelines where appropriate.

---

1   See Table of DGFT's guidelines at p xxv.

1.17 Procedural rules are in preparation which deal with the way in which the DGFT will proceed in the handling of notifications and investigations, as well as rules to deal with appeals to the newly-constituted appeal tribunals of the Competition Commission. The DGFT's directions 'Early guidance' and Form EG for seeking such guidance are set out in Appendix 3.[1]

---

[1]   Two useful websites containing up-to-date information about the preparations for the entry into force of the 1998 Act are that of the DTI (http://www.dti.gov.uk.competition.bill) and that of the OFT (http://www.oft.gov.uk/html/new/act.htm). See para 11.3.

OUTLINE OF THIS BOOK

1.18 As will be clear from the foregoing, the Competition Act 1998, in conjunction with its associated guidelines, rules, etc, amounts to a very large amount of new material for lawyers and their clients to absorb. In the text that follows, we will begin with a description of the Chapter I and Chapter II prohibitions. We will then describe the provisions in the 1998 Act on procedure and enforcement (Ch 4). Chapter 5 deals with institutions and appeals, while Ch 6 considers the extremely important, though somewhat complex, relationship between the provisions in the Act and EC law. In Ch 7 we consider how the 1998 Act will impact upon 'special sectors' (telecommunications, energy, water and railways). Chapter 8 describes the continuing, albeit limited, role that the monopoly provisions in the FTA 1973 will play in domestic competition law. Chapter 9 sets out the very important transitional provisions. After dealing with various miscellaneous matters in Ch 10, we conclude with some thoughts on what lawyers and their clients should be doing between now and 1 March 2000 to prepare for the new legislative regime.

2 Anti-competitive agreements and exemptions

INTRODUCTION

2.1 The Competition Act 1998 (the 1998 Act) controls anti-competitive agreements by means of a new prohibition modelled upon the Treaty of Rome (the EC Treaty), Art 81. The old and very complex system of control of restrictive trade practices and resale price maintenance is abolished.

2.2 The Chapter I prohibition is contained in the 1998 Act, ss 1–16 (Ch I). This Chapter is arranged under five headings as follows—Introduction (s 1); The Prohibition (s 2); Excluded agreements (s 3, together with Schs 1–4); Exemptions (ss 4–11); Notifications (ss 12–16).[1] In addition, s 50 provides for the exclusion of vertical agreements and agreements relating to land. These provisions will also be considered in this chapter (see paras 2.75–2.91).

---

[1]   The provisions on notification are described in paras 4.33–4.48.

2.3   Section 1 provides that the following four Acts will cease to have effect—
   (a) the Restrictive Practices Court Act 1976;
   (b) the Restrictive Trade Practices Act 1976 (RTPA 1976);
   (c) the Resale Prices Act 1976;
   (d) the Restrictive Trade Practices Act 1977.

These repeals will take effect on the appointed day, which is intended to be 1 March 2000.[1] The timing of the coming into force of the 1998 Act and the complex transitional arrangements that it contains are described in detail in Chs 9 and 10.

---

[1]   Statement of Lord Simon of Highbury, Minister for Trade & Industry to House of Lords 20 October 1998 (HL Consideration of Commons' Amendments, 20 October 1998, col 1337).

CHAPTER I PROHIBITION[1]

2.4   Section 2 contains the Chapter I prohibition itself. This prohibition is closely modelled upon the EC Treaty, Art 81(1), although it is by no means identical in every respect.[2] It is worthwhile breaking down s 2 for consideration, and pointing out relevant differences between the Chapter I prohibition and Art 81(1) where appropriate.

---

1   See generally the DGFT's guidelines 'The major provisions', 'The Chapter I prohibition' and 'Trade associations, professions and self-regulating bodies'.
2   For a detailed discussion of Art 81, see *Butterworths Competition Law* I–III; Bellamy and Child *Common Market Law of Competition* (ed Rose) (4th edn, 1993), Chs 2–5, 7.

Section 2(1): the prohibition

2.5   Section 2(1) provides that—

'Subject to section 3, agreements between undertakings, decisions by associations of undertakings or concerted practices which—

(a)   may affect trade within the United Kingdom, and

(b)   have as their object or effect the prevention, restriction or distortion of competition within the United Kingdom,

are prohibited unless they are exempt in accordance with the provisions of this Part.'

'Subject to section 3'

2.6   Section 3 provides for a wide range of agreements to be excluded from the Chapter I prohibition. These exclusions are considered in detail in paras 2.38–2.68. It is also necessary to bear in mind the exclusion for vertical and land agreements under s 50. This is discussed in paras 2.75–2.91 below.

'Agreements between undertakings, decisions by associations of undertakings or concerted practices'

2.7   These words are identical to those in Art 81(1), with the minor exception that the word 'or' in s 2(1) replaces 'and' in Art 81(1). These expressions are ones that have been considered in numerous judgments of the European Court of First Instance (CFI) and the European Court of Justice (ECJ) which, as a general proposition, the DGFT, the Competition Commission (CC) and the domestic courts in the UK are obliged to follow as a result of the 1998 Act, s 60.[1]

---

[1]   For discussion of s 60, see paras 6.15–6.30.

'Undertakings'

2.8   As in the case of Community law,[1] this term will be interpreted broadly by the DGFT to include any natural or legal persons capable of carrying on commercial or economic activities relating to goods or services.[2] Also, depending on the facts of each case, a parent company and its subsidiaries will be treated as one undertaking where the subsidiaries lack economic independence.[3]

---

[1]   On the meaning of undertakings in Community law, see *Butterworths Competition Law* I [107]–[124].

[2]   See DGFT's guidelines 'The major provisions', para 1.9, and 'The Chapter I prohibition', para 2.5.

[3]   DGFT's guidelines 'The Chapter I prohibition', para 2.6.

2.9   The Chapter I prohibition applies to agreements 'between undertakings', but certain provisions of the Act refer to 'persons' rather than undertakings. The reason for this appears to be that in certain contexts the word 'person' is a more appropriate expression. However, in order to prevent undertakings arguing to the contrary, s 59 provides that the expression 'persons' includes 'undertakings'.[1]

1   See HL Report Stage, 23 February 1998, cols 511–512; and see para 4.3.

Agreements

2.10 This term is construed widely in Community law.[1] The Guidelines state that agreements may be spoken or written and need not be legally binding.[2] A reluctant participant to an agreement can still be liable.[3]

1   See *Butterworths Competition Law* I [126]–[129].
2   See DGFT's guidelines 'The major provisions', para 1.9, and 'The Chapter I prohibition', para 2.7.
3   DGFT's guidelines 'The Chapter I prohibition', para 2.8.

'Decisions by associations of undertakings'

2.11 This expression has been broadly interpreted in Community law,[1] and the DGFT will rely heavily on EC law in its interpretation. The term 'decision' will have a broad meaning which includes recommendations, the management decisions of trade associations and their rules.

1   See *Butterworths Competition Law* I [130]–[141].

2.12 The crucial issue for the DGFT is not the form of the decision or the method by which it was adopted, but the possibility of it having the effect of limiting the freedom of action of the associations' members in commercial matters.[1] The guidelines provide examples of 'decisions' as follows—[2]
(a) recommendations to members which can be said to have an appreciable effect on competition in the market in question;
(b) oral statements which are intended to be followed by members;
(c) constitutional rules of an association which are an agreement that all members must follow.

1   DGFT's guidelines 'Trade associations, professional bodies and self-regulatory organisations', para 2.2.
2   Ibid at paras 2.3 and 2.4.

2.13 The effect of these decisions on the UK market will depend to a certain extent on the size of the membership of the association concerned: the broader the membership of an association, the greater the influence of the association is likely to be.[1] If members are required to follow a code of practice, it will have a greater impact on the market if a large number of them are required to follow it.

1   See DGFT's guidelines 'Trade associations, professional bodies and self-regulatory organisations', para 5.3.

'Concerted practices'

2.14 This expression will be interpreted in line with ECJ jurisprudence[1] which identifies the main elements of a concerted practice as a form of practical cooperation, knowingly entered into by the parties, which is intended to amount to a substitution for competition in the market.[2] Furthermore, contacts or communications which influence market behaviour, depending on the nature of the contact or the effect, or even potential effect, on competition, may also be caught if the conduct leads to, or would have led to, a different result had the undertakings not embarked on this conduct.[3]

---

1   See *Butterworths Competition Law* I [142]–161].
2   Case 48/69 *ICI v EC Commission 'Dyestuffs'* [1972] ECR 619, [1972] CMLR 557.
3   Cases 40–48, 50, 54–56, 111, 113 and 114/73 *Suiker Unie v EC Commission* [1975] ECR 1663, [1976] 1 CMLR 295.

2.15 The DGFT will take into account the structure of the relevant market and the nature of the product involved in assessing whether there is a concerted practice. In oligopolistic markets, the DGFT recognises that there may be similar behaviour by undertakings without any type of collusion. But the DGFT will examine the form of any apparent co-ordination in order to determine whether there is a concerted practice or not; for example price leadership on its own may be innocent, but where there is price leadership coupled with frequent communication this could fall foul of the Chapter I prohibition.

2.16 The DGFT recognises that parallel behaviour is not of itself evidence of collusion, and refers to the jurisprudence of the ECJ in *Dyestuffs*.[1] Therefore, it will need to be shown that such behaviour would be inexplicable unless there had been contact between undertakings, in order for the DGFT to be able to conclude that there had been a breach of the Chapter I prohibition.

---

1   See para 2.14, fn 2.

2.17 In any consideration of a concerted practice, the DGFT will conduct an economic assessment. However he will be more likely to conclude that there is a concerted practice where there are few undertakings sharing the market and with similar cost structures and outputs.[1]

---

1   DGFT's guidelines 'The Chapter I prohibition', para 2.13.

'May affect trade within the United Kingdom'

2.18 The obvious point about this expression is that there is no requirement under s 2(1) that trade *between Member States* may be affected, only that trade *within the United Kingdom* should be affected. The result is that in so far as an agreement affects both trade between Member States and trade within the UK, it may be subject both to Art 81(1) and to the Chapter I prohibition.[1] The consequences of this situation are as follows—

  (a) there is a possibility of an undertaking or undertakings being fined more than once in relation to the same agreement. However s 38(9) provides that the DGFT must take into account any fine that has been imposed by the European Commission or any court or body in another Member State (see para 4.65);
  (b) there may be circumstances in which both the DGFT and the European Commission will have jurisdiction in relation to the same agreement.[2] In

that case, the question will arise as to which of the two authorities is the appropriate one to investigate (see paras 6.31–6.46).

(c) there may be circumstances in which the parties to an agreement will consider notifying for an individual exemption both under Art 81(3) and under the 1998 Act, s 4 (see paras 6.31–6.46).

---

1   See DGFT's guidelines 'The Chapter I prohibition', para 7.2.
2   Case 14/68 *Wilhelm v Bundeskartellamt* [1969] ECR 1; Case C–7/97 *Oscar Bronner v Mediaprint* [1999] CMLR 112 at para 19.

Extra-territorial application

2.19 It should be noted that s 2(1) does not deal with the issue of whether the 1998 Act has extra-territorial application: this issue is dealt with in s 2(3) (see paras 2.25–2.29).

Section 2(2): illustrative list

2.20 Section 2(2) provides that—

'Subsection (1) applies, in particular, to agreements, decisions or practices which—

(a)   directly or indirectly fix purchase or selling prices or any other trading conditions;

(b)   limit or control production, markets, technical development or investment;

(c)   share markets or sources of supply;

(d)   apply dissimilar conditions to equivalent transactions with other trading parties, thereby placing them at a competitive disadvantage;

(e)   make the conclusion of contracts subject to acceptance by the other parties of supplementary obligations which, by their nature or according to commercial usage, have no connection with the subject of such contracts.'

2.21 This list, which exemplifies the sorts of agreement which would infringe s 2(1), is identical to the list in Art 81(1). However, it is of vital importance to understand that Art 81(1) has been applied to many other agreements that are *not* explicitly mentioned in the list. For example, an agreement to exchange information about sales, which enables manufacturers to know the market position and strategy of their competitors in an oligopolistic market, has been found by the ECJ to be caught by Art 81(1),[1] although there is no specific reference to information exchanges therein. This is because the list is merely illustrative and in each case the critical issue is whether the agreement has as its object or effect the prevention, restriction or distortion of competition. A further example would be an exclusive purchasing agreement, for example where a brewer of beer requires a retail customer to purchase beer exclusively from it for a period of time. Again there is no specific reference to this kind of agreement in Art 81(1), but the Court of Justice has held that such an agreement is capable in principle of infringement, although a detailed analysis of the factual, legal and economic context in which the agreement is operative is necessary before an assessment can be made of whether it actually does have the effect of restricting competition.[2] The DGFT's guidelines 'The Chapter I prohibition' set out examples of agreements that could infringe s 2(2) at paras 3.5–3.28.

¹   Case C–7/95P *John Deere Limited v EC Commission* [1998] 5 CMLR 311.
²   Case C–234/89 *Delimitis v Henninger Bräu* [1991] ECR I–935, [1992] 5 CMLR 210.

2.22   Section 2(2)(d) and (e) suggest that agreements to discriminate (s 2(2)(d)) and agreements to tie one good or service with another (s 2(2)(e)) may amount to infringements of Art 81 or the Chapter I prohibition. It is fair to point out, however, that in the history of the application of Art 81 by the Commission, there have been very few such cases under Art 81(1)(d) and (e). Discrimination and tie-ins are matters which usually give rise to concern in competition policy only where there is market power on the part of the party which is practising discrimination or which is imposing the tie. For this reason, these phenomena are usually investigated, if at all, under Art 82 rather than under Art 81.[1]

¹   See for example Case 85/76 *Hoffmann-la Roche v EC Commission* [1979] ECR 461; Case T–30/89 *Hilti AG v Commission* [1991] ECR II–1439.

Appreciability

2.23   The Chapter I prohibition will be applicable only where an agreement brings about an *appreciable* restriction of competition. This is a key feature of the prohibition: the Government has no desire that the new legislation should catch agreements that could not, in practice, have a significant impact upon the market. However, the requirement that the impact on competition should be appreciable is not to be found in the legislation itself, but rather is to be found in the case-law of the Court of Justice.[1] This issue was the subject of debate in the House of Lords where it was argued by some of their Lordships that a specific linguistic amendment ought to be made in order to show that a finding of appreciability was needed. Lord Simon however rejected the argument that the wording of the Chapter I prohibition needed to be changed to include 'significant' or 'appreciable',[2] since the relevant EC jurisprudence would apply anyway by virtue of s 60. This view is sensible—s 60 will indeed bring in the jurisprudence of the Court on this matter, which is likely itself to develop over time. Had the UK attempted to legislate specifically for appreciability, there is every possibility that the words used domestically might turn out to be at variance with the evolving case-law in Europe.

¹   Case 5/69 *Völk v Vervaecke* [1969] ECR 295; Case 22/71 *Béguelin Import v GL Import Export* [1971] ECR 949; Cases T–374, 375, 384, 388/94 *European Night Services v EC Commission* [1998] 5 CMLR 718.
²   See for example HL Report Stage, 9 February 1998, cols 884–888.

2.24   The view that the DGFT intends to take in relation to appreciability[1] is that, as a general proposition, an agreement will have no appreciable effect on competition if the undertakings' combined market share of the relevant market[2] does not exceed 25%. However the DGFT will generally consider any agreement which—

   (a)   directly or indirectly fixes prices or shares markets; or
   (b)   imposes minimum resale prices; or
   (c)   is one of a network of similar agreements which have a cumulative effect on the market in question

as being capable of having an appreciable effect, even where the undertakings' combined market share falls below the 25% threshold.[3] In calculating the market share, the DGFT will take into account the parties to the agreement and also parents, subsidiaries and affiliates.[4] The DGFT has said an agreement may still not have an appreciable effect even where the parties have a market share in excess of 25%.[5] The DGFT will not look at turnover when considering appreciability since turnover in itself is unlikely to provide much indication of the parties' market power. However, turnover will be one of the relevant criteria under s 36 in determining whether immunity from fines will be available for small agreements.[6]

---

[1]   See generally DGFT's guidelines 'The Chapter I prohibition', paras 2.18–2.22.
[2]   On market definition, see the European Commission's 'Notice on the definition of relevant market for the purposes of Community competition law' OJ C372, 9.12.97, p 5; DGFT's guidelines 'Market definition', in particular para 1.3, which states that the DGFT, in defining markets for the purposes of this Act, will do so consistently with the Commission Notice. See para 3.15 below.
[3]   DGFT's guidelines 'The Chapter I prohibition', para 2.20.
[4]   Ibid at para 2.22.
[5]   Ibid at para 2.21.
[6]   See paras 4.66–4.67.

Section 2(3): extra-territorial application

2.25   Section 2(3) provides that—

> 'Subsection (1) applies only if the agreement, decision or practice is, or is intended to be, implemented in the United Kingdom.'

As we have already seen, s 2(1) requires that the agreement may affect trade and competition within the UK. However, those requirements do not in themselves answer the jurisdictional question of whether the Act is applicable to undertakings that are located outside the UK. For example, if two US companies were to agree the price that they would charge to UK customers, it would be necessary to know whether they are subject to the Act (so-called 'subject-matter' jurisdiction) and whether they are subject to the provisions in the Act on investigation and enforcement (so-called 'enforcement jurisdiction').

2.26   The traditional view in the UK has been hostile to the extra-territorial application of competition law, in particular on the part of the USA which has claimed the right to jurisdiction in relation to economic behaviour outside its territory, provided that that behaviour produced substantial and foreseeable effects within the USA[1] (the so-called 'effects doctrine'). So hostile has the UK view been to the 'effects doctrine' that diplomatic notes have been exchanged between the UK and the US complaining of wrongful assertions of jurisdiction.[2] As a result, the Protection of Trading Interests Act 1980 was passed, inter alia, to prevent what would be regarded as an excessive claim to jurisdiction.[3] However, the UK has accepted that jurisdiction can be asserted in relation to conduct that is carried out within the territory of a particular Member State.

---

[1]   Restatement (Third) of Foreign Relations Law of the United States § 403.
[2]   See Lowe *Extraterritorial Jurisdiction* (1983), pp 144–147.
[3]   See *Butterworths Competition Law* XII [128]–[147].

2.27   The issue of extra-territoriality in Community law was considered by the Court of Justice in the so-called *Wood Pulp* case.[1] This case was concerned with an alleged cartel between wood-pulp producers in several non-EC states. The Court of

Justice declined to opine on the existence of an 'effects doctrine', despite an invitation in the pleadings of the Commission to hold that such a doctrine did exist in Community law. However, the Court held that Art 81(1) would apply to an agreement or concerted practice entered into between non-EC undertakings outside the EC, if the agreement or concerted practice was to be 'implemented' within the EC. This solution of the problem on the facts of the case was a nimble compromise; without adopting the controversial 'effects doctrine', the Court was able to assert jurisdiction on the basis that something had been done within the Community, in this case the charging of customers at a cartelised price.

---

[1]   Cases 89, 104, 114, 116–117, 125–129/85 etc *A Ahlstrom Oy v EC Commission* [1988] ECR 5913.

2.28   Section 2(3) is intended to give legislative effect in the UK to the *Wood Pulp* doctrine.[1] This is a sensible resolution on the part of the Government: as already mentioned, the *Wood Pulp* doctrine falls short of being an 'effects doctrine', with the result that s 2(3) does not amount to a reversal of the traditional attitude of the UK described above (see para 2.26). At the same time, the 1998 Act is able to adopt a position in relation to jurisdiction which is consistent with EC law as set out in *Wood Pulp*. Agreements implemented in the UK by non-UK undertakings would be caught by the Chapter I prohibition provided that they meet all the other requirements. What will be interesting in the future will be a situation in which the Court of Justice chooses to extend the jurisdictional reach of the competition rules to include an effects doctrine. In such a situation, the basic rule in s 60, ie to ensure that there is no inconsistency between the UK legislation and principles laid down in the Treaty and by the Court, would suggest that the UK should adopt the effects doctrine. However, s 60(1) specifically provides that consistency must be achieved, 'having regard to any relevant differences between the provisions concerned' (see s 60(1) and para 6.18). Presumably this would be a situation in which the clear wording of s 2(3) would indicate a relevant difference between the 1998 Act and the new case-law of the Court, with the consequence that the UK authorities would not be required under the Act to adopt the effects doctrine.

---

[1]   HL Committee, 13 November 1997, col 261 (Lord Simon of Highbury).

2.29   The guidelines are silent on the issue of extra-territoriality, which perhaps is itself indicative of the delicate and complex nature of this particular issue. It is noticeable that there is no equivalent to s 2(3) in the Chapter II prohibition (see para 3.5). Neither the 1998 Act nor the guidelines indicate how export cartels will be treated. They were excluded from RTPA 1976, by Sch 3, para 6, in the case of goods and Sch 3, para 9, in the case of services, provided that the restrictions only had overseas operation. Under the 1998 Act, the key question would be whether an export cartel could affect trade and competition within the UK. This would be an empirical question, turning on the facts of the particular case. For example, if there was a substantial price difference between the UK market and overseas markets, the latter being lower in price, there might be a possibility of parallel imports back into the UK. The ECJ's judgment in *Javico v Yves St Laurent* provides some guidance on this issue.[1]

---

[1]   Case C–306/96 [1998] 5 CMLR 172.

Section 2(4): voidness

2.30   Section 2(4) provides that—

'Any agreement or decision which is prohibited by subsection (1) is void.'

This mirrors the EC Treaty, Art 81(2). The possibility that agreements may be void is of immense significance in Community competition law. The fact that undertakings can be fined for infringing Art 81(1) is a major deterrent—however for many firms it is the possibility that their agreements may turn out to be unenforceable that has as much, and in many cases more, significance. An enormous compliance effort has to be maintained in order to ensure that important commercial transactions will not be undermined by one or more parties to an agreement subsequently reneging on it and claiming it to be unenforceable.

2.31   There seems to be little doubt that the judicial mind is at times unsympathetic to the Art 81(2) defence, where one party to an agreement attempts to walk away from it on the ground that it is void under competition law. *Pacta sunt servanda* has a powerful influence where one person purports, on the basis of a 'technicality' of competition law, to walk away from an agreement. This was attempted in the George Michael case,[1] where the singer sought to argue that his contract with Sony to produce music was in restraint of trade at common law and an infringement of Art 85 (Art 81), and was therefore void and unenforceable. The court rejected both claims in a fairly peremptory manner. There are numerous other examples of this.[2] However, where it is indeed the case that an agreement infringes Art 81(1) and has no possibility of being exempted under Art 81(3), there is no doubt that it, or parts of it, will be unenforceable (see paras 2.32–2.33). Article 81(2) (and the 1998 Act, s 2(4)) are part of the machinery which is intended to ensure that undertakings obey the law: they must bear the risk that transgressions of the competition rules may mean that their agreements are unenforceable. In this sense, therefore, the provision for voidness can be seen as more than merely a consequence of infringement: the possibility of voidness actually operates as a sanction, and is accordingly a deterrent. Voidness in this sense can be seen to be an aspect of public policy, and no matter how instinctively committed a judge might be to the maxim *pacta sunt servanda*, in a clear case of infringement the agreement must be deemed to be void and unenforceable.

---

[1]   *Panayiotou v Sony Music Entertainment (UK) Ltd* [1994] Ch 142, [1994] All ER 755.
[2]   *Inntrepreneur Estates Ltd v Mason* [1993] 2 CMLR 293; see also *Passmore v Morland*, (2 February 1999, unreported) where the Court of Appeal upheld Laddie J in ruling that the voidness of provisions under Art 81(2) is not for all time but depends on the appreciability and economic context of the restriction as applying from time to time; see generally Braakman *The Application of Articles 85 and 86 of the EC Treaty by National Courts in the Member States* (European Commission, July 1997).

Severance

2.32   Section 2(4) provides that 'any agreement' which violates s 2(1) is void. It does not suggest that the voidness might relate only to the provisions in the agreement that violate the Chapter I prohibition, nor does it say anything about the consequence of such voidness on the remaining provisions of the agreement. However, despite the

clear wording of both Art 81(2) and s 2(4) that 'agreements' that infringe are void, it
has been established by the Court of Justice that it may be possible to sever.[1] As
provided for by the 1998 Act, s 60, the intention is that the courts in the UK should
interpret s 2(4) in the same way as the Court of Justice has interpreted Art 81(2).[2]

---

[1] See Case 127/73 *BRT v SABAM* [1974] ECR 51; Case 319/82 *Société de Vente de Ciments et Bétons de l'Est v Kerpen & Kerpen GmbH* [1983] ECR 4173.
[2] HL Report Stage, 9 February 1998, col 890.

2.33 English contract law provides that severance is possible in certain circumstances,
although the rules on this subject are complex.[1] It is presumably a matter for the
applicable law of the contract, rather than the *lex fori* of the court in which the action
is brought, to determine whether, and if so, by what criteria, severance is to be
effected.[2]

---

[1] See *Chitty on Contracts* (27th edn, 1994) paras 16–164 to 16–172.
[2] See Rome Convention on the law applicable to contractual obligations 1980 (consolidated version OJ C27, 26.1.98, p 34); *Dicey and Morris on the Conflict of Laws* (12th edn, 1993), (ed Collins, Lawrence), Chs 32 and 33.

Void or illegal?

2.34 In *Gibbs Mew v Gemmell*[1] the Court of Appeal concluded that an agreement
that infringes Art 81(1) is not only void and unenforceable, but is also illegal. This has
very serious consequences: for example a party who has paid money to another
under an illegal agreement cannot recover that money unless it can be shown that the
parties were not *in pari delicto*.[2] It will presumably follow from this (and assuming that
the House of Lords, before whom the case is now pending, does not reverse the
Court of Appeal decision) that agreements that infringe the Chapter I prohibition
will likewise be held to be illegal. The guidelines do not say anything on this issue,
nor was it discussed in Parliament.

---

[1] [1998] EuLR 588.
[2] See Goff and Jones *Law of Restitution* (5th edn, 1998), Ch 24, p 607. Similarly, in most cases one party to an agreement that is illegal under Art 81(1) cannot claim damages from the other party.

Section 2(5) and (6): interpretation

2.35 These provisions explain that, except where the context otherwise requires, any
reference in the Act to an agreement includes a reference to a concerted practice and
decision by an association of undertakings. This overcomes the clumsiness of having
to use all three expressions throughout the text of the Act.

Section 2(7): the UK

2.36 Section 2(7) provides that—

> 'In this section 'the United Kingdom' means, in relation to an
> agreement which operates or is intended to operate only in a part of the
> United Kingdom, that part.'

The UK for this purpose includes England, Wales, Scotland plus the subsidiary islands (excluding the Isle of Man and the Channel Islands) and Northern Ireland.[1]

---

[1]   DGFT's guidelines 'The Chapter I prohibition', para 2.15.

Section 2(8): the 'Chapter I prohibition'

2.37 Section 2(8) provides that—

> 'The prohibition imposed by subsection (1) is referred to in this Act as 'the Chapter I prohibition'.'

The expression 'the Chapter I prohibition' is therefore a legislative one, and is mirrored by s 18(4) which recognises the companion 'Chapter II prohibition' (see para 3.3).

EXCLUDED AGREEMENTS

2.38 Section 3 provides for a number of exclusions from the Chapter I prohibition. These exclusions will be of considerable importance in practice, and in some cases are complex. Some, but not all, of these exclusions also apply in the case of the Chapter II prohibition (see paras 3.31–3.32).[1] Section 50 also provides for most vertical and land agreements to be excluded (see paras 2.75–2.91). Section 59(2) provides that if the effect of one or other exclusions is that the Chapter I prohibition is inapplicable to one or more provisions of an agreement, those provisions do not have to be disregarded when considering whether the agreement infringes the prohibition for other reasons. In other words, the effect of the agreement as a whole can be considered.

---

[1]   A table, setting out whether these various exclusions apply only to the Chapter I prohibition, or whether they apply to Chapter II as well, will be found in Appendix 8 to this book.

Section 3(1): excluded agreements

2.39 Section 3(1) provides that the Chapter I prohibition does not apply in any of the cases in which it is excluded by or as a result of—
  (a) Schedule 1: mergers and concentrations;
  (b) Schedule 2: competition scrutiny under other enactments;
  (c) Schedule 3: planning obligations and other general exclusions;
  (d) Schedule 4: professional rules.

Section 3(2)–(5) makes provision for the Secretary of State to amend Schs 1 and 3 in certain circumstances, whether by adding additional exclusions or by amending or removing existing ones.[1] Section 3(6) provides that Sch 3 itself enables the Secretary of State himself in certain circumstances to exclude agreements from the Chapter I prohibition.[2]

---

[1]   This order-making power is subject to s 71 which requires an affirmative resolution of each House of Parliament. See para 2.92 and Ch 10.
[2]   See para 2.67 on Sch 3, para 7.

Schedule 1: mergers and concentrations

2.40 Schedule 1 addresses the issue of the extent to which the Chapter I and II prohibitions apply to mergers and concentrations. The basic policy of the Schedule is that the prohibitions will not apply to mergers under FTA 1973 nor to concentrations in respect of which the European Commission has exclusive jurisdiction under the EC Merger Regulation.[1] The exclusion in Sch 1 is automatic and does not require an application to the DGFT or to the Secretary of State. The provisions of Sch 1 are complicated, and require detailed consideration. Draft guidelines have been published by the DGFT on this important issue.[1]

---

[1]   Council Regulation 4064/89/EEC, OJ L257, 21.9.90, p 13.

[2]   DGFT's draft guidelines 'Exclusion for mergers and ancillary restrictions'.

2.41 Schedule 1 is divided into two Parts—Pt I dealing with the relationship between the Act and the UK system of merger control, and Pt II with EC merger control.

Relationship of the Chapter I and II prohibitions with UK merger control

2.42 Schedule 1, para 1(1) provides that the Chapter I prohibition does not apply to an agreement or combination of agreements which results or would result in any two enterprises 'ceasing to be distinct enterprises' for the purposes of FTA 1973, Pt V.[1] It is important to note that the exclusion applies to any transaction whereby enterprises cease to be distinct, irrespective of whether the merger in question would be one that 'qualifies for investigation' for the purposes of FTA 1973.[2] If this were otherwise, the 1998 Act would have revolutionised the control of mergers in the UK by bringing all those transactions that are not subject to FTA 1973 because they fall below the relevant thresholds within the scope of the new Act, which would be an absurdity.

---

[1]   For the meaning of 'ceasing to be distinct', see *Butterworths Competition Law* VII [65]–[67].

[2]   A merger qualifies for investigation under FTA 1973—that is to say the Secretary of State may, in his discretion, refer such a merger to the CC (formerly the Monopolies and Mergers Commission), where it will result in the parties to the transaction having a market share of 25% or more or will result in the acquisition of assets worth £70 million or more: see *Butterworths Competition Law* VII [68]–[81].

2.43 Schedule 1, para 1(2) provides in addition that the exclusion extends to 'any provision directly related and necessary to the implementation of the merger provisions'. Thus, 'ancillary restraints' will also fall outside the Chapter I prohibition.[1] To be ancillary, the restraint must be both 'directly related [to]' and 'necessary to the implementation of' the merger provisions. Examples of ancillary restraints are given in the draft guidelines[2] and include, for example, appropriately limited non-compete clauses, licences of intellectual property rights and purchase and supply agreements. Whether a restraint is to be treated as ancillary is something that will be determined by the OFT's Mergers Secretariat.[3] The expression 'merger provisions' is defined in para 1(3) as being the provisions of the agreement which cause, or if carried out would cause, the agreement to lead to enterprises ceasing to be distinct. The purpose of this definition is to demarcate those provisions which are ancillary to the merger, and therefore fall outside the Chapter I prohibition, from other provisions which would remain subject to its provisions.

1   See *Butterworths Competition Law* VII [1039]–[1051]; useful (although now somewhat dated) guidance can be found in the European Commission's 'Notice regarding restrictions ancillary to concentrations' OJ C203, 14.8.90, p 5.
2   DGFT's draft guidelines 'Exclusion for mergers and ancillary restrictions', paras 4.9–4.16.
3   Ibid paras 4.17–4.21.

2.44   Schedule 1, para 1(4) modifies FTA 1973, s 65(3) and (4), which deal with the meaning of control for the purposes of that Act, by providing that persons, for example, with the ability materially to influence the policy of another company, 'must' be regarded as in control of it, whereas the original text provided only that they 'may' be in control. The explanation for this is that there has to be certainty as to whether or not an agreement or agreements are excluded from the Competition Act 1998.

2.45   Schedule 1, para 2 provides that the Chapter II prohibition does not apply to conduct that results in two enterprises ceasing to be distinct and to any ancillary restraints. Paragraph 2(2) provides for the same modification as para 1(4) (see paras 3.31–3.32).

Newspaper mergers

2.46   Schedule 1, para 3 provides for the same exclusion from the Chapter I and II prohibitions for newspaper mergers as defined in FTA 1973, s 57, and any ancillary restraints. There is no clawback provision in relation to newspaper mergers, which are within the exclusive competence of the Secretary of State.

Clawback

2.47   Schedule 1, para 4 provides for the possibility of 'withdrawal of the paragraph 1 exclusion'. Such a provision is known as a 'clawback', a device that can be found elsewhere in the 1998 Act.[1] The clawback applies only to para 1 (the Chapter I prohibition); there is no clawback in relation to para 2 (the Chapter II prohibition). In the House of Lords Lord Simon explained the reason for the inclusion of the clawback provision: that the breadth of the exclusion—even to include the acquisition of control or material influence by one business over another—'creates some risk of providing a loophole for anti-competitive agreements'.[2] The draft guidelines cite as an example a price-fixing agreement deliberately structured in such a way that it falls within the definition of a merger, but which falls below the thresholds at which it would qualify for investigation.[3] Paragraph 4(5) therefore provides that the DGFT may, by a direction in writing,[4] remove the benefit of the exclusion where he considers that—

  (a) an agreement would, if not excluded, infringe the Chapter I prohibition; and
  (b) he would not be likely to grant it an unconditional exemption (that is to say an exemption to which no conditions or obligations are attached under s 4(3)(a));[5] and
  (c) the agreement is not a protected agreement[6]

The cumulative effect of these provisions is that the clawback power will be exercised only rarely, which is acknowledged in the draft guidelines.[7] Furthermore, exercise of the clawback would not in itself mean that the agreement infringes the Chapter I prohibition: this would have to be the subject of a separate assessment.[8]

1   See for example Sch 3, para 2(3) (clawback possible in relation to agreements that benefit from
    directions under RTPA 1976, s 21(2)); Sch 3, para 9(7) (clawback possible for agreements relating to
    agricultural products).
2   HL Committee, 13 November 1997, col 328.
3   DGFT's draft guidelines 'Exclusion for mergers and ancillary restrictions', para 3.1.
4   Schedule 3, para 4(7)(a); the direction cannot be retrospective: para 4(7)(b).
5   Ibid, para 4(6).
6   Ibid, para 5.
7   DGFT's draft guidelines 'Exclusion for mergers and ancillary restrictions', para 3.6.
8   Ibid, para 3.8.

Protected agreements

2.48 The DGFT cannot exercise the right of 'clawback' in relation to a 'protected agreement'. Protected agreements are defined in Sch 1, para 5 as agreements—

(a) in relation to which the Secretary of State has announced that he will not be making a reference to the CC. The DGFT cannot override a decision by the Secretary of State not to refer a merger under FTA 1973 by instituting his own investigation under the 1998 Act;

(b) in relation to which the CC has found there to be a merger qualifying for investigation;

(c) that would result in enterprises ceasing to be distinct in the sense of FTA 1973, s 65, other than by virtue of the provisions of Sch 1, para 1(4) (see para 2.42);

(d) which the CC has found give rise to a merger in the sense of the Water Industry Act 1991, s 32.

Relationship of the Chapter I and II prohibitions with EC merger control

2.49 Schedule 1, para 6 provides that neither the Chapter I nor the Chapter II prohibitions apply to concentrations which have a Community dimension (para 6(3)) in relation to which the European Commission has exclusive jurisdiction. This provision is necessary in order to comply with Art 21(2) of the Merger Regulation,[1] which provides that no Member State may apply its national legislation on competition law to any concentration that has a Community dimension. Paragraph 6 does not mention ancillary restraints specifically, but since the European Commission can deal with these under the Merger Regulation, it presumably follows that Art 21(2) prevents Member States taking action in relation to them as well.

1   Council Regulation 4064/89/EEC, OJ L257, 21.9.90, p 13.

No clawback

2.50 Since Sch 1, para 6 deals with the exclusive jurisdiction of the European Commission, it follows that the Secretary of State does not in this situation enjoy a right of 'clawback' as he does under para 4, in relation to mergers that are subject to FTA 1973.

Power to amend Sch 1

2.51 Section 3(2) of the 1998 Act gives the Secretary of State the power to amend Sch 1 by order, by providing for one or more additional exclusions or by amending or removing any provisions in it. Section 3(5) provides that any amending order may make provision for the exclusion to cease to apply to a particular agreement.

Schedule 2: competition scrutiny under other enactments

2.52 Schedule 2 excludes agreements which are subject to competition scrutiny under the Financial Services Act 1986, the Companies Act 1989 and its Northern Irish equivalent,[1] the Broadcasting Act 1990 or the Environment Act 1995. The view was taken by the Government that, in so far as particular agreements are subject to competition scrutiny under regimes constructed to deal with the circumstances of specific sectors, it is inappropriate to subject them to the Chapter I prohibition as well, as 'that would just create an unwelcome and unjustified double jeopardy'.[2] In each case, the exclusion from the Chapter I prohibition is effected by amending the provisions of the legislation that provides for 'other' competition scrutiny. It is important to note that there is no exclusion from the Chapter II prohibition for these cases.[3]

---

[1]   Companies (Northern Ireland) Order 1990, SI 1990/593 (NI 5).
[2]   HL Committee, 13 November 1997, col 342.
[3]   But see para 2.53.

Financial Services Act 1986

2.53 The Financial Services Act 1986 deals with the regulation of investment business, and provides for firms to comply with the rules of the regulatory authorities.[1] Schedule 2, para 1 of the 1998 Act amends the 1986 Act, ss 125–127 in order to provide for exclusion from the Chapter I prohibition of agreements and recognised professional bodies that are dealt with according to those provisions. It is understood that these matters will also be excluded from the Chapter II prohibition by the Financial Services and Markets Bill (see para 3.32).

---

[1]   See *Butterworths Competition Law* IX [1204]. 3(1) *Halsbury's Laws* (4th edn reissue) para 158.

Companies Act 1989 and Companies (Northern Ireland) Order 1990 (SI 1990/593)

2.54 Schedule 2, paras 2, 3 of the 1998 Act amend the Companies Act 1989, Sch 14 and the Companies (Northern Ireland) Order 1990, Sch 14 respectively. These Schedules deal with the supervision and qualification of company auditors. The amendments provide for such matters to be dealt with under the rules of recognised professional bodies.[1]

---

[1]   See 7(2) *Halsbury's Laws* (4th edn reissue) para 955.

Broadcasting Act 1990

2.55 The Broadcasting Act 1990, s 194A, deals with the Channel 3 news provision and networking arrangements, and provides for the Secretary of State to exempt agreements from Chapter I which are not considered to pose a threat to competition.[1] Schedule 2, para 4 of the 1998 Act amends the 1990 Act, s 194A in relation to news provision for Channel 3, and para 5 makes provision for the exclusion from the Chapter I prohibition of networking arrangements to the extent that they are subject to the Broadcasting Act 1990, Sch 4, or contain provisions which have been considered thereunder. A list of such arrangements must be published by the Independent Television Commission (Sch 2, para 5(2)), which must consult the DGFT before doing so and must ensure that the list will be brought to the attention of persons who would be affected by it or have an interest in it (Sch 2, para 5(3)).

---

[1]   See *Butterworths Competition Law* IX [2618]–[2636]; 45 *Halsbury's Laws* (4th edn reissue), para 425.

Environment Act 1995

2.56   The Environment Act 1995, s 94, provides for the responsibility of producers in relation to the materials they use.[1] Schedule 2, para 6 of the 1998 Act allows the Secretary of State to exclude agreements from the Chapter I prohibition which relate to exemption schemes.

---

[1]   See 8(2) *Halsbury's Laws* (4th edn reissue) para 458.

No power to amend Sch 2

2.57   There is no power to amend Sch 2. Section 3 of the 1998 Act provides the power to amend only in relation to Sch 1 (see para 2.51) and Sch 3 (see para 2.70).

Schedule 3: planning obligations and other general exclusions

2.58   Schedule 3 is entitled 'General Exclusions' and sets out various matters that are excluded. Some of these provisions are of considerable importance, for example Sch 3, para 2 excludes agreements that are the subject of directions under RTPA 1976, s 21(2), and Sch 3, para 4 excludes 'services of general economic interest'. In some cases the exclusion is from the Chapter I prohibition only, in others from both the Chapter I and II prohibitions. These provisions, therefore, require careful analysis.

Planning obligations

2.59   Schedule 3, para 1 provides that the Chapter I prohibition does not apply to agreements involving planning obligations, for example where planning permission is given subject to the developer agreeing to provide certain services or access to facilities.[1]

---

[1]   See the Town and Country Planning Act 1990, s 106.

Section 21(2) agreements

2.60   Schedule 3, para 2(1) provides that the Chapter I prohibition does not apply to an agreement in respect of which a direction has been given under the RTPA 1976, s 21(2), prior to the coming into force of the 1998 Act, s 2, ie 1 March 2000 (see para 2.3). This provision is clearly of great practical importance. In the course of 1999 and the early months of 2000, the OFT will continue to process agreements and to seek directions where appropriate from the Secretary of State under that section. In so far as the s 21(2) procedure is successfully completed in relation to a particular agreement, it will be excluded from the scope of the Chapter I prohibition, subject to—

(a) cases of material variation to the agreement in question (see para 2.61); and

(b) cases where the DGFT exercises the power of 'clawback' in relation to a particular agreement (see para 2.62 and Ch 9).

Material variation

2.61 Schedule 3, para 2(2) provides that, if a material variation is made to an agreement that has been the subject of directions under the RTPA 1976, s 21(2), the exclusion shall cease to apply from the coming into force of the variation. This provision is a little surprising, since it removes the benefit of exclusion without any reference to the competitive impact of the material variation. It would be odd if a variation that has no impact on competition might nevertheless lead to the loss of the exclusion. However, in so far as the varied agreement has no appreciable impact upon competition, it would not come within the Chapter I prohibition anyway, so that the removal of the exclusion would not in fact make much difference.[1] The DGFT has indicated that a material variation would be one that has an appreciable effect on competition.[2]

---

[1]   See Case C-39/96 *KVB v Free Record Shop BV* [1997] ECR I-2303, [1997] 5 CMLR 521 on the treatment of 'old' agreements under the EC Treaty, Art 81, and the impact on the provisional validity of subsequent variations. The position of the ECJ is more flexible, (admittedly in a somewhat different context) than that set out in the 1998 Act.

[2]   DGFT's guidelines 'Transitional arrangements', para 4.16. See also para 9.4 below.

Clawback

2.62 Schedule 3, para 2(3) provides the DGFT with a power of 'clawback' in relation to excluded s 21(2) agreements. The clawback provisions are similar to those found in Sch 1 in relation to mergers under FTA 1973 (see para 2.47). The DGFT may, by a direction in writing,[1] remove the benefit of the exclusion from a s 21(2) agreement where he considers that—

(a) the agreement would, if not excluded, infringe the Chapter I prohibition; and

(b) he would not be likely to grant it an unconditional exemption (that is to say an exemption to which no conditions or obligations are attached under s 4(3)(a)) (para 2.8).

---

[1]   Schedule 3, para 2(9)(a)—the direction cannot be retrospective: Sch 3, para 2(9)(b).

EEA regulated markets

2.63 Schedule 3, para 3 provides that the Chapter I prohibition does not apply to various matters concerning 'EEA regulated [financial services] markets'. This expression is defined in Sch 3, para 3(5) as meaning a market which is listed by another EEA state[1] and does not require a dealer on the market to have a physical presence where trading facilities are provided or on any other trading floor of that market. This exclusion extends to—

    (a) an agreement for the constitution of an EEA regulated market to the extent to which the agreement relates to any of the rules made, or guidance issued, by that market (Sch 3, para 3(2));

    (b) a decision made by an EEA market to the extent to which it relates to any of the market's regulating provisions (Sch 3, para 3(1));

    (c) practices of an EEA regulated market or any practices which are trading practices in relation to an EEA regulated market (Sch 3, para 3(3));[2]

    (d) an agreement to which the parties are either—

        (i) an EEA regulated market; or

        (ii) a person who is subject to the rules of that market,

to the extent that the agreement consists of provisions, the inclusion of which are required or contemplated by the regulating provisions of that market (Sch 3, para 3(4)).[3] It is understood that these matters will in due course be excluded from the Chapter II prohibition, by amendment of the 1998 Act, in order to ensure consistency of treatment with the provisions on investment business.[4]

---

[1] Pursuant to Council Directive 93/22/EEC, Art 16 (OJ L141, 11.6.93, p 27).

[2] The expression 'trading practices' is defined in para 3(5).

[3] The expression 'regulating provisions' is defined in para 3(5).

[4] See paras 2.53 and 3.32.

Services of general economic interest

2.64 Schedule 3, para 4 provides that neither the Chapter I nor the Chapter II prohibition shall apply to an undertaking—

> 'entrusted with the operation of services of general economic interest or having the character of a revenue-earning monopoly in so far as the prohibition would obstruct the performance, in law or in fact, of the particular tasks assigned to [it]'.

This important provision is modelled on the EC Treaty, Art 86(2),[1] although the language is somewhat less tortuous in the 1998 Act. Experience of the application of Art 86(2) will be important in the interpretation of this exclusion—the Court has considered its meaning in a number of judgments, and the relevant authorities will have to maintain consistency with these by virtue of the 1998 Act, s 60(2) (see paras 6.15–6.30). The Commission has also considered the meaning of Art 86(2), both in its decisions, and in various Directives and Notices, and this experience is something that the authorities must 'have regard to' by virtue of s 60(3) (see paras 6.15–6.30). An amendment was proposed that would have allowed the Secretary of State to certify whether an undertaking complied with this requirement, but the Government rejected this on the grounds that it is a matter for the DGFT, the Commission or the courts to decide upon.[2] However, it is worthwhile pointing out that the Secretary of State does have power under Sch 3, para 7, to exclude an agreement or category of agreements where there are 'exceptional and compelling reasons of public policy' for doing so (see para 2.67). The DGFT may produce guidelines in due course on the meaning of 'general economic interest'.

1   See *Butterworths Competition Law* IX [23]–[46]. See also Ch 7 (Special Sectors), in particular paras 7.20-7.21.
2   HL Report Stage, 9 February 1998, cols 967–968.

Compliance with legal requirements

2.65 Schedule 3, para 5 provides that neither the Chapter I nor the Chapter II prohibition applies to an agreement or to conduct that is required to comply with a legal requirement. For this purpose, a legal requirement is one imposed by or under—

(a) any enactment in force in the UK;

(b) the EC Treaty or the EEA Agreement and having legal effect in the UK without further enactment;

(c) the law in force in another Member State having legal effect in the UK.

The operation of this exclusion could occur where an undertaking in one of the utility sectors was subject to a licence condition requiring it to behave in a certain way.[1] In such circumstances it could not be guilty of infringing the Chapter I or II prohibition, simply for complying with the licence condition. Similarly it could not be found liable under the 1998 Act where it had done something required, for example, by a Commission Directive adopted under the EC Treaty, Art 86(3).

1   HL Committee, 13 November 1997, col 334. See Ch 7.

Avoidance of conflict with international obligations

2.66 Schedule 3, para 6(1) gives the Secretary of State power to make an order to exclude the application of the Chapter I prohibition from an agreement or a category of agreements where this would be appropriate in order to avoid a conflict between the provisions of the 1998 Act and an international obligation of the UK. The order can provide that the exclusion shall apply only in specified circumstances (Sch 3, para 6(2)) and may be retrospective (Sch 3, para 6(3)). Similar provisions are contained in Sch 3, para 6(4) and (5) for exclusion from the Chapter II prohibition. Schedule 3, para 6(6) was introduced in the House of Lords as a Government amendment to extend the meaning of the term 'international obligation' to include inter-governmental arrangements relating to civil aviation. The reason for this is that such arrangements, permitting flights between the UK and other countries, are often not made as treaties[1] and therefore do not give rise to international 'obligations' as such.

1   HL Report Stage, 9 February 1998, cols 972–3.

Public policy

2.67 Schedule 3, para 7 gives the Secretary of State power to make an order to exclude the application of the Chapter I prohibition from an agreement or a category of agreements where there are 'exceptional and compelling reasons of public policy' for doing so. The order can provide that the exclusion shall apply only in specified circumstances (Sch 3, para 7(2)), and may be retrospective (Sch 3, para 7(3)). Similar provisions are contained in Sch 3, para 7(4) and (5) for exclusion from the Chapter II prohibition. It is questionable to what extent this provision will be used in practice—the other exclusions in the 1998 Act are reasonably specific, and the

Secretary of State has power to vary some of them in the manner laid down in the 1998 Act. This provision allows him to make an exclusion on public policy grounds, a concept that is necessarily vague. However, the requirement that the reasons must be 'exceptional and compelling' clearly imposes a heavy burden on the Secretary of State to prove that he needs to exercise the power. It might be that the power would be invoked, for example, in relation to the defence industry. The EC Treaty provides a specific exclusion from the competition articles for certain matters related to defence in Art 296, but there are no specific exclusions for this area in the 1998 Act. In a particular case, therefore, the Secretary of State has the option to proceed under Sch 3, para 7.

Coal and steel

2.68 Schedule 3, para 8 provides that the Chapter I and Chapter II prohibitions do not apply to agreements and conduct within the exclusive jurisdiction of the European Commission under the ECSC (European Coal and Steel Community) Treaty (Sch 3, para 8(1), (3)).[1] These exclusions will cease to have effect when the ECSC Treaty expires (Sch 3, para 8(2), (4)).

---

[1]   See *Butterworths Competition Law* IX [2901]–[3084].

Agricultural products

2.69 Schedule 3, para 9 provides exclusion from the Chapter I prohibition for agreements that fall outside the EC Treaty, Art 81 by virtue of Council Regulation 26/62/EC.[1] If the European Commission decides that an agreement is not thus excluded, the exclusion under Sch 3, para 9 ceases on the same date (Sch 3, para 9(2)). Provision is made for 'clawback'.[2] Schedule 3, para 9(7) provides that the DGFT may make a direction that the agricultural exclusion does not apply where an agreement 'is likely, or is intended, substantially and unjustifiably to prevent, restrict or distort competition in relation to an agricultural product'.[3]

---

[1]   See *Butterworths Competition Law* IX [223]–[249]. Council Regulation 26/62/EC, OJ L30, 21.4.62, p 993.
[2]   Schedule 3, para 9(3)–(8).
[3]   See generally HL Report Stage, 9 February 1998, cols 973–976.

Power to amend Sch 3

2.70 The 1998 Act, s 3(3) gives the Secretary of State the power to amend Sch 3 by order. He can provide for one or more additional exclusions, or amend or remove any additions made under s 3, or any of the provisions in Sch 3, paras 1, 2, 8 or 9.[1] The power in s 3(3)(a) to provide for additional exclusions is subject to s 3(4), which provides that the Secretary of State can provide for an additional exclusion only where it appears to him that agreements within the category to be excluded either do not in general have an adverse effect on competition or are, in general, best considered under the 1998 Act, Ch II or FTA 1973. Section 3(5) provides that any amending order may make provision for the exclusion to cease to apply to a particular agreement.

---

[1] Note therefore that the power to amend Sch 3, paras 3–7 is less extensive than in relation to Sch 3, paras 1, 2, 7, 8 and 9.

Schedule 4: professional rules

2.71 Schedule 4 provides for the exclusion of professional rules. The appropriateness of this exclusion was the subject of debate in the House of Lords.[1] There is no exclusion for professional rules from the application of Arts 81 and 82, but of course if the rules are not anti-competitive or abusive, they would not infringe those provisions. It would have been quite consistent with EC law, therefore, to have subjected the professions and their rule books to the general provisions of the 1998 Act. The view of Lord Simon, however, speaking on behalf of the Government, was that professional rules, the purpose of which is to protect the public, and which contain disciplinary arrangements and are liable to judicial review, should fall outside the Chapter I prohibition.[2] However he did not consider that the 1998 Act should provide an exclusion as wide as that contained in RTPA 1976, which excludes the *services* of solicitors, barristers, accountants etc. The 1998 Act only provides for exclusion of *professional rules*—

> 'The Government believe that, viewed as a whole, it would be unwarranted to apply prohibitions designed primarily for the private sector business to the quasi-public law processes of drawing up and enforcing professional rules'.[3]

---

[1] See HL Committee, 13 November 1997, cols 285–294.
[2] Ibid col 291.
[3] Ibid col 292; see also HL Report Stage, 9 February 1998, cols 896–898.

2.72 Schedule 4 provides that the Chapter I prohibition does not apply to an agreement which—
> '(a) constitutes a designated professional rule,
> (b) imposes obligations arising from designated professional rules, or
> (c) constitutes an agreement to act in accordance with such rules' (Sch 4, para 1(1)).

It is the task of the Secretary of State to designate professional rules for the purposes of the exclusion. Designation, and alterations in such designations, are carried out by order, and the Secretary of State must maintain a list of designated rules (Sch 4, para 2). Professional rules mean rules regulating a professional service of the people providing that service (Sch 4, para 1(2)), and the services in question are listed in Part II of the Schedule, namely barristers, advocates, solicitors, medical practitioners etc. The expression 'rules' for this purpose includes regulations, codes of practice and statements of principle (Sch 4, para 1(2)). Application must be made to the Secretary of State for designation (Sch 4, para 3). Alterations in professional rules must be notified to the Secretary of State as soon as is reasonably practicable, but a rule does not cease to be designated simply because it is altered (Sch 4, para 4). Provision is made for the DGFT to keep the list of professional rules under review and to advise the Secretary of State as to whether the exclusion should be restricted in relation to the rules of a particular body (Sch 4, para 5); and the Secretary of State has power, if he receives such advice from the DGFT, to remove particular rules from the designated list (Sch 4, para 6)).

Inspection

2.73 Any person may inspect the list of professional rules and the rules themselves, and take copies on payment of fees. The DGFT is the person responsible for such inspections (Sch 4, para 7).

No power to amend Sch 4

2.74 The 1998 Act, s 3 does not provide power to amend Sch 4. Section 3 provides the power to amend only in relation to Sch 1 (see para 2.51) and Sch 3 (see para 2.70). Schedule 4 itself gives the Secretary of State power to designate the rules relating to the services in Sch 4, Pt II, but there is no power to *add* to the services set out therein.

Section 50: vertical agreements

2.75 The treatment of vertical agreements is a complex issue which was the subject of considerable debate as the Bill was proceeding through Parliament. Under EC law, it was established by the Court of Justice, in its first substantive judgment on the competition rules, that Art 81 was capable of applying both to horizontal and to vertical agreements, and furthermore that it could apply to restrictions of intra-brand as well as inter-brand competition.[1] A result of this judgment was that a very large number of vertical agreements were brought within the scope of Art 81(1), although they might then be eligible for individual or block exemption under Art 81(3). Several block exemptions are currently in force for vertical agreements for the distribution of goods and, to a limited extent, services.[2] The particular concern of the Commission and the Court of Justice has been that vertical agreements might have the effect of dividing up the single market, preventing the free movement of goods from one Member State to another. This has been a consistent theme since the judgment of the Court in *Consten and Grundig* to the large fine of 102 million ECU imposed by the court in *VW*[3] in 1998.

---

[1]   Cases 56 & 58/64 *Consten and Grundig v Commission* [1966] ECR 299, [1966] CMLR 418.

[2]   See Commission Regulation 1983/83/EEC on exclusive distribution agreements (OJ L173, 30.6.83, p 1), Commission Regulation 1984/83/EEC on exclusive purchasing agreements (OJ L173, 30.6.83, p 5), Commission Regulation 4087/88/EEC on franchising agreements (OJ L359, 28.12.88, p 46), and Commission Regulation 1475/95/EEC on motor car distribution agreements (OJ L145, 29.6.95, p 25).

[3]   Case IV/35.733-VW, OJ L124, 25.4.98, p 60, [1998] 5 CMLR 33.

2.76 The application of Art 81(1) to vertical agreements has been one of the most controversial aspects of competition law for many years. In particular, many commentators have considered that the Commission, in particular, has been too hasty in finding a restriction of competition under Art 81(1). Contractual restrictions—for example to give territorial exclusivity to a dealer or to require a dealer to purchase exclusively from a particular producer—might not have anti-competitive effects at all, and could arguably even be pro-competitive. In such a case, these commentators would argue that Art 81(1) should have no application at all, so that the parties to the agreement should not be required to shape their agreement so as to satisfy the requirements of the Commission for individual or block exemption. As experience of competition law and policy in the EU has increased, many economists have moved towards the consensus that vertical restraints usually present a problem for competition only where at least one of the parties to an agreement has some degree of market power. In this case, argued before the Court in *Consten and Grundig*, Art 81 might not be the appropriate provision for dealing with vertical agreements: perhaps this should be left to Art 82.

The European Commission's proposals for reform of the law on vertical restraints

2.77   The Commission has listened to these arguments over the years and has become more sympathetic towards them. In 1997 it published a Green Paper[1] setting out a variety of options for reforming the law, some entailing very little change, and others slightly more far-reaching. In 1998 the Commission published a Follow-up Document[2] setting out its final proposals, and these are expected to be implemented in the course of 1999—coming into force in 2000. The proposals will lead to the adoption of a much broader and more flexible block exemption for vertical restraints, albeit subject to a market share 'cap' for undertakings which might possess a fairly high degree of market power. This market share 'cap' is the Commission's response to the criticism that historically its approach has been to apply the law to vertical restraints in too formalistic a manner. Precisely what the market share 'cap' should be is the subject of continuing debate, as is the question of whether there should be different caps according to the seriousness of the restraint. It should be added that the Commission's Notice on agreements of minor importance (1997)[3] provides that a vertical agreement between undertakings with a market share of less than 10% would normally fall outside Art 81(1) altogether; and that even above this figure, it remains possible to argue, in particular after *European Night Services v EC Commission*,[4] that any restriction of competition is not sufficiently appreciable to fall within Art 81(1).

---

[1]   'Vertical restraints—Green Paper on vertical restraints in EC competition policy', Com (96) 721, adopted by the Commission on 22 January 1997, [1997] 4 CMLR 519.

[2]   Communication from the Commission on the 'application of the Community competition rules to vertical restraints', Com (98) 544, [1999] 4 CMLR 281.

[3]   OJ C372, 9.12.97, p 13.

[4]   Cases T-374, 375, 384, 388/94 [1998] 5 CMLR 718.

The UK Government's position

2.78   For the Government in the UK, the question of how to treat vertical agreements under the new legislation was a difficult issue. On the one hand, the 1998 Act involves the adoption in the UK of legislation incorporating the wording of Arts 81 and 82, in order to achieve consistency with the position in the rest of the EU. In addition, the 1998 Act, s 60 provides that, as a general proposition, the authorities in the UK should also follow the jurisprudence of the ECJ in interpreting domestic law. It would have been possible for the 1998 Act simply to duplicate the position under EC law, including the adoption of the Commission's new policy proposals (as outlined at para 2.77). On the other hand, as already noted, the application of Art 81 to vertical agreements has been strongly influenced by single market considerations, which are not an issue of concern *within* the UK. General opinion has been very critical of much of EC law on vertical agreements, as economists increasingly agree that vertical agreements normally present problems only where there is a high degree of market power. On a more pragmatic note, the DGFT in the UK is desperately keen to avoid being inundated with thousands of notifications for exemptions for agreements that arguably entail no restriction of competition at all.

2.79 Having weighed up these various arguments, the Government committed itself to providing the Secretary of State with the power to exclude vertical agreements from the scope of the 1998 Act. Technical difficulties in drafting a suitable definition of a vertical agreement meant that it was not possible to include this exclusion in the 1998 Act itself—the commercial world does not usually divide commercial transactions into horizontal and vertical ones, and the danger exists that any definition of a vertical agreement, so as to exclude it from the Chapter I prohibition, might encourage lawyers and their clients to draft horizontal cartel-like agreements in such a way as to benefit from any available exclusion. Also particularly difficult problems arise where networks of agreements produce horizontal effects. Thus the policy of excluding vertical agreements has had to predate the exclusion itself whilst these problems are addressed.

2.80 The argument that the exclusion of vertical agreements from the Chapter I prohibition might be unduly lenient can be countered in at least three ways as follows—[1]

    (a) vertical agreements do not enjoy exclusion from the Chapter II prohibition, therefore, consistently with the views of economists expressed above, a vertical agreement entered into by a firm or firms with market power could be scrutinised under the 1998 Act, s 18;

    (b) the complex monopoly provisions in FTA 1973 remain in force. Where there is a competition problem in a particular sector because of the cumulative effect of the vertical agreements in operation—cars, perfumes or beer might be cited as examples—it would be open to the DGFT to refer the matter to the CC for investigation;

    (c) provision is made in s 50 for any order of the Secretary of State to contain a clawback provision, whereby the DGFT can withdraw the exclusion from any particular vertical agreement (but not from a category of agreements).

---

[1]   See generally HL Report Stage, 9 February 1998, cols 901–903.

The power to exclude vertical agreements

2.81 Section 50(1) states that the Secretary of State may by order provide for any provision of the 1998 Act, Pt I, to apply to vertical agreements with such modifications as may be prescribed. Such an order may provide for exclusions or exemptions, or otherwise provide for prescribed provisions not to apply in relation to such agreements (s 50(2)). The Secretary of State is given power to allow the DGFT to exercise a right of 'clawback' in relation to an individual agreement (s 50(3)). It is worth noting that the power of clawback is not exercisable in relation to categories of agreements. The key expression—'vertical agreement'—has such meaning as may be prescribed by order (s 50(5)). An obvious possibility will be for the Secretary of State to adopt the same definition on the proposal by the European Commission in its own reforms.[1]

---

[1]   See draft 'proposal for a Council Regulation amending 19/65 on the application of art 85(3) of the Treaty to certain categories of agreement and concerted practices and proposal for a Council Regulation amending 17/62: first Regulation implementing arts 85 and 86 of the Treaty' (COM (1998) 546 final—98/0287 and 98/0288 (CNS—OJ C365, 26.11.98, pp 27–30). See HL Consideration of Commons' Amendments, 20 October 1998, col 1379.

2.82 A draft statutory instrument is being prepared and the DTI published a consultation document in February 1999 together with a draft of that Order.[1] The document states that economic analysis suggests that vertical agreements do not generally give rise to competition concerns unless one of the parties has 'significant market power' or there exists a network of similar agreements. It follows that there is a good case for disapplying the Chapter I prohibition from a broad range of vertical agreements. This in turn will reduce the number of precautionary notifications of essentially benign agreements. Vertical agreements that give rise to concern will be dealt with in one of four ways—

    (a) there will be a power of 'clawback';

    (b) there will remain the possibility of a complex monopoly reference under FTA 1973;

    (c) the Chapter II prohibition may apply where there is dominance;

    (d) vertical price-fixing will not be excluded.

The document invites comments on the timing of the adoption of the Order, particularly in view of the fact that the European Commission is itself in the process of reforming the law of vertical restraints under Art 81. The DGFT intends in due course to publish guidelines on 'Vertical agreements and restraints'.

---

[1]   'Exclusion of vertical agreements: consultation on a draft Order' URN 98/1030.

The draft Order

2.83 The draft Order contains four articles. The full text is set out in Appendix 5.

Article 1: title, entry into force and definitions

2.84 The definition of a vertical agreement which, as mentioned above, is not without its difficulties, is given in the draft Order, art 1(2)—

    ' 'vertical agreement' means an agreement—

    (a) between two or more undertakings, each operating at a different stage of the economic process for the purposes of that agreement; and

    (b) in respect of the supply or purchase, or both, of goods for resale or processing or in respect of the marketing of services.'.

As the consultation document states, and as suggested in para 2.81, this definition is drawn from (but is not identical to) the European Commission's proposal for the reform of Council Regulation 19/65/EEC.[1]

---

[1]   OJ L36, 6.3.65, p 533 (S edn 1965–66, p 35).

2.85 The purpose of the definition proposed by the DTI is that any agreement that is genuinely vertical should be excluded, subject to the draft Order, art 3, on price fixing (see para 2.87). The definition differs in some respects from the position of the European Commission—for example it does not disapply the exclusion to reciprocal or non-reciprocal agreements between actual and potential competitors. In addition the DTI's draft contains the words 'for the purposes of that agreement', so that an agreement could be treated as vertical even though, for other purposes, the parties might be considered to be in a horizontal relationship. Views are sought on whether these differences from the position proposed by the Commission are appropriate. Finally it should be noted that the definition of a vertical agreement in art 1 does not extend to licences of intellectual property rights and know-how. The DTI states that in relation to such agreements the boundaries of what is acceptable is 'best established directly from European jurisprudence'. The document points out the possibility that such agreements could benefit from parallel exemption by virtue of the 1998 Act.

Article 2: the disapplication

2.86 The draft Order, art 2, effects the disapplication for vertical agreements—

'The Chapter I prohibition shall not apply to an agreement to the extent that it is a vertical agreement.'.

It will be noted that the exclusion applies 'to the extent that' an agreement is a vertical agreement. Thus, the exclusion is limited 'to the desired width' (as the consultation document puts it); but also the exclusion will be available even though the agreement contains other, non-excluded provisions. If the DGFT were to be called upon to consider the overall impact of an agreement, he would, by virtue of the 1998 Act, s 59(2), be entitled to take into account the excluded vertical agreement in making his assessment, even though that agreement is itself excluded.[1]

---

[1] See para 2.38.

Article 3: price fixing agreements

2.87 Price fixing is not excluded, as art 3 sets out—

'Article 2 shall not apply where—
(a) the vertical agreement, directly or indirectly, in isolation or in combination with other factors under the control of the parties including the exercise of industrial property rights, has the object or effect of—
(i) fixing resale prices or minimum resale prices;
(ii) fixing maximum resale prices or recommended resale prices which have the same effect as fixed resale prices or fixed minimum resale prices.
(b) the vertical agreement takes effect between the same parties and is to the like object or effect to an obligation or restriction contained in an agreement which has been the subject of a direction under Article 4 and is made after the date of the direction in question.'.

In the consultation document the DTI explains that this definition follows the Commission's suggestion in an early draft of its proposed new block exemption, but the DTI welcomes views on the text which, for example, may suffer from uncertainty because of the reference to '*directly or indirectly*' fixing prices. The purpose of art 3(b) is to prevent the clawback power in art 4 being circumvented by the parties entering into a new agreement to the like effect as an agreement already subject to a clawback direction.

Article 4: clawback

2.88 Article 4 gives the DGFT a power of clawback. This provision is modelled upon the other clawback powers found elsewhere in the 1998 Act (see for example para 2.62). As already explained, this provision is an important safeguard in the event that an excluded vertical agreement might in fact be seriously detrimental to competition. The clawback would not have retrospective effect.

Licences of intellectual property rights

2.89 An important practical question will be whether bilateral licences of intellectual property rights will be subject to the Chapter I prohibition. Under RTPA 1976, for various reasons, most bilateral licences would not be registrable.[1] Under the Chapter I prohibition, a licence will infringe the 1998 Act, s 2 only if it has as its object or effect the restriction, prevention or distortion of competition. In so far as any case-law of the Court or statement of the Commission indicates that licences might infringe Art 81(1), the competition authorities in the UK would not be bound to maintain consistency with them to the extent that they were motivated by single-market considerations (see paras 6.15–6.30). For this reason alone, it may be possible to conclude that licences conferring territorial exclusivity in the UK or parts of the UK are not caught by the Chapter I prohibition. However, to the extent that a licence might be found to infringe Chapter I, it is understood that the Government's view is that the power to exclude vertical agreements in s 50 does not extend to licences of intellectual property rights. However, many such agreements would benefit from block exemption in the EC by virtue of Commission Regulation 240/96/EC.[2] In this case, the same agreement would also benefit from parallel exemption under the 1998 Act, s 10(1) (see para 2.106); and if the agreement would benefit from Regulation 240/96/EC but for the fact that it has no effect on trade between Member States, it would benefit from parallel exemption under s 10(2) (see para 2.106). It is also presumably the case that the Secretary of State could, at some future date, take action to exclude licences of intellectual property rights by amending the 'general exclusions' in Sch 3 (see para 2.51). One change that is effected by the 1998 Act in relation to intellectual property matters is that s 70 repeals the Patents Act 1977, ss 44 and 45 which deal with licences (see Ch 10). The DGFT intends in due course to publish guidelines on 'Intellectual property rights'.

---

[1] See *Butterworths Competition Law* V [9]–[27].
[2] OJ L31, 9.2.96, p 2.

Section 50: land agreements

2.90 The House of Lords, when debating land agreements, recognised the difficulties of framing a specific exclusion.[1] Consequently, a broad and flexible exclusion was decided upon to give them special treatment,[2] now contained in the 1998 Act, s 50. As in the case of vertical agreements, this confers power on the Secretary of State to provide the exclusion or exemption of land agreements.

---

[1] HL Committee, 13 November 1997, col 340.
[2] HL Consideration of Commons' Amendments, 20 October 1998, col 1379.

Draft Land Agreements (Exclusion) Order 1998

2.91 The DTI published a consultation document in February 1999 together with a draft of this order.[1] Concern has been expressed in the property industry that the Chapter I prohibition might apply to a large number of property dealings. Such an anxiety might lead to a flood of precautionary notifications, and the exclusion is intended to deal with this potential problem. It applies only to the Chapter I, and not to the Chapter II, prohibition. The structure of the draft order is similar to that for vertical agreements—art 1 contains the definitions, art 2 contains the disapplication itself, art 4 provides for clawback, and art 3 contains further explanatory provisions. A land agreement is defined to mean—

> 'an agreement between undertakings which creates, alters, transfers or terminates, an interest in land, or an agreement to enter into such an agreement, together with any obligation and restriction which in accordance with Article 3 is to be treated as part of the agreement' (art 1(2)).

The DGFT intends in due course to publish guidelines on 'Land agreements'.

---

[1] 'Exclusion of land agreements: consultation on a draft Order' URN 98/1029. See Appendix 5 for full text.

Power to add, amend or remove exclusions in certain circumstances

2.92 The Secretary of State's power under the 1998 Act, ss 3, 19 and 50 to make orders in relation to vertical and land agreements is subject to s 71, which requires there to be an affirmative resolution of both Houses of Parliament. The Government stressed that this was an important safeguard.[1]

---

[1] See HL Committee, 13 November 1997, col 298 (Lord Simon of Highbury).

EXEMPTIONS

Introduction

2.93 As in the case of the EC Treaty, Art 81, the 1998 Act makes provision for exemption from the Chapter I prohibition. The relevant provisions are contained in ss 4–11, and provide for four kinds of exemption—
- (a) individual exemptions, which the DGFT may grant in relation to an agreement that has been notified to him (ss 4, 5);
- (b) block exemptions (ss 6–8);
- (c) parallel exemptions, where an agreement satisfies one of the EC block exemptions,[1] or would do if it were to affect trade between Member States (s 10);
- (d) 'exemptions for other agreements' (s 11).

Each of these will be explained below, after a consideration of the criteria according to which exemption may be available.

---

[1] In addition to the block exemptions referred to in para 2.75, there are also block exemptions for specialisation agreements (Commission Regulation 417/85/EEC OJ L53, 22.2.85, p 1) and for research and development agreements (Commission Regulation 418/85/EEC, OJ L53, 22.2.85, p 5, as amended by Commission Regulation 151/93/EEC), and for technology transfer agreements (Commission Regulation 240/96/EC, OJ L31, 9.2.96, p 2); there are also specific block exemptions for the insurance and transport sectors.

Exemption criteria

2.94 The exemption criteria are set out in the 1998 Act, s 9. Exemption is available for any agreement which—

'(a)   contributes to—

    (i)   improving production or distribution, or

    (ii)   promoting technical or economic progress,

while allowing consumers a fair share of the resulting benefit; but

(b)   does not—

    (i)   impose on the undertakings concerned restrictions which are not indispensable to the attainment of those objectives; or

    (ii)   afford the undertakings concerned the possibility of eliminating competition in respect of a substantial part of the products in question.'

2.95 The wording of s 9 is very similar to, but not identical with, the EC Treaty, Art 81(3). The latter refers to 'improving the production or distribution of goods', but the domestic provision is not so limited, and can therefore be applied to services as well.

2.96 The DGFT has said that parties involved in an agreement are responsible for demonstrating that all the conditions of s 9 are satisfied so that an agreement merits an exemption.[1]

---

[1]   DGFT's guidelines 'The Chapter I prohibition', para 4.10.

2.97 Section 9 sets out the criteria for individual and block exemptions.

The agreement must contribute to an improvement in production or distribution or to technical or economic progress

2.98 The DGFT has given examples of improvements in production or distribution in his guidelines 'The Chapter I prohibition', such as lower costs from longer production or delivery runs, improvements in product quality and increases in the range of products produced or services provided;[1] and examples of the promotion of technical or economic progress such as efficiency gains from economies of scale and specialisation in research and development.[2]

---

[1]   DGFT's guidelines 'The Chapter I prohibition', para 4.11.
[2]   Ibid, para 4.12.

A fair share of any benefits must accrue to consumers

2.99 The DGFT has said that the views of customers and consumers will be an important consideration when deciding whether to give an exemption, and that their views will, in appropriate cases, be sought.[1] 'Consumers' here can mean trade purchasers as well as final consumers.

---

[1]   DGFT's guidelines 'The Chapter I prohibition', para 4.13.

Indispensable restrictions

2.100   The DGFT has said that the agreement should contain the least restrictive means of achieving its aims. The DGFT will look carefully for any restrictions beyond those necessary for securing those benefits.[1]

---
[1]   DGFT's guidelines 'The Chapter I prohibition', para 4.15.

Competition must not be substantially eliminated

2.101   The DGFT has said that an exemption will be unlikely if parties cannot show that there will continue to be effective competition in the market for the goods or services concerned.[1]

---
[1]   DGFT's guidelines 'The Chapter I prohibition', para 4.16.

2.102   Lord Simon stated twice in the House of Lords that he would expect the criteria in the 1998 Act, s 9, to be interpreted in the same broad way as the EC Treaty, Art 81(3).[1]

---
[1]   In doing so, he referred to a report prepared by Richard Whish on the exemption criteria under Art 81(3) which was placed in the Library of the House of Lords: HL Committee, 13 November 1997, col 279; 25 November 1997, col 962.

Individual exemptions

2.103   Individual exemption may be granted by the DGFT if a request has been made under s 14 and if the exemption criteria in s 9 are satisfied (s 4(1)). The DGFT may impose conditions and obligations (s 4(3)(a)) and must specify a period for which the exemption will have effect (s 4(3)(b), (4)). An individual exemption can be given retrospectively (s 4(5)); this can be to a date before the date of the request. Provision is made for the DGFT to extend the period of an individual exemption (s 4(6)). The procedure for notifying agreements to the DGFT is described in paras 4.33–4.48.

2.104   The DGFT may cancel an individual exemption, vary or remove any condition or obligation or impose additional ones (s 5(1)). This can be done by notice in writing where he has a reasonable suspicion that he based his decision to grant an exemption on information that was incomplete, false or misleading (s 5(2)). Breach of a condition has the effect of automatically cancelling an exemption (s 5(3)), whereas breach of an obligation entitles him by notice in writing to take the steps set out in s 5(1) (s 5(4)). Where the DGFT takes any of the steps in s 5(1), he must specify the time from which his decision is to have effect (s 5(5)). Where an exemption is cancelled because the DGFT based his decision on wrong information under s 5(2), or because of breach of an obligation, the time from which his decision is to have effect may be earlier than the date on which he gave his notice in writing (s 5(6)). The DGFT may proceed under s 5 on his own initiative or on a complaint made by any person (s 5(7)).

Block exemptions

2.105   The Secretary of State may adopt block exemptions, acting upon a recommendation from the DGFT (s 6). The block exemption may contain conditions and obligations (s 6(5)) and may be of limited duration (s 6(7)). The block exemption may include an 'opposition procedure', a device that has been used in several of the EC block exemptions (s 7).[1] The procedure for adopting block exemptions is set out in s 8. Given that there are already a number of EC block exemptions, and that these will be available by virtue of the parallel exemption provisions in s 10 (see para 2.106), and given that vertical agreements will be excluded from the legislation so that they will not require exemption anyway (see paras 2.75–2.89), it may be that the block exemption procedure will rarely, if ever, be used under the 1998 Act. One possible use of this device might be for joint gas development agreements, in so far as they might be considered to infringe the Chapter I prohibition.

---

[1]   On the opposition procedure in EC law, see *Butterworths Competition Law* X [319]–[354].

Parallel exemptions

2.106   A novel, but very effective, device in the 1998 Act is the concept of 'parallel exemptions' contained in s 10. Many agreements are block exempted by a Community block exemption, or would be except for the fact that they do not produce an effect on trade between Member States. Since such agreements would not infringe Art 81(1) they would not require or benefit from block exemption under Art 81(3). Section 10(1) and (2) provide that any agreement that benefits from a block exemption, an individual exemption or an opposition or objections procedure under Community law, or would do if it were to affect trade between Member States, will also be exempted from the Chapter I prohibition under domestic law. A consequence of this is that the parties to such agreements will not also need to obtain an individual exemption or to satisfy the provisions of any block exemption under domestic law. Quite apart from the simplicity that this introduces for the parties, it reduces the burden on the DGFT who will not need to grant such agreements individual exemption or to make recommendations to the Secretary of State that a block exemption should be adopted. Section 10(3) provides that such an exemption is to be known as a 'parallel exemption'. The duration of the parallel exemption is in line with the position in EC law (s 10(4)).

Cancelling a parallel exemption

2.107   Section 10(5) makes provision for the DGFT, in accordance with rules made under s 51 (see Ch 4), to impose, vary or remove conditions and obligations subject to which a parallel exemption is to have effect, or even to cancel a parallel exemption. This cancellation could be retrospective from before the date of the DGFT's notice (s 10(6)). It is not entirely clear, as a matter of Community law, whether it is open to the Secretary of State to impose stricter standards than those agreed by the Commission under Art 81(3) of the Treaty,[1] and this is a matter which might, in due course, be the subject of an Art 234 reference.

[1] See paras 6.5–6.8, 6.12. The Secretary of State would presumably be under no constraint in a s 10(2) case, where there is, ex hypothesi, no Community jurisdiction, but a real problem of conflict could arise in a s 10(1) case.

EC comfort letters[1]

2.108   The provisions in the 1998 Act, s 10, will prove important in practice where an agreement is exempt from EC law by virtue of an individual or block exemption. However, it is important to note that parallel exemption is *not* available for an agreement that has been the subject of a so-called 'comfort letter'. However, the DGFT would have regard to such a comfort letter as a result of the 1998 Act, s 60(3).[2]

[1] DGFT's guidelines 'The Chapter I prohibition', paras 7.11 and 7.12.
[2] See Ch 6.

'Exemption for other agreements'

2.109   Section 11 makes provision for 'other' agreements to be exempt: this section, which will rarely be applied in practice, may be applicable in a very narrow range of cases where exemption may be given under the EC Treaty, Art 84.[1] For example, if the Secretary of State[2] or the European Commission were to grant exemption under Art 81(3) to the proposed alliance between British Airways and American Airlines, it could be exempted from the Chapter I prohibition by virtue of the regulations under s 11(2).

[1] As there is still no implementing regulation for air transport between a Community airport and an airport in a third country, exemption can be given only under Art 84.
[2] The Secretary of State took power to give exemptions under Art 81(3) by the EC Competition Law (Articles 88 and 89) Enforcement Regulations 1996, SI 1996/2199, see reg 6(1).

3 Abuse of a dominant position

INTRODUCTION

3.1   The Competition Act 1998 controls the abuse of a dominant position by means of a new prohibition introduced to operate alongside the existing controls on monopoly situations contained in FTA 1973 (see Ch 8). The control of anti-competitive conduct under the Competition Act 1980 is abolished (by the 1998 Act, s 17). For the first time in UK competition law, firms with market power that abuse their position will be subject to the possibility of substantial fines and actions for damages. This reflects the position that has prevailed under EC competition law since 1962, when the EC Treaty, Arts 81 and 82 (former Arts 85 and 86) were brought into effect by Council Regulation 17/62/EEC.[1]

---

[1]   OJ L13, 21.2.62, p 204 (S edn, 1959–62, p 87).

THE PROHIBITION

Section 18

3.2   The prohibition of the abuse of a dominant position is contained in the 1998 Act, s 18. The inclusion of a prohibition system in the new legislation was something of a surprise and came as a result of a relatively recent change in Government thinking. Whilst the need to control the negative effects of market power is central to any effective system of competition law, previous proposals for reform had stopped short of introducing such a system (see paras 1.4, 1.5). Section 18 draws heavily on the text of the EC Treaty, Art 82,[1] and provides—

'(1)   Subject to section 19, any conduct on the part of one or more undertakings which amounts to the abuse of a dominant position in a market is prohibited if it may affect trade within the United Kingdom.

(2)   Conduct may, in particular, constitute such an abuse if it consists in—

(a)   directly or indirectly imposing unfair purchase or selling prices or other unfair trading conditions;

(b)   limiting production, markets or technical development to the prejudice of consumers;

(c)   applying dissimilar conditions to equivalent transactions with other trading parties, thereby placing them at a competitive disadvantage;

(d)   making the conclusion of contracts subject to acceptance by the other parties of supplementary obligations which, by their nature or according to commercial usage, have no connection with the subject of the contracts.

(3)   In this section—
'dominant position' means a dominant position within the United
Kingdom; and
'the United Kingdom' means the United Kingdom or any part of it.

(4)   The prohibition imposed by subsection (1) is referred to in this Act
as 'the Chapter II prohibition'.'

1   For a detailed discussion of EC law on the abuse of dominant position see *Butterworths Competition Law* VI [346]–[748]; Bellamy and Child *Common Market Law of Competition* (ed Rose) (4th edn, 1993), Ch 9.

The 'Chapter II Prohibition'

3.3   As in the case of the 1998 Act, Ch I (see para 2.37), a term has been created for the prohibition set out in s 18, namely 'the Chapter II Prohibition' (s 18(4)).

Affecting trade within the UK

3.4   As with the Chapter I prohibition (see para 2.18), there is a requirement that trade within the UK be affected; however, this is unlikely to have great significance in the context of Ch II, as most conduct that is an abuse of a dominant position within the UK will also affect trade there. This requirement could have the effect of excluding from the scope of the prohibition an abuse of a dominant position within the UK that has its effects entirely outside the UK (see para 3.6).

Jurisdiction

3.5   There is no mention of extra-territorial application in s 18 and in particular there is no equivalent of s 2(3) which limits the ambit of the Chapter I prohibition to agreements that are implemented in the UK.[1] Nevertheless, it is required that the dominant position be within the UK (s 18(3)), and in the debates during the passage of the Bill, Lord Simon explained that this could not be the case if the market in which the dominant position was held was entirely outside the UK. However, it could extend beyond the UK provided it included some part of the UK territory.[2]

1   See paras 2.25–2.29 on the jurisdictional scope of the Chapter I prohibition.
2   HL 3R, 5 March 1998, col 1336 (Lord Simon of Highbury).

3.6   An interesting question is whether the Chapter II prohibition would apply in a case where the dominant position was (wholly or partly) within the UK but the abuse either occurred in a related market outside the UK, or its effects were felt entirely outside the UK (for example a refusal by a UK company to supply an overseas customer). Here the requirement to affect trade within the UK may come into play and determine whether the prohibition applies. Presumably, any effect would have to be appreciable. Given the absence of any express treatment of jurisdictional issues in s 18, such questions, if they arise, will need to be decided in accordance with the principles of EC law under the 1998 Act, s 60 (see Ch 6). No serious issues of this kind have arisen in the jurisprudence so far on the EC Treaty, Art 82.

How the prohibition applies

3.7   For the prohibition to apply, there must therefore be—
   (a) a market,
   (b) one or more undertakings in a dominant position in that market and
   (c) conduct constituting an abuse.

'Conduct' in this context can presumably include a failure to do something, in particular a refusal to supply, which has often been held by the Court of Justice as amounting to an abuse of Art 82.[1] The analysis of these three factors has to take account of their interrelation—in other words, the ability to engage in abusive conduct may be a factor in assessing dominance and even in defining the market in which the abuse is able to occur. Equally, factors such as the ability of other suppliers to switch production to compete may be just as relevant to market definition as to the assessment of dominance. The DGFT's guidelines[2] suggest that he is aware of these issues but that the analysis will in general address each issue separately and in turn. Suffice it to say that defining the relevant market and assessing dominance and abuse are closely-related exercises.

---

[1]   See for example Cases 6&7/73 *Commercial Solvents v Commission* [1974] ECR 223; see further para 3.26.
[2]   DGFT's guidelines 'The Chapter II prohibition', 'Market definition', and his draft guidelines 'Assessment of market power' and 'Assessment of individual agreements and conduct'.

Voidness

3.8   The 1998 Act does not refer explicitly to voidness in the case of Chapter II. Prohibited conduct can nevertheless include agreements. Under EC law, an agreement that is prohibited by Art 82 is most probably void although there is no direct ECJ authority on this point. The same consequence would presumably follow, by virtue of s 60, in the case of an agreement that was prohibited by Chapter II.

Market

3.9   The term 'market' does not appear in Art 82 and its appearance in the 1998 Act is an attempt to define the geographical and substantive context of any dominant position. EC jurisprudence and practice have tended to adopt an economist's approach to markets and when defining the relevant geographical or product market have had reference to economic factors (see para 3.14). The DGFT's likely approach is set out in his guidelines and is discussed further below (see paras 3.15, 3.16).

Market size

3.10 Unlike the terms of Art 82,[1] there is no need for the dominant position to be in the whole or a 'substantial' part of the UK and a relatively small part of the UK could constitute a 'market' within the meaning of s 18.[2] The Chapter II prohibition is thus a potentially far-reaching instrument for competition authorities and litigants alike. Firms that have market power which is only on a local scale and which therefore run little risk of infringing Art 82 for lack of any effect on inter-state trade, or are dominant only in an insubstantial part of the common market, might well find that they are infringing the Chapter II prohibition. Local dominance can be expected to be found in several sectors, such as the operation of bus services.

1   Article 82 refers to a dominant position '. . . within the common market or in a substantial part of it'.
2   DGFT's guidelines 'Market definition', Pt 4.

Dominant position in EC competition law

3.11   The meaning of a 'dominant position' has been the subject of much debate in the EC context, and the jurisprudence of the ECJ and the decisions of the European Commission will inevitably be referred to when applying s 18.[1] Indeed the defeat of Lord McNally's amendment seeking to make special provision for dominance in the newspaper market was justified by the Government on the basis that EC jurisprudence already covered the issue adequately.[2]

1   See *Butterworths Competition Law* VI [346]–[506].
2   See HC 2R, 11 May 1998, col 30 (Margaret Beckett).

3.12   The traditional definition of a dominant position was given in the *United Brands* case[1] where the ECJ stated that it—

> 'relates to a position of economic strength enjoyed by an undertaking which enables it to prevent effective competition being maintained on the relevant market by affording it the power to behave to an appreciable extent independently of its competitors, customers and ultimately of its consumers'.

The definition is one of principle rather than mechanism and does not refer to any specific market share or other factor. Dominance is a relative concept and can be ascertained only by reference to a relevant market or by reference to the exercise of market power over other operators.

1   Case 27/76 [1978] ECR 207.

The relevant market

3.13   The relevant market has two main aspects: product and geography.[1] Most of the EC's jurisprudence has concentrated on determining the relevant product (or service) market rather than the geographic market. The Commission in cases under Art 82 has tended to argue the existence of narrow markets while the undertakings concerned have usually argued that the relevant market is wide. This process may be reversed in a merger case, where the merging parties might attempt to demonstrate that their transaction will not result in their attaining a disproportionate amount of market share since they operate on separate markets. It is also true to say that merger decisions of the Commission, rather than its practice under Art 82, have shed further light on the relevant geographic market, no doubt because in a merger analysis it is necessary to consider generally how a transaction will impact upon the single market.

1   A third component is the temporal aspect, but this has rarely been a significant issue under Art 82. The DGFT's guidelines 'Market definition' mention this, giving the example of the difference between peak and off-peak travel in assessing transport markets (see Pt 5).

The product market in EC law

3.14   The relevant product market is analysed in terms of demand side and supply side factors. On the demand side, the ECJ laid down a test of 'limited interchangeability' of products within a relevant market according to the consumer's perception of their price, characteristics and intended use. Similar formulations of this test, which dates at least from the *Continental Can* case in 1972,[1] have appeared in numerous different contexts in EC competition law.[2] The test provides a useful framework but is often difficult to apply and can be subjective. Its principal component, namely substitutability in terms of price, is measured by testing the cross-elasticity of demand (ie the extent to which consumers react to an increase in price of one product by switching to others). In 1997 the European Commission published a Notice on market definition[3] which summarises and explains its practice in defining the market for competition law purposes. The Notice sometimes appears to represent an ideal rather than an actual picture. For example it refers to the use of economic measures such as the so-called 'SSNIP' test (whether the product in question can undergo a 'Small but Sustained Non-transitory Increase in Prices' without customers switching to other products). The application of this test has hitherto been principally confined to merger cases. Some recent economic thinking questions the need to establish conclusively the limits of the relevant market where there is evidence of abusive behaviour which causes harm to competitors or consumers.[4] On the supply side, the ability of other suppliers to enter the market in competition with the allegedly dominant undertaking can be an important part of the market analysis and is sometimes overlooked when concentrating on consumer choice.[5]

---

[1]   Case 6/72R [1972] ECR 157.

[2]   See for example Commission Notice on agreements of minor importance, para 14 (OJ C372, 9.12.97, p 13).

[3]   Commission Notice on the definition of relevant market for the purposes of Community Competition Law (OJ C372, 9.12.97, p 5).

[4]   See eg Williams and Yarrow 'Market Definition and the Hypothetical Monopolist', Regulatory Policy Institute 1999.

[5]   In the *Continental Can* case, the Commission's failure to consider fully cross-entry of supply was a factor in its decision being overturned; the Commission's Notice on market definition sets out in paras 20–23 the circumstances in which it considers that supply-side substitutability could be taken into account when defining the relevant market.

The product market in UK law

3.15   The DGFT has issued guidelines[1] which set out how the market will be defined when the prohibitions are applied. The guidelines purport to follow the approach of the European Commission's Notice but under the 1998 Act, s 60, the DGFT and other regulators are not obliged to apply the Notice but rather must 'have regard' to it. It is only in relation to principles laid down by the EC Treaty and judgments of the ECJ that the UK authorities are obliged under s 60 to operate 'consistently' with EC law. In situations where the market unifying objectives of EC law are not relevant, there is some scope for departing from the European Commission's approach to market definition (see Ch 6 for discussion of s 60).

---

[1]   See DGFT's guidelines 'Market definition'.

3.16 The DGFT describes market definition as important because it 'sets the stage on which competition takes place'.[1] He will start by trying to identify products which can be substituted for each other so that competing undertakings can be identified.[2] In ascertaining the relevant product market, he will 'usually' use the 'hypothetical monopolist' test to ascertain which group of products could be supplied at prices maintained above competitive levels, and will usually apply the narrowest potential definition.[3] On the demand side, he will consider the proportion of captive customers, whether the 'hypothetical monopolist' is able to discriminate between customers and, sometimes, issues arising from chains of substitution. On the supply side, he will consider whether other suppliers could switch relatively quickly (say within one year) to supplying products to compete with the 'hypothetical monopolist'. The DGFT will add the estimated market shares of the products that could be switched when trying to ascertain total market size, accepting that this may not be easy.[4]

---

[1]   DGFT's guidelines 'Market definition', para 2.3.
[2]   Ibid para 2.6.
[3]   Ibid para 2.9 and Pt 3 (The 'hypothetical monopolist' test is the name given by the OFT to the SSNIP test in the EC Notice).
[4]   Ibid para 3.21.

The geographic market in EC law

3.17 The relevant geographic market has been an issue in some EC cases (see para 3.13). The best exposition of the law is in the *United Brands* case where the ECJ said that the analysis must be—

> 'with reference to a clearly defined geographic area in which (the product) is marketed and where the conditions of competition are sufficiently homogenous for the effect of the economic power of the undertaking concerned to be able to be evaluated'.[1]

This assessment requires account to be taken of legal and technical factors[2] as well as economic factors such as the prevalence of vertical links and particular purchasing patterns. The cost of transport, the value of the product and the ease with which it may be traded are equally relevant.[3] The ECJ's findings have not always been free from criticism—in the *Michelin* case, the ECJ confirmed the Commission's designation of the Netherlands as the relevant market without considering whether the customers of the tyre dealers in question could obtain supplies from outside that country.[4]

---

[1]   Case 27/76 [1978] ECR 207. Compare the Commission Notice on agreements of minor importance, para 15 (OJ C372, 9.12.97, p 13).
[2]   See eg Case 26/75 *General Motors*, [1975] ECR 1367, where the geographical market was defined by national type approval certification.
[3]   See eg Case T-30/89 *Hilti* [1990] ECRII-163, a case where the product could easily be traded through the EC.
[4]   Case 322/81 [1983] ECR 3461.

3.18 The Commission Notice on market definition[1] also goes into some detail on the geographic market, listing the categories of evidence to be used in the assessment and placing some emphasis on the increasing integration of the common market.

1   OJ C372, 9.12.97, p 13 (paras 44–52).

The geographic market under UK law

3.19 The DGFT indicates he will consider demand side and supply side issues and the possibility of imports in assessing the geographic market. Demand side factors include the value of the product, the mobility of customers and chains of substitution. Supply side factors include transport costs and the time within which supply could be switched from one area to another. The DGFT stresses that the prevalence of imports does not necessarily mean a market is international and that the lack of imports need not mean it is not international.[1]

1   DGFT's guidelines 'Market definition', Pt 4.

Assessing dominance

Dominant position under EC law

3.20 The definition of a dominant position that was given by the ECJ has already been mentioned (see para 3.12). In practice, the EC authorities have considered numerous factors in assessing whether a particular undertaking holds a dominant position. These include—

(a) absolute market shares: substantial market shares are evidence (although not conclusive evidence) of the existence of a dominant position.[1] In the *AKZO* case,[2] the ECJ said a dominant position would be presumed if the market share of the company in question exceeded 50%;

(b) relative market shares: the importance of the market share of the allegedly dominant firm will be increased if it is far greater than that of its nearest competitor;[3]

(c) statutory monopolies and other legal regulation;[4]

(d) intellectual property rights[5] and technology;[6]

(e) access to financial resources;[7]

(f) product differentiation.[8]

Many other factors ranging from economies of scale to the undertaking's own behaviour on the market may also be relevant. The focus of the whole analysis is the assessment of the potential for competition and the assessment of barriers to entry.

1   Case 85/76 *Hoffmann-La Roche* [1979] ECR 461 (where the share was 80%).
2   Case C-62/86 *AKZO Chemie* [1991] ECR 1–3359.
3   Case 322/81 *Michelin* [1983] ECR 3461.
4   See the *AKZO* case (note 2 above).
5   Case 238/87 *Volvo v Veng* [1988] ECR 6211.
6   See the *Hoffmann-La Roche* case (note 1 above).
7   Ibid.
8   This was a major factor in the *United Brands* case itself.

Dominant position under UK law

3.21 The DGFT's intentions are described in the guidelines on the Chapter II prohibition and will be explained further in the specific draft guidelines on 'Assessing

Market Power'. As with market definition, the DGFT will take into account the statements and decisions of the European Commission but may apply a different approach in circumstances where EC market-unifying objectives are not relevant. However, the DGFT will be obliged under s 60 to act consistently with the principles applied by the ECJ having regard to any relevant differences (see para 3.15).

3.22 The DGFT will take into account two main factors, namely the market share of the supposedly dominant undertaking and the extent to which it faces, or may face, competition from new entrants. He will consider entry barriers in terms of absolute and strategic advantages and in terms of the undertaking's exclusionary behaviour. He will also look at other constraints such as buyer power or government regulation and may also consider whether the undertaking is jointly dominant with others.[1] It should be noted that the DGFT will generally consider that an undertaking with a market share below 40% will not be individually dominant (unless there is other evidence to the contrary).[1]

---

[1] On joint dominance, see para 3.29.
[2] This is a lower threshold than that of the ECJ in presuming the existence of a dominant position, but is not materially different from European Commission practice.

Abuse

Section 18(2)

3.23 Section 18(2) provides—[1]

> 'Conduct may, in particular, constitute such an abuse if it consists in—
> (a) directly or indirectly imposing unfair purchase or selling prices or other unfair trading conditions;
> (b) limiting production, markets or technical development to the prejudice of consumers;
> (c) applying dissimilar conditions to equivalent transactions with other trading parties, thereby placing them at a competitive disadvantage;
> (d) making the conclusion of contracts subject to acceptance by the other parties of supplementary obligations which, by their nature or according to commercial usage, have no connection with the subject of the contracts.'

---

[1] The non-exclusive list of abuses reflects exactly the terms of Art 82.

Abuse of dominant position under EC law

3.24 EC jurisprudence has not developed solely by reference to the corresponding list of conduct set out in Art 82 but has instead concentrated on the more general purpose and scope of the prohibition.[1] The ECJ has defined abuse in a number of cases, including *Hoffmann-La Roche,*[2] where it stated—

> 'The concept of abuse is an objective concept relating to the behaviour of an undertaking in a dominant position which is such as to influence the structure of the market where, as a result of the very presence of the undertaking in question, the degree of competition is weakened . . . '.

¹ See *Butterworths Competition Law* VI [548].
² Case 85/76 [1979] ECR 461.

3.25 Practices condemned under EC law include the following—
  (a) discriminatory prices;[1]
  (b) unfair or 'predatory' pricing;[2]
  (c) refusal to supply;[3]
  (d) unfair termination of contracts;[4]
  (e) misuse of intellectual property rights;[5]
  (f) loyalty or 'fidelity' rebates;[6]
  (g) the acquisition of a principal competitor;[7]
  (h) the 'leveraging' of market power from one market to a separate but associated market.[8]

The list of possible abuses is not closed and there is no doubt that a firm in a dominant position, which the ECJ has repeatedly said has 'special responsibility' not to harm unfettered competition, must tread carefully to avoid an infringement of Art 82.

¹ Case 27/76 *United Brands* [1978] ECR 207.
² Case C-62/86 *AKZO Chemie* [1991] ECR I–3359.
³ Cases 6 and 7/73 *Commercial Solvents* [1974] ECR 223.
⁴ *United Brands* (see above).
⁵ Cases C-241, 242/91P *RTE and ITP* [1995] ECR 1–743.
⁶ Case 85/76 *Hoffmann-La Roche* [1979] ECR 461.
⁷ Case 6/72R *Continental Can* [1972] ECR 157.
⁸ Case C-333/94P *Tetra Pak International* [1996] ECR I–5951.

Abuse under UK law—conduct

3.26 Unlike Art 82, s 18(1) refers to 'conduct' which amounts to an abuse, rather than merely an abuse. It is hard to see how this improves on the EC version, although it could possibly lead to a narrower interpretation in situations where the abuse stems from inactivity rather than from any actual conduct. Would failure to respond to requests, for example, for the grant of rights under a patent, amount to 'conduct'? This is probably the case, but the discrepancy is not justified by any difficulty in EC jurisprudence.

The DGFT's guidelines

3.27 The DGFT is issuing specific guidelines on the assessment of individual agreements and conduct, much of which is relevant to the application of s 18 and which supplements the explanations in the general guidelines on the Chapter II prohibition.[1] These guidelines describe the DGFT's approach to—
  (a) excessive prices;
  (b) price discrimination;
  (c) predation;
  (d) other pricing issues (subsidies, cross-subsidies and discounts);
  (e) vertical restraints;
  (f) refusal to supply and access to essential facilities;
  (g) actions in related markets.

The guidelines discuss the approach of the ECJ and the European Commission to these issues and show an intention to apply UK law consistently with EC law.

---

[1]   The guidelines are also relevant, albeit to a much lesser extent, to the Chapter I prohibition—see the discussion in Ch 2.

Vertical restraints

3.28 The discussion of vertical restraints is particularly important in view of the proposed disapplication of the Chapter I prohibition to many of them (see paras 2.75–2.89).[1] Such restraints remain subject to the Chapter II prohibition and indeed are much more likely to cause concern when they are considered in connection with the exercise of market power.[2] The restraints discussed are—

   (a) resale price maintenance;
   (b) selective distribution;
   (c) exclusive distribution;
   (d) tie-in sales and bundling;
   (e) full-line forcing;
   (f)   quantity forcing;
   (g) fidelity discounts;
   (h) non-linear pricing.

The guidelines discuss each of these practices in detail.[3]

---

[1]   Some practices such as resale price maintenance will not be excluded from the Chapter I prohibition.
[2]   This was a factor in retaining monopoly controls under FTA 1973 also; see Ch 8.
[3]   DGFT's guidelines 'The Chapter II prohibition', paras 4.31–4.46; see also draft guidelines 'Assessment of individual agreements and conduct', Pt 6.

Joint dominance

3.29 Section 18 refers to 'conduct on the part of one or more undertakings', raising the question of whether the abuse or the dominant position, or both, needs to be confined to a single undertaking. EC jurisprudence and practice on this point[1] will be relevant but it should be noted that the Government did not feel that the developing EC doctrine of joint dominance, the precise scope of which remains unclear, was a sufficient replacement for the complex monopoly provisions of FTA 1973.[2] The DGFT's guidelines[3] confirm that he will aim to follow the EC jurisprudence on this subject.

---

[1]   See for example Cases T-68, 77-8/89 *Italian Flat Glass* 1992 ECR II-1403; Cases T- 24–26 and 28/93 *CMBT v Commission* [1996] ECR II-1201; Case C-393/92 *Almelo* [1994] ECRI-1477 and also Cases C-68/94 and C-30/95 *France v Commission* [1998] 4 CMLR 829 on the application of the Merger Regulation to joint dominance.
[2]   HL Committee, 13 November 1997, col 300 (Lord Simon of Highbury).
[3]   DGFT's guidelines 'The Chapter II prohibition', paras 3.19–3.21 and 4.13; see also draft guidelines 'Assessment of market power', paras 2.9, 2.10.

Undertaking

3.30 This term will have the same meaning as in the case of the Chapter I prohibition (see Ch 2).

EXCLUSIONS[1]

Exclusions for mergers subject to UK or EC merger control

3.31 The Chapter II prohibition does not apply to conduct resulting in a merger situation[2] or in a concentration with a Community dimension (Sch 1, para 6). The first of these exclusions applies to all conduct resulting in enterprises 'ceasing to be distinct' (the FTA 1973 merger test) and is not limited to those mergers that qualify for investigation under the 1973 Act. It also includes 'ancillary' conduct (directly related to and necessary to the attainment of the merger). The second exclusion (for conduct subject to the Commission's exclusive jurisdiction under the EC Merger Regulation)[3] does not expressly extend to 'ancillary' conduct but provided such conduct falls within the Commission's jurisdiction, it is effectively excluded. Situations in which the so-called 'Continental Can' doctrine[4] would otherwise be applicable (ie, the strengthening of an existing dominant position by the acquisition of a competing undertaking) are also excluded. If the concentration is not one in relation to which the Commission has exclusive jurisdiction under the EC Merger Regulation, it will be excluded under Sch 1, Pt I; if the Commission does have exclusive jurisdiction, it will be excluded under Sch 1, Pt II.

---

[1] See the detailed discussion of exclusions in the context of the Chapter I prohibition at paras 2.38–2.92.

[2] Section 19, Sch 1, paras 2, 3(2) (covering newspaper mergers); unlike the Chapter I exclusion, this exclusion cannot be withdrawn by the DGFT but by s 19(2) the Secretary of State may by order amend Sch 1 with respect to the Chapter II prohibition by providing additional exclusions or amending or removing any existing ones.

[3] Council Regulation 4064/89/EEC, OJ L257, 21.9.90, p 13 (as amended by Council Regulation 1310/97/EC, OJ L180, 9.7.97, p 1).

[4] Case 6/72 *Continental Can* [1972] ECR 157; see para 3.25.

Other exclusions

3.32 Section 19(1) refers to Sch 3 which contains a list of further exclusions. This list is shorter than the list of those exclusions applicable to the Chapter I prohibition (see paras 2.38–2.92), but the following are common to both prohibitions—

    (a) services of general economic interest (Sch 3, para 4);[1]

    (b) compliance with legal requirements (Sch 3, para 5);

    (c) avoidance of conflict with international obligations (Sch 3, para 6);

    (d) exceptional and compelling reasons of public policy (Sch 3, para 7);

    (e) conduct subject to the exclusive jurisdiction of the Commission under the ECSC (European Coal and Steel Community) Treaty (Sch 3, para 8).[2]

The ECSC Treaty expires in 2001 and s 19(3) empowers the Secretary of State by order to amend the exclusion relating to the ECSC. A table setting out exclusions from both the Chapter I and Chapter II prohibitions is set out in Appendix 8.[3]

---

[1] See the discussion in Ch 7 on this provision which is intended to reflect the EC Treaty, Art 86.

[2] The relevant ECSC Treaty article is Art 66(7) which is formulated in less clear-cut terms than the EC Treaty, Art 82.

[3] It is understood that the Chapter I exclusions relating to the Financial Services Act 1986 and EEA regulated markets will be extended to include the Chapter II prohibition by amendment to the Competition Act 1998 (see paras 2.53 and 2.63).

Conduct of minor significance

3.33 Section 40 provides limited immunity from penalties only for 'conduct of minor significance'. The immunity may be withdrawn by the DGFT if, after investigation, he considers the conduct may nonetheless infringe Chapter II. The DGFT proposes to use only the turnover threshold provided by s 40(2) to define minor significance—the limit is not yet decided—rather than market share. The immunity does not go to substance and does not prevent claims by third parties.[1]

---

[1]   See the discussion on immunity from penalties at paras 4.66–4.67; and on third party actions, see paras 4.71–4.74.

COMMENT

3.34 The main difference between the Chapter II prohibition and the EC Treaty, Art 82 is the absence of any requirement of size or scale. Although EC jurisprudence on Art 82 has sometimes concerned isolated practices in very narrow markets,[1] in general the law has been applied to the practices of economically powerful undertakings operating on a substantial scale in the European territory. Chapter II contains no such requirement and action under Chapter II will depend heavily on the authorities' (and courts') practice in relation to the relevant geographic market.[2] At the same time it is likely that Chapter II will prove much more effective than the Competition Act 1980 in combating short-term exclusionary conduct where the likely complainant cannot sustain opposition to the exercise of market power and may succumb before the authorities can act effectively, not least because of the possibility of taking interim measures under s 35.[3]

---

[1]   See for example the *General Motors* case (Case 26/75 1975 [ECR] 1367) which concerned type approval certificates for GM cars imported into Belgium.

[2]   See DGFT's guidelines 'Market definition', Pt 4, which refer to markets possibly as small as a few square miles and as large as the whole of the UK.

[3]   See paras 4.56–4.58.

3.35 The other difference between Chapter II and its EC equivalent is the fact that it is buttressed by the monopoly provisions contained in FTA 1973. The Government has confirmed[1] that the purpose of retaining these provisions is to provide additional remedies and to avoid certain practices escaping competition scrutiny altogether. However, it is conceivable that action under Ch II could follow a monopoly investigation by the reporting function of the Competition Commission, as an alternative to, or even in addition to, ministerial action. Thus the potential scope for intervention using the new prohibition seems to be increased.

---

[1]   HL Committee, 13 November 1997, col 300 (Lord Simon of Highbury). See also Ch 8.

4 Procedure and enforcement

INTRODUCTION

4.1   The need to apply and enforce the new prohibitions requires major changes to the procedures operated by the UK competition authorities. The power to impose penalties carries with it a responsibility to ensure that the fact-finding and assessment of cases is rigorous, accountable and fair. In addition, the major increase in the authorities' powers to obtain information and to conduct investigations is a further reason why procedure and enforcement are central to the 1998 Act. This chapter considers the investigation and decision-making powers of the DGFT and regulators, the conduct of investigations, notifications for guidance or exemption, the powers of enforcement, and the right of third parties to take action. Appeals are dealt with in Ch 5.

INQUIRIES AND INVESTIGATIONS

Investigations under s 25

4.2   The DGFT may conduct an investigation if there are 'reasonable grounds for suspecting' that either of the prohibitions has been infringed (s 25).[1] The terms of the section anticipate the DGFT's likely delegation to authorised officers and do not require his personal suspicion in each case.[2] This new power deals with one of the DGFT's complaints about the previous regime under which he had to have 'reasonable cause to believe'[3] that an infringement had occurred before he could investigate it (in other words, he had to be able to show it existed before he could find out whether or not it did).

---

[1]   The DGFT's powers apply equally to the sector regulators listed in s 54 and it should be assumed throughout this chapter that anything which applies to the DGFT applies equally to them, unless otherwise stated.

[2]   See HL Report Stage, 9 February 1998, cols 986–7 (Lord Haskel).

[3]   RTPA 1976, s 36 (cf FTA 1973, s 44 (as amended) 'Where it appears to the Director that there are grounds for believing . . .').

Written inquiries

4.3   An investigation under s 25 can involve requests for information in writing or take the form of an on-the-spot investigation. A written request is made by a notice under s 26 requiring a person to produce to the DGFT a specified document or specified information which the DGFT considers relevant to the investigation (s 26(1), (2)). The notice must indicate the subject matter and purpose of the investigation (s 26(3)(a)) and the offences involved in non-compliance (s 26(3)(b)). Specification can be by reference to a particular item or by category and the notice may state when and where the document or information is to be provided as well as how and in what form (s 26(4) and (5)).[1] The DGFT has the further power to take copies or extracts from a document produced in response to the notice and to ask for an explanation of it, or, if the document is not produced, to ask where it is believed to be (s 26(6)).[2] Notices can be addressed to any person, which is defined to include an undertaking[3] and the DGFT regards this as extending to an association of undertakings.[4]

---

[1] Section 59(3) provides that if information is not in legible form, the DGFT may require a copy in legible form.

[2] See paras 4.18–4.19 for discussion of the scope of the power to request explanations and the EC law on self-incrimination.

[3] Section 59(1), which refers to the Interpretation Act 1978 ('person' includes a body of persons corporate or unincorporate). See paras 2.8–2.9.

[4] DGFT's guidelines 'Powers of investigation', para 3.11. In the case of an undertaking or an association, an authorised person should respond on its behalf.

4.4   A s 26 notice is therefore similar to an Art 11 request by the European Commission[1] and it is likely that a similar format (with the offences for non-compliance printed at the bottom of the page) will be used. It should be noted that while s 26 applies to documents and to information equally, the DGFT's guidelines make it clear that the power to obtain information can effectively require a person to create a document comprising that information 'using the knowledge or experience of the sales manager'.[2]

---

[1] See Council Regulation 17/62/EEC, OJ L13, 21.2.62, p 204 (S edn 1959–62, p 87) and *Butterworths Competition Law* X [491]–[531].

[2] DGFT's guidelines 'Powers of investigation', para 3.7.

Entry without warrant

4.5   Section 27 provides—

'(1)   Any officer of the Director[1] who is authorised in writing by the Director to do so ('an investigating officer') may enter any premises in connection with an investigation under section 25.'[2]

This equates to the provisions of Art 14 (investigation by the European Commission).[3]

---

[1] Director means the DGFT and the sector regulators listed in s 54. Officer means a member of his staff.

[2] The Secretary of State may certify in the interests of national security that specified Crown premises may not be entered under this section (see s 73(8)).

[3] See *Butterworths Competition Law* X [532]–[592].

Party under investigation

4.6   The operation of the power of entry varies depending on whether the premises are occupied by a party under investigation for possible infringement of the Chapter I or Chapter II prohibitions or by a 'third party', that is to say someone who is not suspected of an offence. In the case of the former, the investigating officer must have written authority from the DGFT, together with a document including details of the subject matter and purpose of the investigation and the offences involved in non-compliance. On entry, he must produce this document and show evidence of his authorisation (s 27(3), (4)). There is no requirement to give prior warning or notice.

Third party premises

4.7   In the case of entry to third party premises, the investigating officer must give two working days' prior written notice and the notice itself must indicate the subject matter and purpose of the investigation (s 27(2)). If, however, the officer has taken all reasonable steps to give notice but has been unable to do so, he may dispense with the notice requirement and enter as if the premises were occupied by a party under investigation.[1]

---

[1]   Presumably this situation will only occur rarely.

4.8   When entering the premises,[1] the officer may—
  (a) take with him any necessary equipment;
  (b) require 'any person'[2] to produce any documents which the officer considers relevant, to say where a document may be found, and, in relation to any document produced, require an explanation of it;
  (c) take copies of or extracts from any document produced (but not take the originals);
  (d) require the production in visible, legible and portable form of any relevant information that is held on computer (s 27(5)).[3]

---

[1]   See para 4.9.
[2]   In this instance, this term presumably (although not necessarily) refers to an individual rather than to an undertaking but there is no restriction as to who the person needs to be; it could include secretaries, IT personnel and messengers as well as directors. See HL Committee, 17 November 1997, col 391 (Lord Simon of Highbury).
[3]   See also s 59(3).

Premises

4.9   Premises are defined in s 59(1) as not including domestic premises unless they are also used in connection with an undertaking's affairs or an undertaking's documents are kept there, but are taken to include any vehicle. Relevant documents cannot therefore safely be hidden at home or in a car. Documents kept at the offices of an undertaking's lawyers would be disclosable also, subject to legal professional privilege.[1]

---

[1]   See DGFT's guidelines 'Powers of investigation', para 4.6.

Practical effect

4.10 From the point of view of a party being investigated, investigating officers may turn up at their premises without warning (normally during business hours) and demand entry.[1] The only document that the officers need produce is evidence of their authority from the DGFT and a document indicating what the investigation is about. They may bring necessary equipment with them and require documents to be produced, copy them in whole or in part and ask 'any person' for an explanation of them. They may not, however, use any force either to enter or once on the premises and permitted equipment would not therefore include crowbars or other tools.[2] Section 27 entry may therefore be described as a 'right of peaceable entry'.[3]

1   DGFT's guidelines 'Powers of investigation', para 4.9.
2   See ibid, para 4.5 which refers to portable computers and recording equipment.
3   See paras 4.16–4.19 below for discussion of legal professional privilege, the right of access to lawyers and the right against self-incrimination.

Entry with a warrant

4.11 In certain situations, the DGFT has a power of entry with a warrant issued by a Judge of the High Court (Court of Session in Scotland) and in this case he may use reasonable force to obtain entry (s 28). The circumstances are as follows—

  (a) there are reasonable grounds for suspecting that a document sought by written notice or by an investigation without warrant but not produced is on the premises;

  (b) there are reasonable grounds for suspecting that a document that the DGFT could obtain by written notice is on the premises but would be interfered with if it were required to be produced; or

  (c) entry without warrant for the purpose of investigation has been impossible and there are reasonable grounds for suspecting that documents are on the premises that could have been required if entry had been obtained (s 28(1)).

The s 28 powers are therefore a 'right of forcible entry'.[1]

1   The possible exclusion of specified Crown premises applies to s 28 also (s 73(8)).

The warrant

4.12 Investigation by warrant is a serious matter and the investigator's powers are more extensive than under ss 26 or 27. The warrant must authorise the investigating officer and any others delegated by the DGFT by name (s 28(2)). The subject matter and purpose of the investigation, and the offences for non-compliance, must be indicated in the warrant itself (s 29(1)). Therefore, the party being investigated should inspect this document closely.

Reasonable force

4.13 The investigators may use reasonable force to gain entry, but must lock the premises up in as secure a manner as they found them before leaving (s 28(2), (5)). They may take 'equipment' to exercise such force but may not use force against any person.[1]

1   DGFT's guidelines 'Powers of investigation', paras 5.4 and 5.5.

Documents

4.14 As with investigations without warrant, the authorised officer may require documents to be produced but the scope of this power depends on the situation in which the warrant was issued. The warrant will accordingly specify documents of 'the relevant kind' (s 28(2)(b)) ie those subject to a specific request under ss 26 or 27, or those of the kind that could have been required on investigation under s 27 but were not provided. The DGFT envisages the second category as requiring a generic definition only.[1]

---

[1] DGFT's guidelines 'Powers of investigation', para 5.6.

Other powers when entry is with a warrant

4.15 In addition to all the powers investigators would have on entry without a warrant, including the power to require information to be accessed from computers (s 28(3)), they can also take away *originals* of documents and retain them for three months if copying them on the premises is not practicable or if taking them away appears necessary to prevent their disappearance (s 28(2)(c), (7)). The investigators can also take any other necessary steps to preserve the existence of documents (s 28(2)(d)).

Legal professional privilege

4.16 The requirement to produce documents whether by written notice or on investigation does not extend to privileged communications (s 30). These are defined as communications either between a professional legal adviser and his client or those made in connection with, or in contemplation of, legal proceedings and which, for the purposes of those proceedings, would be protected from disclosure in High Court proceedings (Court of Session in Scotland) on grounds of legal professional privilege (confidentiality of communications in Scotland).[1] 'Professional legal adviser' includes professionally qualified lawyers employed by firms (in-house counsel) as well as those practising in their own right, and in this respect privilege under the 1998 Act is more extensive than under EC competition law.[2]

---

[1] For the law of privilege in court proceedings see 13 *Halsbury's Laws* (4th edn) paras 71–85.
[2] See DGFT's guidelines 'Powers of investigation' paras 6.1 and 6.2 and HL Committee, 17 November 1997, col 416 (Lord Haskel). See para 4.31 for the difficulties this difference may create.

Access to lawyers

4.17 In the case of an investigation with or without a warrant, there is no statutory right to obtain outside legal help, and certainly none to delay the start of an investigation, until a firm's external lawyer arrives on the scene. Such situations are familiar in the context of EC investigations and, during the passage of the Bill through Parliament, the Government asserted that even though there was nothing in the statute itself, the DGFT would follow European Commission practice in this regard, by giving a firm without internal legal assistance a reasonable period (in practice usually no more than a couple of hours) to obtain external help.[1] The DGFT has accepted that this is required and the guidelines and draft Rules reflect this, although the investigating officer will still have considerable latitude.[2]

---

[1] HL Committee, 17 November 1997, col 404 (Lord Simon of Highbury). For a description of European Commission practice see *Butterworths Competition Law* Div X [582]–[635].
[2] See DGFT's guidelines 'Powers of investigation' paras 4.10 and 4.11 which show an intention to be no more generous than the European Commission in this regard and allow the investigating officer to take steps to prevent documents being destroyed or tampered with in the meantime. The investigating

officer also need not delay at all if the firm being investigated has an internal legal adviser, however non-specialised he or she may be. The DGFT's draft Procedural Rules provide expressly for this right 'if the officer considers it reasonable in the circumstances to do so and if he is satisfied that such conditions as he considers . . . appropriate . . . will be complied with' (See r 13(1)).

Limits on the explanation of documents

4.18 The power to provide an 'explanation' of a document is expressly linked to and limited to documents that are produced (ss 26(6)(a)(ii), 27(5)(b)(ii)). The only area of uncertainty is in relation to investigations under warrant, where the requirement to provide an explanation applies to 'any document appearing to be of the relevant kind' (s 28(2)(e)) without any specific reference to the document having been produced. The investigator could in theory require explanation of a document that appears to exist but which he has been unable to find, but the DGFT's guidelines do not indicate any intention to act in this way.[1]

[1] The DGFT's draft Procedural Rules provide (at r 13(3)) that any person required under s 26(6)(a)(ii) (ie by written notice) to provide an explanation of a document may be accompanied by a legal adviser. Note that they do not offer such a right during an on-the-spot investigation. (See Appendix 4 for full text of the draft rules.)

Self-incrimination

4.19 The DGFT acknowledges the EC jurisprudence on the subject of self-incrimination[1] and accepts that it will apply to his actions by virtue of s 60.[2] It remains to be seen how this difficult area will be addressed in practice. The DGFT indicates that he may not ask for explanations that might involve admissions of an infringement and will instead seek explanations of matters of fact,[3] but the distinction between these two will not always be clear-cut.

[1] See *Butterworths Competition Law* X paras [593]–[596].
[2] DGFT's guidelines 'Powers of investigation', para 6.3.
[3] Ibid, para 6.4: the example given is whether a particular employee attended a particular meeting.

Confidentiality

4.20 There are detailed provisions in the 1998 Act about the disclosure of information obtained during the course of an investigation (and as a result of the operation of Part I generally)[1] and these provide a degree of reassurance to disclosing parties. However, parties subject to an investigation or to a request for information would be well advised to identify any confidential information that is supplied to the DGFT or to his investigators in order to support any subsequent claim that it should not be published or disclosed to anyone else. There is, moreover, no right to withhold information from the investigators on grounds of confidentiality.[2] The DGFT's guidelines explain his rights and obligations as regards publication.[3]

[1] See s 55 (together with Sch 11), and s 56; see Ch 10.
[2] See r 25 of the DGFT's draft Procedural Rules in relation to information provided by third parties.
[3] DGFT's guidelines 'Powers of investigation' paras 6.5–6.9. See para 4.73 for discussion of disclosure to facilitate court proceedings brought by third parties.

Offences

4.21 There are criminal sanctions for non-compliance with the power of investigation. The relevant offences are set out in the 1998 Act, ss 42–44. They fall into five main categories as follows—

(a) failing to comply with a requirement imposed under ss 26, 27 or 28 (s 42(1));

(b) intentionally obstructing an officer investigating without a warrant (s 42(5));

(c) intentionally obstructing an officer investigating with a warrant (s 42(7));

(d) intentionally or recklessly destroying, disposing of, falsifying or concealing documents, or causing or permitting those things to happen (s 43(1));

(e) knowingly or recklessly supplying information which is false or misleading in a material particular either directly to the DGFT or to anyone else knowing it is for the purpose of providing information to the DGFT (s 44(1), (2)).

Defences

4.22 The Act allows various defences to these rather all-embracing penal provisions. Thus, if a person is charged with not producing a document, it is a defence to show that he did not have it in his possession or control and it was not reasonably practical for him to get it (s 42(2), (3)). A similar defence applies to failure to provide information. In relation to all requirements under ss 26 and 27 (written notice and investigation without a warrant) there is a general defence if the investigator failed to act in accordance with the section (s 42(4)). This shows the importance of ensuring that all the procedural steps are properly taken, but there is no such defence in relation to investigations with a warrant, although it is possible to appeal against the issue of the warrant itself. There are no statutory defences to the charges of knowingly or recklessly destroying documents or providing false or misleading information.

Penalties

4.23 The penalties can be substantial and depend on whether the offence is tried summarily or is serious enough to be taken on indictment to the High Court (or High Court of the Justiciary in Scotland). Usually the penalties are financial but in the case of any obstruction of investigators with a warrant, destruction of documents or provision of false or misleading information, imprisonment for up to two years is possible (as well as a fine in some cases).[1]

---

[1]   See ss 42(6), (7), 43(2), 44(3). The DGFT's guidelines 'Powers of investigation' describe the penalties in detail (see para 7.7 thereof).

Persons affected

4.24 As already described, the powers of investigation, and the offences, are applicable to 'persons', which can include an undertaking (s 59(1); see para 4.3). In addition, under s 72, officers of bodies corporate are liable to punishment if they have consented to or connived at an offence or it is due to neglect on their part (s 72(2)).[1]

Officer means a director, manager, secretary or other similar officer, or anyone purporting to act as such (s 72(3)). There are similar provisions applicable to companies managed by their members (who can be liable) and, in Scotland, to partners and partnerships (s 72(4)–(6)). A table of offences and penalties affecting individuals appears in Appendix 7 to this book. The fact that individuals themselves can be liable in certain circumstances under the 1998 Act and that there is even a possibility of imprisonment will no doubt concentrate the minds of those responsible for ensuring compliance with the legislation.

---

[1]   See DGFT's guidelines 'Powers of investigation', para 7.4. Similar provisions were contained in the RTPA 1976 (see s 38(6), (7) of that Act) but never attracted particular attention.

Investigations under FTA 1973

4.25 As explained in Ch 8 (at para 8.8), the powers to obtain information and to investigate under FTA 1973 have been substantially strengthened to assist the DGFT in applying the continuing monopoly control legislation. These powers are similar to those provided in relation to the provisions of the 1998 Act but no power to enter premises with a warrant using force is provided.

Scope and exercise of FTA 1973 powers

4.26 The amendments made to FTA 1973 include the creation of new powers to assist the DGFT in determining whether to take a decision to make a monopoly reference or to accept undertakings in lieu (FTA 1973, s 44(1), (1A)). Powers to require the production of documents and information and the power to enter premises are now contained in FTA 1973, s 44, with differences in detail from the powers contained in the 1998 Act, ss 26–28. Thus, the powers may be exercised in relation to any person carrying on a business in the production or supply of goods or services of the relevant (ie the DGFT's) description in the UK (FTA 1973, s 44(2)(b), (3)); and the information requested can include 'estimates, forecasts [or] returns' (FTA 1973, s 44(2)(b)).[1] The reservations for privilege and the other qualifications on the DGFT's powers that apply in the context of the prohibitions are equally applicable to the exercise of these powers (FTA 1973, s 44(6)).[2]

---

[1]   The 1998 Act, s 59(1) defines information as including 'estimates and forecasts' but makes no mention of 'returns'.
[2]   See DGFT's guidelines 'Powers of investigation', paras 9.1–9.5, particularly 9.4.

Penalties under FTA 1973

4.27 FTA 1973, s 46 is amended to introduce similar penalties to those otherwise applicable, bearing in mind the absence of any power to enter with a warrant. Thus a serious offence of document destruction could attract a prison sentence of two years.[1]

---

[1]   See DGFT's guidelines 'Powers of investigation', para 9.5.

Assisting the European Commission

4.28 Although the European Commission's powers of investigation have been applicable in the UK for some 25 years, the 1998 Act provides for the first time specific powers for the DGFT to assist the Commission in this respect. The reason for this change is that the new powers given to the DGFT[1] to investigate possible breaches of UK competition law expose the fact that no similar express powers have existed to give effect to the UK's obligations under Art 14(6) of Council Regulation 17/62/EEC[2] for the past quarter century. This omission is now remedied.[3]

---

[1]   Note that in this instance the powers are given to the DGFT alone and not to any regulator.
[2]   Council Regulation 17/62/EEC, OJ L13, 21.2.62, p 204 (S edn 1959–62, p 87).
[3]   Note, however, that the 1998 Act does *not* give the DGFT himself the power to enforce the EC Treaty, Arts 81 and 82, a power that has been given to the competition authorities in some Member States (see para 6.1).

Warrant

4.29 The DGFT is given power to enter premises with a warrant, using reasonable force as necessary, in the event of obstruction of either—

(a) a European Commission investigation which the DGFT is assisting (a 'Commission investigation')

(b) an investigation carried out by the DGFT under EC law at the request of the European Commission (a 'Director's investigation')

(c) a Director's investigation carried out by the DGFT in connection with a Commission investigation (a 'Director's special investigation').[1]

---

[1]   See the 1998 Act, s 61. Note that the possible exclusion of Crown premises in the interests of national security is applicable (s 73(8)) and that the right of entry does not in any event apply to land occupied by the Crown or a Government department unless the suspected infringement is by the Crown or a public servant (s 73(6), (7)); see also Ch 10.

Powers, offences and penalties

4.30 The details of the powers and the offences and penalties are very similar to those in the case of investigation by warrant under the 1998 Act, s 28 and the reader is referred to the description of that section.[1]

---

[1]   See paras 4.21–4.23. Sections 62–65 set out the DGFT's power to obtain a warrant, the DGFT's authorised officer's powers, the offences and the prescribed penalties. See also DGFT's guidelines 'Powers of investigation' paras 10.1 and 10.9.

Legal professional privilege

4.31 The scope of legal professional privilege allowed for investigations into breaches of UK competition law is wider than is allowed under EC law.[1] Not only does EC law not extend to 'in-house' (ie employed) lawyers but independent professional lawyers have to be qualified in an EU Member State.[2] Thus a document required to be produced could legitimately be withheld in one investigation but not in another, and if the investigators were combining an EC and a UK investigation into a single visit under dual authority, the situation could become quite Gilbertian. This is exacerbated by the fact that disputed claims of privilege in an EC context are referred to the Court of First Instance, but a dispute under UK law would either be 'stored up' for an appeal against the DGFT's final decision, or be subject to an application for judicial review.[3] The UK authorities can hardly be blamed for this situation but it is one where the operation of s 60 will not lead to the application of the principles of EC law and where this is perhaps beneficial. It is to be hoped that those conducting investigations will do their best to prevent such undesirable situations from arising.

---

1   DGFT's guidelines 'Powers of investigation', paras 10.7 and 10.8.
2   For a discussion of privilege in EC competition law, see *Butterworths Competition Law* X [1377]–[1410].
3   See Ch 6. But the actions of an official authorised by the DGFT in the context of a Director's investigation or special investigation at the behest of the European Commission could be susceptible to judicial review in the UK courts (possibly leading to an Art 234 reference to the ECJ).

Transitional provisions and exclusions

4.32 The DGFT has the power to obtain information to enable him to take action in relation to the application of transitional periods to particular agreements and in connection with exclusions from the prohibitions. These powers are described in the DGFT's guidelines.[1]

---

1   DGFT's guidelines 'Powers of investigation', Pt 8. For description of the transitional arrangements see Ch 9.

NOTIFICATION TO THE AUTHORITIES

Introduction

4.33 An agreement may be notified to the DGFT[1] for the purpose of assessing whether it infringes the Chapter I prohibition or whether it falls within an exclusion or qualifies for exemption (s 12). Conduct may be notified to the DGFT for the purpose of assessing whether it infringes the Chapter II prohibition or whether it falls within an exclusion (s 20). The procedure to be followed is outlined in the 1998 Act (Schs 5, 6) and further indications are contained in the draft Director's Rules[2] and the notification Form N.[3] There are two sorts of notification provided for by the 1998 Act, namely for guidance and for a decision and these are explained below.[4]

---

1   The regulators have all the powers of the DGFT to receive and process notifications to give guidance and make decisions granting exemption. For a discussion of these concurrent powers see Ch 7. See para 4.2, fn 1.
2   DGFT's draft Procedural Rules to be enacted under s 51.
3   See DGFT's draft Form N 'Form for Notifications for Guidance or Decision under Chapters I and II of the Competition Act 1998', set out in Appendix 4.
4   For discussion of dual notifications to the European Commission and to the DGFT see paras 6.31–6.46.

Notification of agreements for guidance

4.34 Notification for guidance must be made by a party to the agreement and when the DGFT has received such a notification he may give the applicant guidance as to whether or not the agreement is likely to infringe the Chapter I prohibition (s 13(1), (2)). If he considers that an infringement is likely (in the absence of any exemption) the guidance may indicate either whether a block, parallel or s 11 exemption applies (see paras 2.105–2.109) or whether he would grant individual exemption (see paras 2.103, 2.104) if asked to do so.

Effect of notification of agreements for guidance

4.35 If the DGFT determines an application under s 13 by giving guidance to the effect either that—
  (a) the agreement is unlikely to infringe; or
  (b) it benefits from block, parallel or s 11 exemption; or
  (c) he would be likely to exempt it individually,
the consequences listed in s 15 follow.

4.36 The first of these consequences is that the DGFT cannot proceed further against the agreement unless—
  (a) he has reasonable grounds to believe there has been a material change of circumstance; or
  (b) he has a reasonable suspicion that he was given information that was incomplete, false or misleading in a material particular; or
  (c) one of the parties asks him for a decision under s 14; or
  (d) he receives a complaint from a third party (s 15(2)).
The second is that he may impose no penalty (s 15(3)).[1]

---

[1]   For discussion of immunity from penalties on notification and receipt of guidance, and on the possibility of the DGFT withdrawing that immunity by provisional decision, see paras 4.66–4.69.

Notification of conduct for guidance and its effect

4.37 Notification of conduct for guidance must be made by the person whose conduct is at issue, and when the DGFT has received the notification he may give the person guidance as to whether the Chapter II prohibition is likely to be infringed (s 21). The effect of guidance is similar to that given under the Chapter I prohibition (s 23; see paras 4.35, 4.36).

Notification of an agreement for a decision

4.38 For an agreement to be examined under s 14 a party to the agreement must notify the DGFT, who may then take a decision as to whether the Chapter I prohibition has been infringed and, if not, whether that is because of the effect of an exclusion or because the agreement is exempt (s 14(1), (2)).[1] The 1998 Act provides that the application 'may include' a request for individual exemption (s 14(3)) although in practice it is likely that this will be the rule rather than the exception. If the agreement benefits from a block, parallel or s 11 exemption, notifying is unlikely to be justified, first as the exemptions are automatic and secondly because the benefits of a further decision on the subject are small. A decision confirming that an agreement falls within one of the exclusions could have benefits in some situations of doubt, but the main purpose of s 14 notifications is likely to be for individual exemption.

Effect of notification of an agreement for a decision

4.39 If the DGFT takes a decision as a result of a notification under s 14 to the effect that the agreement has not infringed the Chapter I prohibition, then the consequences set out in s 16 follow (s 16(1)). If he takes a decision that the agreement has infringed the prohibition (because no exemption or exclusion applies and the agreement restricts competition to an appreciable extent) the enforcement procedure will apply (see paras 4.49–4.70).

4.40 The consequences set out in s 16 are as follows. First, the DGFT cannot proceed further against the agreement unless—

(a) he has reasonable grounds to believe there has been a material change of circumstance since his decision; or

(b) he has a reasonable suspicion that he was given information that was incomplete, false or misleading in a material particular (s 16(2)).

Secondly, he may impose no penalty (s 16(3)).[1]

[1]   For discussion of immunity from penalties on notification and the making of decisions and on the possibility of the DGFT withdrawing that immunity by provisional decision, see paras 4.66–4.69.

Notification of conduct for a decision and its effect

4.41 Notification of conduct for a decision to be considered must be made by the person whose conduct is at issue, and when the DGFT has received the notification he may make a decision as to whether the Chapter II prohibition has been infringed and, if not, whether that is on account of an exclusion (s 22) (there are no exemptions from Ch II of the 1998 Act; see Ch 3). The effect of a decision on conduct is the same as that given under the Chapter I prohibition (s 24).

Procedure

Notification

4.42 Notification in all cases must be made using Form N,[1] and an original must be supplied together with two copies (and an extra copy for any relevant regulator) (see para 4.43). Copies must be duly certified by the applicant. Joint applications may be made by a jointly nominated representative, and notifications made by an representative of an applicant must include written proof of the authority to act. Time starts to run on the date the notification is received by the DGFT provided that this is before 6.00pm. If Form N is incomplete, the DGFT must inform the applicant(s) in writing and the effective date of the notification is delayed until full information is received. The DGFT has one month within which to inform the applicant of incomplete information, otherwise the notification is deemed to be complete. Confidential information should be put in a separate annex marked 'confidential information' together with an explanation.[2] Material changes to the relevant facts must be communicated without delay to the DGFT or the relevant regulator, as the case may be.

---

¹   See para 4.33 and Appendix 4. Form N (which is more a check list of headings than a form to be filled out) is similar to Form A/B used by the European Commission but, for example, omits reference to an effect on inter-state trade. The main differences in the two procedures in practice will be the numbers of copies required. See DGFT's draft Procedural Rules, rr 1–7 and the 1998 Act, Sch 5, para 2.

²   See the DGFT's obligations of confidentiality. See para 4.20 and paras 10.2–10.5.

Concurrency

4.43   In the case of concurrent jurisdiction,¹ all Forms N must still be sent to the DGFT with an *extra copy* for any relevant sectoral regulator. It is advisable to send an additional copy direct to the regulator in question. The DGFT must inform the applicant that he has passed the Form N to the relevant regulator (there may be more than one) and the applicant is to be kept informed of which regulator is handling the case. There is an element of circularity in this as the applicant really needs this information in advance of making the notification, but in most cases this will be obvious.²

---

¹   For the allocation of tasks between the DGFT and regulators, and consideration of concurrency generally, see Ch 7.

²   DGFT's draft Procedural Rules, r 8.

Notification of other parties

4.44   The applicant must take all reasonable steps to notify all other parties that he is aware of that an application has been made, and what sort of application it is.¹ This must be in writing and given within seven working days of receipt of the DGFT's acknowledgement of receipt. In addition a copy of the notice must be given to the DGFT.

---

¹   For guidance or a decision, see DGFT's draft Procedural Rules, r 6 and the 1998 Act, Sch 5, para 2 and Sch 6, para 2.

Public register

4.45   The DGFT will keep a register containing a summary of the agreement or conduct, and an indication of the result of the application.¹ However there will be nothing under the new regime which resembles the practice under RTPA 1976 where the actual agreements submitted for registration under that Act could be scrutinised and copied. Form N contains a section in which the applicants are asked to provide the necessary summary.

---

¹   DGFT's draft Procedural Rules, r 7.

Provisional decisions

4.46   Schedules 5 and 6 provide for the DGFT to make provisional decisions after a preliminary investigation (Sch 5, para 3; Sch 6, para 3).¹ In the case of agreements, he must consider it likely that the Chapter I prohibition will be infringed and that individual exemption would not be appropriate (Sch 5, para 3(1)). In the case of conduct, he must simply consider it likely that the Chapter II prohibition will be infringed (Sch 6, para 3(1)). In each case, he must inform the applicant as to his intention,[2] notify the applicant in writing of the decision (Sch 5, para 3(2)(a); Sch 6, para 3(2)) together with an account of his facts and reasons.[3] Provisional decisions in relation to notified agreements remove the provisional immunity from penalties (see para 4.69; Sch 5, para 3(2)(b)). There is no such immunity for notified conduct. Provisional decisions are not subject to appeal to the Competition Commission (CC) appeal tribunals (s 46; see Ch 5), and do not affect the final determination of the application, which the DGFT may continue until his decision (Sch 5, para 3(4), (5); Sch 6, paras 3(4), (5)). Provisional decisions following notifications should be distinguished from interim measures (s 35; see paras 4.56, 4.58).

---

1   DGFT's draft Procedural Rules, r 9.
2   Ibid, para 9(1).
3   Ibid, para 9(2).

Procedure on giving of guidance

4.47 Guidance given to the applicant must be given without delay after the determination together with the supporting facts and reasons.[1] Guidance is not published, although an 'indication' of it will appear on the public register. It may be negative, or favourable.[2] If the DGFT proposes to take further action after favourable guidance, for example because he has received a complaint, he must consult the recipient of the guidance.[3] Having given negative guidance, he is, of course, free to enforce the prohibitions against the applicants by taking either a provisional decision or a final decision, or both, and in either case with directions which would be considered appropriate to bring any infringement to an end (see paras 4.49–4.70).

---

1   DGFT's draft Procedural Rules, r 10.
2   Negative guidance would be to the effect that the agreement or conduct is likely to infringe a prohibition and is not subject to an exclusion or (for an agreement only) an exemption. The limitations on DGFT action under ss 15, 16, 23 and 24 only apply in the event of favourable guidance.
3   DGFT's draft Procedural Rules, r 11.

Consultation of the public

4.48 When an agreement or conduct is notified for a decision, the DGFT's rules of procedure provide for varying degrees of consultation as follows[1]—
  (a) if the DGFT proposes to grant an exemption for an agreement subject to conditions or obligations, he *must* consult the applicant;
  (b) if he proposes to grant an exemption for an agreement even without conditions or obligations he *must* consult the public;
  (c) if he proposes to decide that no prohibition is infringed either by an agreement or by conduct he *may* consult the public.

---

1   See the DGFT's draft Procedural Rules, r 12. These broadly reflect similar requirements under EC law but Council Regulation 17/62/EEC, Art 19(3) (OJ L13, 21.2.62, p 204 (S edn 1959–62, p 87)) requires publication of the intention to grant both negative clearance and exemption.

ENFORCEMENT BY THE AUTHORITIES

Introduction

4.49 The DGFT and the regulators[1] will enforce the prohibitions by making the decision that they have (ss 31–33) or have not been infringed (ss 16, 24).[2] In the case of an infringement, the DGFT may give directions to bring the infringement to an end (ss 32, 33) and may require an infringing undertaking to pay him a penalty (s 36). Provisions are included to deal with enforcement of directions (s 34) and recovery of penalties (s 37). There are also immunities from penalties, and these immunities can be withdrawn (see paras 4.66, 4.67). There are provisions for interim measures (s 35). The following paragraphs discuss each of these matters in turn. Private actions for damages or injunctive relief are discussed at para 4.72.

---

[1]   As defined in s 54. All the enforcement powers apply to the DGFT and regulators alike (see para 4.2). The DGFT has published guidelines on 'Enforcement' and will issue guidance under s 38 on the appropriate amount of penalties.

[2]   The effect of these decisions is discussed in paras 4.33–4.47.

Decisions

4.50 The importance of the expression 'decisions' in the scheme of the 1998 Act cannot be overstated. Not only are decisions the culmination of most (although not all) of the DGFT's activity but it is decisions that are for the most part appealable to the appeal tribunal (see para 5.16). References to decisions of the DGFT are scattered around the Act but fall under three main headings—

    (a)   infringement of Ch I;

    (b)   exemption under Ch I;

    (c)   infringement of Ch II.

4.51   Relevant decisions may follow from—

    (a)   an application under Ch I;[1] the DGFT may make a decision either that Ch I is or is not infringed and, if not,

        —   that this is because of an exclusion; or

        —   because it is exempt from the prohibition.

    (b)   an application under Ch II;[2] the DGFT may decide either that Ch II is infringed or that it is not infringed and, if not, whether that is on account of an exclusion;

    (c)   an investigation under s 25.

In the latter case, the 1998 Act requires the DGFT to give written notice to the person or persons 'likely to be affected' (s 31(2)) and give that person (or persons) an opportunity to make representations (s 31(2)). There is no such statutory requirement in relation to infringement decisions following an application under ss 14 or 22, although the DGFT's Rules of Procedure provide for this.[3]

---

[1]   Section 14(1), (2). See paras 4.33–4.47.

[2]   Section 22(1),(2). See paras 4.33–4.47.

[3]   DGFT's draft Procedural Rules, r 14.

Reasons

4.52 The statutory requirement for the DGFT to give reasons in the case of decisions following notifications is contained in Schs 5 and 6.[1] There is no express requirement in the case of decisions following investigations but under the 1998 Act, s 60, EC law principles in this respect will be applicable and the DGFT has indicated that reasons will be given in published decisions.[2] Indeed, it would be difficult to make the appeal system work effectively if they were not given.

[1]   Schedule 5, para 6; Sch 6, para 6.
[2]   DGFT's guidelines 'Enforcement', para 2.6; DGFT's draft Procedural Rules, r 15.

Directions

4.53 Section 32(1) provides that—

'If the Director has made a decision that an agreement infringes the Chapter I prohibition, he may give to such person or persons as he considers appropriate such directions as he considers appropriate to bring the infringement to an end.'

Section 32(3) provides that—

'A direction under this section may, in particular, include provision—
(a)   requiring the parties to the agreement to modify the agreement; or
(b)   requiring them to terminate the agreement'.

There are corresponding provisions in s 33 for directions in the case of infringements of Chapter II but in this case the direction may include a provision—

'(a) requiring the person concerned to modify the conduct in question; or
(b) requiring him to cease that conduct'.

In either case, directions may include other provisions also, such as positive action (informing third parties) and reporting obligations.[1] Directions under s 32(3) would not be able to require divestment or transfer of part of the undertaking or assets of the dominant firm found to have abused its position contrary to s 18; structural remedies could follow only from a monopoly investigation under provisions of FTA 1973 (see paras 8.5–8.7).

[1]   DGFT's guidelines 'Enforcement', para 2.3.

Persons who may be the subject of directions

4.54 It should be noted that the directions may be given to appropriate persons, who are not necessarily the parties to the agreement or perpetrators of the conduct. The purpose of this is to enable the DGFT to direct parents, affiliates or private individuals with the ability to influence or procure actions by the infringing persons.[1] However, the DGFT will need to be careful not to issue directions to persons where this is not justified.

[1]   See DGFT's guidelines 'Enforcement', para 2.2.

Jurisdiction

4.55 The physical location of persons who may be the subject of directions is not restricted under the 1998 Act and the DGFT may therefore seek to give directions to persons not present within the UK, although he will not be able to enforce such directions directly.[1] There is relevant jurisprudence under EC law on such matters which may be useful in determining the limit of what may be directed by the DGFT in such circumstances.[2]

---

[1] Section 34 allows the court to order an undertaking or its officers to obey a direction relating to the management of that undertaking if the person subject to the direction has failed to comply, see para 5.43.

[2] See *Butterworths Competition Law* XII [69]–[122].

Interim measures

Grounds

4.56 If the DGFT has a 'reasonable suspicion' that either a Chapter I or Chapter II prohibition has been infringed but has not completed his investigation he may give directions for the purpose either—

    (a) of preventing serious, irreparable damage to a particular person; or

    (b) of protecting the public interest,

if he considers the necessity so to act as a matter of urgency (s 35(1), (2)). Interim measures therefore require a reasonable suspicion of infringement, a valid purpose and a need for urgent action.[1]

---

[1] For EC law on interim measures see *Butterworths Competition Law* X [780]–[830]. The DGFT's guidelines 'Enforcement' (see para 3.3) suggest that the burden of proof in EC law is too high to make the use of interim measures effective and that they will feature to a greater extent under the UK law. See also HL Report Stage, 19 February 1998, col 354 (Lord Simon of Highbury).

Procedure

4.57 The DGFT must give notice to the affected persons before giving directions, thus giving them an opportunity to make representations (s 32(3)). Such notice must indicate the nature of the proposed direction and the DGFT's reasons (s 32(4)). Any direction given may be similar in terms to a final direction and can be enforced in a similar way (s 32(5)–(7)). The DGFT attaches considerable importance to the power to take interim measures.[1] Under the FTA, a serious problem was the lack of any power to adopt interim measures pending the outcome of an MMC investigation, with the result that in some cases a complainant had gone out of business long before any remedial steps could be taken to assist it.[2]

---

[1] DGFT's guidelines 'Enforcement', Pt 3.

[2] See in particular 'Highland Scottish Omnibuses Ltd' Cm 1129 (1990).

Public interest

4.58 It is somewhat anomalous that whereas the DGFT's powers to make final decisions under the prohibitions are based on damage to competition, he may give interim directions to protect the public interest. This term is not defined in the Act.[1] During the Parliamentary debates on the Bill the Government said that, in accordance with EC principles of proportionality, the DGFT's interim measures should not exceed what was necessary to achieve the proposed objective.[2]

---

[1]   Although a definition exists in FTA 1973, s 84, for the purposes of that Act. See the DGFT's guidelines 'Enforcement', para 3.6, which refer to the need to protect an 'industry'.

[2]   HL Report Stage, 19 February 1998, col 356 (Lord Simon of Highbury).

Enforcement

4.59 If a person subject to directions (whether final or interim) fails to comply without reasonable excuse, the DGFT may apply to the court (defined in s 59(1)) for an order requiring compliance within a specified time or, if the direction concerns the management of an undertaking, ordering another officer to carry it out (s 34). Breach of such an order would be contempt of court, punishable by fines or imprisonment, at the court's discretion.[1]

---

[1]   DGFT's guidelines 'Enforcement', para 2.9.

Penalties

4.60 Section 36(1) provides that—

'On making a decision that an agreement has infringed the Chapter I prohibition, the Director may require an undertaking which is a party to the agreement to pay him a penalty in respect of the infringement.'

Section 36(2) provides correspondingly for infringement of the Chapter II prohibition.

Intention or negligence

4.61 The DGFT must be satisfied that the infringement has been committed intentionally or negligently (s 36(3)).[1] Intention may be deduced from internal documents, or from deliberate concealment of the agreement or conduct in question.[2]

---

[1]   This requirement was added at a late stage of the Bill's passage through Parliament after debate as to whether the 1998 Act, s 60 imported the principles of Council Regulation 17/62/EEC into the 1998 Act (the better view being that it does not)—HL Consideration of Commons' Amendments, 20 October 1998, cols 1373–1376 (Lord McIntosh of Haringey).

[2]   DGFT's guidelines 'Enforcement' paras 4.6–4.8. For negligence see paras 4.9–4.10 and for duress see para 4.11.

Compliance programmes and other factors

4.62 The DGFT will take into account the existence and effectiveness of competition compliance programmes[1] although it is emphasised that such programmes must be kept up-to-date and effectively promulgated to influence penalties to any significant extent. Similarly, the co-operation of the undertaking in the DGFT's investigation will presumably be a mitigating factor.[2] Ignorance of the law will not be a defence but the DGFT may be expected to be cautious in imposing penalties where the legal doctrine being applied or developed is new and therefore without precedent.[3]

---

[1]   DGFT's guidelines 'Enforcement', paras 4.35–4.36.

[2]   At least it has been in European Commission practice (the leading case is Case C-277/87 *Sandoz* [1990] I–ECR 45 where the fine was reduced by the ECJ on this basis). There is no direct reference to this point in the DGFT's guidelines.

[3]   As with the practice of the European Commission. See *Butterworths Competition Law* X paras [996]–[1031] for the factors that the European Commission takes into account in setting the level of fines.

'Whistleblowing'

4.63   The DGFT has indicated[1] that he will take into account the conduct of a party to an infringing agreement in disclosing the infringement to him and subsequent co-operation. This reflects similar policy by the European Commission[2] and, like EC practice, the concession is limited to the first 'whistleblower'.

---

[1]   DGFT's guidelines 'Enforcement', paras 4.37–4.39.

[2]   European Commission Notice on the non-imposition or reduction of fines in cartel cases (OJ C207, 18.7.96, p 4). See also European Commission Decision in *Cartonboard* OJ L243, 19.9.94, p 1.

Amount of penalty

4.64   Penalties may not exceed 10% of the turnover of the penalised undertaking (s 36(8)). In Parliament, this was confirmed as turnover arising in the UK,[1] a position which is different from that under Council Regulation 17/62/EEC[2] where worldwide turnover can be taken into account. Turnover is to be determined in accordance with provisions specified by order of the Secretary of State.[3] The DGFT has indicated that he will use his powers to impose penalties to the extent sufficient to deter as well as to punish infringement.[4] Factors to be taken into account include the duration and gravity of the infringement and the degree of culpable intention or negligence.[5] The DGFT is required under s 38 to prepare and publish guidance on the appropriate level of any penalty. Such guidance must first be approved by the Secretary of State. The DGFT must have regard to this guidance in setting penalties,[6] as must the appeal tribunals and appellate courts.

---

[1]   HC SC G, 16 June 1998, col 454 (Nigel Griffiths). 'The power to penalise an undertaking by up to 10% of its UK turnover will give the new prohibition regime real teeth'. See also HL Committee, 17 November 1997, col 425 (Lord Haskel) and HL Consideration of Commons' Amendments, 20 October 1998, cols 1373–6 (Lord McIntosh of Haringey).

[2]   Council Regulation 17/62/EEC, OJ L13, 21.2.62, p 204 (S edn 1959–62, p 87).

[3]   No such order has yet been made.

[4]   DGFT's guidelines 'Enforcement', para 4.2.

[5]   Ibid para 4.32.

[6]   No guidance has yet been published. The regulators must also observe this guidance, prepared after consultation with them, in setting penalties under their concurrent powers.

Double jeopardy

4.65   In setting penalties, the DGFT must take account of fines imposed by the European Commission or by a court or other body in another Member State (though apparently not a Contracting State of the EEA), as must the appeal tribunals or any court hearing appeals on levels of penalties (s 38(9)).[1] This raises interesting questions concerning whether the same agreement or conduct is at issue, as there may be different effects in different Member States. EC principles applied through s 60 may assist in resolving them.[2]

---

[1]   Fines under US anti-trust law are not covered.
[2]   See eg the ECJ ruling in Case 45/69 *Boehringer Mannheim* [1970] ECR 769.

Immunity

4.66   In addition to providing for the level of penalties and the conditions for their application, the Act confers immunity from penalties in some cases, namely—

  (a) 'small agreements' where the DGFT is satisfied that an undertaking acted on the reasonable assumption that being party to such an agreement gave it immunity (ss 36(4), 39; see also para 2.24);
  (b) 'conduct of minor significance', where the DGFT is similarly so satisfied (ss 36(5), 40; see also para 3.33);
  (c) in an application for Chapter I (but not Chapter II) guidance or a decision, for the period from the date of notification to the date specified by a notice (which cannot be retrospective) from the DGFT (ss 13(4), (5), 14(4), (5));
  (d) where guidance has been given under either prohibition (ss 15(3), 23(3));
  (e) where a decision has been made that neither prohibition is infringed (ss 16(3), 24(3));
  (f) where an agreement has been notified to the European Commission for exemption under Art 81(3), for the period from notification until the Commission determines the matter (s 41).[1]

---

[1]   The meaning of 'determines' is not stated; for discussion of its significance see para 6.33.

Withdrawing immunities

4.67   The immunities in respect of small agreements and conduct of minor significance are liable to be withdrawn by the DGFT if, after investigation, he considers an infringement is likely, after all, subject to his observation of some basic procedures (ss 39(4), 40(4)).[1]

---

[1]   The DGFT must give the parties or persons in respect of which the immunity is withdrawn written notice of his decision and must specify a date which gives them time to adjust (ss 39(5), (8), 40(5), (8)).

4.68   In the case of guidance or decisions following notification, the grounds for withdrawing the immunity are that the DGFT—

  (a) has reasonable grounds for believing there is a material change of circumstances; or
  (b) has a reasonable suspicion that the information on which he based his guidance or decision was incomplete, false or misleading in a material particular (ss 15(2), 16(2), 23(2) and 24(2)).

In the case of guidance, additional grounds are that—

  (a) (in the case of an agreement) one of the notifying parties has applied for a decision; or

(b) a complaint has been made by a non-party (ss 15(2), 23(2)).

In each case, the DGFT must take action in one of these circumstances (ss 15(4), 16(4), 23(4) and 24(4)) and he must consider it likely that Chapter I or Chapter II will be infringed. He must give notice of removal and specify a date. If he reasonably suspects that information was provided which was false, incomplete or misleading in a material particular, the DGFT may backdate the notice of withdrawal (ss 15(5), 16(5), 23(5) and 24(5)).

Provisional decisions

4.69 In the case of notification of agreements, the notification itself gives immunity from penalties while the application is being considered (see para 4.66). This 'provisional' immunity may be withdrawn by a provisional decision of the DGFT, which has the effect of deeming the immunity never to have existed (Sch 5, para 3(2)(b); see para 4.46). This is similar to a decision of the European Commission under Council Regulation 17/62/EEC, Art 15(6) but, unlike the position under EC law, such a decision is not subject to appeal.[1]

---

[1]   See Council Regulation 17/62/EEC, OJ L13, 21.2.62, p 204 (S edn 1959–62, p 87). See also para 4.70 and paras 5.28–5.30 for consideration of whether an application for judicial review could be made. Provisional decisions under Sch 5 (or Sch 6) do not appear in the list of appealable decisions in s 46.

Immunity after notification to European Commission

4.70 Immunity from penalties under the Act following a notification to the European Commission cannot be withdrawn by the DGFT, but if the European Commission takes an interim decision under Council Regulation 17/62/EEC,[1] Art 15(6), to remove the provisional immunity from penalties under that Regulation,[2] this has the effect of withdrawing the corresponding immunity under UK law (s 41).[3]

---

[1]   Council Regulation 17/62/EEC, OJ L13, 21.2.62, p 204 (S edn 1959–62, p 87).
[2]   Such a decision can be appealed to the CFI under EC law (Cases 8-11/66 *Cimenteries Belges* [1967] ECR 75, see Ch 6).
[3]   The DGFT is not precluded from investigating the agreement and the phrase 'provisional immunity from penalties' may be given a meaning as prescribed by order of the Secretary of State.

THIRD PARTY ACTIONS

4.71 In its consultation paper prior to the Competition Bill,[1] the Government envisaged third party action as an important buttress to the deterrent effect of the prohibitions and as a safeguard for the victims of anti-competitive behaviour. Third party rights fall into two categories—
(a) rights to appeal DGFT decisions to the appeal tribunals;[2]
(b) the bringing of civil actions in the courts based on breach of the prohibitions.[3]

The Government had intended to provide expressly that decisions of the DGFT are admissible in private actions as evidence of a breach of the prohibitions, but no such provision appears in the Act.[4] What is provided is that the DGFT's findings of fact are binding on the parties in court proceedings brought by the infringing parties or third parties.[5] This means that parties bringing such proceedings will not have to go through the process of producing all the evidence once again, and will be a substantial boost to so-called 'coat-tail' actions.

---

[1]   'A prohibition approach to anti-competitive agreements and abuse of dominant position' (URN 97/803) (August 1997), para 7.26.

[2]   Section 47, discussed in Ch 5.

[3]   Not expressly provided for in the 1998 Act apart from an oblique reference in s 60(6)(b).

[4]   Decisions of the European Commission have been held to be admissible in English court proceedings as evidence of the correctness of the conclusions they contain; see *Iberian UK Ltd v BPB Industries and British Gypsum* [1997] EuLR1 at 21 (per Laddie J).

[5]   Section 58, provided that the time for appeal has expired, or the DGFT's findings are confirmed on appeal. The court hearing the proceedings may direct that the DGFT's findings are not binding; the DGFT may be called on to assist the court in such cases. 'Court' for this purpose does not have the meaning given in s 59(1) and presumably means any court in which an action is brought and to which UK legislation applies.

Private actions

4.72   The apparent explanation for the absence from the 1998 Act itself of any express right to bring civil actions is that such a right exists under EC competition law and thus providing expressly for it might prevent private litigants from benefitting from developments in EC law in this respect.[1] Although it is probably the case that the ECJ will eventually rule that in principle there should be damages in some cases where Arts 81 and/or 82 are infringed, it does not follow that damages should be available in every case. The ECJ may wish to consider issues such as causation, remoteness of damage and the degree of intention or recklessness that must be demonstrated before there is a financial liability. Such an approach might resemble a number of cases beginning with *Francovich v Italian Republic*[2] on state liability. From the UK's perspective, therefore, it may be preferable to leave the law to develop consistently with the case law in the EU, such consistency to be achieved through the 'general principles' clause in s 60.

---

[1]   For discussion of private actions for breach of EC competition law and the remedies that may be available see *Butterworths Competition Law* XI [169]–[230]. The leading UK case is *Garden Cottage Foods v Milk Marketing Board* [1984] AC 130, where a right of damages was assumed by the House of Lords to be available.

[2]   Cases C-6 and 9/90 [1991] ECR I-5357.

Statements in Parliament

4.73   During the passage of the Bill through Parliament, the Government was at pains to confirm that the right of third parties to seek redress in the courts was available. Thus, Lord Simon stated '(I)t is an important part of the new regime that businesses and consumers who have been seriously harmed by anti-competitive behaviour should be able to seek redress. To that end, we are including provisions to facilitate rights of private action in the courts for damages'.[1] The then Secretary of State, Margaret Beckett, similarly confirmed that 'Companies and individuals who have been harmed by infringements of the prohibitions will be entitled to seek damages in the Courts'.[2] The DTI also issued a press release confirming the Government's intention that private actions for damages should be available.[3]

1   HL 2R, 30 October 1997, col 1148. The provisions are s 58 (see para 4.71); s 55(3)(b) (disclosure of information allowed if 'made with a view to the institution of, or otherwise for the purposes of, civil proceedings brought under or in connection with this Part') (see para 10.3) and s 60(6)(b) (decisions to which the courts must have regard include a decision as to 'the civil liability of an undertaking for harm caused by its infringement of Community law') (see para 6.21).

2   HC 2R, 11 May 1998, col 35. The Government 'considered carefully' whether the appeals tribunals of the CC should be the forum for private actions but decided against it for reasons of economy and speed of process (Consultation Paper, Aug 1997, para 7.25).

3   DTI press release P/98/552 (9 July 1998).

Comment

4.74   For all this Ministerial exhortation, anyone studying the 1998 Act will not be convinced that the right of third party action is an important part of the scheme of the new legislation. The scattered and obscure references referred to in the preceding description hardly add up to a ringing endorsement of the right of those affected by the prohibitions to obtain redress. It will probably be some time before there is significant progress in this area.[1]

1   The DGFT's guidelines 'Enforcement' contain only one paragraph on this aspect (para 5.1).

5 Institutions and appeals

INTRODUCTION

5.1   The Competition Act 1998 creates a new institution called the Competition Commission (CC) and in doing so changes the roles that are played by the Office of Fair Trading (OFT) and the Secretary of State (and consequently the Department of Trade and Industry (DTI)) in the operation of UK competition policy. The 1998 Act also affects the powers of the sectoral regulators[1] and abolishes the Restrictive Practices Court (RPC), which is the existing specialist competition court. Institutional aspects are therefore important in the overall scheme of the Act. This Chapter describes the institutional changes brought about by the Act and the new appeal mechanism.

---

[1]   See Ch 7.

5.2   One of the most important innovations in the 1998 Act is the establishment, within the new CC, of appeal tribunals, which will hear appeals against decisions of the Director General of Fair Trading (DGFT) and regulators.[1] For the first time it will be possible to appeal against the substance, as opposed to the legality or reasonableness, of a decision of a UK competition authority, and a tribunal may be invited to reconsider the economic and legal analysis which has been applied by that authority. The appeal tribunals will therefore be actively involved in the development of UK law, and will not merely review the activities of other bodies.

---

[1]   Ie the regulators given competition powers under s 54.

5.3   The establishment of appeal tribunals is a response to the fact that power has been conferred on the DGFT and regulators to impose penalties on undertakings. In order to safeguard the rights of such undertakings, something more than the existing judicial review process is considered necessary. While the most immediate model is the control exercised by the European Court of First Instance (CFI) over the European Commission, the appeal tribunals in the UK will in fact have more extensive powers than the CFI. At the same time it is hoped that the tribunals will be able to avoid some of the problems encountered by the CFI in applying that control.

INSTITUTIONAL CHANGES

The overall framework

5.4   The tripartite structure of the OFT, Monopolies and Mergers Commission (MMC) and DTI that has characterised the UK system for many years remains largely intact, although the OFT now plays an enhanced role, the MMC's former role is subsumed into that of the new CC and the DTI's role is diminished. With the abolition of the RPC, the role of specialist competition 'court' passes to the CC, although the role of the court system generally in relation to judicial review and third party actions is also significant.[1]

---

[1]   See Ch 4.

The OFT

5.5   The 1998 Act itself never refers to the OFT which is deemed to operate through the DGFT, who is its head.[1] The DGFT receives considerable new powers under the Act and this inevitably changes the OFT's role, methods of operation and structure. As explained elsewhere,[2] the DGFT plays the principal role in enforcing the prohibitions contained within the Act, and has increased powers to obtain information, as well as new powers to enter premises to conduct investigations, make interim and final decisions and impose substantial financial penalties. Instead of acting as a filter for cases to be passed to other bodies to make a decision on them, the DGFT can now decide things for himself.

---

[1]   The personalisation of competition institutions is an endearing and enduring feature of the UK system.
[2]   See Ch 4.

5.6   As a consequence of this enhanced role, the OFT has increased in size[1] and its competition division is being restructured to enable it to carry out its role more effectively. This new structure comprises of four branches organised by industrial sectors, each with a mix of disciplines, which are devoted to case handling. There is also a 'cartel' branch that handles investigations as well as a policy co-ordination branch. The specialist economic and legal functions have been allocated between the case handling branches, and the new structure bears a considerable resemblance to that of DGIV of the European Commission.[2] The mergers' secretariat and consumer affairs functions continue essentially as before.[3] A structure chart of the OFT is given at Figure 1 in Appendix 6 to this book.

---

[1]   An extra 50 officials have been authorised making a total of 200 working on competition regulation. OFT officials have also received training in competition law and economics.
[2]   Although DGIV does not have a separate investigations unit and the OFT does not have the equivalent of a Hearing Officer. The Commission's Legal Service is also separate from DGIV.
[3]   The OFT is to publish a weekly hard copy Gazette in addition to the information it makes available on the Internet.

5.7   The new structure of the OFT enables the DGFT to address more effectively his task of enforcing the prohibitions, while in other respects his role remains as before. He is still required to make recommendations to the Secretary of State on mergers,[1] to consider monopoly references[2] (albeit as a measure of last resort) and to carry out his general functions under FTA 1973.[3] It is thought that the need to operate in a procedurally more rigorous manner in relation to the prohibitions could possibly affect OFT practice in these other areas.

---

[1]   FTA 1973, ss 76(1) and 86(1).
[2]   FTA 1973, s 50.
[3]   Particularly pursuant to FTA 1973, s 2.

Fees

5.8   A further innovation is the power given by the 1998 Act, s 53 which allows the DGFT to charge fees for the exercise of his functions (guidance, decisions, exemptions, etc).[1] The details have not yet been revealed, but these powers are expected to be exercised and must be effected through rules made by the DGFT under s 51.

---

[1]   Fees are already charged by the Secretary of State in the context of merger control.

The MMC and the Competition Commission

5.9   Section 45(3) of the 1998 Act provides that—

> 'The Monopolies and Mergers Commission is dissolved and its functions
> are transferred to the Competition Commission.'

The CC is itself established by s 45(1) and comes into existence in April 1999. The old MMC functions are taken over by the reporting panel of the CC while new appeal functions are discharged by the appeal panel, which will operate one or more appeal tribunals under the control of the President of the Competition Commission Appeal Tribunals, which is a new post. The members of the former MMC take on corresponding functions under the CC, as does the MMC Chairman who becomes Chairman of the CC.

5.10   The 1998 Act contains some detail about the CC.[1] In addition to reporting panel and appeal panel members, there are specialist panel members who will conduct investigations in particular sectors. The Commission Chairman must be a reporting panel member as must any deputy chairman. The President of the Competition Commission Appeal Tribunals must be legally qualified with ten years' standing and with appropriate experience and knowledge of competition law and practice. A panel of chairmen of appeal tribunals, comprising lawyers with seven years' standing and with appropriate specialised knowledge and experience, will assist the President. An appeal tribunal must comprise a (legally qualified) Chairman and two other appeal panel members but the details of the tribunals' procedures remain to be worked out.[2] It is clear that the position of President of the Competition Commission Appeal Tribunals is an important one in the new structure and how he or she works in conjunction with the CC Chairman will be a crucial factor. The appointment is made by the Secretary of State in consultation with the Lord Chancellor and is of similar status to a puisne judge.

---

[1]   See s 45 and Sch 7. The Council of the CC, established by Sch 7, para 5, is a management board only, and has no substantive function in the conduct of appeals or investigations.

[2]   Section 48 provides for rules to be made by the Secretary of State. Sch 8 makes provision for what these rules may include.

5.11   The CC is clearly a more important and influential body than the former MMC. This is mainly because of its new appeal function, but the combining of this function with the other functions of the former MMC may have created a whole which is greater than the sum of its parts. Whilst concern has been expressed[1] about the need to keep the appeal and reporting functions separate, and for the appeal function to be completely independent, combining the two gives the appeal tribunals access to specialist support and advice should they require it. It is also possible that the combination will have virtuous results, by encouraging the reporting panel members to consider whether their procedures meet the standards that will have to be applied in the context of appeals under the prohibition system. A structure chart of the new CC is given at Appendix 6, Figure 2.

---

[1]   For example by the Confederation of British Industry.

The regulators

5.12   The important new powers conferred on the sectoral regulators[1] also affect the institutional structure. Any appeal against their decisions in the exercise of their competition powers lies to the appeal tribunals of the CC. However, the existing arrangements for references to the MMC in relation to the regulators' licensing functions continue, although they become references to the reporting panel of the CC.[2] Regulators' decisions may therefore come up for review by the CC through two different routes and one of the more interesting problems to be worked out in practice will be ensuring that the CC avoids any problems that may arise in such a situation. For example, it is possible that an 'MMC' reference could be made, and pursued, in parallel with an appeal against a regulator's decision under the 1998 Act on a similar or related issue.

---

[1]   See Ch 7.
[2]   See *Butterworths Competition Law* IX for a fuller discussion of these powers and duties.

The Secretary of State and the DTI

5.13   Enhancing the powers of the DGFT and CC has a corresponding effect on the role of the Secretary of State in the administration and enforcement of UK competition policy. In turn this must affect the role of the competition policy division of the DTI and possibly its influence and status.

5.14   The Secretary of State retains a central role in—
  (a)   merger control (the making of references and action following MMC/CC reports);
  (b)   appointments (all the main MMC/CC appointments and the DGFT's appointment are made by the Secretary of State);
  (c)   the enactment of rules (particularly for the procedures of the appeal tribunals), guidance on penalties and exclusions from the prohibitions;
  (d)   monopoly references (action following MMC/CC reports, but used as a measure of last resort).

The Secretary of State's central role in administering the RTPA (through the giving of directions under s 21(2) and through control of the special section of the register) has been removed and he has no function in relation to the enforcement of the Chapter I and II prohibitions. It remains to be seen how the institutional balance will develop, but it is significant that it has at least been mooted that the Secretary of State's role in merger control may be less sacrosanct than was thought hitherto and if that role were devolved even in part to the CC, then the balance would have been further tilted towards the specialist institutions and away from political involvement.

APPEALS

What can be appealed

5.15 The 1998 Act provides for appeals to be made against a decision by the DGFT or any sectoral regulators exercising their respective powers. However, not all decisions can be appealed and not all acts of the DGFT or regulators may constitute decisions. In that respect, precedents under EC law may come to be considered if the position under EC law would be different.

5.16 The appealable decisions are set out in s 46(3) and comprise decisions as to—

(a) infringements of the Chapter I and II prohibitions (ss 14(2) or 22(2));
(b) whether to grant individual exemption (s 4(1));
(c) whether to impose conditions on the grant (s 4(3)(a)) or review (s 5(1)(c)) of an individual exemption;
(d) the terms of such conditions or obligations;
(e) how long an individual exemption may last (s 4(3)(b) and (4)) and when it should start (s 4(5));
(f) whether, and for how long, an individual exemption should be extended (s 4(6));
(g) the cancellation of an exemption;[1]
(h) the imposition and amount of any penalty under s 36;
(i) the withdrawing or varying of any of those decisions following a third party application under s 47(1);
(j) directions under ss 32 and 33 (bringing an infringement to an end);
(k) interim measures (s 35).

The list is not closed as it extends to 'such other decision as may be prescribed'.[2] In addition to the matters listed in s 46(3), s 47(6) provides that an unsuccessful third party applicant under s 47(1) can appeal to the CC against the rejection of his application.

---

[1] This is not limited to cancelling an individual exemption under s 5(1)(a) and so appears to extend to parallel exemptions under s 10(5) and block exemptions under s 6(6).

[2] By regulations made by the Secretary of State (s 59(1)). However, not all the 'decisions' appealable under s 46(3) are described as decisions in the relevant part of the Act, and s 46(3) does not list all those acts which could be characterised as decisions.

What is not appealable

5.17 Although the scope of appealable decisions is quite wide, there are some notable exceptions. For example, in relation to acts which are associated with investigations or enquiries, it seems that there is no right of appeal to the CC when the DGFT or a sectoral regulator—

(a) starts an investigation (s 25);
(b) requires documents to be produced (s 26);
(c) authorises entry onto premises (s 27); and
(d) applies for a judge's warrant under s 28.

The position here is in contrast to EC competition law where such acts, if made by decision of the European Commission, are appealable under Art 230 (former Art 173).[1] Another exception is any decision which imposes or varies conditions or obligations on a parallel exemption under s 10(5) or a block exemption under s 6(6). This anomaly arises from the terms of s 46(3) which largely refers to individual exemptions only, and is probably an error.[2] A further exception is a notice under s 16 which removes immunity from penalties for an agreement that has been previously found not to infringe. The same applies to a provisional decision under Sch 5 where the provisional immunity from penalties on notification of an agreement is removed. Again, this contrasts with the position under EC competition law.[3] Finally, it should be noted that the giving or withholding of guidance is not appealable.[4]

---

[1]   See eg Cases 46/87, 227/88 *Hoechst v EC Commission* [1989] ECR 2859.
[2]   In each case, the decision would be as to the application of the parallel or block exemption to an individual agreement, which is not the same as an individual exemption.
[3]   Cases 8-11/66 *Cimenteries Belges v EC Commission* [1967] ECR 75 where a letter sent under Art 15(6) of Regulation 17/62/EEC was held to constitute an appealable decision.
[4]   Under ss 13(2) and 21(2).

5.18   The approach taken in s 46(3) of listing appealable decisions appears to be a deliberate departure from EC law, under which any act that alters the legal position of an undertaking, provided that it definitively lays down the authority's position, can be appealed.[1] By excluding from the scope of appeals to the CC acts done, for example in the course of investigations, the legislator may nevertheless still face being attacked—but the focus will instead be on judicial review and compatibility with the Human Rights Act 1998.[2]

---

[1]   Case 60/81 *IBM v EC Commission* [1981] ECR 2639 where the statement of objections sent by the Commission to the parties was held not to be an appealable act. Cases 8-11/66 *Cimenteries Belges v EC Commission* [1967] ECR 75.
[2]   Whether and to what extent procedural issues will influence appeals to the CC, as opposed to forming the basis for judicial review applications, remains to be seen. Excluding investigations from the scope of s 46(3) is only one element of this matter because the conduct of investigations may form grounds of appeals to the CC against the Chapter I or II decision itself; see paras 5.28–5.35.

Who may appeal

5.19   Appeals may be made by—
(a)   any party to an agreement who is the subject of a decision (s 46(1));
(b)   any person whose conduct is the subject of a decision (s 46(2));
(c)   a third party applicant under s 47(1) in relation to any rejection by the DGFT of his application (s 47(6)).

It is hardly surprising that parties subject to a decision should have a right to appeal against it, but the right of interested third parties to request the withdrawing or varying of a decision raises some interesting questions.

5.20   Under EC law, there is a wealth of jurisprudence which deals with the position of third parties who are directly or indirectly concerned by a particular case and who may have a right to appeal it.[1] Under the 1998 Act the DGFT (or sectoral regulator) decides whether or not a particular third party has a sufficient interest to justify withdrawing or varying the relevant decision and whether sufficient reason has been shown for the variation or withdrawal and it is against that decision that a third party's right of appeal lies. If the DGFT or regulator proceeds to withdraw or change the decision, the parties may appeal against that under s 46(3)(h).

---

[1]   See Case 27/76 *Metro* [1977] ECR 1875 and Case 75/84 *Metro II* [1986] ECR 3021. See also *Butterworths Competition Law* X [1171].

5.21 Section 47 envisages that applications may be made by representative bodies because the grounds for refusing an application include the fact that 'in the case of an applicant claiming to represent persons who have such[1] an interest, the applicant does not represent such persons' (s 46(3)(b)) and that 'the persons represented by the applicant do not have such[1] an interest (s 46(3)(c)).

---

[1] Ie a sufficient interest in the relevant decision—s 46(3)(a).

How will appeals work?

Appeal tribunals

5.22 Appeals made to the CC must be determined by an appeal tribunal (s 48(1)). The details of how these tribunals will operate remains to be seen but Sch 8 provides some guidance as to what might emerge.[2]

---

[1] Section 48(4) makes it clear that when making Rules for the appeal tribunals the Secretary of State is not limited by the terms of Sch 8. Previous proposals for an independent tribunal envisaged that the Deregulation (Model Appeal Provisions) Order 1996, SI 1996/1678, would apply and in any event supervision by the Council on Tribunals, as envisaged by art 37 of that Order, would be beneficial.

Procedure

5.23 Schedule 8 sets out what may be contained in the relevant Rules[1] and includes provisions for—
  (a) a Registrar;
  (b) the period within which appeals must be brought;
  (c) the form and content of notices of appeal;
  (d) amendments to and acknowledgements of a notice of appeal;
  (e) the rejection of notices of appeal;
  (f) pre-hearing reviews;
  (g) the payment of a deposit by way of security;
  (h) the conduct of hearings including—
    — privacy;
    — who may represent parties;
    — attendance of witnesses;
    — evidence;
    — time limits;
    — disclosure of documents between the parties;
    — appointment of experts;
    — award and taxation of costs;
    — reference back to the DGFT for further investigation;
    — breach of rules on attendance of witnesses or requirements for disclosure is an offence.
  (i) payment of interest;
  (j) fees;
  (k) withdrawal of appeals;
  (l) interim or suspensory orders;
  (m) joining of parties.

1   See Sch 8, Pt II, paras 5–14.

Notice of appeal

5.24 Appeals are started by sending to the CC within the specified period a notice of appeal, which must set out grounds of appeal in sufficient detail to indicate—
  (a) what provision of the Act is at issue;
  (b) to what extent the appeal is based on error of fact or of law;
  (c) to what extent the appeal is against the exercise of the Director's discretion;

and the grounds of appeal identified in the notice may be amended with the leave of the tribunal.[1]

1   See Sch 8, Pt I, para 2.

The tribunals' powers

5.25 The appeal tribunals must determine the appeal 'on the merits' by reference to the grounds of appeal (Sch 8, para 3(1)). This is a major innovation in UK competition law enforcement. A tribunal has very wide powers and may—
  (a) confirm or set aside all or part of the decision;
  (b) remit the matter to the DGFT or relevant regulator;
  (c) impose, revoke or vary the amount of any penalty;
  (d) grant or cancel an individual exemption or vary any condition or obligation;
  (e) give any direction, take any step or make any other decisions which the DGFT (or regulator) could have given, taken or made (Sch 8, para 3(2)).

Publication of decisions

5.26 The tribunals' decisions are enforceable as if they were decisions of the DGFT or relevant regulator (Sch 8, para 3(3)). They may be made by majority (Sch 8, para 4(1)) (each tribunal comprising three people) and must be recorded with a statement of reasons (Sch 8, para 4(2)) to which the s 56 restrictions on disclosure of information apply (Sch 8, para 4(3)).[1] Decisions must be published (Sch 8, para 4(4)). There will therefore be a growing body of UK competition jurisprudence in the form of published, reasoned decisions of the appeal tribunals.

1   See Ch 10.

Further appeal

5.27 Under s 49, there is a further right of appeal from decisions of an appeal tribunal either on a point of law or as to the amount of any penalty (s 49(1)(a) and (b)). Any such appeal is to the Court of Appeal for a tribunal in England and Wales, to the Court of Session in Scotland and to the Court of Appeal in Northern Ireland for proceedings in that province[1] and must be with leave either of the appeal tribunal or of the appropriate court. From the relevant appellate court, further appeal lies to the House of Lords under the normal rules.[2]

---

[1] Changed from the High Court in earlier proposals. Note that this reference to different parts of the UK is the only hint in the 1998 Act that appeal tribunals may sit outside London. This was one of the suggestions in the DTI's August 1997 consultation paper, 'A prohibition approach to anti-competitive agreements and abuse of dominant position' (URN 97/803), at para 7.13.

[2] HL Report Stage, 19 February 1998, col 361 (Lord Simon of Highbury).

Judicial review

5.28 In addition to the new appeal regime, judicial review will continue to be available. In the House of Lords, Lord Simon stated '. . . we are doing nothing in the Bill to prevent the application of the normal rules of judicial review. Therefore, the lawfulness of decisions may be tested in the courts'.[1] The grounds of judicial review are not directed towards the substance of the disputed decisions but rather to their rationality, legality and procedural fairness. Nevertheless, there is scope for overlap and confusion in the juxtaposition of the appeal regime and judicial review.

---

[1] HL Report Stage, 19 February 1998, col 381.

5.29 It remains to be seen how the CC will approach its role but it would be understandable if it sought to give priority to reviewing the substance of the disputed decision. The paradox is that, in the early stages at least, it is likely to be procedural issues that give the greater ground for concern. An undertaking may argue that the DGFT ignored evidence that it presented, or unfairly refused an oral hearing, or disclosed confidential information to a competitor in the course of an investigation. More fundamentally, it may claim bias or general unfairness in the way the case has been handled. It remains to be seen whether the appeal tribunals will refuse to consider these points altogether. If they refuse to do so, there is a danger that their role in controlling the activities of the DGFT and sectoral regulators will be seriously diminished.

5.30 There is the further danger of multiple suits and waste of public money. The appeal tribunals and the courts will need to be extremely vigilant to prevent a situation of confusion arising. One of the problems is that events that give rise to judicial review may occur during a procedure, for example, in the course of an on-the-spot investigation. The affected party is unlikely to take the risk of waiting until the DGFT (or regulator) has made a decision that is appealable to the CC, as the appeal tribunal may decide the point has no merit. A way of dealing with this risk would be for judges considering whether to grant leave to apply for judicial review to keep in mind the need to maintain a coherent competition appeal system (and to refuse leave if there appears to be another avenue for appeal).[1] At the same time it would be necessary for the appeal tribunals to give due consideration to procedural issues, particularly those falling under the broad umbrella of 'rights of defence'[2] when hearing appeals.

---

[1] It will only be in exceptional circumstances that leave to bring judicial review proceedings will be granted if a statutory right of appeal exists. *Harley Development Inc v Commission of Inland Revenue* [1006] 1 WLR 727 at 736C (per Lord Jauncey). See also *R v Secretary of State for the Home Department ex p Capti-Mehmet* [1997] COD 61 and *R v Leeds City Council ex p Hendy* [1994] 6 Admin LR 439.

[2]   The Government regards Community law on rights of defence as relevant to the UK system, and applicable under s 60 (see eg Lord Simon of Highbury in HL Committee, 17 November 1997, col 404) and so this might suggest that appeal tribunals should consider such rights as well.

HUMAN RIGHTS ACT 1998

The Convention

5.31 The European Convention on the Protection of Human Rights and Fundamental Freedoms ('the Convention') will be relevant to the 1998 Act indirectly through its penetration of the principles of EC competition law[1] (applicable through s 60) and directly through the Human Rights Act 1998 (HRA 1998). From the date that the main provisions of HRA 1998 take effect[2] the Convention will affect the way the DGFT, the sectoral regulators, the CC and the courts apply the law, and to some extent its substance.

[1]   Although the European Union is not itself a party to the Convention, its terms form part of the body of fundamental rights forming part of European Community law. See Case 11/70 *Internationale Handelsgesellschaft* [1970] ECR 1125, and also Case 374/87 *Orkem v EC Commission* 1989 ECR 3283 and Case 27/88 *Solvay v EC Commission* [1989] ECR 3355.
[2]   Expected sometime in 1999.

The UK statute

5.32 HRA 1998 will require the courts to apply the Competition Act 1998 in such a way that is compatible with Convention rights, and will also make it unlawful for competition authorities to act in a way that is incompatible with those rights. The rules for the DGFT's procedures and for those of the appeal tribunals of the CC will similarly have to take account of these rights.

5.33 So far as the appeal tribunals are concerned, in order to comply with HRA 1998, they will have to respect Convention rights both in their own proceedings and in exercising control over those of the DGFT and the sectoral regulators (s 6). It would appear that the appeal tribunals cannot make a damages award (s 8) or a declaration of incompatibility with the Convention (s 4). These matters are reserved for the courts. However, in proceedings before an appeal tribunal, a party, provided that he is the 'victim', may rely on Convention rights, and may similarly do so in appealing against an appeal tribunal's ruling (s 7). Acts of an appeal tribunal fall within the definition of 'judicial act' (s 5) and may therefore be subject to appeal or judicial review on Convention grounds.

Substance

5.34 The Convention confers a number of rights but the main rights relevant to undertakings subject to Competition Act 1998 procedures (and they will for the most part be corporations) are—

  (a) the right to a fair trial within a reasonable time by an independent and impartial tribunal established by law (Art 6(1));

(b) the right to privacy (Art 8);[1]
(c) the right against self-incrimination;[2]
(d) various rights associated with criminal proceedings (Art 6(3)).[3]

---

[1]   Which could be affected by on-the-spot investigations.
[2]   The ECJ in the *Orkem* and *Solvay* cases (loc cit) held that the Convention did not confer an absolute right against self-incrimination. See now the Court of Human Rights' judgments in *Funke* (Case 82/1991/334/407) Series A No 256A [1993] 1 CMLR 897 and *Saunders* TLR 18/12/96 ILR 14/1/97 Application 19187/91 (1997).
[3]   This depends on whether the procedures and penalties for breach of the prohibitions under the 1998 Act are criminal in nature. This point is not free from doubt.

5.35 These rights are not absolute and they are qualified by HRA 1998, particularly if it can be shown that the primary legislation required the authorities to act in a way inconsistent with the Convention (s 6(2)(a)). Nevertheless, the issues which the authorities will have to consider include—

(a) what body gives the 'fair trial' under the Convention? The DGFT, the CC or the courts?
(b) whether a 'fair trial' is available in all cases where sectoral regulators apply their powers?
(c) whether or not the measures for investigating the affairs of undertakings are compatible with the Convention?
(d) whether the authorities' procedures for reaching decisions are compatible with the Convention?

It may be anticipated that objections based on HRA 1998 and on the Convention will be raised by judicial review application against the DGFT's and regulators' decisions and will also form a part of the grounds of appeals to the Commission, appeals from decisions of appeal tribunals to the Court of Appeal, and other such appeals.

6 Relationship with EC law

INTRODUCTION

Overlap and consistency

6.1 UK national competition authorities are not empowered to enforce Arts 81 and 82 of the EC Treaty,[1] although under Art 10 they have a duty not to jeopardise the attainment of the Treaty objectives (of which the application of Arts 81 and 82 is one). The 1998 Act does not extend to these authorities the power to apply EC competition provisions and Chs I and II of the 1998 Act are purely domestic in nature. There is no jurisdictional rule that defines which agreements and practices are subject to EC law and which are subject to UK competition law,[2] and it is possible that both systems of law may apply to the same case. It is necessary therefore to deal with the problem of overlap so as to ensure consistency in interpretation and clarity of process. It is also in no-one's interest to have the same matter investigated twice as this is a waste of resources. One of the objectives of the 1998 Act therefore is to minimise the differences between EC and UK competition law so as to reduce the compliance burden on businesses.

---

[1] An exception is the EC Competition Law (Articles 88 and 89) Enforcement Regulations 1996, SI 1996/2199 which apply in the field of air transport and give the UK authorities the power to apply Arts 81 and 82 (including Art 81(3)).

[2] See in contrast the position under Italian law where the overlap between EC and domestic competition law is excluded (see Law No 287 10 October 1990 art 1.1).

6.2   There are three separate issues—
   (a) how issues of conflict in the application of the two systems are to be resolved;
   (b) how consistency in the interpretation of the law itself is to be achieved; and
   (c) how the handling of individual cases is to be allocated between the EC and UK authorities.

AVOIDANCE OF CONFLICT BETWEEN EC AND NATIONAL COMPETITION LAW

The Community approach—supremacy of Community law

6.3   The basic principle when dealing with conflicts between national and Community law is that Community law takes precedence. This flows from the EC Treaty, Art 10, which states that Member States must 'abstain from any measure which could jeopardise the attainment of the objectives of this Treaty'. This principle was affirmed in *Wilhelm v Bundeskartellamt*[1] in which the ECJ held that conflicts between Community and national rules in the matter of the law on cartels must be resolved by applying the principle that Community law takes precedence. The application of this principle is not always straightforward and the following situations need to be considered.

---

[1]   Case 14/68 [1969] ECR 1. See *Butterworths Competition Law* I [909]–[931] for a full discussion.

Community prohibition: domestic authorisation

6.4   This is the simplest area of potential conflict to resolve. The principle of the supremacy of Community law prevents a national authority from authorising conduct which has been condemned by the Commission pursuant to the competition provisions. By the same token, an agreement which has previously been authorised by a national competition authority can still be condemned by the Commission under Community law.[1]

---

[1]   See Case T-66/89 *Publishers' Association v Commission (No 2)* [1992] 4 All ER 70.

Community exemption: domestic prohibition

6.5   There is no direct guidance from the ECJ as to whether national competition authorities must approve conduct which has been exempted by the Commission. The Commission's historical view, which it has reaffirmed over the years,[1] was that a national authority is bound to respect the exemption and refrain from applying its own stricter standards.

---

[1]   4th Report on Competition Policy, para 45. Notice on co-operation between national competition authorities and the Commission in handling cases falling within the scope of Articles 85 or 86 [81 or 82] of the EC Treaty, OJ C313, 15.10.97, p 3, para 19. See *Butterworths Competition Law* I [922]–[924.2].

6.6   The ECJ appears to favour this approach. Dicta in *Wilhelm* suggest strongly that national authorities should not condemn conduct which enjoys individual exemption. For example—

> '. . . if the ultimate general aim of the Treaty is to be respected, this parallel application of the national system can only be allowed in so far as it does not prejudice the uniform application throughout the Common Market of the Community rules on cartels and of the full effect of the measures adopted in implementation of those rules.'[1]

---

[1]   Case 14/68 [1969] ECR 1 at 14 (para 4).

6.7   In addition, Advocates General VerLoren Van Themaat in *Metro-SB-Grossmarkte GmbH v Commission*[1] and Tesauro in *BMW v ALD Auto-Leasing* and *BKA v Volkswagen ACT and VAG Leasing GmbH*[2] have both considered that the existence of an exemption would preclude the contrary application of national law.

---

1   Case 75/84 [1986] ECR 3021 at p 3071.
2   Cases C-70/93 [1995] ECR I-3439 and C-266/93 [1995] ECR I-3477. The Commission supported this view in its submission to the Court in these cases, but the Court did not rule on the point. The relevant block exemptions were not applicable in either case anyway.

6.8   In contrast, the European Commission indicated in its evidence to the *British Airways/Sabena* Monopolies and Mergers Commission (MMC) enquiry[1] that it would not object if the MMC recommended stricter conditions than the European Commission itself intended to apply in the same case, provided that these conditions did not conflict with or frustrate the Commission's decision. The Commission has also recently proposed, in a paper to the Council of Ministers on vertical restraints, that the authorities of a Member State should be permitted to cancel, or limit the application of, a block exemption in their national territory.[2]

---

[1]   Cm 1155 (1990) Appendix 7.1.

[2]   'Communication from the Commission on the application of the Community competition rules to vertical restraints' (Com 98 (544)), 30.9.98, p 34, [1999] 4 CMLR 281, although later proposals seek to circumscribe this possibility.

6.9   It was stated in the Commission Notice on co-operation with national competition authorities[1] that where the Commission has indicated in a comfort letter that an agreement falling foul of Art 85(1) [Art 81(1)] qualifies for exemption, it will call upon those authorities to consult the Commission before they decide whether or not to adopt a different decision under national law.

---

[1]   Notice on co-operation between national competition authorities and the Commission in handling cases falling within the scope of Articles 85 or 86 [81 or 82] of the EC Treaty, OJ C313, 15.10.97, p 3; see para 6.5 above.

Non-application of Community law: domestic prohibition

6.10   The leading case in this area is *Procureur de la Republique v Giry and Guerlain*.[1] In that case, the Commission had notified the parties in a comfort letter that the agreements at issue did not fall within Art 85(1) (now Art 81(1)) because they had no effect on trade between Member States and that it was accordingly closing the case file. On this basis, the ECJ held that the French authorities were entitled to apply their stricter competition provisions to those agreements. Even though the case concerned a comfort letter rather than a formal decision, it is generally considered that it lays down a general principle that national authorities should be free to apply their stricter national provisions to arrangements which have been given negative clearance by the Commission, either formally or informally, at least where the Commission's decision was based on the lack of effect on inter-state trade, or that the arrangements came within the scope of the notice on agreements of minor importance.[2]

---

[1]   Case 253/78 [1980] ECR 2327.

[2]   See *Butterworths Competition Law* I [925].

6.11   It is less clear whether this principle extends to decisions granted on the basis that the arrangements did not distort competition. To allow a national authority to condemn an agreement in these circumstances would arguably be inconsistent with its duty under EC Treaty, Art 10, not to interfere with the uniform application of Community law. At the moment, there is no case law dealing with this specific point.

The approach of the 1998 Act—parallel exemption

6.12 The approach of the 1998 Act in relation to these issues is not without difficulty. Acknowledgement of Community exemptions is contained in s 10 and this gives parallel exemption to agreements which have either been granted an individual exemption by the Commission, or which are covered by a block exemption, subject to certain derogations. However, the DGFT's power to cancel or limit a parallel exemption (s 10(5))[1] does raise the question of whether the supremacy of EC law is to be respected. Provided that this power is exercised in relation to agreements exempted under s 10(2) which benefit from parallel exemption even though they do not affect trade between Member States, the point may never need addressing. However, there is nothing in the 1998 Act that limits the exercise of the DGFT's power to this situation.[2]

---

[1]   See paras 2.106, 2.107 for parallel exemptions.
[2]   Nor, so far, any guidance in the DGFT's guidelines.

Negative clearance

6.13 Section 10(9) states that—

> '. . . references to an agreement being exempt from the Community prohibition are to be read as including references to the prohibition being inapplicable to the agreement by virtue of a Regulation or a decision by the Commission.'

This precludes agreements given negative clearance (as opposed to individual exemption by way of a formal decision) from benefiting from parallel exemption—as Art 81(1) is not inapplicable to them by virtue of the Commission's decision, but because they did not breach its prohibition in the first place.[1] There is nothing in the 1998 Act which places a positive obligation on the DGFT to grant negative clearance under UK law to an agreement already granted a negative clearance decision under Council Regulation 17/62/EEC.[2] Section 60(3) provides that the DGFT must *have regard to* any relevant decision or statement of the Commission while, as a matter of Community law, a decision is binding only upon the persons to whom it is addressed, and this would not include the DGFT.[3] The DGFT is not obliged to draw the same conclusions in an assessment of an agreement under UK law as those drawn by the Commission in its assessment of that agreement under Art 81.

---

[1]   The DGFT's guidelines 'Major provisions' also imply that it is intended that agreements which have been granted negative clearance decisions by the Commission should not benefit from parallel exemption (see paras 3.9 and 6.7).
[2]   OJ L13, 21.2.62, p 204 (S edn, 1959–62, p 87).
[3]   See para 6.22.

EC prohibition

6.14 The question must also be raised as to whether it would be possible for the UK authorities to authorise an agreement prohibited under EC law. Nothing in the 1998 Act expressly prohibits the UK authorities from seeking to do this, but there is little doubt that the operation of s 60[1] combined with the UK's general obligations under the EC Treaty, Art 10, would rule out such a course.

---

[1]   See paras 6.15–6.23.

CONSISTENT INTERPRETATION OF EC AND UK LAW

The principle

6.15   In recognition of the potential for conflict and the need for consistency in interpretation, s 60 sets out the principles to be applied in determining questions which arise in relation to competition within the UK. Section 60(1) explains the purpose of the section, whereas s 60(2) actually imposes the obligation.

Section 60(1)

6.16   Section 60(1) provides that—

> 'The purpose of this section is to ensure that so far as is possible (having regard to any relevant differences between the provisions concerned), questions arising under this Part in relation to competition within the UK are dealt with in a manner which is consistent with the treatment of corresponding questions arising in Community law in relation to competition within the Community'.[1]

---

[1]   For the meaning of the Community, see the Interpretation Act 1978 and European Communities Act 1972.

'. . . so far as is possible'

6.17   The objective of consistency is not absolute and the 1998 Act envisages that there will be circumstances in which different interpretations may apply. However, if there are no relevant differences between the provisions under consideration, it is hard to see why a consistent interpretation should not be possible.[1]

---

[1]   The Government stated that 'we are satisfied that the drafting of [section] 60 accurately expresses the concept that Community jurisprudence is to be followed unless the court is driven to some different interpretation by some provision in that part of the [Act]'—HL Consideration of Commons' Amendments, 20 October 1998, col 1383 (Lord Simon of Highbury).

'. . . having regard to any relevant differences'

6.18   A critical issue will evidently therefore be the identification of any relevant differences, with an obvious example being the application of the EC competition rules in order to achieve single market purposes. UK law presumably does not have to be applied with single market considerations in mind, which could lead to the Chapter I and II prohibitions and Arts 81 and 82 being applied in significantly different ways.[1] Another example would be differences in the actual treatment of vertical agreements under the law that will emerge from the European Commission's green paper proposals (giving rise to a broad block exemption) and the statutory instrument to be made under s 50.[2] A third example is the wider exclusion under the 1998 Act for mergers than that provided for under EC law.[3]

---

[1]   For example, an agreement restricting exports might not restrict competition within the UK but would be a cardinal offence under EC competition law. See the Report prepared by Bill Bishop and Richard Whish for the Government on the Treatment of Vertical Agreements under the Competition Bill (3 February 1998) (referred to at HL Consideration of Commons' Amendments, 9 February 1998, cols 901–3 (Lord Simon of Highbury)).

[2]   The UK law may follow EC law as closely as possible but an exclusion by the Competition Act is different in kind from an exemption under Art 81(3) in the form of a block exemption. See paras 2.75–2.91.

[3]   HL 3R, 5 March 1998, col 1365 (Lord Simon of Highbury). This exclusion under the 1998 Act, Sch 1, Pt 1 would extend to some joint ventures not regarded as concentrations under EC merger control.

'. . . questions arising . . . in relation to competition'

6.19   It is unclear how far this expression extends to procedural questions arising in relation to the enforcement of the competition rules, as well as the substantive competition rules themselves. The Government obviously has no desire to make the DGFT (or regulators) follow exactly the same procedures as the European Commission (indeed that might be undesirable), and the draft Procedural Rules make it clear that they will not do so.[1] A further issue is whether this expression imports the general principles of Community law—which can be of considerable significance in determining the scope of the competition rules—as well as the specific interpretation of Arts 81 and 82 themselves. In the House of Lords, Lord Simon of Highbury stated that the general principles of Community law are to be imported, save where there is a relevant difference.[2]

---

[1]   See DGFT's draft 'Procedural Rules', introductory para 4. Some important procedural principles are subject to this section. Civil remedies are covered by s 60(6) and the Government stated in Parliament that Community law on rights of defence will apply to the UK law—see HL Committee, 17 November 1997, col 404 (Lord Simon of Highbury). These presumably include the right to a hearing, the right to be informed of the matters relied on by the authorities and the right to obtain professional legal advice in confidence.

[2]   HL Committee, 25 November 1997, cols 960–963. Relevant principles include proportionality, legitimate expectations and, possibly, the principles of purposive or teleological interpretation of legislation applied by the Community courts.

'. . . are dealt with in a manner which is consistent with the treatment of corresponding questions arising in Community law in relation to competition within the Community'

6.20   The objective of consistent treatment is clearly stated.[1] Questions of Community law do not only arise in the proceedings of Community institutions and these words could also refer to the treatment of Community law questions by UK courts, or the courts of other Member States.

---

[1]   The Government confirmed in Parliament that 'one cannot construe the prohibitions and then compare them (with Community law). They must be construed from the outset on the basis of (section) 60'—HC 3R, 8 July 1998, col 1204 (Mr Ian McCartney).

Section 60(2)–(6)

6.21   The remainder of s 60 provides that—

'(2) At any time when the court[1] determines a question arising under this Part, it must act (so far as is compatible with the provisions of this Part[2] and whether or not it would otherwise be required to do so)[3] with a view to securing that there is no inconsistency[4] between—

   (a) the principles applied, and decision reached, by the court in determining that question; and

   (b) the principles laid down by the Treaty[5] and the European Court,[6] and any relevant decision of that Court, as applicable at that time in determining any corresponding question arising in Community law.

(3) The court must, in addition, have regard to any relevant decision or statement of the Commission.

(4) Subsections (2) and (3) also apply to—

   (a) the Director; and

   (b) any person acting on behalf of the Director, in connection with any matter arising under this Part.

(5) In subsections (2) and (3), 'court' means any court or tribunal.

(6) In subsections (2)(b) and (3), 'decision' includes a decision as to—

   (a) the interpretation of any provision of Community law;

   (b) the civil liability of an undertaking for harm caused by its infringement of Community law.'[7]

---

[1]   'Court' in this context means any court or tribunal (s 60(5)) and the provisions of s 60(2) apply also to the DGFT and the relevant regulators.

[2]   All matters to do with the prohibitions and their enforcement but not investigations under FTA 1973.

[3]   Member States are under a general obligation not to jeopardise the objectives of the EC Treaty (Art 10).

[4]   Section 60(1) puts the objective positively and is preferable to this double negative.

[5]   The EC Treaty (s 59(1)).

[6]   The ECJ and the European Court of First Instance (CFI) (s 59(1)).

[7]   For consideration of third party rights under the 1998 Act, see paras 4.71–4.74.

Decisions and statements of the Commission

6.22   The authorities under s 60(3) must have regard to any relevant decision[1] or statement of the Commission, ie UK authorities must take these into account, although this is a lesser obligation than the obligation to ensure that there is no inconsistency under s 60(2). Decisions and statements of other bodies such as the Council of Ministers[2] or the European Parliament are not included.

---

[1]   See s 60(6).

[2]   Documents such as the Minutes of the Council's deliberations about the European Merger Control Regulation would therefore not need to be considered—although they could be highly relevant in a particular case.

6.23   There is no explanation as to what is meant by Commission statements, which could range from a formal notice to any off-the-cuff remarks made by the Commissioner responsible for competition. It is likely that considerable regard will be paid to formal Commission notices[1] but press releases will carry less authority.

Comfort letters are also 'statements' which the DGFT is likely to take considerable notice of when deciding what attitude to take to an agreement that is subject to the UK prohibitions. Notices issued by the Commission under Art 19(3) are often the principal 'statement' made on an individual case, although they may also be followed by a comfort letter.[2] A Commission statement could only be made by someone with the authority to speak or write on the Commission's behalf [3] and Commission officials habitually make it clear in which capacity they are speaking. An official at a conference will not normally make a Commission statement, but a formal policy statement made by the Commissioner may well qualify.

---

[1]   See, however, the qualification entered in the DGFT's guidelines 'Major provisions', para 6.3, in relation to the non-applicability of the EU's market unifying objectives to the UK context.
[2]   As to whether the DGFT will follow 'comfort letters', see paras 6.35 and 6.41.
[3]   The DGFT's guidelines 'Major provisions' refer to 'decisions or statements which have the authority of the European Commission as a whole' and lists Commission Notices and guidelines and statements published in the Annual Report on Competition Policy (para 6.2).

Article 234 references

6.24 An important aid to the consistency of the application of EC law in Member States is the preliminary ruling procedure of EC Treaty, Art 234 (former Art 177) which enables the ECJ to rule on any questions referred to them by national courts or tribunals.[1] Given the objective of consistency between the 1998 Act and EC competition law, an important question is whether it is possible for a UK court or tribunal, when applying the provisions of the 1998 Act rather than EC competition law, to make a reference to the Court of Justice from a case involving domestic law, in circumstances where that law is to be interpreted consistently with the Treaty.[2] A secondary question might be which of the courts or tribunals could refer a question.[3]

---

[1]   Article 234 gives the ECJ jurisdiction to rule on the interpretation of the EC Treaty, the validity and interpretation of acts of Community institutions and the interpretation of statutes of certain Community bodies.
[2]   Having regard to any relevant differences, etc.
[3]   See para 6.30.

EC jurisprudence

6.25 The jurisprudence of the ECJ strongly suggests that references under Art 234 could be made in cases involving the UK prohibitions. The ECJ has faced the problem in the past that its rulings are intended to be binding—it does not give merely advisory opinions, and its rulings must not be only indicative. However the ECJ would not want the position to develop in which national laws based upon Arts 81 and 82 might be interpreted in a substantially different way from the meaning given to them by Community institutions. *Inter alia* this could lead a national court, when called upon to apply the Community rules, to do so by reference to a prior and different interpretation of the national rules, which could jeopardise the uniformity of Community law. In *Kleinwort Benson v City of Glasgow District Council* [1] the ECJ declined to give a ruling on the interpretation of the Civil Jurisdiction and Judgments Act 1982 in so far as it related to the allocation of jurisdiction as between the courts of England and Wales and the courts in Scotland. In this case the ECJ noted that the domestic court in the UK, when applying the so-called 'modified Convention' (dealing with intra-UK matters) had only an obligation 'to have regard to the Court's case law'. There was no obligation to apply it 'absolutely and unconditionally' which therefore sets up the possibility of distinguishing *Kleinwort Benson*. Indeed subsequent judgments have suggested that the ECJ may be willing to deal with a reference where a ruling on a point of Community law is necessary so as to enable a proper interpretation to be made where the situation to which the rules will be applied is exclusive to a particular Member State. This can be seen, for example in *Bernd Giloy v Hauptzollamt Frankfurt am Main-Ost*[2] and *Leur Bloem v Inspecteur der Belastingdienst*,[3] citing earlier judgments in *Dzodzi v Belgian State*[4] and *Gmurzynska-Bscher*.[5]

---

[1] Case C-346/93 [1995] ECR I-615.
[2] Case C-130/95 [1997] ECR I-4291.
[3] Case C-28/95 [1997] ECR I-4161.
[4] Cases C-297/88 and C-197/89 [1990] ECR I-3763.
[5] Case C-231/89 [1990] ECR I-4003.

6.26 In *Leur-Bloem*, the ECJ was asked to interpret provisions of domestic Dutch law on income tax, but the national court asked the ECJ whether that domestic law should be interpreted in conformity with Arts 2 and 11 of Council Directive 90/434/EEC on the common system of taxation applicable to mergers, etc. The Court held that—

> '. . . the Court of Justice has jurisdiction under Article 177 of the Treaty to interpret Community law where the situation in question is not governed directly by Community law but the national legislature, in transposing the provisions of a directive into domestic law, has chosen to apply the same treatment to purely internal situations and to those governed by the directive, so that it has aligned its domestic legislation to Community law.'.[1]

Again, in *Giloy*, the ECJ was asked to interpret provisions of domestic German law on the levying of turnover taxes, but the national court asked the ECJ whether that domestic law should be interpreted in conformity with Art 244 of Council Regulation 2913/92/EEC which establishes the Community Customs Code.[2] The Court repeated the *Leur-Bloem* formulation.[3] Interestingly, Advocate General Jacobs had advised the Court in a joint Opinion on these two cases that it ought to overrule *Dzodzi*, but the Court declined to take this advice and expressly approved *Dzodzi* in the *Bronner* case.[4]

---

[1] Case C-28/95 [1997] ECR I-4161 at para 34.
[2] OJ L302, 19.10.92, p 1.
[3] Case C-130/95 [1997] ECR I-4291 at para 23.
[4] See para 6.27.

6.27 In the *Bronner* case,[1] the Austrian court of first instance for competition matters referred questions to the ECJ in relation to the interpretation of Art 82 (former Art 86) in the context of a refusal of access to a daily newspaper distribution system. Although the court was applying its own domestic law to the case, and although this was not written in the same terms as EC law, it nevertheless felt that an interpretation of Art 82 would enable it to reach a decision, because it could hardly apply its own law inconsistently with EC competition law. The European Commission argued that the reference was inadmissible as the Austrian court was not applying EC law. The Advocate General advised that the Austrian court was competent to apply EC law and that an interpretation of EC law could be permitted on this basis. The Court of Justice held as follows—

'. . . a request from a national court may be rejected only if it is quite obvious that the interpretation of Community law . . . bears no relation to the actual facts of the case or to the subject matter of the main action' [17].

'. . . the fact that a national court is dealing with a restrictive practices dispute by applying national competition law should not prevent it from making a reference to the Court on the interpretation of Community law on the matter, and in particular on the interpretation of Article 86 [Art 82] of the Treaty in relation to that same situation, when it considers that a conflict between Community law and national law is capable of arising.' [20].

---

[1]   Case C-7/97 *Oscar Bronner GmbH v Mediaprint Zeitungs und Zeitsschriftenverlag* [1999] 4 CMLR 112.

6.28 This ruling would appear to establish conclusively that references may be made to the ECJ on the interpretation of Arts 81 and 82 where the domestic court or tribunal is considering corresponding issues under Chs I and II of the 1998 Act. The ruling is remarkable because the definition in Austrian law of dominance is quite different from that contained in Art 82 and abuse can only be prohibited following a court order to terminate it. However, the ruling is in generous terms and should not be confined to Art 82 issues. In addition it refers to the need to avoid conflict between domestic law and EC competition law and it is to that extent an encouragement for national courts and tribunals to make use of Art 234. It is not clear whether the ECJ has assessed the likely number of Art 234 references which will follow from this ruling, the impact that this may have on its workload, or the delay (normally about 21 months) in obtaining an answer to a reference question.

6.29 Despite the wide scope of the *Bronner* ruling, there will be cases where the EC provisions do not correspond to the UK law at issue and where an EC interpretation will not be relevant. For example, given the importance in EC law of the market unifying objective, asking the ECJ how Art 81 would apply to a market sharing agreement when that objective is not relevant to the UK law might not be fruitful.[1] In practice, it may be possible to avoid these conceptual difficulties: the ECJ's interpretation of questions such as the extent of joint or collective dominance, the meaning of 'implemented' in the context of territorial jurisdiction or on various permutations of 'abuse' would be common to both systems and, in the light of the *Bronner* case, will apparently be freely given.

---

[1]   Another example might be the contrasting formulation of Art 86(2) and Sch 3, para 4 (see Ch 7). Nevertheless the UK courts might be obliged under the EC Treaty, Art 10, not to pursue an interpretation which conflicts with EC law in a manner which jeopardised attainment of the Treaty objectives.

Which bodies may use Article 234?

6.30 The bodies administering UK competition law which would be able to make a reference include the Court of Appeal and the House of Lords, as well as any other court or tribunal which meet the necessary criteria. A court or tribunal must be established by permanent and independent law so as to be able to refer questions under Art 234. It must also have been called upon to give judgment in proceedings which require a judicial decision to be made and which it is under a legal duty to try.[1]

The Competition Commission's appeal tribunals are expected to meet these tests and thus to be eligible to use the Art 234 procedure.[2] The DGFT and utility regulators, when making decisions in exercise of their powers under the 1998 Act, would appear not to be so eligible because their procedures[3] are unlike those of an ordinary court, and their decisions will be administrative rather than judicial in nature.[4]

---

[1]   See Case C-54/96 *Dorsch Consult Ingenieurgesellschaft v Bundesbaugesellschaft Berlin* [1997] ECR I-4961 and C-111/94 *Job Centre* [1995] ECR I-3361 (at para 9), cited by Jacobs AG in the *Bronner* case (Opinion para 11); see para 6.27 above.

[2]   The intriguing possibility also arises from the Advocate General's opinion in the *Bronner* case (see para 6.27) that the appeals tribunals will themselves be able to apply Arts 81 and 82 in those cases where there is the necessary effect on trade between Member States.

[3]   At least on the basis of the draft rules of procedure so far made available.

[4]   The Government put on record its view that the appeals tribunals of the Commission would be eligible to refer questions to the ECJ but the DGFT and regulators would not 'necessarily' be able to do so—HL Committee, 25 November 1997, col 975 (Lord Simon of Highbury).

ALLOCATION OF TASKS BETWEEN UK AND EC AUTHORITIES

6.31   The DGFT's guidelines give some indication as to how cases that fall under both UK and EC competition law should be dealt with. The objective appears to be to keep the number of so-called 'dual notifications' (ie notifications to both authorities) to a minimum by encouraging parties who are involved in any agreements that affect trade between Member States to deal with the European Commission.[1] This is for two main reasons. First because an agreement obtaining EC exemption will automatically enjoy 'parallel exemption' under UK law (s 10(1), (2))[2] and secondly because any notification to the European Commission confers protection from penalties under UK law (s 41(2)).[3] Exemption under EC law applies throughout the territory of the EC while exemption under UK law does not affect the possible application of EC law and its effects are confined to the UK.

---

[1]   See DGFT's guidelines 'The Chapter I prohibition', paras 7.1-7.13.

[2]   See paras 2.106, 2.107 for consideration of 'parallel exemptions'.

[3]   See para 4.66.

Parallel exemptions

6.32   The problem with parallel exemption is that it is rare for the European Commission actually to grant an individual exemption pursuant to a notification. The European Commission is much more likely to close a file with a comfort letter which in some cases will be a so-called 'Art 85(3) [Art 81(3)] comfort letter'.[1] In such a case there will be no parallel exemption, since a comfort letter is not listed in s 10(1), but a comfort letter is a statement of the Commission to which regard must be had by virtue of the 1998 Act, s 60(3). Another problem is that obtaining an individual exemption decision, in the few cases that this is possible, takes months if not years, and during this time there is no provisional validity for the agreement in question.

---

[1]   In 1997 there were only eight individual exemption decisions (of which six were under special procedures relating to maritime transport) and 210 cases closed by comfort letter (see European Commission XXVIIth Report on Competition Policy 1997, pp 156-163).

Protection for penalties

6.33 Penalties may not be imposed under the 1998 Act from the time an agreement is notified to the European Commission until the Commission has reached a determination (s 41(2)).[1] What is meant by this is not clear. The guidelines published by the DGFT on the Chapter I prohibition refer to the Commission having 'determined' the matter,[2] but the guidelines on enforcement refer to the Commission determining the matter 'either formally or informally through a 'comfort' letter' '.[3] A further question is whether an appeal to the European Court of First Instance (CFI) and the ECJ will extend the period for the Commission's determination. Logically it should do so and a useful parallel would be the definition of 'determined' in the 1998 Act, Sch 13 in the context of continuing proceedings before the Restrictive Practices Court, where appeals and the time for lodging an appeal are included (Sch 13, para 15(4), (5)).[4]

---

[1]   See also para 4.66.
[2]   DGFT's guidelines 'The Chapter I prohibition', para 7.4.
[3]   DGFT's guidelines 'Enforcement', para 4.19.
[4]   See also para 4.66.

Affecting trade between Member States

6.34 The DGFT has stressed the broad interpretation given by the ECJ to the concept of 'effect on trade between Member States' and his belief that many agreements will be caught by both EC competition law and by the Chapter I prohibition.[1] He also suggests that the parties should conduct an assessment of this issue before notifying an agreement to him.[2]

---

[1]   DGFT's guidelines 'The Chapter I prohibition', para 7.2.
[2]   Ibid, para 7.3.

The approach normally taken

6.35 In the event of a dual notification, the DGFT will liaise closely with the European Commission to determine the appropriate forum for assessment. If the Commission decides to deal with the agreement by formal or informal means, the DGFT will suspend action until the Commission has completed its assessment and informed the parties of its conclusions. If the Commission grants an exemption, the agreement will benefit from parallel exemption (see para 6.32). If the Commission delivers a formal negative clearance decision, the DGFT and the courts 'are obliged to have regard [to that decision]' (see para 6.22). Otherwise, the DGFT will generally follow the Commission's assessment as set out in the relevant comfort letter.[1]

---

[1]   See DGFT's guidelines 'The Chapter I prohibition', paras 7.11 and 7.12. See also para 6.41 below.

Action by the DGFT

6.36 In some circumstances the DGFT will proceed with the notification, for example where—[1]

(a) the agreement raises particular concerns in the UK which it does not in other Member States (probably a rare occurrence, although networks of agreements operating solely within the UK, but deemed to affect trade between Member States because of their prevalence within their market sector, could fall within this category);

(b) the DGFT considers the agreement involves important legal, economic or policy developments.

Another possible circumstance is where the European Commission decides as a matter of its internal priorities not to consider the matter.[2] However there is always the danger here that an agreement could escape proper scrutiny by either authority if it is likely to come within the scope of Art 81(1), since the UK authorities do not have the power to apply EC competition law and in particular to grant Art 81(3) exemptions.

---

[1]   See DGFT's guidelines 'The Chapter I prohibition', para 7.10.
[2]   The Commission has a discretion in deciding which cases are of sufficient Community interest (see Case T-24/90 *Automec Srl* [1992] ECR II-2223).

Policy conflict between the Commission and the DGFT

6.37 The essential problem with these arrangements appears to be that both the European Commission[1] and the DGFT[2] have an inclination to defer judgment in borderline jurisdictional cases to each other.

---

[1]   See eg Commission Notice on co-operation between national competition authorities and the Commission in handling cases falling within the scope of Articles 85 or 86 [81 or 82] of the EC Treaty, OJ C313, 15.10.97, p 3, para 10 and 28.
[2]   See eg DGFT's guidelines 'The Chapter I prohibition', para 7.4.

6.38 The DGFT suggests that parties in borderline cases may wish to consult with the OFT as to the most appropriate forum for notification.[1] This may be helpful if the DGFT were to liaise with the European Commission at this stage on this matter, but the more prudent course of action would generally be to notify the European Commission in any event because anything that the DGFT might have to say would not necessarily affect the approach that the European Commission might take.

---

[1]   DGFT's guidelines 'The Chapter I prohibition', para 7.6.

Other problems

Delay

6.39 A further potential problem with only notifying the European Commission is the inevitable time delay between the European Commission's formal response and the parties' subsequent notification to the DGFT. This leaves the parties potentially exposed to penalties pursuant to UK law during this interim period. Although this is unlikely to cause many problems in practice, there may be situations in which this could be unsatisfactory. For instance, in cases where the Commission has formally refused jurisdiction on the basis of lack of effect on trade between Member States, it seems unfair that the parties cannot benefit from a period of grace within which to furnish a notification to the DGFT. Immunity from fines is a factor to be considered in determining whom to notify and parties will judge their possible exposure and notify accordingly. The DGFT has indicated that he will try to give priority to any notifications received in such circumstances.[1]

---

[1]   See DGFT's guidelines 'The Chapter I prohibition', para 7.7.

Retroactive effect

6.40 Where a party notifies an agreement to the DGFT, for example in circumstances where it has been previously been notified to the European Commission, but where the Commission has declined jurisdiction, it is important for any exemption to be granted with retroactive effect. The DGFT's guidelines state that he has the power to grant retroactive exemptions in all cases.[1]

---

[1]   See DGFT's guidelines 'The Chapter I prohibition', para 7.5.

Lack of reasons

6.41 In some cases European Commission 'comfort letters' merely state that the Commission is of the opinion that the agreement does not contravene Art 81(1), and do not elaborate any further. The parties may need to notify to the DGFT in those circumstances as the Commission may have simply considered that the agreement does not affect trade between Member States, rather than that it does not restrict competition.

Commission negative clearance decisions

6.42 The 1998 Act, s 60(3), obliges the DGFT to have regard to a final negative clearance decision but it is not clear that EC law would require him to follow it.[1] The DGFT has indicated that he will not seek to adopt a different approach from that of the European Commission.[2]

---

[1]   See paras 6.10 and 6.11.
[2]   DGFT's guidelines 'The Chapter I prohibition', para 7.9.

Chapter II and Article 82 notifications

6.43 The DGFT has not stated how he will approach notifications for negative clearance of a potential breach of both Chapter II and Art 82. The circumstances in which this will be an issue are likely to be rare.

Commission's refusal to act

6.44 It is debatable whether a refusal by the Commission to reach a formal decision on a notified agreement is actionable under Art 232 (formerly Art 175). The Commission has indicated in the Notice on co-operation with national authorities[1] that it will process Art 81(3) applications where the agreements are being litigated on Art 81(1) issues. The DGFT has not indicated what his approach would be to agreements where the Commission is simply not proceeding with the application, and is unlikely to issue a comfort letter. Although the parties are immune from fines, the enforceability of their agreements under UK law could still seriously be in question. If the DGFT takes no action at all then the parties are at the mercy of the Commission's inactivity. It is suggested that the DGFT should be willing to take action, if necessary after liaising with the Commission, to resolve the status of the agreement, at least under UK competition law.

---

[1]   See para 6.37 above.

Proceedings in the UK courts

6.45 The DGFT has confirmed, however, that in cases where an agreement has received an EC comfort letter but is nevertheless challenged in the UK courts under Ch I, he will accept and consider as a priority any notifications made to him, provided always that he considers the agreement to be capable of exemption. In these circumstances, exemption is likely to be retroactive.[1]

---

[1]   DGFT's guidelines 'The Chapter I prohibition', para 7.13.

General comment

6.46 The UK authorities' reluctance to encourage dual notifications is understandable, given the legendary tales of the thousands of notifications made to the European Commission in 1963. These fears may be misplaced if the law applying to vertical agreements is clarified prior to the prohibitions coming into force in March 2000; it was the overwhelming number of distribution agreements notified in 1962 that inundated the Commission and this can be avoided in the UK by excluding vertical agreements from the Chapter I prohibition. It is necessary to recognise that immunity from penalties is an important factor in any decision to notify and that there are loopholes in the protection provided by notifying only to the European Commission. Moreover, depending on how the DGFT addresses the task before him, the speedy turnaround of notifications will be a high priority, whereas the European Commission's record in that respect is not uniformly good. Finally, the apparent eagerness of the UK authorities to direct applications to Brussels sits uncomfortably beside the vigour with which the enactment of a separate but overlapping UK competition law was pursued. If most cases will affect interstate trade and should be dealt with by the European Commission, do we need the elaborate apparatus of the Competition Act 1998 at all?

7 Special sectors

INTRODUCTION

Concurrency

7.1   The Competition Act 1998 (the 1998 Act) significantly increases the powers of the various utility regulators to apply competition law. They will have the power to investigate any anti-competitive behaviour in their relevant sectors which fall within the scope of the Chapter I and II prohibitions. Under the previous legislation, the regulators had similar functions to those of the DGFT in relation to the monopoly provisions contained in the Fair Trading Act 1973 (FTA 1973) but had no role in relation to agreements subject to the Restrictive Trade Practices Act 1976 (RTPA 1976). The effectiveness of the powers that they enjoyed under the Competition Act 1980 (CA 1980) was limited by the weaknesses of that Act.[1] Under the new legislation, the powers available to the regulators (and to the DGFT) are far broader than those under the old competition regime, and include the rights to obtain information, to carry out on-the-spot investigations and to impose fines.[2]

---

[1]   See para 8.11.

[2]   Regulators already have the power to obtain information as part of their licensing functions, and in some cases (eg in the gas industry) may impose financial penalties for breach of licence. These powers, however, are very different from those now conferred.

7.2   The relationship between the various regulators and their regulated undertakings is likely to change profoundly once these powers come into effect.[1] Providing for the functions of the DGFT to be exercisable concurrently by the regulators was a controversial matter as the Bill went through Parliament, and was the subject of extensive debate. Of particular concern were—

(a)   the effect on the general duties of the various regulators and the incompatibility of some of them with competition objectives;[2]

(b)   the attenuation or removal of previous exemptions from the RTPA 1976;[3]

(c)   the danger that sectoral regulators would apply competition powers in a different manner from the DGFT;[4] and

(d)   the danger of double (or treble) jeopardy where the DGFT and one or more of the regulators would be investigating the same issue, particularly in the case of conglomerate utilities.[5]

---

[1]   The imposition on all the main regulators of a statutory duty to protect the interests of consumers, following the 1998 Green Paper 'A fair deal for consumers: modernising the framework for utility regulation', Cm 3898 (March 1998), para 4.9, may also have an important effect.

[2]   HL Consideration of Commons' Amendments, 20 October 1998, col 1388 (Lord Simon of Highbury).

[3]   Ibid, col 1390 (Lord McIntosh of Haringey).

[4]   HL Committee, 25 November 1997, col 907 (Lord Ezra). See para 7.16.

[5]   Ibid, col 908 (Lord Ezra); col 913 (Lord Simon of Highbury).

Outline

7.3   The role of the regulators is set out in the 1998 Act, s 54 and Sch 10. The general scheme of these provisions is that—

(a) regulators[1] are given the power to apply the Chapter I and Chapter II prohibitions 'concurrently' with the DGFT in relation to the activities over which they have licensing powers and commercial activities connected with those activities;[2]

(b) previous exemptions for agreements in regulated sectors are dealt with under the transitional provisions;[3]

(c) the regulators may have regard to their general duties when exercising their competition powers in some circumstances but they are not obliged to do so;

(d) the making of rules, directions and guidance as to penalties is reserved to the DGFT, subject to his having consulted the regulators if their sectors are affected and subject to the approval of the Secretary of State (ss 38, 51);

(e) regulations may be made by the Secretary of State to co-ordinate the concurrent application of the 1998 Act by the DGFT and the various regulators;[4]

(f) regulators may issue their own guidelines explaining how they will apply the 1998 Act in their own sectors;[5]

(g) agreements or conduct specifically required by the terms of relevant sectoral licences are excluded from the 1998 Act by the operation of Sch 3, para 5.

Amendments to the legislation governing the functions of the regulators and the DGFT are set out in the 1998 Act, Sch 10. The treatment of each regulated sector follows a similar pattern but there are differences in some of the details. The list of affected regulators in Sch 10, para 1, does not include the Independent Television Commission, the Radio Authority and the Civil Aviation Authority (CAA), each of which also exercises competition functions. The first two of these are already required to have regard to the need to maintain fair and effective competition when exercising their licensing functions,[6] while the CAA has competition powers under the Airports Act 1986, Pt IV. The DTI canvassed the inclusion of the CAA in the list in Sch 10 in its Green Paper on utilities regulation,[7] and seems to have concluded that the CAA should also be given concurrent powers under the 1998 Act.[8]

---

[1]   The 1998 Act, s 54(1), Sch 10, para 1 lists the relevant regulators as—
  (a) the Director General of Telecommunications;
  (b) the Director General of Electricity Supply;
  (c) the Director General of Electricity Supply for Northern Ireland;
  (d) the Director General of Water Services;
  (e) the Rail Regulator;
  (f) the Director General of Gas Supply; and
  (g) the Director General of Gas for Northern Ireland.
  Note that the two Northern Ireland posts are currently held by the same person as are the posts of Electricity and Gas Supply regulators. It is intended to merge the latter into a single Energy Regulator (see para 7.8).

[2]   Section 54(2)–(7). For the specific functions given to regulators see para 7.17. The regulators' powers under the monopoly control provisions of the FTA 1973 are retained.

[3]   See paras 9.24–9.25.

[4]   Section 54(4) which was added to the Bill at a late stage of the Parliamentary process; the DGFT's guidelines 'Concurrent application to regulated industries' describe mechanics and allocation of cases rather than provide for any substantive co-ordination of approach. A consultation paper 'Concurrency—consultation on possible need and scope for regulations' (URN 99/586) was issued by the DTI in February 1999.

[5]   See eg the draft guidelines issued by the Director General of Telecommunications (see para 7.4).

THE REGULATORS

Telecommunications

Concurrent powers

7.4 The 1998 Act provides that the functions of the Director General of Telecommunications (DGT) under CA 1980 cease to be exercisable.[1] Schedule 10, para 2(6) substitutes the Telecommunications Act 1984, s 50(3), (3A), thus entitling the DGT to exercise concurrently with the DGFT the functions of the DGFT so far as they relate to agreements, decisions and concerted practices caught by the Chapter I prohibition, and conduct caught by the Chapter II prohibition which relate to 'commercial activities connected with telecommunications'.[2] The DGT will issue guidelines explaining how he will apply his powers under the 1998 Act.[3]

---

1 Schedule 10, para 2(1). The functions were those transferred under the Telecommunications Act 1984, s 50(3).
2 This phrase is defined in the Telecommunications Act 1984, s 4(3). The 1998 Act, Sch 10, para 2(7)–(10) provides for other consequential amendments to the 1984 Act.
3 See DGT's draft guidelines 'Application in the telecommunications sector', particularly Pt 3, in which the DGT emphasises that the distinctive features of the sector require a slightly different emphasis or approach when applying competition rules.

Interplay with licensing powers

7.5 If the DGT is satisfied that it would be better to deal with an agreement or practice under his competition powers, rather than his licensing powers, he may do so provided he gives notice that he is doing this.[1] The DGT may, but need not, have regard to his general duties[2] when exercising his competition powers, provided that the matter for which the general duty is imposed is one that the DGFT could himself have regard to.[3] This complex formulation was the subject of considerable debate during the Bill's passage through Parliament.[4] It is designed to bridge the gap between the DGT's licensing functions and his competition powers, which operate on different (if overlapping) principles and are subject to different procedures (for example, the DGT's decisions on licence matters are not appealable to the appeal tribunals of the Competition Commission).[5]

---

1 See the 1998 Act, Sch 10, para 9(4). The notice is given under the Telecommunications Act 1984, s 16(5).
2 Telecommunications Act 1984, s 3(1) and (2).
3 Schedule 10, para 2(4) adding new subsections (3B) and (3C) to the Telecommunications Act 1984, s 3.
4 HC 3R, 8 July 1998, col 1198.
5 Other differences include the lack of penalties for breach of licence, limitations on third party actions and on provisional orders and the need for a series of licence breaches; see DGT's draft guidelines 'Application in the telecommunications sector', para 4.4.

7.6   The DGT's duties to maintain and promote effective competition and to promote efficiency and economy on the part of those engaged in telecommunications commercial activity are matters for which the DGT has a general duty to which the DGFT could have regard.[1] It is more difficult to envisage that the DGFT could have regard to the ability of service providers to finance their activities[2] or the encouragement of investment in the UK.[3] Accordingly, the DGT may not have regard to these matters when exercising his competition, rather than licensing, powers. It remains to be seen how carefully these distinctions will be drawn in practice. The DGT intends to take into account the principles established by the sector specific regulatory rules when applying his competition powers and by doing so will follow the approach of the European Commission in its application of competition law to the telecommunications sector.[4] Matters specifically required by the terms of a licence condition are excluded from the application of the 1998 Act by Sch 3, para 5.[5]

---

[1]   Telecommunications Act 1984, s 3(2)(b) and (c).
[2]   Ibid, s 3(1)(b).
[3]   Ibid, s 3(2)(e).
[4]   DGT's draft guidelines 'Application in the telecommunications sector', para 4.7, referring to the European Commission's Notice on the application of the competition rules to access agreements in the telecommunications sector (OJ C265, 22.8.98, p 2).
[5]   DGT's draft guidelines 'Application in the telecommunications sector', para 4.2. (The example given is the condition in BT's licence requiring it to provide services to deaf users). See also para 2.65.

Fair Trading Condition

7.7   The DGT has included in the principal PTO[1] licences a so-called Fair Trading Condition (FTC) based on the EC Treaty, Arts 81 and 82, which is designed to enable him to apply competition rules through the medium of the licence. The FTC contains a 'sunset' clause rendering it inapplicable once suitable competition legislation comes into force in the UK and the DGT has indicated that he considers that the 1998 Act fulfils that requirement; as a result of this the FTC will accordingly cease to apply from 1 March 2000.[2]

---

[1]   Public Telecommunications Operator.
[2]   DGT's draft guidelines 'Application in the telecommunications sector', paras 4.10–4.11.

Gas and electricity

Merging of regulators

7.8   The 1998 Act makes separate provision for the giving of concurrent powers to the Director General of Gas Supply (DGGS) and to the Director General of Electricity Supply (DGES). However, the Government's intention is to merge these two regulators with effect from a date in 1999.[1] This will involve consequential amendment to the current provisions on competition as described below.

---

[1]   Green Paper 'A fair deal for consumers: modernising the framework for utility regulation' Cm 3898 (March 1998), para 4.9. 'The Response to Consultation' (July 1998), para 47. However, primary legislation will be needed to effect this merger and the date may slip.

Gas

7.9   The DGGS loses his competition powers under CA 1980 and, as with the DGT (see paras 7.4–7.6), receives concurrent competition powers under the 1998 Act.[1] The DGGS may apply the prohibitions to the shipping, conveyance or supply of gas and activities ancillary thereto.[2] The DGGS may decide that if appropriate he should act under his competition powers, rather than his licensing powers[3] and need not have regard to his general duties[4] when applying his competition powers, but may do so if they are matters to which the DGFT could have regard.[5] The DGGS will issue guidelines on how the Act is to be applied in the gas sector. There are similar provisions for Northern Ireland conferring power on the Director General of Gas for Northern Ireland.[6]

[1]   See the Gas Act 1986, s 36A, as amended by the 1998 Act, Sch 10, para 3.
[2]   Gas Act 1986, ss 5(1) and 36A(4), as amended.
[3]   The 1998 Act, Sch 10, para 10(5).
[4]   Gas Act 1986, s 4(1)–(3).
[5]   See the Gas Act 1986, ss 4(3A), (3B), as inserted by the 1998 Act, Sch 10, para 3(3).
[6]   The 1998 Act, Sch 10, para 8. In this case the powers are applicable to the conveyance, storage or supply of gas in Northern Ireland.

Electricity

7.10   The DGES receives new competition powers in the same way as the DGT (see paras 7.4–7.6) and the DGGS.[1] The DGES's powers apply to commercial activities connected with the generation, transmission or supply of electricity.[2] This applies also to the Director General of Electricity Supply for Northern Ireland. [3]

[1]   See the Electricity Act 1989, ss 3, 43, as amended by the 1998 Act, Sch 10, para 4. Note that the DGES and DGGS are the same person.
[2]   Electricity Act 1989, s 43, as amended.
[3]   The 1998 Act, Sch 10, para 7. The scope of powers applicable in Northern Ireland is the same as for Great Britain.

Water

7.11   The Director General of Water Supply (DGWS) receives new competition powers in the same way as the other regulators.[1] The DGWS's powers apply to commercial activities connected with the supply (or securing a supply) of water or of sewerage services.[2]

[1]   See the Water Industry Act 1991, ss 2, 31, as amended by the 1998 Act, Sch 10, para 5.
[2]   Water Industry Act 1991, s 31, as amended.

Railways

7.12   Competition powers are conferred on the Rail Regulator in relation to the supply of railway services with similar terms to those for the other regulators.[1] However, the application of these new powers to access agreements[2] is limited, as is the power of the DGFT. Access agreements are largely excluded from the application of the Chapter I prohibition by virtue of the 'compliance with legal requirements' exclusion in the 1998 Act, Sch 3, para 5 (as they can only be entered into as directed by the Rail Regulator) (see para 2.65). In addition, neither the Rail Regulator nor the DGFT may take final or interim enforcement measures under Ch I in respect of access agreements, although they may do so in respect of conduct connected with an access agreement which is subject to the Chapter II prohibition.[3]

---

[1]   See the Railways Act 1993, ss 4, 67, as amended by the 1998 Act, Sch 10, para 6. See also the Channel Tunnel Rail Link Act 1996, s 22 (amended by the 1998 Act, Sch 10, para 16(1) and (2)) in relation to the Rail Regulator's duties as to the exercise of regulatory functions.

[2]   Ie agreements under which train operators are given rights to use the rail network, stations and light maintenance depots (Railways Act 1993, ss 17 and 18). Such agreements may only be entered into pursuant to directions from the Rail Regulator although they may be amended subject to his approval, rather than his direction.

[3]   See the Railways Act 1993, s 22(6A) and (6B), which are inserted by the 1998 Act, Sch 10, para 15(5). These provisions were included to prevent the Rail Regulator or DGFT from ordering amendments to access agreements (to the extent that they were not already excluded from Ch I by Sch 3(5)) as a remedy for breach of Ch I. See HL Consideration of Commons' Amendments, 20 October 1998, col 1390 (Lord McIntosh of Haringey).

Channel tunnel rail link

7.13   Agreements, decisions or concerted practices entered into or taken by a rail link undertaker, and conduct engaged in by such an undertaker in connection with the supply of railway services so far as relating to the rail link[1] are excluded from the Rail Regulator's concurrent 1998 Act powers.[2] The exemption from the Rail Regulator's jurisdiction enjoyed under the previous legislation is thus retained.

---

[1]   For the definition of these terms see Channel Tunnel Rail Link Act 1996, s 56.

[2]   See the Channel Tunnel Rail Link Act 1996, s 22(3), as substituted by the 1998 Act, Sch 10, para 16(3).

CONCURRENCY AND CO-ORDINATION

Section 54 regulations

7.14   The overlap and potential for confusion between the powers of the DGFT and those conferred on the sectoral regulators is recognised, and the solution adopted by the legislator is partly statutory and partly political. A new subsection was added to s 54 at a relatively late stage during the Bill's passage through Parliament, giving the Secretary of State the power to make regulations 'for the purpose of co-ordinating the performance of functions under [the Act]'.[1] The DGFT also has the power to make procedural rules, which have to be approved by an order made by the Secretary of State (s 51(5))[2] and, by s 51(4), rules relating to regulators' concurrent jurisdiction can only be made subject to prior consultation with them. There are therefore quite sufficient powers to regulate the allocation of functions amongst the various authorities.

---

[1]   Section 54(4), which was introduced during the 3rd Reading in the House of Commons; see HC 3R, 8 July 1998, col 1199. A consultation paper 'Concurrency—consultation on possible need and scope for regulations (URN 99/586) was issued by the DTI in February 1999.

[2]   See para 4.33.

The Concurrency Working Party

7.15 In addition to legislative powers, there is also provision for the working party which comprises representatives of the DGFT and the various regulators, to continue in existence as the 'Concurrency Working Party'.[1] Its functions will cover information sharing, working arrangements and the issue and revision of guidelines. To the uninitiated, this reliance on a non-statutory body may seem strange but it is really no different from the non-statutory mergers panel which co-ordinates the giving of advice to the Secretary of State on mergers. It is to be hoped that the deliberations of the Concurrency Working Party will be less shrouded in mystery than its mergers equivalent.

---

[1]   The DGFT's guidelines on 'Concurrent application to regulated industries' explain the Working Party's role.

Allocation of tasks

7.16 The general principle that the authorities will seek to apply is that a case will be dealt with by the authority which is better or best placed to do so. Unless there are reasons for doing otherwise, the relevant regulator, rather than the DGFT, will apply the prohibitions to matters falling within his sector.[1]

---

[1]   See the DGFT's guidelines 'Concurrent application to regulated industries'.

Regulators' functions

7.17 The competition functions of the regulators will therefore comprise—
    (a) giving individual guidance on the 1998 Act;
    (b) considering notifications for a decision;[1]
    (c) granting exemptions;
    (d) receiving complaints;[2]
    (e) imposing interim measures;
    (f) carrying out inquiries and investigations;
    (g) imposing penalties;
    (f) enforcing deadlines; and
    (h) issuing advice and information on the application of the 1998 Act in the relevant sector.[3]

For notifications, there is a 'one stop shop' in that only the DGFT can accept applications for guidance and notifications. In addition, only the DGFT may issue guidance on penalties, although he must consult with the regulators before doing so. This consultation requirement also applies to any procedural rules made by the DGFT under s 51.[4]

---

[1]   On receipt of notifications passed to him by the DGFT, notifying parties should include an extra copy of Form N (see Appendix 3) for the DGFT to pass to the regulator and also send an extra copy direct to the relevant regulator.
[2]   Complaints may be made direct to the regulators but the DGFT urges complainants to complain to one authority only.
[3]   For example, the DGT's draft guidelines 'Application in the telecommunications sector'.
[4]   In other words, the regulators should all operate the same procedures as the DGFT when applying the prohibitions.

Co-ordination of approach

7.18 While the above measures may ensure that cases are handled by the body which is best equipped to do so, the difficulty remains that the interpretation placed on the prohibitions by the various bodies with concurrent powers may differ. For example a regulator may analyse predatory pricing in a different way than the DGFT may, or may indeed apply the DGFT's guidelines on 'Market definition' so as to produce a result which is different from that which the DGFT himself may have previously reached in a decision covering similar issues. It is regrettable that the 1998 Act does not place a duty on the DGFT and regulators to apply their concurrent powers in a way that ensures, so far as possible, a consistent approach to the application of the prohibitions. What the 1998 Act does provide is for—

> (a) input from the regulators on the DGFT's guidelines and particularly on the s 36 guidance on penalties (see para 7.3) as well as input from the DGFT and other regulators on each regulator's own guidelines.
> (b) the regulators to operate the DGFT's rules of procedure (see para 7.14);
> (c) the Secretary of State to make regulations on co-ordination under s 54;[1]
> (d) an appeal system common to all bodies;[2]
> (e) the regulators, like the DGFT, to act consistently with EC law (s 60).[3]

The task of ensuring consistency of approach in actual cases appears to fall outside the remit of the Concurrency Working Party and there is no other body expressly charged with achieving consistency in this way.

---

[1]   See paras 7.3 and 7.14.

[2]   See para 7.19 and Ch 5.

[3]   See para 7.19.

Appeals

7.19 All decisions[1] of regulators are subject to appeal to an appeal tribunal of the Competition Commission (as are all decisions of the DGFT) and must be made having regard to the requirement of consistency with EC law imposed by the 1998 Act, s 60.[2] Regulators, like the DGFT, do not, however, have the necessary jurisdiction to allow them to refer questions to the ECJ under the EC Treaty, Article 234.[3]

---

[1]   For the list of appealable decisions, see s 46(3) (discussed at para 5.16).

[2]   See para 6.16.

[3]   See para 6.30.

SERVICES OF GENERAL ECONOMIC INTEREST

Exclusion

7.20 The 1998 Act excludes from the scope of the prohibitions any acts of undertakings 'entrusted with the operation of services of general economic interest or having the character of a revenue-producing monopoly in so far as the prohibition would obstruct the performance, in law or in fact, of the particular task assigned to that undertaking' (Sch 3, para 4).[1] This exclusion is based on EC Treaty, Art 86(2) (former Art 90(2)), but translation into statutory language, although clearer than its EC equivalent, is inverted and this may lead to a different interpretation. Article 86(2) *extends* to such undertakings the prohibitions of Arts 81 and 82 unless the performance of their tasks would be thereby obstructed. This has encouraged a strict interpretation of any exceptions in the voluminous case law.[2] The phrasing of the 1998 Act, which *excludes* such undertakings from the prohibitions, suggests that a wider interpretation may be appropriate, and, to that extent, may be one of the provisions the legislator had in mind when including in s 60 the phrase 'having regard to any relevant differences between the provisions concerned'.[3]

---

[1]   See para 2.64. The DGFT intends to publish a guideline on 'General economic interest'.
[2]   For discussion of Art 86 (ex Art 90) see *Butterworths Competition Law IX* [23]–[87]; Bellamy and Child: *Common Market Law of Competition* (ed Rose) (4th edn 1993), Ch 13.
[3]   Section 60(1); see also s 60(2) 'so far as is compatible with the provisions of this Part'. See Ch 6.

Practical effects

7.21   If this is indeed the case, regulated utilities that fall within the definition in Sch 3 (and this could include the principal operators in the various sectors)[1] could claim that the exclusion applies to their activities. This would not help them in the case of blatant breaches of the prohibitions,[2] but agreements for the sharing of pipelines and other means of conveyance, or the refusal to grant access to infrastructure networks, might be said to be necessary for the attainment of the task assigned to that undertaking.[3] The regulators' sector specific powers will continue to apply and are not excluded by Sch 3.

---

[1]   For example, Railtrack is described by the Rail Regulator as having a role of 'stewardship' of the network.
[2]   A price fixing agreement with competitors would be difficult to establish as necessary for the attainment of the utility company's task—but it is not inconceivable.
[3]   No formal decision has ever been taken by the European Commission disapplying the EC Treaty, Arts 81 and 82. The argument may therefore be described as more brave than reliable. It is not enough for a restrictive agreement merely to assist the undertaking in achieving its tasks—it must be indispensable; see eg Commission Decision *NAVEWA-ANSEAU* (OJ L167, 15.6.82, p 39). The DGT has indicated that he believes it is unlikely that the exception would apply to any telecommunications companies (draft guidelines 'Application in the telecommunications sector', para 7.15).

8 Existing powers

INTRODUCTION

8.1   The Competition Act 1998 (the 1998 Act) repeals the Restrictive Trade Practices Acts 1976 and 1977, the Resale Prices Act 1976 and the Restrictive Practices Court Act 1976 in their entirety together with the provisions of the Competition Act 1980 covering anti-competitive practices. However, certain provisions of the current system of competition law in the UK are retained. In particular, the merger provisions of the Fair Trading Act 1973 (FTA 1973) are left in place,[1] as are the provisions for investigating scale and complex monopolies under that Act. The Competition Commission (CC) will also take over the functions of the former Monopolies and Mergers Commission (MMC) in relation to efficiency audits under the Competition Act 1980, s 11 and in relation to licence modifications in regulated sectors, although these are not, strictly speaking, competition law.

---

[1]   The Government's White Paper 'Our competitive future: building the knowledge driven economy', Cm 4176 (December 1998) referred to a consultation paper on possible reform of the UK merger regime to be published 'early 1999' (para 4.7).

Merger control

8.2   The statutory provisions controlling mergers[1] (including the stricter provisions for newspaper[2] and water industry[3] mergers) are not repealed and as a consequence UK merger control will continue to operate as before, with the OFT, the CC and the Secretary of State retaining their respective roles. Arrangements and conduct comprising or ancillary to merger situations are excluded from the Chapter I and II prohibitions and there are corresponding exclusions for concentrations with a Community dimension.[4]

---

[1]   FTA 1973, ss 63–80.
[2]   FTA 1973, ss 57–62.
[3]   Water Industry Act 1991, s 14.
[4]   See paras 2.40–2.51, 3.31.

8.3   The functions of the former MMC are taken over by the CC; the reporting function will ostensibly operate in the same way as the MMC did, but it is hard to imagine that its method of proceeding will not be influenced by the activities of the appeal tribunals, which with their legally qualified Chairman and Deputy Chairmen and non-legal members, will operate separately from, but within, the same organisation as the reporting function of the CC.

Scale and complex monopolies

8.4   Both the so-called 'scale' and 'complex' monopolies are retained. Scale monopolies are those where one firm has a share of supply of a given description of goods or services at or exceeding one quarter. Complex monopolies are those where that 'market' share is accounted for by several firms who act, if not necessarily in collusion, in a way that distorts competition. Both these tests are jurisdictional in nature and simply lead to a requirement that a monopoly situation be referred to the CC for investigation.[1]

---

[1] See *Butterworths Competition Law* VI [106]–[149] for a full description of these provisions.

Scale monopolies

8.5 Where there has been an infringement of the Chapter II prohibition, the DGFT will be able to impose a fine under the 1998 Act, s 36 and to make directions under s 33.[1] However, such directions can only require a modification or cessation of the condemned conduct and cannot, for example, include an order of divestment.[2] There may be circumstances where divestment would be a suitable remedy and this is the reason that the scale monopoly provisions of FTA 1973 have been retained, since the power of divestment is among the powers available to the Secretary of State under FTA 1973, Sch 8, Pt II. The Government indicated during the Bill's passage through Parliament that the use of the scale monopoly provisions would be rare and that they would 'essentially become reserve powers to deal with situations where the problem is market structure rather than abuse'.[3]

---

[1] See para 4.53.
[2] Compare the similar position in EC law under Council Regulation 17/62/EEC, OJ L13, 21.2.62, p 204 (S edn, 1959–62, p 87).
[3] HL Committee, 13 November 1997, col 300 (Lord Simon of Highbury). See also HL 3R, 5 March 1998, col 1333 'We intend that these powers should be used in the future only in circumstances where there has already been proven abuse under the prohibitions, and where the director believes that there is a real prospect of further abuses by the same firm'.

Complex monopolies

8.6 The principal reason given by the Government for retaining the complex monopoly controls (a long cherished feature of UK competition legislation), was the need to control situations of competitive failure in an industry where neither Ch I nor Ch II might apply.[1] However there are other considerations which also help to explain why the retention of these FTA 1973 powers was attractive to the Government as follows—

(a) the acknowledged difficulty in EC competition law in dealing with networks of similar agreements;[2]
(b) the exclusion of most so-called vertical agreements from the Chapter I prohibition[3] and the non-applicability of Ch II to them in the absence of dominance;
(c) uncertainty over the development of EC jurisprudence on joint dominance.[4]

---

[1] HL Report Stage, 19 February 1998, col 351 (Lord Simon of Highbury), '. . . the Fair Trading Act complex monopoly provisions may enable the authorities to deal with problems that fall outside the Chapter I and Chapter II prohibitions, particularly where there is parallel behaviour by companies in a market but no actual agreement.'
[2] Case 23/67 *Brasserie de Haecht* [1967] ECR 407; Case C-234/89 *Delimitis v Henninger Bräu* [1991] ECR I-935.
[3] See para 2.75–2.88
[4] See para 3.29.

Comment

8.7   The retention of FTA 1973 monopoly controls in addition to the prohibitions attracted the comment that industry would be subjected to double jeopardy and that the authorities had retained more power than they reasonably needed.[1] However, the perceived danger in discarding structural remedies altogether and the flexibility given by the complex monopoly provisions to investigate sectors or whole industries,[2] coupled with the responses to the Government's consultation prior to tabling the Bill, made the retention of these provisions inevitable.

---

[1]   The combination of prohibition and FTA 1973 monopoly controls was referred to in the pre-enactment consultations as 'hybridity'. It had been one of the options canvassed in the 1992 Green Paper 'Abuse of market power: a consultative document on possible legislative options', Cm 2100 (November 1992) and discussed at length in the 1995 Commons Trade and Industry Committee Report 'UK Policy on Monopolies' (TIC Fifth Report HC 249–I) (17 May 1995) (see para 1.4).

[2]   See eg MMC Inquiries *Beer* (Cm 651); *Petrol* (Cm 972); *Carbonated Drinks* (Cm 1625); *Contact Lens Solutions* (Cm 2242).

Powers of inquiry and investigation

8.8   The DGFT (and the sectoral regulators) are given new powers to obtain information for the purpose of deciding whether to make a monopoly reference (or to seek undertakings in lieu).[1] These include the power to require the production of documents, to enter premises and take copies of documents, but do not extend to the making of a forced entry with a judge's warrant. They do, however, represent a substantial increase in the information-gathering powers under FTA 1973, particularly as they are backed by criminal sanctions.[2]

---

[1]   The 1998 Act, s 66, adding new provisions to ss 44 and 46 of the FTA 1973 (see paras 4.25–4.27). The previous powers were limited to inquiry by written notice for certain specified categories of information. This amendment is now in force.

[2]   The 1998 Act, s 67.

Publication of reports

8.9   Another change is the removal of the obligation in FTA 1973, s 83, to provide the parties to a monopoly situation with an advance copy of the MMC's report (the 1998 Act, s 69).[1]

---

[1]   The period of grace had been 24 hours: see FTA 1973, s 83(1A). The continued existence of this practice, which does not occur in the case of mergers, was thought to be anomalous and to carry the risk of misuse of price sensitive information.

Services relating to the use of land

8.10   As a consequence of introducing the possibility of an exclusion from the prohibitions for agreements relating to land, the Secretary of State is permitted to modify the definition of supply of services relating to the use of land, by means of statutory instrument.[1] This enables him to extend the scope of what can be investigated under the monopoly provisions of FTA 1973. There have in the past been difficulties in applying the definition contained in FTA 1973, s 137 to situations involving the use of land.[2]

¹   The 1998 Act, s 68, modifying FTA 1973, s 137(3). See paras 2.90–2.92 for a discussion of the exclusions in relation to land agreements.

²   See eg Competition Act 1980, s 23, which extended the definition to include caravan sites. See also the MMC's 1990 Report on *Electrical Contracting at Exhibition Halls in London* (Cm 995).

Anti-competitive practices

8.11   One consequence of the introduction of the Chapter II prohibition is the repeal of the main part of the Competition Act 1980, controlling anti-competitive practices by single firms. These provisions, hailed on their introduction as a radical innovation, have consistently failed to make any significant impact on corporate or administrative behaviour.[1] Attenuated in 1994,[2] their deletion will be neither greatly noticed nor lamented.

¹   Mainly because no sanction followed from an adverse finding by the OFT other than a reference to the MMC.

²   The Anti-Competitive Practices (Exclusions) (Amendment) Order 1994, SI 1994/1557.

9 Transitional arrangements

INTRODUCTION

9.1 Transitional provisions are contained in the Competition Act 1998 (the 1998 Act), Sch 13,[1] which takes effect pursuant to s 74(2) of the Act. Transition has two main purposes. First it provides a fair means of transferring the control of agreements under RTPA 1976 and the Resale Prices Act 1976 to the new Chapter I prohibition, with sufficient time provided for undertakings to adapt and adjust. Secondly it allows a period of time to prepare for the introduction of the new Chapter II prohibition. The transitional scheme is therefore to delay the entry into force of the Chapter I and II prohibitions until March 2000 and to provide additional transitional periods for existing agreements.[2] There is no additional period for the Chapter II prohibition, which will take effect on 1 March 2000.[3] There are special provisions for agreements which are subject to proceedings of the Restrictive Practices Court (RPC) and for certain agreements in the regulated utility sectors. The DGFT is issuing guidelines on the transitional arrangements. The 1998 Act is not retrospective.[4]

---

[1] Schedule 13 in its present form was introduced towards the end of the Parliamentary process of the Bill and replaced an earlier version. This was in part because of the need to provide for transition in relation to regulated sectors and partly because of the complexity of the arrangements themselves.

[2] See DGFT's guidelines 'Transitional arrangements' which provide an excellent and comprehensive account of the DGFT's approach to transition.

[3] Ibid, Pt 9. See also para 10.10.

[4] HC SC G, 16 June 1998, col 448 (Nigel Griffiths).

DEFINITIONS

9.2 The 1998 Act, Sch 13, para 1 sets out some essential definitions, the most important of which to note are—

  (a) **'enactment date'**—the date of Royal Assent (9 November 1998);
  (b) **'starting date'**—the date on which s 2 comes into force: intended to be 1 March 2000;[1]
  (c) **'interim period'**—the period beginning on the enactment date and ending immediately before the starting date; and
  (d) **'transitional period'**—the period after the starting date designated for various types of agreement; generally one year, but in some cases five years.

There are also some other important definitions but the relevance of these is better understood in their context. As a further aid to understanding the exceedingly complex terms of Sch 13 it may be helpful to adopt three further working definitions, namely—

  (a) **'existing agreements'**—agreements made before the enactment date;
  (b) **'interim agreements'**—agreements made during the interim period (after enactment but before the starting date); and
  (c) **'new agreements'**—agreements made after the starting date;

and the following paragraphs of this Chapter use these terms where it is helpful to do so.

¹ Consideration of Commons' Amendments, 20 October 1998, col 1337. See also para 10.10.

THE INTERIM PERIOD

9.3   During the interim period, the principal administrative concern is to deal with existing agreements (ie those made prior to the enactment date) and to prepare for the new prohibitions to take effect. However, it is also necessary to provide a mechanism for dealing with interim agreements (ie those made during the interim period).

RTPA 1976

Existing agreements

9.4   RTPA 1976 continues in force during the interim period but its procedural application is relaxed, although this differs according to whether an agreement is an existing or an interim one. Existing agreements that receive directions under RTPA 1976, s 21(2) before the starting date will be excluded indefinitely from the Chapter I prohibition by virtue of the 1998 Act, Sch 3, para 2.[1] Such s 21(2) directions can (and arguably must) be given in appropriate cases for existing agreements where particulars have been duly furnished, even if the furnishing takes place after the enactment date, and the DGFT will seek to have them processed as quickly as possible during the interim period. The DGFT will not, however, extend the deadlines for furnishing particulars.[2]

---

¹ See DGFT's guidelines 'Transitional arrangements', paras 4.13–4.16. The exclusion can be withdrawn by direction of the DGFT in some circumstances (Sch 3, para 2(3)–(9)) and ceases to apply if the agreement is subject to a material variation (see Sch 3, para 2(2)). A material variation is one that has appreciable effect on competition (see para 4.16 of the guidelines). See also paras 2.60–2.62.

² See DGFT's guidelines 'Transitional arrangements', para 2.4.

Interim agreements

9.5   The DGFT is no longer bound to refer interim agreements to the RPC, although he may do so (Sch 13, para 6(a)). The 's 21(2)' procedure (whereby the DGFT is relieved of his duty to take proceedings in relation to agreements which contain restrictions of no significance) does not apply (Sch 13, para 6(b)) and the DGFT can no longer grant extensions of time for furnishing of particulars (Sch 13, para 6(c)).[1] Most importantly, however, the category of non-notifiable agreements is greatly expanded to cover virtually all commercial agreements with the exception of those which involve price fixing.[2]

---

¹ Note that variations to existing agreements are treated as subject to the previous regime under RTPA 1976 even if the variation is made after the enactment date—see DGFT's guidelines 'Transitional arrangements', paras 2.3, 2.7.

² Schedule 13, para 5 and RTPA 1976, s 27A(1)(a), (c), (d). A price fixing agreement is essentially an agreement subject to RTPA 1976 by virtue of containing a restriction as to prices to be charged etc for goods or services, or as to prices to be recommended or suggested as prices to be quoted on the resale

of goods supplied (RTPA s 27A(3)). It may therefore also contain other relevant restrictions, although the DGFT's guidelines 'Transitional arrangements', para 2.3.1.

Notifiable agreements

9.6   Notifiable interim agreements (ie price fixing agreements) remain subject to the duty to furnish particulars. There can be no extension in the time allowed for furnishing particulars and the DGFT retains a discretion to refer them to the RPC.[1] The last date on which particulars can be validly furnished to the DGFT under RTPA 1976 is 29 February 2000.[2]

---

[1]   See DGFT's guidelines 'Transitional arrangements', para 2.6. This also applies to variations to existing agreements (see para 2.7 of the guidelines).
[2]   For the effect of Sch 13, para 25, see para 9.11, fn 1 below.

Summary

9.7   The practical consequences of these complex provisions are that—

(a) existing agreements, where particulars are duly furnished to the DGFT, will continue to be dealt with in the normal way, including the use of RTPA 1976, s 21(2);[1]

(b) interim agreements will in most cases be non-notifiable and the DGFT need not refer them to the RPC. On the other hand, s 21(2) directions will not be available;

(c) existing agreements which have obtained the benefit of s 21(2) directions before the starting date (whenever those directions were given) are excluded from the Chapter I prohibition unless subject to a material variation or 'clawed back' by the DGFT.

---

[1]   See *Butterworths Competition Law* X [1622]–[1660].

Early guidance

9.8   The other important task during the interim period is to give guidance on the treatment of interim agreements under the new prohibition. In anticipation of the coming into force of the provisions for guidance,[1] the DGFT can receive applications and give 'early guidance', which, on expiry of the interim period, is deemed to have been properly given under the relevant provisions that come into force at that point.[2] The DGFT has issued directions covering the early guidance procedure as well as issuing Form EG which is to be used for the requisite notification.[3] It should be noted that this applies to guidance under ss 13 and 15 of the 1998 Act only and it is not possible to notify an agreement for decision under ss 14 and 16 during the interim period. Early guidance is not available for possible breaches of the Chapter II prohibition.

---

[1]   Schedule 13, para 7. See also ss 13 and 15 and the DGFT's guidelines 'Transitional arrangements', Pt 3.
[2]   An earlier draft of Sch 13 would have required a fresh application for guidance on the starting date, greatly reducing the value of early guidance. Applications still being considered at the starting date will be treated as if made under the 1998 Act, s 13.
[3]   See Appendix 3. The application is similar to the application using Form N but is only for guidance under Ch I. The DGFT does not wish to encourage unnecessary applications for early guidance.

THE TRANSITIONAL PERIOD

After the starting date

9.9   After the starting date, ie 1 March 2000, RTPA 1976 and RPA 1976 are repealed and the new prohibition applies. However, a number of provisions of RTPA 1976 remain in force for certain purposes (Sch 13, paras 10–13). For example, the DGFT has to continue the register of restrictive trading agreements[1] to cover—

(a)   those agreements already entered in it;

(b)   notifiable agreements which were furnished to the DGFT before the starting date, but that are not yet entered in the register;

(c)   agreements subject to 'continuing proceedings';[2] and

(d)   agreements subject to court[3] directions as to whether they are registrable.[4]

---

[1]   See DGFT's guidelines 'Transitional arrangements', Pt 7.
[2]   See para 9.17.
[3]   See Sch 13, para 10(6).
[4]   See Sch 13, para 10(2)–(4).

The general rule

9.10   The general rule is that a transitional period of one year applies to any agreement made before the starting date (Sch 13, para 19(1)).[1] The Chapter I prohibition does not apply to the agreement during that transitional period to the extent that the period applies (Sch 13, para 19(2)). There are cases where no transitional period applies and there are cases where a longer period applies.[2] These exceptions are mainly the result of factors that applied under RTPA 1976, RPA 1976, and the various utility regimes.

---

[1]   See DGFT's guidelines 'Transitional arrangements', Pt 4.
[2]   It is possible for one agreement to benefit from different transitional periods for different restrictions; see DGFT guidelines 'Transitional arrangements', paras 4.5–4.6.

Exceptions—no transitional period

9.11   In the following cases there is no transitional period to the extent to which—

(a)   agreements are void under RTPA 1976 for failure to furnish particulars (Sch 13, para 20(1)(a)) (but if the time for furnishing particulars expires on or after the starting date, the special provisions of Sch 13, para 25 apply);[1]

(b)   agreements are prohibited by a court order under RTPA 1976 (Sch 13, para 20(1)(b));[2]

(c)   agreements are unlawful or void under RPA 1976 (Sch 13, para 20(1)(c)); and

(d)   agreements are, as a result of continuing proceedings,[3] declared void or unlawful (Sch 13, para 20(4)).

---

[1]   This paragraph provides for a one year transitional period for agreements or variations where the time for furnishing particulars expires on or after the starting date if particulars of the relevant agreement (or relevant variation) are in fact furnished to the DGFT before the starting date. If particulars are not furnished before the starting date there is no transitional period (see Sch 13, para 20(3)) but the agreement is not void under RTPA 1976, s 35(1). However, if the parties have, in either situation, unlawfully given effect to the restrictions before the starting date, not only is the

agreement to that extent void under s 35(1)(a), but even if particulars have been duly furnished, there is no transitional period (see Sch 13, para 20(2)). See DGFT's guidelines 'Transitional arrangements', paras 2.9, 2.10 and 4.1.
2   This would include undertakings to the court if they form part of a court order (as is usually the case); see para 9.2.2, fn 2.
3   See 9.17.

Exceptions—a five year period

9.12 In the following cases a five year transitional period is available—[1]
   (a) agreements already found by the RPC not to be contrary to the public interest (Sch 13, para 23(1));
   (b) agreements so found as a result of continuing proceedings (Sch 13, para 23(3));
   (c) agreements covering exempt goods[2] either before the starting date or as a result of continuing proceedings;[3]
   (d) various utilities' agreements;[4]
   (e) certain broadcasting agreements exempted from RTPA 1976 (Sch 13, para 26(1)(b));[5]
   (f) certain financial services agreements subject to a favourable direction or Treasury declaration (Sch 13, para 26(1)(a) and (2)).[6]

1   'to the extent to which', Sch 13, para 19(2).
2   Under RPA, s 14.
3   See 9.17.
4   See 9.31.
5   See the Broadcasting Act 1990, s 194A(3).
6   See the Financial Services Act 1986, s 127(2) and (3).

Extensions

9.13 There are provisions for extending transitional periods (Sch 13, para 36).[1] This may follow an application by a party, made not less than three months before the end of the period, or may be made on the DGFT's own initiative. Only one extension is allowed—a one year period may be extended by not more than a year and a five year period by not more than six months (Sch 13, para 36(2)). The DGFT must give notice of his decision on the extension in accordance with rules made under s 51 (Sch 13, para 36(4)).[2]

1   See DGFT's guidelines 'Transitional arrangements', paras 5.2–5.5.
2   See DGFT's draft 'Procedural rules', r 24. The DGFT will aim to notify his decision within two months of the application. If he fails to do so, the maximum extension is granted.

Termination

9.14 The DGFT's power to terminate the transitional period for any agreement does not apply to excluded agreements (Sch 13, para 37(2)) other than any exclusions for UK merger agreements,[1] section 21(2) agreements[2] or agreements relating to agricultural products.[3] In addition, it appears that the DGFT cannot terminate the five year transitional periods provided by Sch 13, para 24(1) or (3) for exempt goods under RPA 1976.[4]

1   See Sch 1, para 1.
2   See Sch 3, para 2.
3   See Sch 3, para 9.
4   Sch 13, para 39(5).

Termination procedure

9.15   Where the DGFT has the power to terminate the transitional period he should do so by direction in writing (Sch 13, para 37(1)).[1] This power applies—

(a)   where a party has failed to provide information that the DGFT has requested in connection with that agreement (Sch 13, para 38(2)); or

(b)   where the DGFT considers that the agreement would, but for the transitional period or relevant exclusion, infringe the Chapter I prohibition and that he would not be likely to grant an unconditional exemption.[2]

The direction must give at least 28 days' notice of termination (Sch 13, para 39(1)) and there are other procedural safeguards in place (Sch 13, para 39(2)). The direction can be revoked before the termination takes effect but a further direction may only be given if there is a material change of circumstances (Sch 13, para 39(3) and (4)).

1   See DGFT's guidelines 'Transitional arrangements', paras 5.6–5.12.
2   See Sch 13, para 38(3). Note that 'unconditional exemption' means an exemption to which no conditions or obligations under s 4(3)(a) are attached.

Comment

9.16   Although the DGFT is required to operate by means of particular procedures, the power to terminate given by the 1998 Act, Sch 13, para 37 is wide. All the DGFT is required to do is to be of the opinion that the agreement in question infringes Ch I (which it must do in any event if it needs to benefit from the transitional period) and that he would not be likely to grant *unconditional* exemption. A direction under Sch 13, para 37 is not included in the list of appealable decisions under s 46(3) but such a direction could be subject to judicial review and any action taken by the DGFT following the termination of the transitional period could of course give rise to an appealable decision.

CONTINUING PROCEEDINGS

9.17   There are detailed provisions governing the situation where an agreement is the subject of proceedings resulting from certain applications to the RPC under RTPA 1976 or RPA 1976 (Sch 13, para 15), and which are made but not determined[1] before the starting date (referred to as 'continuing proceedings'). Sch 13, para 14 provides[2] that Ch I does not apply to such agreements while the proceedings continue; therefore transitional periods apply from the date of determination of the proceedings (if they find in favour of the agreement) if that is later than the starting date.

1   See Sch 13, para 15(4) which provides for appeals to run their course before proceedings are 'determined'.
2   See also DGFT's guidelines 'Transitional arrangements', paras 6.3–6.8.

Scope

9.18 The scope of proceedings defined as 'continuing proceedings' should be noted. Proceedings under RTPA 1976, s 3 (interim orders of the Court) and s 26 (Court's power to rectify the register) are excluded[1] but the 1998 Act, Sch 13 otherwise refers generally to applications made to the RPC (Sch 13, para 15(1)). Enforcement proceedings under RTPA 1976, ss 2(2) (including those relating to variations under ss 4(1)), 35(3), 37(1), 40(1) and Sch 4, para 5, cease on the starting date if still undetermined (Sch 13, para 8). Other proceedings under RTPA 1976, s 4 (variation of the Court's decisions) continue, however, provided that appropriate steps have been taken before the starting date (Sch 13, para 16(a) and (b)). Proceedings under RPA 1976 are also generally included but again enforcement proceedings under RPA 1976, s 25(2) cease on the starting date (Sch 13, para 8). Specific provision is made for new applications under RPA 1976, s 16, and change of circumstance applications under s 17, if appropriate steps are taken before the starting date (Sch 13, para 17(a) and (b)).

---

[1]   See Sch 13, para 15(2), but see para 9.19.

Continuing applications

9.19 Applications under RTPA 1976, s 3 (interim orders of the Court) are not 'continuing proceedings', but are 'continuing applications' (Sch 13, para 11(2)).[1] The 1998 Act, Sch 13 provides that RTPA 1976, s 3, and so far as necessary the whole Act, remain in force to allow such applications to be made and to continue after the starting date (Sch 13, para 11(1)). RTPA 1976 similarly continues to apply after the starting date to applications under s 26 (rectifications etc) which were made before that date, and any determination is deemed to have been made immediately before the starting date (so that the register is rectified before RTPA 1976 is repealed) (Sch 13, para 12). Similarly the right to bring civil proceedings under RTPA 1976 or RPA 1976 in relation to any period before the starting date or in relation to any continuing proceedings is expressly preserved despite the repeal of the relevant sections (Sch 13, para 13).

---

[1]   This means that the Chapter I prohibition applies subject to any transitional period or exclusion.

Discontinuance

9.20 Continuing proceedings can be discontinued by means of a joint application by all parties to the RPC (Sch 13, para 18). If, for this or any other reason, proceedings are ordered to be discontinued, the 1998 Act, Sch 13 applies on the date of discontinuance as if the proceedings had never been instituted. Otherwise, the transitional period begins on the date that continuing proceedings are determined (Sch 13, paras 21 and 22).

9.21 There is no transitional period to the extent to which the determination of continuing proceedings is unfavourable to the parties. However, where the determination is favourable, the five year transitional period can apply to agreements with provisions which are found not to be against the public interest, or which relate to goods found to be exempt (Sch 13, paras 23 and 24).

COURT ORDERS

9.22 On the starting date, most orders made by the RPC lapse.[1] However, such orders remain in force during the interim period and are relevant to possible contempt of court actions and any actions by third parties which are brought after the starting date.[2]

---

[1]   Schedule 13, para 9 lists the orders which lapse. Interim orders under RTPA, s 3 are not included—see the discussion of 'continuing applications' in para 9.19.

[2]   DGFT's guidelines 'Transitional arrangements', paras 6.1, 6.2. The guidelines state that undertakings given to the Court in lieu of orders also lapse; such undertakings are normally either embodied in, or form the basis of, an order made by the court. It is hard to see how other undertakings could be covered.

EXAMPLES

9.23 The application of the transitional arrangements can be illustrated by the following examples.

Agreement A—An existing agreement caught by RTPA 1976

9.24 The agreement is subject to an obligation to furnish particulars within three months and if this is done it will be processed by the OFT in the normal way. If s 21(2) directions are given, the agreement will be safe from any reference to the RPC and will be excluded from the scope of Ch I on the starting date, unless the DGFT issues a direction withdrawing the exclusion, or unless the agreement is subject to a 'material variation'.

Agreement B—An agreement similar to A but executed less than three months prior to the enactment date, so that particulars are not required to be furnished until after that date

9.25 Exactly the same regime applies as with *A*, but the DGFT will not in principle extend the time for furnishing particulars.

Agreement C—An interim agreement that is a non-notifiable agreement

9.26 This agreement is not subject to the obligation to furnish particulars, will not therefore be placed on the register and cannot be the subject of s 21(2) directions. The agreement will, if caught by the Chapter I prohibition on the starting date (which is not necessarily the case), receive a one year (or where applicable a five year) transitional period. Early guidance can be sought from the DGFT which will be deemed to constitute actual guidance from the starting date. Contrast this with the corresponding existing agreement (A or B) which can receive s 21(2) directions and escape Ch I altogether.

Agreement D—An agreement of a restrictive nature but which is not caught by RTPA 1976 (for example due to one of the formalistic anomalies)

9.27 This agreement will not be subject to the Chapter I prohibition on the starting date to the extent that it benefits from the one year (or five year) transitional period. That will apply whether the agreement was made before or after the enactment date.

Agreement E—A notifiable interim agreement caught by RTPA 1976 (ie one containing a price restriction)

9.28   There will be a duty to furnish particulars and the agreement may, but need not, be referred to the RPC. Any application for early guidance will be unlikely to receive favourable treatment. If the agreement having been placed on the register is not referred to the RPC it will in theory receive a one year (or five year) transitional period but this is liable to be withdrawn by the DGFT. If it is referred, it will be the subject of continuing proceedings and will continue to be valid until these are determined (also see Agreement G at para 9.30).

Agreement F—A new agreement that is restrictive in nature and made after the starting date

9.29   This will be subject to the prohibition of Ch I from the moment it is concluded.

Agreement G—An agreement which is the subject of proceedings under RTPA 1976 after having been duly furnished to the DGFT, registered and referred to the RPC

9.30   If these proceedings result in a favourable ruling, the agreement will have a five year transitional period from that date. If the agreement is condemned, the Chapter I prohibition will apply from the date of the RPC's final determination.

UTILITIES

9.31   In the case of agreements in certain regulated utilities sectors, ie electricity and gas (including Northern Ireland) and railways, there are special provisions for transitional periods framed by reference to 'the relevant period' (Sch 13, para 27).[1] The regulators[2] may also exercise, in their relevant sector,[3] the DGFT's functions under Sch 13.

---

[1]   These provisions are detailed and specific—they are summarised in para 9.32 but should be scrutinised with care. See also DGFT's guidelines 'Transitional arrangements', paras 4.8–4.12 and Pt 10.

[2]   See Sch 13, para 35. The regulators are listed in Sch 10, para 1(a)–(g) and the list applies to the 1998 Act, Pt I. It presumably applies to Sch 13 also, as para 35(2) to Sch 13 specifies the 'sectoral matters' in relation to each of the regulators. See also Ch 7 for a discussion of the regulators' powers.

[3]   The relevant DGFT's functions exercisable by the regulators are—
    (a)   Sch 13, para 3—advice and information;
    (b)   Sch 13, para 7—guidance (but the power to give directions is reserved to the DGFT, subject to an obligation to consult the relevant regulator including pre-enactment consultation);
    (c)   Sch 13, para 19(3)—regulations for guidance made by the Secretary of State;
    (d)   Sch 13, para 36—extending the transitional period;
    (e)   Sch 13, paras 37–39—terminating the transitional period.

Types of agreement

9.32   The 'relevant period' is in most cases five years (Sch 13, para 27) and the agreements benefiting from it comprise—
    (a)   in the *electricity* sector, agreements covered by the Electricity Act 1989, s 100 (Sch 13, para 28) or agreements which benefit from a transitional

order made by the Secretary of State after consultation with the Director General of Electricity Supply and the DGFT (Sch 13, para 29);

(b) in the *gas* sector, agreements covered by the Gas Act 1986, s 62, an order made under that section (Sch 13, para 30), or an agreement which benefits from a transitional order made by the Secretary of State after consulting the Director General of Gas Supply and the DGFT (Sch 13, para 31)—there are corresponding provisions in relation to the Gas (Northern Ireland) Order 1996, SI 1996/275 (NI 2), Art 41, and the relevant regulator in Northern Ireland (Sch 13, paras 32, 33);

(c) in relation to *railways*, agreements covered by the Railways Act 1993, s 131, or directions made thereunder (Sch 13, para 34),[1] and railway services agreements not so covered but otherwise required or approved by the Secretary of State or the Rail Regulator or by a Pt I licence (any variation of a s 131 agreement removes it from that section's protection).

---

[1] See the discussion in the DGFT's guidelines 'Transitional arrangements', para 4.12 as to 'the extent to which' the relevant agreement is required or approved.

FTA 1973

9.33 There are some obscure provisions which regulate the transition from RTPA 1976 to the 1998 Act, Ch I in relation to matters which are dealt with under FTA 1973. These provisions require careful scrutiny.[1]

---

[1] DGFT's guidelines 'Transitional arrangements', para 8.1.

9.34 The 1998 Act, Sch 13 seeks to provide for the situation where an MMC investigation is continuing (on a reference made before the relevant date) so as to enable the investigation to consider questions that it would previously have been prevented from considering due to those questions falling within the scope of RTPA 1976 or particular sectoral legislation (Sch 13, para 40). The relevant date is the date of repeal of the respective exclusionary provisions.[1]

---

[1] The provisions are listed in Sch 13, para 40(2) and include the FTA 1973, ss 10(2), 54(5) and 78(3) as well as corresponding sections in other sectoral statutes.

9.35 Similarly, where there is an order in force under FTA 1973, ss 56 or 73, following an MMC report, there is a one year transitional period from the starting date following which the limiting provisions of FTA 1973, Sch 8 (which prevents the order from extending to matters within the scope of RTPA 1976) are deemed never to have had effect (Sch 13, para 41).

9.36 It is notable that Ch I has not been substituted for RTPA 1976 by these changes, which extend the scope of the MMC's[1] activities and FTA 1973, Sch 8, in the particular instances.

---

[1] Ie the reporting function of the CC.

9.37 There are provisions in the 1998 Act which cover court proceedings under FTA 1973, Pt III, in relation to the DGFT's consumer functions (Sch 13, para 42).

COMPETITION ACT 1980

9.38 The 1998 Act, Sch 13, para 43(2), provides that in the event of continuing proceedings, undertakings given to the DGFT under the Competition Act 1980, ss 4 or 9 continue in force until the proceedings are determined.[1] The 1998 Act, Sch 13, para 44 also provides that the repeals in the 1998 Act, s 1, do not affect the Competition Act 1980, ss 25 and 26, in relation to applications made before the starting date.

---

[1]   See the DGFT's guidelines 'Transitional arrangements', para 8.2. Otherwise they lapse when these sections are repealed.

INFORMATION

9.39 The 1998 Act, s 55 which imposes restrictions on the disclosure of information by the competition authorities, is extended to apply to information subject to RTPA 1976, s 41, immediately before the starting date, subject to certain exemptions.[1] Information entered in the special section of the register of restrictive agreements is governed by s 56 (Sch 13, para 45(3)); and a similar provision to RTPA 1976, s 41(2) (maintenance of the register) is incorporated into s 55 (Sch 13, para 45(4)).

---

[1]   See Sch 13, para 45(1) and (2). For a discussion of s 55 see paras 10.2–10.5.

10 Miscellaneous provisions

INTRODUCTION

10.1 The Competition Act 1998 (the 1998 Act) contains a number of miscellaneous provisions which affect the operation of other parts of the Act. These relate to confidentiality, immunity from defamation, amendments to the Patents Act 1977, and the Secretary of State's powers to make orders, as well as provisions for the entry into force of the Act over time.

CONFIDENTIALITY

10.2 There is a general restriction on disclosure of information which is obtained pursuant to the 1998 Act.[1] No such information relating to the affairs of an individual, or any particular business or undertaking, is to be disclosed during the individual's lifetime or while the business is carried on unless consent is obtained. Consent can come from the person from whom the information was originally obtained and (if different) from the person to whose affairs the information relates or who is carrying on the business to which it relates (s 55(2)).

---

[1]   See s 55 and Sch 11.

10.3 This general restriction does not apply to disclosure made for the purpose of—
    (a) facilitating the performance of any relevant function of a designated person (ie regulators and competition authorities generally—see s 55(4), Sch 11);
    (b) helping the European Commission apply EC competition law;
    (c) helping the Comptroller and Auditor General;
    (d) criminal proceedings in the UK or in connection with investigating a criminal offence;
    (e) meeting a Community obligation; and
    (f) bringing civil proceedings for breach of the prohibitions.[1]

The Secretary of State can add specified persons and functions to the list of those to whom the restriction does not apply (s 55(5) and (6)). Breach of the obligation is a criminal offence (s 55(8)).

---

[1]   See the discussion of third party actions in paras 4.71–4.74.

10.4 Quite apart from this general restriction (which does not apply where the DGFT, regulators or the Secretary of State are carrying out their respective functions) the DGFT, the regulators and the Secretary of State have further obligations when considering whether to disclose information under the Act (s 56(1)), in particular they must have regard to the need to exclude from disclosure—
    (a) information if it would be contrary to the public interest;

    (b) commercial information if it would significantly harm the relevant undertaking's business interests; and

    (c) information about the private affairs of an individual if it would, or might, significantly harm his interests,

and they must also consider the extent to which the disclosure is necessary for the relevant purpose (s 56(2) and (3)).

10.5 These provisions provide some protection for parties who are being investigated or who are submitting notifications or making complaints. They do, however, reserve a large measure of discretion to the authorities provided that they pay due regard to the s 56 considerations. It is likely that disclosure of information by the DGFT to a regulator would be facilitating the performance of his functions, but when disclosing information about one person's business to another person who may be a competitor, great care needs to be taken not only to avoid damaging legitimate business interests but also to avoid damaging competition itself.

DEFAMATION

10.6 Advice, guidance, notices, directions given and decisions made by the DGFT or a regulator in the exercise of any of their respective functions enjoy absolute privilege for the purposes of the law of defamation (s 57).

PATENTS ACT 1977

10.7 The Patents Act 1977, ss 44, 45 will cease to have effect by virtue of the 1998 Act, s 70. Section 44 renders void any term of a patent licence or contract for supply of a patented product that extended to unpatented items, while s 45 makes it possible to determine on three months' notice patent licences or supply agreements for patented products after the expiry of the original patents. Given the broad scope of the prohibitions in the 1998 Act, special treatment for these 'tie-in' and 'post-expiry' contracts is no longer appropriate and they will now be included for consideration along with other provisions in intellectual property licences.[1]

---

[1]   See para 2.89 for the consideration of intellectual property agreements.

ORDER-MAKING POWERS

10.8 The provisions governing the exercise of the Secretary of State's powers to make orders or regulations are contained in the 1998 Act, s 71. Some orders (for example those relating to exclusions under ss 3 and 19) must be subject to affirmative resolution of both Houses of Parliament. The Secretary of State enjoys a general order-making power for incidental, consequential, transitional or supplemental purposes (s 75).

APPLICATION TO THE CROWN

10.9 The Act applies to the Crown save that—
      (a) the Crown cannot be criminally liable (although public servants can be);
      (b) the Crown is not liable for any penalty; and
      (c) Her Majesty is not affected in her private capacity (s 73).[1]

There are also provisions limiting investigations on Crown land which include a right for the Secretary of State to restrict such investigations in the interests of national security (s 73(8)).[2]

---

[1] See also the Crown Proceedings Act 1947, s 38(3).
[2] See paras 4.2–4.32 for a discussion of investigations.

ENTRY INTO FORCE

10.10 Under s 76(2) of the 1998 Act, the provisions containing order-making powers (ss 71 and 75) and certain parts of Sch 13 (transitional provisions and savings) came into force on the enactment date (9 November 1998). The remainder of the Act will come into force during the period up to 1 March 2000. The commencement orders so far made[1] are included in Appendix 1 to this book. They brought into force those provisions of the Act which provide for—
      (a) the DGFT to make rules about procedural and other matters in connection with Part I of the Act;
      (b) the preparation and issuing of guidelines and information about the Chapter I and II prohibitions and their enforcement;
      (c) the exercise by the regulators of their functions; and
      (d) interpretation (ss 59 and 60); and
      (e) some transitional aspects (the modified application of RTPA 1976).

The prohibitions themselves, and the associated powers of investigation, enforcement and penalties, are to take effect on 1 March 2000.

---

[1] The Competition Act 1998 (Commencement No 1) Order 1998, SI 1998/2750 and the Competition Act 1998 (Commencement No 2) Order 1998, SI 1998/3166.

11 Practical steps

INTRODUCTION

11.1 Undertakings in the UK will be affected more severely by the new competition legislation. Prohibitions, investigations and penalties add a new dimension to corporate exposure and give a new focus to the benefits of knowledge and legal compliance. Although the law may seem in some respects draconian, it is not greatly different in its application from the EC competition law on which it is based, and experience of that system shows that there are many steps companies can take to reduce the risk of infringement as well as some useful opportunities for companies damaged by anti-competitive behaviour.

MINIMISING EXPOSURE

11.2 Steps to minimise exposure include—
- (a) understanding the effect of the new competition legislation;
- (b) setting up a competition law compliance programme;
- (c) establishing procedures to handle investigations;
- (d) conducting an audit of agreements during the transitional period up to March 2000;
- (e) reviewing the risk of abuse of a dominant position.

Understanding

11.3 It is an unavoidable, if obvious, requirement that companies must understand the implications of the new legislation, and must ensure that all their relevant staff understand the implications also, in particular sales and purchasing staff and those who deal directly with customers and suppliers. The publication of guidelines by the DGFT is a concerted effort to provide help with this process,[1] while the transitional period allows time to adjust.

---

[1] The DGFT's guidelines on 'Enforcement' make clear that ignorance of the law will not serve to reduce penalties. The DGFT has prepared audio tapes and a video explaining the new law and is making available material by Internet (http://www.oft.gov.uk/html/new/act.htm (e-mail address: enquiries@oft.gov.uk)) particularly on updates to and progress on guidelines, etc. It is also advertising an information telephone number (0171-211-8989). See also para 1.17.

Compliance programmes

11.4 As an extension of this understanding, companies need to consider adding, if they have not already done so, competition law to the other programmes they may have[1] to ensure that legal compliance is built into their corporate values and conditions of employment. A compliance programme should not simply take the form of a manual[2] that people read once and then file or throw away. It is a programme of cascading education under which officers and employers are briefed at the appropriate level of detail. It should be reinforced and repeated regularly for existing employees and all relevant new employees should be exposed to it. Above all, the programme must be endorsed by the Board of Directors.

1   Eg Environmental or Health and Safety programmes.
2   Although a clear, plainly written manual is the starting point for a programme.

11.5 Compliance programmes will have a mitigating effect when it comes to penalties,[1] the paradox being that if penalties are at issue at all, the programme will have failed. A programme instituted after a breach has been identified is nevertheless evidence of an intention to prevent further breaches and, as part of a co-operative attitude, will lessen the severity of any penalty.[2]

1   The DGFT's guidelines on 'Enforcement' make this clear but emphasise the need for compliance programmes to be genuinely supported and actively implemented (paras 4.35–4.36 of the guidelines).
2   For discussion of penalties, see paras 4.60–4.70.

Investigations

11.6 Given that there are criminal sanctions for obstructing an on-the-spot investigation even without warrant,[1] it is in the interests of a company and its individual officers to set up procedures to ensure that such situations are properly handled. Not only can a badly handled investigation prove extremely embarrassing for the company personnel involved,[2] it may also lead to damaging and unnecessary admissions or disclosures,[3] as well as to confusion over what has been said and which documents have been disclosed. Whether as part of the compliance programme, or as a separate exercise, investigation procedures are highly desirable.

1   See para 4.21.
2   Other personnel may assume the investigation concerns fraudulent or criminal conduct.
3   For example, claims for legal professional privilege may be overlooked.

11.7 There is a need for care as it is possible to be over zealous in preparation. In some quarters it is fashionable to conduct 'dummy-run' investigations with the company's legal advisers taking the role of the investigators, which, if done as part of compliance education and training, is laudable. However, if, having received advance notice of an inspection, such a dummy run were to be carried out prior to the inspection, the inspectors may feel that the company's files have been prepared and organised and that they are no longer being shown the material that they need to see.[1] In practice, the principles of fairness and reasonableness must apply, and a company must avoid giving any cause for suspicion that its records have been interfered with or documents removed or suppressed.

1   See the European Commission decision in *Cartonboard* [1994] OJ L243, 19.9.94, p 1 where one or more of the defendant's external legal advisers had conducted a 'mock' investigation review of files of which the Commission appears not entirely to have approved (see para 23 of the decision).

Review of agreements

11.8 Companies will no doubt be bombarded with advice that they need to conduct (at great effort and expense) a comprehensive review of all existing agreements to see whether they are exposed to liability and risk under the 1998 Act. Whilst there is some merit in this, a degree of caution is also appropriate. Such a review would have two main purposes—

(a) to ascertain which agreements have in the past been furnished to the DGFT under RTPA 1976 and what their fate has been; and

(b) to verify whether agreements not previously subject to UK competition law will become subject to the Chapter I prohibition and whether early guidance should be sought.[1]

---

[1]   For discussion of early guidance and other transitional aspects see Ch 9 (in particular para 9.8).

11.9 It is likely that many agreements previously subject to RTPA 1976 will appear on the DGFT's register, but many will also have been the subject of directions under s 21(2) of that Act. Such agreements are excluded from Ch I[1] but a material variation (either in one of the restrictive provisions or in the form of a further restriction) would imperil that exclusion and would bring Ch I into play again. An extension of the period of a non-competition obligation in an agreement for the sale of a business would be an example of this. The best time to consider the application of the 1998 Act to such agreements is probably at the time of the variation.

---

[1]   See paras 2.60–2.62.

11.10   Agreements not previously subject to RTPA 1976 may also need to be reviewed. Given the formalism inherent in the test of registrability, it is quite conceivable that Ch I will apply to agreements that escaped the old law. Examples would include agreements where the relevant restriction was accepted by only one of the parties or where only one of the parties was carrying on business in the UK but the agreement had been 'implemented' in the UK. Such agreements need to be considered carefully. Once the prohibitions take effect in March 2000 the agreements will benefit from a transitional period of one year[1] and after that they will be prohibited. The DGFT can investigate them during the transitional period and decide that the period should be curtailed. An application for early guidance can, if necessary or appropriate, be made prior to March 2000. All these factors point to the advisability of some element of review by a company of its main contracts, but a well run business should not find this either difficult or unusual.

---

[1]   For discussion of the transitional arrangements, see Ch 9.

Review of abuse of a dominant position

11.11   A review of possible exposure to Ch II is a more difficult exercise. The holding of a dominant position is not prohibited and, given the legal definition, many companies will be liable to be found dominant, and may indeed regard such a finding as recognition of their efficiency and success. Nevertheless, it is the precursor to being accused of conduct that is an abuse and is therefore something of which companies may need to be aware. One step that can be taken is a review of each of the company's activities against its own market definitions and categories and an assessment of what market share it might claim to hold, both nationally and in those regions where it makes business sense to view the market regionally. That at least would enable and encourage further investigation of these matters. Another useful step is to see what market studies have been published which might assist (or undermine) the company's own assessment.

11.12   A review of possible abusive conduct is even more difficult as the dividing line between fair and unfair practices is often unclear. One approach, which should be viewed as part of on-going compliance, is to question whether a particular practice is likely to provoke complaint from consumers, customers, suppliers or competitors and to consider what the company's response to such a complaint might be.

OPPORTUNITIES

11.13   'If you think that one of your competitors, customers, suppliers, or any other undertaking has breached either of the prohibitions, you will be able to take your complaint to the OFT'.[1] The 1998 Act provides considerable opportunities for complainants and it is likely that numerous complaints will be made both to the OFT and to the sectoral regulators. The 1998 Act provides mechanisms for relatively speedy and effective intervention in cases where a company cannot obtain supplies of an essential product or is being otherwise excluded or damaged. It remains to be seen how effective the operation of these mechanisms will be.

---

[1]   'What your business needs to know' (OFT, 27 Nov 1998) p 11.

11.14   The emphasis placed by Ministers on third party rights also suggests that private actions for damages, either separately from or as a result of findings by the authorities, may become an increasingly important part of corporate activity in the competition law field. Recognition of the possibility of such suits should become a noticeable feature of corporate awareness.

CONCLUSION

11.15   The Competition Act 1998 represents a fundamental reform of competition law as it affects businesses and individuals in the UK. Only the foolhardy will ignore its impact and the prudent will seek to understand it, become familiar with the risks and opportunities and ensure that their companies and colleagues appreciate these also. The initial rhetoric of Ministers and officials suggests an emphasis on breaking up horizontal cartels but the acid test of the new legislation is whether it comes to be seen by business as fair and acceptable. In that process, the way in which the law is applied and enforced will play a critical role and this in turn depends on the analytical rigour of decisions and fairness of procedures giving rise to them. All the participants in this exercise, whether they be investigators, businessmen, advisers, regulators or members of appeal tribunals, have an important part to play in the operation of a workable system. It is hoped that this Guide will contribute to that process.

Appendix 1

Competition Act 1998

Competition Act 1998

(1998 c 41)

ARRANGEMENT OF SECTIONS

PART I
COMPETITION

CHAPTER I
AGREEMENTS

CHAPTER II
ABUSE OF DOMINANT POSITION

CHAPTER V
MISCELLANEOUS

PART II
INVESTIGATIONS IN RELATION TO ARTICLES 85 AND 86

PART III
MONOPOLIES

PART IV
SUPPLEMENTAL AND TRANSITIONAL

SCHEDULES:

An Act to make provision about competition and the abuse of a dominant position in the market; to confer powers in relation to investigations conducted in connection with Article 85 or 86 of the treaty establishing the European Community; to amend the Fair Trading Act 1973 in relation to information which may be required in connection with investigations under that Act; to make provision with respect to the meaning of "supply of services" in the Fair Trading Act 1973; and for connected purposes.

[9 November 1998]

Parliamentary debates.
House of Lords:
2nd Reading 30 October 1997: 582 HL Official Report (5th series) col 1144.
Committee Stage 13 November 1997: 583 HL Official Report (5th series) cols 256, 325;

17 November 1997: 583 HL Official Report (5th series) cols 367, 432; 25 November 1997: 583 HL Official Report (5th series) cols 868, 897, 946.

Report Stage 9 February 1998: 585 HL Official Report (5th series) cols 873, 955; 19 February 1998: 586 HL Official Report (5th series) col 327; 23 February 1998: 586 HL Official Report (5th series) cols 453, 491.

3rd Reading 5 March 1998: 586 HL Official Report (5th series) col 1301.

Consideration of Commons' Amendments 20 October 1998: 593 HL Official Report (5th series) col 1336.

House of Commons:

2nd Reading 11 May 1998: 312 HC Official Report (6th series) col 23.

Committee Stage 19 May–25 June 1998: HC Official Report, SC G (Competition Bill).

3rd Reading 8 July 1998: 315 HC Official Report (6th series) col 1100.

PART I
COMPETITION

CHAPTER I
AGREEMENTS

Introduction

1 Enactments replaced

The following shall cease to have effect—
- (a) the Restrictive Practices Court Act 1976 (c 33),
- (b) the Restrictive Trade Practices Act 1976 (c 34),
- (c) the Resale Prices Act 1976 (c 53), and
- (d) the Restrictive Trade Practices Act 1977 (c 19).

References   See paras 2.3, 9.38.

The prohibition

2 Agreements etc preventing, restricting or distorting competition

(1)   Subject to section 3, agreements between undertakings, decisions by associations of undertakings or concerted practices which—
- (a) may affect trade within the United Kingdom, and
- (b) have as their object or effect the prevention, restriction or distortion of competition within the United Kingdom,

are prohibited unless they are exempt in accordance with the provisions of this Part.

(2)   Subsection (1) applies, in particular, to agreements, decisions or practices which—
- (a) directly or indirectly fix purchase or selling prices or any other trading conditions;
- (b) limit or control production, markets, technical development or investment;
- (c) share markets or sources of supply;
- (d) apply dissimilar conditions to equivalent transactions with other trading parties, thereby placing them at a competitive disadvantage;
- (e) make the conclusion of contracts subject to acceptance by the other parties of supplementary obligations which, by their nature or according to commercial usage, have no connection with the subject of such contracts.

(3)   Subsection (1) applies only if the agreement, decision or practice is, or is intended to be, implemented in the United Kingdom.

(4)   Any agreement or decision which is prohibited by subsection (1) is void.

(5)   A provision of this Part which is expressed to apply to, or in relation to, an agreement is to be read as applying equally to, or in relation to, a decision by an association of undertakings or a concerted practice (but with any necessary modifications).

(6)   Subsection (5) does not apply where the context otherwise requires.

(7)   In this section "the United Kingdom" means, in relation to an agreement which operates or is intended to operate only in a part of the United Kingdom, that part.

(8)   The prohibition imposed by subsection (1) is referred to in this Act as "the Chapter I prohibition".

References   See paras 2.4, 2.5, 2.7–2.37.

Excluded agreements

3 Excluded agreements

(1)   The Chapter I prohibition does not apply in any of the cases in which it is excluded by or as a result of—
    (a)   Schedule 1 (mergers and concentrations);
    (b)   Schedule 2 (competition scrutiny under other enactments);
    (c)   Schedule 3 (planning obligations and other general exclusions); or
    (d)   Schedule 4 (professional rules).

(2)   The Secretary of State may at any time by order amend Schedule 1, with respect to the Chapter I prohibition, by—
    (a)   providing for one or more additional exclusions; or
    (b)   amending or removing any provision (whether or not it has been added by an order under this subsection).

(3)   The Secretary of State may at any time by order amend Schedule 3, with respect to the Chapter I prohibition, by—
    (a)   providing for one or more additional exclusions; or
    (b)   amending or removing any provision—
        (i)   added by an order under this subsection; or
        (ii)   included in paragraph 1, 2, 8 or 9 of Schedule 3.

(4)   The power under subsection (3) to provide for an additional exclusion may be exercised only if it appears to the Secretary of State that agreements which fall within the additional exclusion—
    (a)   do not in general have an adverse effect on competition, or
    (b)   are, in general, best considered under Chapter II or the Fair Trading Act 1973.

(5)   An order under subsection (2)(a) or (3)(a) may include provision (similar to that made with respect to any other exclusion provided by the relevant Schedule) for the exclusion concerned to cease to apply to a particular agreement.

(6)   Schedule 3 also gives the Secretary of State power to exclude agreements from the Chapter I prohibition in certain circumstances.

Definitions   For "the Chapter I prohibition", see s 2(8).
References   See paras 2.6, 2.38–2.68, 2.70, 2.74, 2.92.

Exemptions

4 Individual exemptions

(1)   The Director may grant an exemption from the Chapter I prohibition with respect to a particular agreement if—

    (a)   a request for an exemption has been made to him under section 14 by a party to the agreement; and

    (b)   the agreement is one to which section 9 applies.

(2)   An exemption granted under this section is referred to in this Part as an individual exemption.

(3)   The exemption—

    (a)   may be granted subject to such conditions or obligations as the Director considers it appropriate to impose; and

    (b)   has effect for such period as the Director considers appropriate.

(4)   That period must be specified in the grant of the exemption.

(5)   An individual exemption may be granted so as to have effect from a date earlier than that on which it is granted.

(6)   On an application made in such way as may be specified by rules under section 51, the Director may extend the period for which an exemption has effect; but, if the rules so provide, he may do so only in specified circumstances.

Definitions   For "the Chapter I prohibition", see s 2(8); for "the Director", see s 59(1).
References   See paras 2.18, 2.62, 2.93, 2.103, 5.16.

5 Cancellation etc of individual exemptions

(1)   If the Director has reasonable grounds for believing that there has been a material change of circumstance since he granted an individual exemption, he may by notice in writing—

    (a)   cancel the exemption;

    (b)   vary or remove any condition or obligation; or

    (c)   impose one or more additional conditions or obligations.

(2)   If the Director has a reasonable suspicion that the information on which he based his decision to grant an individual exemption was incomplete, false or misleading in a material particular, he may by notice in writing take any of the steps mentioned in subsection (1).

(3)   Breach of a condition has the effect of cancelling the exemption.

(4)   Failure to comply with an obligation allows the Director, by notice in writing, to take any of the steps mentioned in subsection (1).

(5)   Any step taken by the Director under subsection (1), (2) or (4) has effect from such time as may be specified in the notice.

(6)   If an exemption is cancelled under subsection (2) or (4), the date specified in the notice cancelling it may be earlier than the date on which the notice is given.

(7)   The Director may act under subsection (1), (2) or (4) on his own initiative or on a complaint made by any person.

Definitions   For "individual exemption", see s 4(2); for "the Director" and as to "information" and "person", see s 59(1).
References   See paras 2.93, 2.104, 5.16.

6 Block exemptions

(1)   If agreements which fall within a particular category of agreement are, in the opinion of the Director, likely to be agreements to which section 9 applies, the Director may recommend that the Secretary of State make an order specifying that category for the purposes of this section.

(2)   The Secretary of State may make an order ("a block exemption order") giving effect to such a recommendation—

    (a)   in the form in which the recommendation is made; or

    (b)   subject to such modifications as he considers appropriate.

(3)   An agreement which falls within a category specified in a block exemption order is exempt from the Chapter I prohibition.

(4)   An exemption under this section is referred to in this Part as a block exemption.

(5)   A block exemption order may impose conditions or obligations subject to which a block exemption is to have effect.

(6)   A block exemption order may provide—

    (a)   that breach of a condition imposed by the order has the effect of cancelling the block exemption in respect of an agreement;

    (b)   that if there is a failure to comply with an obligation imposed by the order, the Director may, by notice in writing, cancel the block exemption in respect of the agreement;

    (c)   that if the Director considers that a particular agreement is not one to which section 9 applies, he may cancel the block exemption in respect of that agreement.

(7)   A block exemption order may provide that the order is to cease to have effect at the end of a specified period.

(8)   In this section and section 7 "specified" means specified in a block exemption order.

Definitions   For "the Chapter I prohibition", see s 2(8); for "the Director", see s 59(1).
References   See paras 2.93, 2.105, 5.16, 5.17.

---

7 Block exemptions: opposition

(1)   A block exemption order may provide that a party to an agreement which—

    (a)   does not qualify for the block exemption created by the order, but

    (b)   satisfies specified criteria,

may notify the Director of the agreement for the purposes of subsection (2).

(2)   An agreement which is notified under any provision included in a block exemption order by virtue of subsection (1) is to be treated, as from the end of the notice period, as falling within a category specified in a block exemption order unless the Director—

    (a)   is opposed to its being so treated; and

    (b)   gives notice in writing to the party concerned of his opposition before the end of that period.

(3)   If the Director gives notice of his opposition under subsection (2), the notification under subsection (1) is to be treated as both notification under section 14 and as a request for an individual exemption made under subsection (3) of that section.

(4)   In this section "notice period" means such period as may be specified with a view to giving the Director sufficient time to consider whether to oppose under subsection (2).

Definitions   For "block exemption order", see s 6(2); for "specified", see s 6(8); for "the Director", see s 59(1).
References   See paras 2.93, 2.105.

8 Block exemptions: procedure

(1)   Before making a recommendation under section 6(1), the Director must—
    (a)   publish details of his proposed recommendation in such a way as he thinks most suitable for bringing it to the attention of those likely to be affected; and
    (b)   consider any representations about it which are made to him.

(2)   If the Secretary of State proposes to give effect to such a recommendation subject to modifications, he must inform the Director of the proposed modifications and take into account any comments made by the Director.

(3)   If, in the opinion of the Director, it is appropriate to vary or revoke a block exemption order he may make a recommendation to that effect to the Secretary of State.

(4)   Subsection (1) also applies to any proposed recommendation under subsection (3).

(5)   Before exercising his power to vary or revoke a block exemption order (in a case where there has been no recommendation under subsection (3)), the Secretary of State must—
    (a)   inform the Director of the proposed variation or revocation; and
    (b)   take into account any comments made by the Director.

(6)   A block exemption order may provide for a block exemption to have effect from a date earlier than that on which the order is made.

Definitions   For "block exemption order", see s 6(2); for "the Director", see s 59(1).
References   See paras 2.93, 2.105.

9 The criteria for individual and block exemptions

This section applies to any agreement which—
    (a)   contributes to—
        (i)   improving production or distribution, or
        (ii)   promoting technical or economic progress,
    while allowing consumers a fair share of the resulting benefit; but
    (b)   does not—
        (i)   impose on the undertakings concerned restrictions which are not indispensable to the attainment of those objectives; or
        (ii)   afford the undertakings concerned the possibility of eliminating competition in respect of a substantial part of the products in question.

References   See paras 2.93–2.95, 2.97, 2.102, 2.103.

10 Parallel exemptions

(1)   An agreement is exempt from the Chapter I prohibition if it is exempt from the Community prohibition—

     (a)   by virtue of a Regulation,

     (b)   because it has been given exemption by the Commission, or

     (c)   because it has been notified to the Commission under the appropriate opposition or objection procedure and—

          (i)   the time for opposing, or objecting to, the agreement has expired and the Commission has not opposed it; or

          (ii)   the Commission has opposed, or objected to, the agreement but has withdrawn its opposition or objection.

(2)   An agreement is exempt from the Chapter I prohibition if it does not affect trade between Member States but otherwise falls within a category of agreement which is exempt from the Community prohibition by virtue of a Regulation.

(3)   An exemption from the Chapter I prohibition under this section is referred to in this Part as a parallel exemption.

(4)   A parallel exemption—

     (a)   takes effect on the date on which the relevant exemption from the Community prohibition takes effect or, in the case of a parallel exemption under subsection (2), would take effect if the agreement in question affected trade between Member States; and

     (b)   ceases to have effect—

          (i)   if the relevant exemption from the Community prohibition ceases to have effect; or

          (ii)   on being cancelled by virtue of subsection (5) or (7).

(5)   In such circumstances and manner as may be specified in rules made under section 51, the Director may—

     (a)   impose conditions or obligations subject to which a parallel exemption is to have effect;

     (b)   vary or remove any such condition or obligation;

     (c)   impose one or more additional conditions or obligations;

     (d)   cancel the exemption.

(6)   In such circumstances as may be specified in rules made under section 51, the date from which cancellation of an exemption is to take effect may be earlier than the date on which notice of cancellation is given.

(7)   Breach of a condition imposed by the Director has the effect of cancelling the exemption.

(8)   In exercising his powers under this section, the Director may require any person who is a party to the agreement in question to give him such information as he may require.

(9)   For the purpose of this section references to an agreement being exempt from the Community prohibition are to be read as including references to the prohibition being inapplicable to the agreement by virtue of a Regulation or a decision by the Commission.

(10)   In this section—

     "the Community prohibition" means the prohibition contained in—

          (a)   paragraph 1 of Article 85;

          (b)   any corresponding provision replacing, or otherwise derived from, that provision;

          (c)   such other Regulation as the Secretary of State may by order specify; and

     "Regulation" means a Regulation adopted by the Commission or by the Council.

(11) This section has effect in relation to the prohibition contained in paragraph 1 of Article 53 of the EEA Agreement (and the EFTA Surveillance Authority) as it has effect in relation to the Community prohibition (and the Commission) subject to any modifications which the Secretary of State may by order prescribe.

Definitions   For "the Chapter I prohibition", see s 2(8); for "Article 85", "the Commission", "the Council", "the Director", "the EEA Agreement" and as to "information", "person", and "prescribe", see s 59(1).
References   See paras 2.89, 2.93, 2.105–2.108, 5.16, 5.17, 6.12, 6.31, 6.32.

11 Exemption for certain other agreements

(1)   The fact that a ruling may be given by virtue of Article 88 of the Treaty on the question whether or not agreements of a particular kind are prohibited by Article 85 does not prevent such agreements from being subject to the Chapter I prohibition.

(2)   But the Secretary of State may by regulations make such provision as he considers appropriate for the purpose of granting an exemption from the Chapter I prohibition, in prescribed circumstances, in respect of such agreements.

(3)   An exemption from the Chapter I prohibition by virtue of regulations under this section is referred to in this Part as a section 11 exemption.

Definitions   For "the Chapter I prohibition", see s 2(8); for "Article 85", "prescribed" and "the Treaty", see s 59(1).
References   See paras 2.93, 2.109, 4.34, 4.35, 4.38.

Notification

12 Requests for Director to examine agreements

(1)   Sections 13 and 14 provide for an agreement to be examined by the Director on the application of a party to the agreement who thinks that it may infringe the Chapter I prohibition.

(2)   Schedule 5 provides for the procedure to be followed—
    (a)   by any person making such an application; and
    (b)   by the Director, in considering such an application.

(3)   The Secretary of State may by regulations make provision as to the application of sections 13 to 16 and Schedule 5, with such modifications (if any) as may be prescribed, in cases where the Director—
    (a)   has given a direction withdrawing an exclusion; or
    (b)   is considering whether to give such a direction.

Definitions   For "the Chapter I prohibition", see s 2(8); for "the Director" and "prescribed" and as to "person", see s 59(1).
References   See para 4.33.

13 Notification for guidance

(1)   A party to an agreement who applies for the agreement to be examined under this section must—
    (a)   notify the Director of the agreement; and
    (b)   apply to him for guidance.

(2)   On an application under this section, the Director may give the applicant guidance as to whether or not, in his view, the agreement is likely to infringe the Chapter I prohibition.

(3)   If the Director considers that the agreement is likely to infringe the prohibition if it is not exempt, his guidance may indicate—

    (a)   whether the agreement is likely to be exempt from the prohibition under—

        (i)   a block exemption;

        (ii)   a parallel exemption; or

        (iii)   a section 11 exemption; or

    (b)   whether he would be likely to grant the agreement an individual exemption if asked to do so.

(4)   If an agreement to which the prohibition applies has been notified to the Director under this section, no penalty is to be imposed under this Part in respect of any infringement of the prohibition by the agreement which occurs during the period—

    (a)   beginning with the date on which notification was given; and

    (b)   ending with such date as may be specified in a notice in writing given to the applicant by the Director when the application has been determined.

(5)   The date specified in a notice under subsection (4)(b) may not be earlier than the date on which the notice is given.

Definitions   For "the Chapter I prohibition", see s 2(8); for "indivdual exemption", see s 4(2); for "block exemption", see s 6(4); for "parallel exemption", see s 10(3); for "section 11 exemption", see s 11(3); for "the Director", see s 59(1).

References   See paras 4.34, 4.35, 4.66, 9.8.

---

14 Notification for a decision

(1)   A party to an agreement who applies for the agreement to be examined under this section must—

    (a)   notify the Director of the agreement; and

    (b)   apply to him for a decision.

(2)   On an application under this section, the Director may make a decision as to—

    (a)   whether the Chapter I prohibition has been infringed; and

    (b)   if it has not been infringed, whether that is because of the effect of an exclusion or because the agreement is exempt from the prohibition.

(3)   If an agreement is notified to the Director under this section, the application may include a request for the agreement to which it relates to be granted an individual exemption.

(4)   If an agreement to which the prohibition applies has been notified to the Director under this section, no penalty is to be imposed under this Part in respect of any infringement of the prohibition by the agreement which occurs during the period—

    (a)   beginning with the date on which notification was given; and

    (b)   ending with such date as may be specified in a notice in writing given to the applicant by the Director when the application has been determined.

(5)   The date specified in a notice under subsection (4)(b) may not be earlier than the date on which the notice is given.

Definitions   For "the Chapter I prohibition", see s 2(8); for "individual exemption", see s 4(2); for "the Director", see s 59(1).
References   See paras 2.103, 4.38, 4.39, 4.51, 4.66, 5.16.

15 Effect of guidance

(1)   This section applies to an agreement if the Director has determined an application under section 13 by giving guidance that—

    (a)   the agreement is unlikely to infringe the Chapter I prohibition, regardless of whether or not it is exempt;

    (b)   the agreement is likely to be exempt under—

        (i)   a block exemption;

        (ii)   a parallel exemption; or

        (iii)   a section 11 exemption; or

    (c)   he would be likely to grant the agreement an individual exemption if asked to do so.

(2)   The Director is to take no further action under this Part with respect to an agreement to which this section applies, unless—

    (a)   he has reasonable grounds for believing that there has been a material change of circumstance since he gave his guidance;

    (b)   he has a reasonable suspicion that the information on which he based his guidance was incomplete, false or misleading in a material particular;

    (c)   one of the parties to the agreement applies to him for a decision under section 14 with respect to the agreement; or

    (d)   a complaint about the agreement has been made to him by a person who is not a party to the agreement.

(3)   No penalty may be imposed under this Part in respect of any infringement of the Chapter I prohibition by an agreement to which this section applies.

(4)   But the Director may remove the immunity given by subsection (3) if—

    (a)   he takes action under this Part with respect to the agreement in one of the circumstances mentioned in subsection (2);

    (b)   he considers it likely that the agreement will infringe the prohibition; and

    (c)   he gives notice in writing to the party on whose application the guidance was given that he is removing the immunity as from the date specified in his notice.

(5)   If the Director has a reasonable suspicion that information—

    (a)   on which he based his guidance, and

    (b)   which was provided to him by a party to the agreement,

was incomplete, false or misleading in a material particular, the date specified in a notice under subsection (4)(c) may be earlier than the date on which the notice is given.

Definitions   For "the Chapter I prohibition", see s 2(8); for "indivdual exemption", see s 4(2); for "block exemption", see s 6(4); for "parallel exemption", see s 10(3); for "section 11 exemption", see s 11(3); for "the Director" and as to "information" and "person", see s 59(1).
References   See paras 4.35, 4.36, 4.47, 4.66, 4.68, 9.8.

16 Effect of a decision that the Chapter I prohibition has not been infringed

(1)   This section applies to an agreement if the Director has determined an application under section 14 by making a decision that the agreement has not infringed the Chapter I prohibition.

(2) The Director is to take no further action under this Part with respect to the agreement unless—

    (a) he has reasonable grounds for believing that there has been a material change of circumstance since he gave his decision; or

    (b) he has a reasonable suspicion that the information on which he based his decision was incomplete, false or misleading in a material particular.

(3) No penalty may be imposed under this Part in respect of any infringement of the Chapter I prohibition by an agreement to which this section applies.

(4) But the Director may remove the immunity given by subsection (3) if—

    (a) he takes action under this Part with respect to the agreement in one of the circumstances mentioned in subsection (2);

    (b) he considers that it is likely that the agreement will infringe the prohibition; and

    (c) he gives notice in writing to the party on whose application the decision was made that he is removing the immunity as from the date specified in his notice.

(5) If the Director has a reasonable suspicion that information—

    (a) on which he based his decision, and

    (b) which was provided to him by a party to the agreement,

was incomplete, false or misleading in a material particular, the date specified in a notice under subsection (4)(c) may be earlier than the date on which the notice is given.

Definitions   For "the Chapter I prohibition", see s 2(8); for "the Director" and as to "information", see s 59(1).
References   See paras 4.39, 4.40, 4.47, 4.49, 4.66, 4.68, 5.17, 9.8.

CHAPTER II
ABUSE OF DOMINANT POSITION

Introduction

17 Enactments replaced

Sections 2 to 10 of the Competition Act 1980 (control of anti-competitive practices) shall cease to have effect.

References   See para 3.1.

The prohibition

18 Abuse of dominant position

(1) Subject to section 19, any conduct on the part of one or more undertakings which amounts to the abuse of a dominant position in a market is prohibited if it may affect trade within the United Kingdom.

(2) Conduct may, in particular, constitute such an abuse if it consists in—

    (a) directly or indirectly imposing unfair purchase or selling prices or other unfair trading conditions;

    (b) limiting production, markets or technical development to the prejudice of consumers;

    (c) applying dissimilar conditions to equivalent transactions with other trading parties, thereby placing them at a competitive disadvantage;

  (d) making the conclusion of contracts subject to acceptance by the other parties of supplementary obligations which, by their nature or according to commercial usage, have no connection with the subject of the contracts.

(3) In this section—

  "dominant position" means a dominant position within the United Kingdom; and

  "the United Kingdom" means the United Kingdom or any part of it.

(4) The prohibition imposed by subsection (1) is referred to in this Act as "the Chapter II prohibition".

References See paras 2.80, 3.2–3.30.

Excluded cases

19 Excluded cases

(1) The Chapter II prohibition does not apply in any of the cases in which it is excluded by or as a result of—

  (a) Schedule 1 (mergers and concentrations); or

  (b) Schedule 3 (general exclusions).

(2) The Secretary of State may at any time by order amend Schedule 1, with respect to the Chapter II prohibition, by—

  (a) providing for one or more additional exclusions; or

  (b) amending or removing any provision (whether or not it has been added by an order under this subsection).

(3) The Secretary of State may at any time by order amend paragraph 8 of Schedule 3 with respect to the Chapter II prohibition.

(4) Schedule 3 also gives the Secretary of State power to provide that the Chapter II prohibition is not to apply in certain circumstances.

Definitions For "the Chapter II prohibition", see s 18(4).
References See paras 2.92, 3.31.

Notification

20 Requests for Director to consider conduct

(1) Sections 21 and 22 provide for conduct of a person which that person thinks may infringe the Chapter II prohibition to be considered by the Director on the application of that person.

(2) Schedule 6 provides for the procedure to be followed—

  (a) by any person making an application, and

  (b) by the Director, in considering an application.

Definitions For "the Chapter II prohibition", see s 18(4); for "the Director" and as to "person", see s 59(1).
References See para 4.33.

21 Notification for guidance

(1) A person who applies for conduct to be considered under this section must—

  (a) notify the Director of it; and

  (b) apply to him for guidance.

(2)   On an application under this section, the Director may give the applicant guidance as to whether or not, in his view, the conduct is likely to infringe the Chapter II prohibition.

Definitions   For "the Chapter II prohibition", see s 18(4); for "the Director" and as to "person", see s 59(1).
References   See para 4.37.

22 Notification for a decision

(1)   A person who applies for conduct to be considered under this section must—
    (a)   notify the Director of it; and
    (b)   apply to him for a decision.

(2)   On an application under this section, the Director may make a decision as to—
    (a)   whether the Chapter II prohibition has been infringed; and
    (b)   if it has not been infringed, whether that is because of the effect of an exclusion.

Definitions   For "the Chapter II prohibition", see s 18(4); for "the Director" and as to "person", see s 59(1).
References   See paras 4.41, 4.51, 5.10.

23 Effect of guidance

(1)   This section applies to conduct if the Director has determined an application under section 21 by giving guidance that the conduct is unlikely to infringe the Chapter II prohibition.

(2)   The Director is to take no further action under this Part with respect to the conduct to which this section applies, unless—
    (a)   he has reasonable grounds for believing that there has been a material change of circumstance since he gave his guidance;
    (b)   he has a reasonable suspicion that the information on which he based his guidance was incomplete, false or misleading in a material particular; or
    (c)   a complaint about the conduct has been made to him.

(3)   No penalty may be imposed under this Part in respect of any infringement of the Chapter II prohibition by conduct to which this section applies.

(4)   But the Director may remove the immunity given by subsection (3) if—
    (a)   he takes action under this Part with respect to the conduct in one of the circumstances mentioned in subsection (2);
    (b)   he considers that it is likely that the conduct will infringe the prohibition; and
    (c)   he gives notice in writing to the undertaking on whose application the guidance was given that he is removing the immunity as from the date specified in his notice.

(5)   If the Director has a reasonable suspicion that information—
    (a)   on which he based his guidance, and
    (b)   which was provided to him by an undertaking engaging in the conduct,
was incomplete, false or misleading in a material particular, the date specified in a notice under subsection (4)(c) may be earlier than the date on which the notice is given.

Definitions For "the Chapter II prohibition", see s 18(4); for "the Director" and as to "information", see s 59(1).
References See paras 4.37, 4.47, 4.66, 4.68.

24 Effect of a decision that the Chapter II prohibition has not been infringed

(1)   This section applies to conduct if the Director has determined an application under section 22 by making a decision that the conduct has not infringed the Chapter II prohibition.

(2)   The Director is to take no further action under this Part with respect to the conduct unless—

(a)   he has reasonable grounds for believing that there has been a material change of circumstance since he gave his decision; or

(b)   he has a reasonable suspicion that the information on which he based his decision was incomplete, false or misleading in a material particular.

(3)   No penalty may be imposed under this Part in respect of any infringement of the Chapter II prohibition by conduct to which this section applies.

(4)   But the Director may remove the immunity given by subsection (3) if—

(a)   he takes action under this Part with respect to the conduct in one of the circumstances mentioned in subsection (2);

(b)   he considers that it is likely that the conduct will infringe the prohibition; and

(c)   he gives notice in writing to the undertaking on whose application the decision was made that he is removing the immunity as from the date specified in his notice.

(5)   If the Director has a reasonable suspicion that information—

(a)   on which he based his decision, and

(b)   which was provided to him by an undertaking engaging in the conduct,

was incomplete, false or misleading in a material particular, the date specified in a notice under subsection (4)(c) may be earlier than the date on which the notice is given.

Definitions For "the Chapter II prohibition", see s 18(4); for "the Director" and as to "information", see s 59(1).
References See paras 4.41, 4.47, 4.49, 4.66, 4.68.

CHAPTER III

INVESTIGATION AND ENFORCEMENT

Investigations

25 Director's power to investigate

The Director may conduct an investigation if there are reasonable grounds for suspecting—

(a)   that the Chapter I prohibition has been infringed; or

(b)   that the Chapter II prohibition has been infringed.

Definitions For "the Chapter I prohibition", see s 2(8); for "the Chapter II prohibition", see s 18(4); for "the Director", see s 59(1).
References See paras 4.2, 4.3, 4.51, 5.17.

26 Powers when conducting investigations

(1)   For the purposes of an investigation under section 25, the Director may require any person to produce to him a specified document, or to provide him with specified information, which he considers relates to any matter relevant to the investigation.

(2)   The power conferred by subsection (1) is to be exercised by a notice in writing.

(3)   A notice under subsection (2) must indicate—
  (a)   the subject matter and purpose of the investigation; and
  (b)   the nature of the offences created by sections 42 to 44.

(4)   In subsection (1) "specified" means—
  (a)   specified, or described, in the notice; or
  (b)   falling within a category which is specified, or described, in the notice.

(5)   The Director may also specify in the notice—
  (a)   the time and place at which any document is to be produced or any information is to be provided;
  (b)   the manner and form in which it is to be produced or provided.

(6)   The power under this section to require a person to produce a document includes power—
  (a)   if the document is produced—
    (i)   to take copies of it or extracts from it;
    (ii)   to require him, or any person who is a present or past officer of his, or is or was at any time employed by him, to provide an explanation of the document;
  (b)   if the document is not produced, to require him to state, to the best of his knowledge and belief, where it is.

Definitions   For "the Director", and as to "document", "information" and "person", see s 59(1).
References   See paras 4.3, 4.4, 4.18, 4.22, 5.17.

27 Power to enter premises without a warrant

(1)   Any officer of the Director who is authorised in writing by the Director to do so ("an investigating officer") may enter any premises in connection with an investigation under section 25.

(2)   No investigating officer is to enter any premises in the exercise of his powers under this section unless he has given to the occupier of the premises a written notice which—
  (a)   gives at least two working days' notice of the intended entry;
  (b)   indicates the subject matter and purpose of the investigation; and
  (c)   indicates the nature of the offences created by sections 42 to 44.

(3)   Subsection (2) does not apply—
  (a)   if the Director has a reasonable suspicion that the premises are, or have been, occupied by—
    (i)   a party to an agreement which he is investigating under section 25(a); or
    (ii)   an undertaking the conduct of which he is investigating under section 25(b); or
  (b)   if the investigating officer has taken all such steps as are reasonably practicable to give notice but has not been able to do so.

(4)   In a case falling within subsection (3), the power of entry conferred by subsection (1) is to be exercised by the investigating officer on production of—

    (a)   evidence of his authorisation; and

    (b)   a document containing the information referred to in subsection (2)(b) and (c).

(5)   An investigating officer entering any premises under this section may—

    (a)   take with him such equipment as appears to him to be necessary;

    (b)   require any person on the premises—

        (i)   to produce any document which he considers relates to any matter relevant to the investigation; and

        (ii)   if the document is produced, to provide an explanation of it;

    (c)   require any person to state, to the best of his knowledge and belief, where any such document is to be found;

    (d)   take copies of, or extracts from, any document which is produced;

    (e)   require any information which is held in a computer and is accessible from the premises and which the investigating officer considers relates to any matter relevant to the investigation, to be produced in a form—

        (i)   in which it can be taken away, and

        (ii)   in which it is visible and legible.

Definitions   For "the Director" and as to "document", "information" and "premises", see s 59(1).
References   See paras 4.5–4.8, 4.10, 4.18, 4.22, 5.17.

---

28 Power to enter premises under a warrant

(1)   On an application made by the Director to the court in accordance with rules of court, a judge may issue a warrant if he is satisfied that—

    (a)   there are reasonable grounds for suspecting that there are on any premises documents—

        (i)   the production of which has been required under section 26 or 27; and

        (ii)   which have not been produced as required;

    (b)   there are reasonable grounds for suspecting that—

        (i)   there are on any premises documents which the Director has power under section 26 to require to be produced; and

        (ii)   if the documents were required to be produced, they would not be produced but would be concealed, removed, tampered with or destroyed; or

    (c)   an investigating officer has attempted to enter premises in the exercise of his powers under section 27 but has been unable to do so and that there are reasonable grounds for suspecting that there are on the premises documents the production of which could have been required under that section.

(2)   A warrant under this section shall authorise a named officer of the Director, and any other of his officers whom he has authorised in writing to accompany the named officer—

    (a)   to enter the premises specified in the warrant, using such force as is reasonably necessary for the purpose;

    (b)   to search the premises and take copies of, or extracts from, any document appearing to be of a kind in respect of which the application under subsection (1) was granted ("the relevant kind");

    (c)   to take possession of any documents appearing to be of the relevant kind if—

         (i)   such action appears to be necessary for preserving the documents or preventing interference with them; or

        (ii)   it is not reasonably practicable to take copies of the documents on the premises;

    (d)   to take any other steps which appear to be necessary for the purpose mentioned in paragraph (c)(i);

    (e)   to require any person to provide an explanation of any document appearing to be of the relevant kind or to state, to the best of his knowledge and belief, where it may be found;

    (f)   to require any information which is held in a computer and is accessible from the premises and which the named officer considers relates to any matter relevant to the investigation, to be produced in a form—

        (i)   in which it can be taken away, and

        (ii)   in which it is visible and legible.

(3)   If, in the case of a warrant under subsection (1)(b), the judge is satisfied that it is reasonable to suspect that there are also on the premises other documents relating to the investigation concerned, the warrant shall also authorise action mentioned in subsection (2) to be taken in relation to any such document.

(4)   Any person entering premises by virtue of a warrant under this section may take with him such equipment as appears to him to be necessary.

(5)   On leaving any premises which he has entered by virtue of a warrant under this section, the named officer must, if the premises are unoccupied or the occupier is temporarily absent, leave them as effectively secured as he found them.

(6)   A warrant under this section continues in force until the end of the period of one month beginning with the day on which it is issued.

(7)   Any document of which possession is taken under subsection (2)(c) may be retained for a period of three months.

Definitions   For "investigating officer", see s 27(1); for "the Director" and "the court" and as to "document", "information" and "premises", see s 59(1).
References   See paras 4.11–4.15, 4.18, 4.30.

29 Entry of premises under warrant: supplementary

(1)   A warrant issued under section 28 must indicate—

    (a)   the subject matter and purpose of the investigation;

    (b)   the nature of the offences created by sections 42 to 44.

(2)   The powers conferred by section 28 are to be exercised on production of a warrant issued under that section.

(3)   If there is no one at the premises when the named officer proposes to execute such a warrant he must, before executing it—

    (a)   take such steps as are reasonable in all the circumstances to inform the occupier of the intended entry; and

    (b)   if the occupier is informed, afford him or his legal or other representative a reasonable opportunity to be present when the warrant is executed.

(4)   If the named officer is unable to inform the occupier of the intended entry he must, when executing the warrant, leave a copy of it in a prominent place on the premises.

(5)   In this section—

        "named officer" means the officer named in the warrant; and

        "occupier", in relation to any premises, means a person whom the named officer reasonably believes is the occupier of those premises.

Definitions   As to "person" and "premises", see s 59(1).
References   See para 4.12.

30 Privileged communications

(1)   A person shall not be required, under any provision of this Part, to produce or disclose a privileged communication.

(2)   "Privileged communication" means a communication—
    (a)   between a professional legal adviser and his client, or
    (b)   made in connection with, or in contemplation of, legal proceedings and for the purposes of those proceedings,

which in proceedings in the High Court would be protected from disclosure on grounds of legal professional privilege.

(3)   In the application of this section to Scotland—
    (a)   references to the High Court are to be read as references to the Court of Session; and
    (b)   the reference to legal professional privilege is to be read as a reference to confidentiality of communications.

Definitions   As to "person", see s 59(1).
References   See para 4.16.

31 Decisions following an investigation

(1)   Subsection (2) applies if, as the result of an investigation conducted under section 25, the Director proposes to make—
    (a)   a decision that the Chapter I prohibition has been infringed, or
    (b)   a decision that the Chapter II prohibition has been infringed.

(2)   Before making the decision, the Director must—
    (a)   give written notice to the person (or persons) likely to be affected by the proposed decision; and
    (b)   give that person (or those persons) an opportunity to make representations.

Definitions   For "the Chapter I prohibition", see s 2(8); for "the Chapter II prohibition", see s 18(4); for "the Director" and as to "person", see s 59(1).
References   See para 4.51.

Enforcement

32 Directions in relation to agreements

(1)   If the Director has made a decision that an agreement infringes the Chapter I prohibition, he may give to such person or persons as he considers appropriate such directions as he considers appropriate to bring the infringement to an end.

(2)   Subsection (1) applies whether the Director's decision is made on his own initiative or on an application made to him under this Part.

(3)   A direction under this section may, in particular, include provision—
    (a)   requiring the parties to the agreement to modify the agreement; or
    (b)   requiring them to terminate the agreement.

(4)   A direction under this section must be given in writing.

Definitions   For "the Chapter I prohibition", see s 2(8); for "the Director" and as to "person", see s 59(1).
References   See paras 4.53, 4.54, 4.57, 5.16.

33   Directions in relation to conduct

(1)   If the Director has made a decision that conduct infringes the Chapter II prohibition, he may give to such person or persons as he considers appropriate such directions as he considers appropriate to bring the infringement to an end.

(2)   Subsection (1) applies whether the Director's decision is made on his own initiative or on an application made to him under this Part.

(3)   A direction under this section may, in particular, include provision—
    (a)   requiring the person concerned to modify the conduct in question; or
    (b)   requiring him to cease that conduct.

(4)   A direction under this section must be given in writing.

Definitions   For "the Chapter II prohibition", see s 18(4); for "the Director" and as to "person", see s 59(1).
References   See paras 4.53, 5.16, 8.5.

34   Enforcement of directions

(1)   If a person fails, without reasonable excuse, to comply with a direction under section 32 or 33, the Director may apply to the court for an order—
    (a)   requiring the defaulter to make good his default within a time specified in the order; or
    (b)   if the direction related to anything to be done in the management or administration of an undertaking, requiring the undertaking or any of its officers to do it.

(2)   An order of the court under subsection (1) may provide for all of the costs of, or incidental to, the application for the order to be borne by—
    (a)   the person in default; or
    (b)   any officer of an undertaking who is responsible for the default.

(3)   In the application of subsection (2) to Scotland, the reference to "costs" is to be read as a reference to "expenses".

Definitions   For "the court", "the Director" and as to "officer" and "person", see s 59(1).
References   See paras 4.55, 4.59.

35   Interim measures

(1)   This section applies if the Director—
    (a)   has a reasonable suspicion that the Chapter I prohibition has been infringed, or
    (b)   has a reasonable suspicion that the Chapter II prohibition has been infringed,
but has not completed his investigation into the matter.

(2)   If the Director considers that it is necessary for him to act under this section as a matter of urgency for the purpose—
    (a)   of preventing serious, irreparable damage to a particular person or category of person, or
    (b)   of protecting the public interest,
he may give such directions as he considers appropriate for that purpose.

(3)   Before giving a direction under this section, the Director must—

    (a)   give written notice to the person (or persons) to whom he proposes to give the direction; and

    (b)   give that person (or each of them) an opportunity to make representations.

(4)   A notice under subsection (3) must indicate the nature of the direction which the Director is proposing to give and his reasons for wishing to give it.

(5)   A direction given under this section has effect while subsection (1) applies, but may be replaced if the circumstances permit by a direction under section 32 or (as appropriate) section 33.

(6)   In the case of a suspected infringement of the Chapter I prohibition, sections 32(3) and 34 also apply to directions given under this section.

(7)   In the case of a suspected infringement of the Chapter II prohibition, sections 33(3) and 34 also apply to directions given under this section.

Definitions   For "the Chapter I prohibition", see s 2(8); for "the Chapter II prohibition", see s 18(4); for "the Director" and as to "person", see s 59(1).
References   See paras 3.34, 4.56, 5.16.

---

36 Penalty for infringing Chapter I or Chapter II prohibition

(1)   On making a decision that an agreement has infringed the Chapter I prohibition, the Director may require an undertaking which is a party to the agreement to pay him a penalty in respect of the infringement.

(2)   On making a decision that conduct has infringed the Chapter II prohibition, the Director may require the undertaking concerned to pay him a penalty in respect of the infringement.

(3)   The Director may impose a penalty on an undertaking under subsection (1) or (2) only if he is satisfied that the infringement has been committed intentionally or negligently by the undertaking.

(4)   Subsection (1) is subject to section 39 and does not apply if the Director is satisfied that the undertaking acted on the reasonable assumption that that section gave it immunity in respect of the agreement.

(5)   Subsection (2) is subject to section 40 and does not apply if the Director is satisfied that the undertaking acted on the reasonable assumption that that section gave it immunity in respect of the conduct.

(6)   Notice of a penalty under this section must—

    (a)   be in writing; and

    (b)   specify the date before which the penalty is required to be paid.

(7)   The date specified must not be earlier than the end of the period within which an appeal against the notice may be brought under section 46.

(8)   No penalty fixed by the Director under this section may exceed 10% of the turnover of the undertaking (determined in accordance with such provisions as may be specified in an order made by the Secretary of State).

(9)   Any sums received by the Director under this section are to be paid into the Consolidated Fund.

Definitions   For "the Chapter I prohibition", see s 2(8); for "the Chapter II prohibition", see s 18(4); for "the Director", see s 59(1).
References   See paras 4.60, 4.61, 4.64, 4.66, 5.16, 8.5.

---

37 Recovery of penalties

(1) If the specified date in a penalty notice has passed and—

(a) the period during which an appeal against the imposition, or amount, of the penalty may be made has expired without an appeal having been made, or

(b) such an appeal has been made and determined,

the Director may recover from the undertaking, as a civil debt due to him, any amount payable under the penalty notice which remains outstanding.

(2) In this section—

"penalty notice" means a notice given under section 36; and

"specified date" means the date specified in the penalty notice.

Definitions   For "the Director", see s 59(1).
References   See para 4.49.

38 The appropriate level of a penalty

(1) The Director must prepare and publish guidance as to the appropriate amount of any penalty under this Part.

(2) The Director may at any time alter the guidance.

(3) If the guidance is altered, the Director must publish it as altered.

(4) No guidance is to be published under this section without the approval of the Secretary of State.

(5) The Director may, after consulting the Secretary of State, choose how he publishes his guidance.

(6) If the Director is preparing or altering guidance under this section he must consult such persons as he considers appropriate.

(7) If the proposed guidance or alteration relates to a matter in respect of which a regulator exercises concurrent jurisdiction, those consulted must include that regulator.

(8) When setting the amount of a penalty under this Part, the Director must have regard to the guidance for the time being in force under this section.

(9) If a penalty or a fine has been imposed by the Commission, or by a court or other body in another Member State, in respect of an agreement or conduct, the Director, an appeal tribunal or the appropriate court must take that penalty or fine into account when setting the amount of a penalty under this Part in relation to that agreement or conduct.

(10) In subsection (9) "the appropriate court" means—

(a) in relation to England and Wales, the Court of Appeal;

(b) in relation to Scotland, the Court of Session;

(c) in relation to Northern Ireland, the Court of Appeal in Northern Ireland;

(d) the House of Lords.

Definitions   For "regulator", see s 54(1); for "appeal tribunal", "the Commission" and "the Director" and as to "person", see s 59(1).
References   See paras 2.18, 4.64, 4.65, 7.3.

39 Limited immunity for small agreements

(1)   In this section "small agreement" means an agreement—
   (a)   which falls within a category prescribed for the purposes of this section; but
   (b)   is not a price fixing agreement.

(2)   The criteria by reference to which a category of agreement is prescribed may, in particular, include—
   (a)   the combined turnover of the parties to the agreement (determined in accordance with prescribed provisions);
   (b)   the share of the market affected by the agreement (determined in that way).

(3)   A party to a small agreement is immune from the effect of section 36(1); but the Director may withdraw that immunity under subsection (4).

(4)   If the Director has investigated a small agreement, he may make a decision withdrawing the immunity given by subsection (3) if, as a result of his investigation, he considers that the agreement is likely to infringe the Chapter I prohibition.

(5)   The Director must give each of the parties in respect of which immunity is withdrawn written notice of his decision to withdraw the immunity.

(6)   A decision under subsection (4) takes effect on such date ("the withdrawal date") as may be specified in the decision.

(7)   The withdrawal date must be a date after the date on which the decision is made.

(8)   In determining the withdrawal date, the Director must have regard to the amount of time which the parties are likely to require in order to secure that there is no further infringement of the Chapter I prohibition with respect to the agreement.

(9)   In subsection (1) "price fixing agreement" means an agreement which has as its object or effect, or one of its objects or effects, restricting the freedom of a party to the agreement to determine the price to be charged (otherwise than as between that party and another party to the agreement) for the product, service or other matter to which the agreement relates.

Definitions   For "the Chapter I prohibition", see s 2(8); for "the Director" and "prescribed", see s 59(1).
References   See paras 2.24, 4.66, 4.67.

40 Limited immunity in relation to the Chapter II prohibition

(1)   In this section "conduct of minor significance" means conduct which falls within a category prescribed for the purposes of this section.

(2)   The criteria by reference to which a category is prescribed may, in particular, include—
   (a)   the turnover of the person whose conduct it is (determined in accordance with prescribed provisions);
   (b)   the share of the market affected by the conduct (determined in that way).

(3)   A person is immune from the effect of section 36(2) if his conduct is conduct of minor significance; but the Director may withdraw that immunity under subsection (4).

(4)   If the Director has investigated conduct of minor significance, he may make a decision withdrawing the immunity given by subsection (3) if, as a result of his investigation, he considers that the conduct is likely to infringe the Chapter II prohibition.

(5)   The Director must give the person, or persons, whose immunity has been withdrawn written notice of his decision to withdraw the immunity.

(6)   A decision under subsection (4) takes effect on such date ("the withdrawal date") as may be specified in the decision.

(7)   The withdrawal date must be a date after the date on which the decision is made.

(8)   In determining the withdrawal date, the Director must have regard to the amount of time which the person or persons affected are likely to require in order to secure that there is no further infringement of the Chapter II prohibition.

Definitions   For "the Chapter II prohibition", see s 18(4); for "the Director" and "prescribed", and as to "person", see s 59(1).
References   See paras 3.33, 4.66, 4.67.

41 Agreements notified to the Commission

(1)   This section applies if a party to an agreement which may infringe the Chapter I prohibition has notified the agreement to the Commission for a decision as to whether an exemption will be granted under Article 85 with respect to the agreement.

(2)   A penalty may not be required to be paid under this Part in respect of any infringement of the Chapter I prohibition after notification but before the Commission determines the matter.

(3)   If the Commission withdraws the benefit of provisional immunity from penalties with respect to the agreement, subsection (2) ceases to apply as from the date on which that benefit is withdrawn.

(4)   The fact that an agreement has been notified to the Commission does not prevent the Director from investigating it under this Part.

(5)   In this section "provisional immunity from penalties" has such meaning as may be prescribed.

Definitions   For "the Chapter I prohibition", see s 2(8); for "Article 85", "the Commission", "the Director" and "prescribed", see s 59(1).
References   See paras 4.66, 4.70, 6.31, 6.33.

Offences

42 Offences

(1)   A person is guilty of an offence if he fails to comply with a requirement imposed on him under section 26, 27 or 28.

(2)   If a person is charged with an offence under subsection (1) in respect of a requirement to produce a document, it is a defence for him to prove—

    (a)   that the document was not in his possession or under his control; and

    (b)   that it was not reasonably practicable for him to comply with the requirement.

(3)   If a person is charged with an offence under subsection (1) in respect of a requirement—

    (a)   to provide information,

    (b)   to provide an explanation of a document, or

    (c)   to state where a document is to be found,

it is a defence for him to prove that he had a reasonable excuse for failing to comply with the requirement.

(4)   Failure to comply with a requirement imposed under section 26 or 27 is not an offence if the person imposing the requirement has failed to act in accordance with that section.

(5)   A person is guilty of an offence if he intentionally obstructs an officer acting in the exercise of his powers under section 27.

(6)   A person guilty of an offence under subsection (1) or (5) is liable—
  (a)   on summary conviction, to a fine not exceeding the statutory maximum;
  (b)   on conviction on indictment, to a fine.

(7)   A person who intentionally obstructs an officer in the exercise of his powers under a warrant issued under section 28 is guilty of an offence and liable—
  (a)   on summary conviction, to a fine not exceeding the statutory maximum;
  (b)   on conviction on indictment, to imprisonment for a term not exceeding two years or to a fine or to both.

Definitions   As to "document", "information" and "person", see s 59(1).
References   See paras 4.21–4.23.

43 Destroying or falsifying documents

(1)   A person is guilty of an offence if, having been required to produce a document under section 26, 27 or 28—
  (a)   he intentionally or recklessly destroys or otherwise disposes of it, falsifies it or conceals it, or
  (b)   he causes or permits its destruction, disposal, falsification or concealment.

(2)   A person guilty of an offence under subsection (1) is liable—
  (a)   on summary conviction, to a fine not exceeding the statutory maximum;
  (b)   on conviction on indictment, to imprisonment for a term not exceeding two years or to a fine or to both.

Definitions   As to "document" and "person", see s 59(1).
References   See paras 4.21, 4.23.

44 False or misleading information

(1)   If information is provided by a person to the Director in connection with any function of the Director under this Part, that person is guilty of an offence if—
  (a)   the information is false or misleading in a material particular, and
  (b)   he knows that it is or is reckless as to whether it is.

(2)   A person who—
  (a)   provides any information to another person, knowing the information to be false or misleading in a material particular, or
  (b)   recklessly provides any information to another person which is false or misleading in a material particular,

knowing that the information is to be used for the purpose of providing information to the Director in connection with any of his functions under this Part, is guilty of an offence.

(3)   A person guilty of an offence under this section is liable—
  (a)   on summary conviction, to a fine not exceeding the statutory maximum;

(b) on conviction on indictment, to imprisonment for a term not exceeding two years or to a fine or to both.

Definitions For "the Director" and as to "information" and "person", see s 59(1).
References See paras 4.21, 4.23.

CHAPTER IV
THE COMPETITION COMMISSION AND APPEALS

The Commission

45 The Competition Commission

(1) There is to be a body corporate known as the Competition Commission.

(2) The Commission is to have such functions as are conferred on it by or as a result of this Act.

(3) The Monopolies and Mergers Commission is dissolved and its functions are transferred to the Competition Commission.

(4) In any enactment, instrument or other document, any reference to the Monopolies and Mergers Commission which has continuing effect is to be read as a reference to the Competition Commission.

(5) The Secretary of State may by order make such consequential, supplemental and incidental provision as he considers appropriate in connection with—
    (a) the dissolution of the Monopolies and Mergers Commission; and
    (b) the transfer of functions effected by subsection (3).

(6) An order made under subsection (5) may, in particular, include provision—
    (a) for the transfer of property, rights, obligations and liabilities and the continuation of proceedings, investigations and other matters; or
    (b) amending any enactment which makes provision with respect to the Monopolies and Mergers Commission or any of its functions.

(7) Schedule 7 makes further provision about the Competition Commission.

Definitions As to "document", see s 59(1).
References See para 5.9.

Appeals

46 Appealable decisions

(1) Any party to an agreement in respect of which the Director has made a decision may appeal to the Competition Commission against, or with respect to, the decision.

(2) Any person in respect of whose conduct the Director has made a decision may appeal to the Competition Commission against, or with respect to, the decision.

(3) In this section "decision" means a decision of the Director—
    (a) as to whether the Chapter I prohibition has been infringed,
    (b) as to whether the Chapter II prohibition has been infringed,
    (c) as to whether to grant an individual exemption,
    (d) in respect of an individual exemption—
        (i) as to whether to impose any condition or obligation under section 4(3)(a) or 5(1)(c),

(ii) where such a condition or obligation has been imposed, as to the condition or obligation,

(iii) as to the period fixed under section 4(3)(b), or

(iv) as to the date fixed under section 4(5),

(e) as to—

(i) whether to extend the period for which an individual exemption has effect, or

(ii) the period of any such extension,

(f) cancelling an exemption,

(g) as to the imposition of any penalty under section 36 or as to the amount of any such penalty,

(h) withdrawing or varying any of the decisions in paragraphs (a) to (f) following an application under section 47(1),

and includes a direction given under section 32, 33 or 35 and such other decision as may be prescribed.

(4) Except in the case of an appeal against the imposition, or the amount, of a penalty, the making of an appeal under this section does not suspend the effect of the decision to which the appeal relates.

(5) Part I of Schedule 8 makes further provision about appeals.

Definitions   For "the Chapter I prohibition", see s 2(8); for "individual exemption", see s 4(2); for "the Chapter II prohibition", see s 18(4); for "the Director" and "prescribed" and as to "person", see s 59(1). **References**   See paras 5.16–5.21.

47 Third party appeals

(1) A person who does not fall within section 46(1) or (2) may apply to the Director asking him to withdraw or vary a decision ("the relevant decision") falling within paragraphs (a) to (f) of section 46(3) or such other decision as may be prescribed.

(2) The application must—

(a) be made in writing, within such period as the Director may specify in rules under section 51; and

(b) give the applicant's reasons for considering that the relevant decision should be withdrawn or (as the case may be) varied.

(3) If the Director decides—

(a) that the applicant does not have a sufficient interest in the relevant decision,

(b) that, in the case of an applicant claiming to represent persons who have such an interest, the applicant does not represent such persons, or

(c) that the persons represented by the applicant do not have such an interest,

he must notify the applicant of his decision.

(4) If the Director, having considered the application, decides that it does not show sufficient reason why he should withdraw or vary the relevant decision, he must notify the applicant of his decision.

(5) Otherwise, the Director must deal with the application in accordance with such procedure as may be specified in rules under section 51.

(6) The applicant may appeal to the Competition Commission against a decision of the Director notified under subsection (3) or (4).

(7) The making of an application does not suspend the effect of the relevant decision.

Definitions For "the Director" and "prescribed" and as to "person", see s 59(1).
References See paras 4.71, 5.16, 5.19, 5.21.

48 Appeal tribunals

(1)   Any appeal made to the Competition Commission under section 46 or 47 is to be determined by an appeal tribunal.

(2)   The Secretary of State may, after consulting the President of the Competition Commission Appeal Tribunals and such other persons as he considers appropriate, make rules with respect to appeals and appeal tribunals.

(3)   The rules may confer functions on the President.

(4)   Part II of Schedule 8 makes further provision about rules made under this section but is not to be taken as restricting the Secretary of State's powers under this section.

Definitions For "appeal tribunal" and as to "person", see 59(1).
References See para 5.22.

49 Appeals on point of law etc

(1)   An appeal lies—
      (a)   on a point of law arising from a decision of an appeal tribunal, or
      (b)   from any decision of an appeal tribunal as to the amount of a penalty.

(2)   An appeal under this section may be made only—
      (a)   to the appropriate court;
      (b)   with leave; and
      (c)   at the instance of a party or at the instance of a person who has a sufficient interest in the matter.

(3)   Rules under section 48 may make provision for regulating or prescribing any matters incidental to or consequential upon an appeal under this section.

(4)   In subsection (2)—
    "the appropriate court" means—
      (a)   in relation to proceedings before a tribunal in England and Wales, the Court of Appeal;
      (b)   in relation to proceedings before a tribunal in Scotland, the Court of Session;
      (c)   in relation to proceedings before a tribunal in Northern Ireland, the Court of Appeal in Northern Ireland;
    "leave" means leave of the tribunal in question or of the appropriate court; and
    "party", in relation to a decision, means a person who was a party to the proceedings in which the decision was made.

Definitions For "appeal tribunal" and as to "person", see 59(1).
References See para 5.27.

CHAPTER V
MISCELLANEOUS

Vertical agreements and land agreements

50 Vertical agreements and land agreements

(1)   The Secretary of State may by order provide for any provision of this Part to apply in relation to—

(a) vertical agreements, or
(b) land agreements,

with such modifications as may be prescribed.

(2) An order may, in particular, provide for exclusions or exemptions, or otherwise provide for prescribed provisions not to apply, in relation to—
    (a) vertical agreements, or land agreements, in general; or
    (b) vertical agreements, or land agreements, of any prescribed description.

(3) An order may empower the Director to give directions to the effect that in prescribed circumstances an exclusion, exemption or modification is not to apply (or is to apply in a particular way) in relation to an individual agreement.

(4) Subsections (2) and (3) are not to be read as limiting the powers conferred by section 71.

(5) In this section—
    "land agreement" and "vertical agreement" have such meaning as may be prescribed; and
    "prescribed" means prescribed by an order.

Definitions For "the Director", see s 59(1).
References See paras 2.75–2.92.

Director's rules, guidance and fees

51 Rules

(1) The Director may make such rules about procedural and other matters in connection with the carrying into effect of the provisions of this Part as he considers appropriate.

(2) Schedule 9 makes further provision about rules made under this section but is not to be taken as restricting the Director's powers under this section.

(3) If the Director is preparing rules under this section he must consult such persons as he considers appropriate.

(4) If the proposed rules relate to a matter in respect of which a regulator exercises concurrent jurisdiction, those consulted must include that regulator.

(5) No rule made by the Director is to come into operation until it has been approved by an order made by the Secretary of State.

(6) The Secretary of State may approve any rule made by the Director—
    (a) in the form in which it is submitted; or
    (b) subject to such modifications as he considers appropriate.

(7) If the Secretary of State proposes to approve a rule subject to modifications he must inform the Director of the proposed modifications and take into account any comments made by the Director.

(8) Subsections (5) to (7) apply also to any alteration of the rules made by the Director.

(9) The Secretary of State may, after consulting the Director, by order vary or revoke any rules made under this section.

(10) If the Secretary of State considers that rules should be made under this section with respect to a particular matter he may direct the Director to exercise his powers under this section and make rules about that matter.

Definitions For "regulator", see s 54(1); for "the Director" and as to "person", see 59(1).
References See paras 2.107, 7.3, 7.14, 7.17, 9.13.

52 Advice and information

(1)   As soon as is reasonably practicable after the passing of this Act, the Director must prepare and publish general advice and information about—

   (a)   the application of the Chapter I prohibition and the Chapter II prohibition, and

   (b)   the enforcement of those prohibitions.

(2)   The Director may at any time publish revised, or new, advice or information.

(3)   Advice and information published under this section must be prepared with a view to—

   (a)   explaining provisions of this Part to persons who are likely to be affected by them; and

   (b)   indicating how the Director expects such provisions to operate.

(4)   Advice (or information) published by virtue of subsection (3)(b) may include advice (or information) about the factors which the Director may take into account in considering whether, and if so how, to exercise a power conferred on him by Chapter I, II or III.

(5)   Any advice or information published by the Director under this section is to be published in such form and in such manner as he considers appropriate.

(6)   If the Director is preparing any advice or information under this section he must consult such persons as he considers appropriate.

(7)   If the proposed advice or information relates to a matter in respect of which a regulator exercises concurrent jurisdiction, those consulted must include that regulator.

(8)   In preparing any advice or information under this section about a matter in respect of which he may exercise functions under this Part, a regulator must consult—

   (a)   the Director;

   (b)   the other regulators; and

   (c)   such other persons as he considers appropriate.

Definitions For "the Chapter I prohibition", see s 2(8); for "the Chapter II prohibition", see s 18(4); for "regulator", see s 54(1); for "the Director" and as to "person", see s 59(1).

53 Fees

(1)   The Director may charge fees, of specified amounts, in connection with the exercise by him of specified functions under this Part.

(2)   Rules may, in particular, provide—

   (a)   for the amount of any fee to be calculated by reference to matters which may include—

      (i)   the turnover of any party to an agreement (determined in such manner as may be specified);

      (ii)   the turnover of a person whose conduct the Director is to consider (determined in that way);

   (b)   for different amounts to be specified in connection with different functions;

   (c)   for the repayment by the Director of the whole or part of a fee in specified circumstances;

   (d)   that an application or notice is not to be regarded as duly made or given unless the appropriate fee is paid.

(3)   In this section—
      (a)   "rules" means rules made by the Director under section 51; and
      (b)   "specified" means specified in rules.

Definitions   For "the Director" and as to "person", see s 59(1).
References   See para 5.8.

Regulators

54 Regulators

(1)   In this Part "regulator" means any person mentioned in paragraphs (a) to (g) of paragraph 1 of Schedule 10.

(2)   Parts II and III of Schedule 10 provide for functions of the Director under this Part to be exercisable concurrently by regulators.

(3)   Parts IV and V of Schedule 10 make minor and consequential amendments in connection with the regulators' competition functions.

(4)   The Secretary of State may make regulations for the purpose of co-ordinating the performance of functions under this Part ("Part I functions") which are exercisable concurrently by two or more competent persons as a result of any provision made by Part II or III of Schedule 10.

(5)   The regulations may, in particular, make provision—
      (a)   as to the procedure to be followed by competent persons when determining who is to exercise Part I functions in a particular case;
      (b)   as to the steps which must be taken before a competent person exercises, in a particular case, such Part I functions as may be prescribed;
      (c)   as to the procedure for determining, in a particular case, questions arising as to which competent person is to exercise Part I functions in respect of the case;
      (d)   for Part I functions in a particular case to be exercised jointly—
         (i)   by the Director and one or more regulators, or
         (ii)   by two or more regulators,
   and as to the procedure to be followed in such cases;
      (e)   as to the circumstances in which the exercise by a competent person of such Part I functions as may be prescribed is to preclude the exercise of such functions by another such person;
      (f)   for cases in respect of which Part I functions are being, or have been, exercised by a competent person to be transferred to another such person;
      (g)   for the person ("A") exercising Part I functions in a particular case—
         (i)   to appoint another competent person ("B") to exercise Part I functions on A's behalf in relation to the case; or
         (ii)   to appoint officers of B (with B's consent) to act as officers of A in relation to the case;
      (h)   for notification as to who is exercising Part I functions in respect of a particular case.

(6)   Provision made by virtue of subsection (5)(c) may provide for questions to be referred to and determined by the Secretary of State or by such other person as may be prescribed.

(7)   "Competent person" means the Director or any of the regulators.

Definitions   For "the Director" and "prescribed", see s 59(1).
References   See paras 4.2, 7.3, 7.14, 7.18.

Confidentiality and immunity from defamation

55 General restrictions on disclosure of information

(1)   No information which—

    (a)   has been obtained under or as a result of any provision of this Part, and

    (b)   relates to the affairs of any individual or to any particular business of an undertaking,

is to be disclosed during the lifetime of that individual or while that business continues to be carried on, unless the condition mentioned in subsection (2) is satisfied.

(2)   The condition is that consent to the disclosure has been obtained from—

    (a)   the person from whom the information was initially obtained under or as a result of any provision of this Part (if the identity of that person is known); and

    (b)   if different—

        (i)   the individual to whose affairs the information relates, or

        (ii)   the person for the time being carrying on the business to which the information relates.

(3)   Subsection (1) does not apply to a disclosure of information—

    (a)   made for the purpose of—

        (i)   facilitating the performance of any relevant functions of a designated person;

        (ii)   facilitating the performance of any functions of the Commission in respect of Community law about competition;

        (iii)   facilitating the performance by the Comptroller and Auditor General of any of his functions;

        (iv)   criminal proceedings in any part of the United Kingdom;

    (b)   made with a view to the institution of, or otherwise for the purposes of, civil proceedings brought under or in connection with this Part;

    (c)   made in connection with the investigation of any criminal offence triable in the United Kingdom or in any part of the United Kingdom; or

    (d)   which is required to meet a Community obligation.

(4)   In subsection (3) "relevant functions" and "designated person" have the meaning given in Schedule 11.

(5)   Subsection (1) also does not apply to a disclosure of information made for the purpose of facilitating the performance of specified functions of any specified person.

(6)   In subsection (5) "specified" means specified in an order made by the Secretary of State.

(7)   If information is disclosed to the public in circumstances in which the disclosure does not contravene subsection (1), that subsection does not prevent its further disclosure by any person.

(8)   A person who contravenes this section is guilty of an offence and liable—

    (a)   on summary conviction, to a fine not exceeding the statutory maximum; or

    (b)   on conviction on indictment, to imprisonment for a term not exceeding two years or to a fine or to both.

Definitions   For "the Commission" and as to "information" and "person", see s 59(1).
References   See paras 4.20, 4.73, 9.39, 10.2, 10.3.

56 Director and Secretary of State to have regard to certain matters in relation to the disclosure of information

(1)   This section applies if the Secretary of State or the Director is considering whether to disclose any information acquired by him under, or as a result of, any provision of this Part.

(2)   He must have regard to the need for excluding, so far as is practicable, information the disclosure of which would in his opinion be contrary to the public interest.

(3)   He must also have regard to—
    (a)   the need for excluding, so far as is practicable—
        (i)   commercial information the disclosure of which would, or might, in his opinion, significantly harm the legitimate business interests of the undertaking to which it relates, or
        (ii)   information relating to the private affairs of an individual the disclosure of which would, or might, in his opinion, significantly harm his interests; and
    (b)   the extent to which the disclosure is necessary for the purposes for which the Secretary of State or the Director is proposing to make the disclosure.

Definitions   For "the Director" and as to "information", see s 59(1).
References   See paras 4.20, 9.39, 10.4, 10.5.

57 Defamation

For the purposes of the law relating to defamation, absolute privilege attaches to any advice, guidance, notice or direction given, or decision made, by the Director in the exercise of any of his functions under this Part.

Definitions   For "the Director", see s 59(1).
References   See para 10.6.

Findings of fact by Director

58 Findings of fact by Director

(1)   Unless the court directs otherwise or the Director has decided to take further action in accordance with section 16(2) or 24(2), a Director's finding which is relevant to an issue arising in Part I proceedings is binding on the parties if—
    (a)   the time for bringing an appeal in respect of the finding has expired and the relevant party has not brought such an appeal; or
    (b)   the decision of an appeal tribunal on such an appeal has confirmed the finding.

(2)   In this section—
    "a Director's finding" means a finding of fact made by the Director in the course of—
        (a)   determining an application for a decision under section 14 or 22, or
        (b)   conducting an investigation under section 25;
    "Part I proceedings" means proceedings—
        (a)   in respect of an alleged infringement of the Chapter I prohibition or of the Chapter II prohibition; but
        (b)   which are brought otherwise than by the Director;

"relevant party" means—
- (a) in relation to the Chapter I prohibition, a party to the agreement which is alleged to have infringed the prohibition; and
- (b) in relation to the Chapter II prohibition, the undertaking whose conduct is alleged to have infringed the prohibition.

(3) Rules of court may make provision in respect of assistance to be given by the Director to the court in Part I proceedings.

Definitions For "the Chapter I prohibition", see s 2(8); for "the Chapter II prohibition", see s 18(4); for "appeal tribunal" and "the Director", see s 59(1).
References See paras 4.71, 4.73.

Interpretation and governing principles

59 Interpretation

(1) In this Part—
"appeal tribunal" means an appeal tribunal established in accordance with the provisions of Part III of Schedule 7 for the purpose of hearing an appeal under section 46 or 47;
"Article 85" means Article 85 of the Treaty;
"Article 86" means Article 86 of the Treaty;
"block exemption" has the meaning given in section 6(4);
"block exemption order" has the meaning given in section 6(2);
"the Chapter I prohibition" has the meaning given in section 2(8);
"the Chapter II prohibition" has the meaning given in section 18(4);
"the Commission" (except in relation to the Competition Commission) means the European Commission;
"the Council" means the Council of the European Union;
"the court", except in sections 58 and 60 and the expression "European Court", means—
- (a) in England and Wales, the High Court;
- (b) in Scotland, the Court of Session; and
- (c) in Northern Ireland, the High Court;
"the Director" means the Director General of Fair Trading;
"document" includes information recorded in any form;
"the EEA Agreement" means the Agreement on the European Economic Area signed at Oporto on 2nd May 1992 as it has effect for the time being;
"the European Court" means the Court of Justice of the European Communities and includes the Court of First Instance;
"individual exemption" has the meaning given in section 4(2);
"information" includes estimates and forecasts;
"investigating officer" has the meaning given in section 27(1);
"Minister of the Crown" has the same meaning as in the Ministers of the Crown Act 1975;
"officer", in relation to a body corporate, includes a director, manager or secretary and, in relation to a partnership in Scotland, includes a partner;
"parallel exemption" has the meaning given in section 10(3);
"person", in addition to the meaning given by the Interpretation Act 1978, includes any undertaking;
"premises" does not include domestic premises unless—
- (a) they are also used in connection with the affairs of an undertaking, or
- (b) documents relating to the affairs of an undertaking are kept there,
but does include any vehicle;

"prescribed" means prescribed by regulations made by the Secretary of State;

"regulator" has the meaning given by section 54;

"section 11 exemption" has the meaning given in section 11(3); and

"the Treaty" means the treaty establishing the European Community.

(2)   The fact that to a limited extent the Chapter I prohibition does not apply to an agreement, because of an exclusion provided by or under this Part or any other enactment, does not require those provisions of the agreement to which the exclusion relates to be disregarded when considering whether the agreement infringes the prohibition for other reasons.

(3)   For the purposes of this Part, the power to require information, in relation to information recorded otherwise than in a legible form, includes power to require a copy of it in a legible form.

(4)   Any power conferred on the Director by this Part to require information includes power to require any document which he believes may contain that information.

References   See para 10.10.

---

60 Principles to be applied in determining questions

(1)   The purpose of this section is to ensure that so far as is possible (having regard to any relevant differences between the provisions concerned), questions arising under this Part in relation to competition within the United Kingdom are dealt with in a manner which is consistent with the treatment of corresponding questions arising in Community law in relation to competition within the Community.

(2)   At any time when the court determines a question arising under this Part, it must act (so far as is compatible with the provisions of this Part and whether or not it would otherwise be required to do so) with a view to securing that there is no inconsistency between—

(a)   the principles applied, and decision reached, by the court in determining that question; and

(b)   the principles laid down by the Treaty and the European Court, and any relevant decision of that Court, as applicable at that time in determining any corresponding question arising in Community law.

(3)   The court must, in addition, have regard to any relevant decision or statement of the Commission.

(4)   Subsections (2) and (3) also apply to—

(a)   the Director; and

(b)   any person acting on behalf of the Director, in connection with any matter arising under this Part.

(5)   In subsections (2) and (3), "court" means any court or tribunal.

(6)   In subsections (2)(b) and (3), "decision" includes a decision as to—

(a)   the interpretation of any provision of Community law;

(b)   the civil liability of an undertaking for harm caused by its infringement of Community law.

Definitions   For "the Director" and "the Treaty", see s 57(1).
References   See paras 2.23, 2.28, 6.15–6.30, 6.42, 7.18–7.20.

PART II
INVESTIGATIONS IN RELATION TO ARTICLES 85 AND 86

61 Introduction

(1)   In this Part—

"Article 85" and "Article 86" have the same meaning as in Part I;

"authorised officer", in relation to the Director, means an officer to whom an authorisation has been given under subsection (2);

"the Commission" means the European Commission;

"the Director" means the Director General of Fair Trading;

"Commission investigation" means an investigation ordered by a decision of the Commission under a prescribed provision of Community law relating to Article 85 or 86;

"Director's investigation" means an investigation conducted by the Director at the request of the Commission under a prescribed provision of Community law relating to Article 85 or 86;

"Director's special investigation" means a Director's investigation conducted at the request of the Commission in connection with a Commission investigation;

"prescribed" means prescribed by order made by the Secretary of State;

"premises" means—

(a)   in relation to a Commission investigation, any premises, land or means of transport which an official of the Commission has power to enter in the course of the investigation; and

(b)   in relation to a Director's investigation, any premises, land or means of transport which an official of the Commission would have power to enter if the investigation were being conducted by the Commission.

(2)   For the purposes of a Director's investigation, an officer of the Director to whom an authorisation has been given has the powers of an official authorised by the Commission in connection with a Commission investigation under the relevant provision.

(3)   "Authorisation" means an authorisation given in writing by the Director which—

(a)   identifies the officer;

(b)   specifies the subject matter and purpose of the investigation; and

(c)   draws attention to any penalties which a person may incur in connection with the investigation under the relevant provision of Community law.

References   See para 4.29.

---

62 Power to enter premises: Commission investigations

(1)   A judge of the High Court may issue a warrant if satisfied, on an application made to the High Court in accordance with rules of court by the Director, that a Commission investigation is being, or is likely to be, obstructed.

(2)   A Commission investigation is being obstructed if—

(a)   an official of the Commission ("the Commission official"), exercising his power in accordance with the provision under which the investigation is being conducted, has attempted to enter premises but has been unable to do so; and

(b)   there are reasonable grounds for suspecting that there are books or records on the premises which the Commission official has power to examine.

(3)   A Commission investigation is also being obstructed if there are reasonable grounds for suspecting that there are books or records on the premises—

(a)   the production of which has been required by an official of the Commission exercising his power in accordance with the provision under which the investigation is being conducted; and

(b)   which have not been produced as required.

(4)   A Commission investigation is likely to be obstructed if—

(a)   an official of the Commission ("the Commission official") is authorised for the purpose of the investigation;

(b)   there are reasonable grounds for suspecting that there are books or records on the premises which the Commission official has power to examine; and

(c)   there are also reasonable grounds for suspecting that, if the Commission official attempted to exercise his power to examine any of the books or records, they would not be produced but would be concealed, removed, tampered with or destroyed.

(5)   A warrant under this section shall authorise—

(a)   a named officer of the Director,

(b)   any other of his officers whom he has authorised in writing to accompany the named officer, and

(c)   any official of the Commission authorised for the purpose of the Commission investigation,

to enter the premises specified in the warrant, and search for books and records which the official has power to examine, using such force as is reasonably necessary for the purpose.

(6)   Any person entering any premises by virtue of a warrant under this section may take with him such equipment as appears to him to be necessary.

(7)   On leaving any premises entered by virtue of the warrant the named officer must, if the premises are unoccupied or the occupier is temporarily absent, leave them as effectively secured as he found them.

(8)   A warrant under this section continues in force until the end of the period of one month beginning with the day on which it is issued.

(9)   In the application of this section to Scotland, references to the High Court are to be read as references to the Court of Session.

Definitions   For "the Commission", "Commission investigation", "the Director" and "premises", see s 61(1).
References   See para 4.30.

63 Power to enter premises: Director's special investigations

(1)   A judge of the High Court may issue a warrant if satisfied, on an application made to the High Court in accordance with rules of court by the Director, that a Director's special investigation is being, or is likely to be, obstructed.

(2)   A Director's special investigation is being obstructed if—

(a)   an authorised officer of the Director has attempted to enter premises but has been unable to do so;

(b)   the officer has produced his authorisation to the undertaking, or association of undertakings, concerned; and

      (c)   there are reasonable grounds for suspecting that there are books or records on the premises which the officer has power to examine.

(3)   A Director's special investigation is also being obstructed if—

      (a)   there are reasonable grounds for suspecting that there are books or records on the premises which an authorised officer of the Director has power to examine;

      (b)   the officer has produced his authorisation to the undertaking, or association of undertakings, and has required production of the books or records; and

      (c)   the books and records have not been produced as required.

(4)   A Director's special investigation is likely to be obstructed if—

      (a)   there are reasonable grounds for suspecting that there are books or records on the premises which an authorised officer of the Director has power to examine; and

      (b)   there are also reasonable grounds for suspecting that, if the officer attempted to exercise his power to examine any of the books or records, they would not be produced but would be concealed, removed, tampered with or destroyed.

(5)   A warrant under this section shall authorise—

      (a)   a named authorised officer of the Director,

      (b)   any other authorised officer accompanying the named officer, and

      (c)   any named official of the Commission,

to enter the premises specified in the warrant, and search for books and records which the authorised officer has power to examine, using such force as is reasonably necessary for the purpose.

(6)   Any person entering any premises by virtue of a warrant under this section may take with him such equipment as appears to him to be necessary.

(7)   On leaving any premises which he has entered by virtue of the warrant the named officer must, if the premises are unoccupied or the occupier is temporarily absent, leave them as effectively secured as he found them.

(8)   A warrant under this section continues in force until the end of the period of one month beginning with the day on which it is issued.

(9)   In the application of this section to Scotland, references to the High Court are to be read as references to the Court of Session.

Definitions   For "authorised officer", "the Commission", "the Director", "Director's special investigation" and "premises", see s 61(1); for "authorisation", see s 61(3).
References   See para 4.30.

64 Entry of premises under sections 62 and 63: supplementary

(1)   A warrant issued under section 62 or 63 must indicate—

      (a)   the subject matter and purpose of the investigation;

      (b)   the nature of the offence created by section 65.

(2)   The powers conferred by section 62 or 63 are to be exercised on production of a warrant issued under that section.

(3)   If there is no one at the premises when the named officer proposes to execute such a warrant he must, before executing it—

      (a)   take such steps as are reasonable in all the circumstances to inform the occupier of the intended entry; and

(b)   if the occupier is informed, afford him or his legal or other representative a reasonable opportunity to be present when the warrant is executed.

(4)   If the named officer is unable to inform the occupier of the intended entry he must, when executing the warrant, leave a copy of it in a prominent place on the premises.

(5)   In this section—

"named officer" means the officer named in the warrant; and

"occupier", in relation to any premises, means a person whom the named officer reasonably believes is the occupier of those premises.

Definitions   For "premises", see s 61(1).
References   See para 4.30.

---

65 Offences

(1)   A person is guilty of an offence if he intentionally obstructs any person in the exercise of his powers under a warrant issued under section 62 or 63.

(2)   A person guilty of an offence under subsection (1) is liable—
(a)   on summary conviction, to a fine not exceeding the statutory maximum;
(b)   on conviction on indictment, to imprisonment for a term not exceeding two years or to a fine or to both.

PART III
MONOPOLIES

66 Monopoly investigations: general

(1)   Section 44 of the Fair Trading Act 1973 (power of the Director to require information about monopoly situations) is amended as follows.

(2)   In subsection (1), for the words after paragraph (b) substitute—

"the Director may exercise the powers conferred by subsection (2) below for the purpose of assisting him in determining whether to take either of the following decisions with regard to that situation."

(3)   After subsection (1) insert—

"(1A)   Those decisions are—
(a)   whether to make a monopoly reference with respect to the existence or possible existence of the situation;
(b)   whether, instead, to make a proposal under section 56A below for the Secretary of State to accept undertakings."

(4)   For subsection (2) substitute—

"(2)   In the circumstances and for the purpose mentioned in subsection (1) above, the Director may—
(a)   require any person within subsection (3) below to produce to the Director, at a specified time and place—
(i)   any specified documents, or
(ii)   any document which falls within a specified category,
which are in his custody or under his control and which are relevant;

    (b)   require any person within subsection (3) below who is carrying on a business to give the Director specified estimates, forecasts, returns, or other information, and specify the time at which and the form and manner in which the estimates, forecasts, returns or information are to be given;

    (c)   enter any premises used by a person within subsection (3) below for business purposes, and—

        (i)   require any person on the premises to produce any documents on the premises which are in his custody or under his control and which are relevant;

        (ii)   require any person on the premises to give the Director such explanation of the documents as he may require.

(3)   A person is within this subsection if—

    (a)   he produces goods of the description in question in the United Kingdom;

    (b)   he supplies goods or (as the case may be) services of the description in question in the United Kingdom; or

    (c)   such goods (or services) are supplied to him in the United Kingdom.

(4)   The power to impose a requirement under subsection (2)(a) or (b) above is to be exercised by notice in writing served on the person on whom the requirement is imposed; and "specified" in those provisions means specified or otherwise described in the notice, and "specify" is to be read accordingly.

(5)   The power under subsection (2)(a) above to require a person ("the person notified") to produce a document includes power—

    (a)   if the document is produced—

        (i)   to take copies of it or extracts from it;

        (ii)   to require the person notified, or any person who is a present or past officer of his, or is or was at any time employed by him, to provide an explanation of the document;

    (b)   if the document is not produced, to require the person notified to state, to the best of his knowledge and belief, where it is.

(6)   Nothing in this section confers power to compel any person—

    (a)   to produce any document which he could not be compelled to produce in civil proceedings before the High Court or, in Scotland, the Court of Session; or

    (b)   in complying with any requirement for the giving of information, to give any information which he could not be compelled to give in evidence in such proceedings.

(7)   No person has to comply with a requirement imposed under subsection (2) above by a person acting under an authorisation under paragraph 7 of Schedule 1 to this Act unless evidence of the authorisation has, if required, been produced.

(8)   For the purposes of subsection (2) above—

    (a)   a document is relevant if—

        (i)   it is relevant to a decision mentioned in subsection (1A) above; and

        (ii)   the powers conferred by this section are exercised in relation to the document for the purpose of assisting the Director in determining whether to take that decision;

    (b)   "document" includes information recorded in any form; and

    (c)   in relation to information recorded otherwise than in legible form, the power to require its production includes power to require production of it in legible form, so far as the means to do so are within the custody or under the control of the person on whom the requirement is imposed."

(5)   The amendments made by this section and section 67 have effect in relation to sectoral regulators in accordance with paragraph 1 of Schedule 10.

Definitions   For "the Director", see Fair Trading Act 1973, s 1(1), for "monopoly reference", see s 5(3) of that Act, for "business", "goods" and "supply", see s 137(2) thereof, as to "supply of services", see s 137(3), (3A) thereof, as inserted in the case of s 137(3A) by s 68 of this Act.
References   See para 8.8.

67 Offences

(1)   Section 46 of the Fair Trading Act 1973 is amended as follows.

(2)   Omit subsections (1) and (2).

(3)   At the end insert—

"(4) Any person who refuses or wilfully neglects to comply with a requirement imposed under section 44(2) above is guilty of an offence and liable—
  (a)   on summary conviction, to a fine not exceeding the prescribed sum, or
  (b)   on conviction on indictment, to imprisonment for a term not exceeding two years or to a fine or to both.

(5)   If a person is charged with an offence under subsection (4) in respect of a requirement to produce a document, it is a defence for him to prove—
  (a)   that the document was not in his possession or under his control; and
  (b)   that it was not reasonably practicable for him to comply with the requirement.

(6)   If a person is charged with an offence under subsection (4) in respect of a requirement—
  (a)   to provide an explanation of a document, or
  (b)   to state where a document is to be found,

it is a defence for him to prove that he had a reasonable excuse for failing to comply with the requirement.

(7)   A person who intentionally obstructs the Director in the exercise of his powers under section 44 is guilty of an offence and liable—
  (a)   on summary conviction, to a fine not exceeding the prescribed sum;
  (b)   on conviction on indictment, to a fine.

(8)   A person who wilfully alters, suppresses or destroys any document which he has been required to produce under section 44(2) is guilty of an offence and liable—
  (a)   on summary conviction, to a fine not exceeding the prescribed sum;
  (b)   on conviction on indictment, to imprisonment for a term not exceeding two years or to a fine or to both."

Definitions   For "the Director", see Fair Trading Act 1973, s 1(1).
References   See para 8.8.

68 Services relating to use of land

In section 137 of the Fair Trading Act 1973, after subsection (3) insert—

"(3A) The Secretary of State may by order made by statutory instrument—

    (a)   provide that "the supply of services" in the provisions of this Act is to include, or to cease to include, any activity specified in the order which consists in, or in making arrangements in connection with, permitting the use of land; and

    (b)   for that purpose, amend or repeal any of paragraphs (c), (d), (e) or (g) of subsection (3) above.

(3B) No order under subsection (3A) above is to be made unless a draft of the order has been laid before Parliament and approved by a resolution of each House of Parliament.

(3C) The provisions of Schedule 9 to this Act apply in the case of a draft of any such order as they apply in the case of a draft of an order to which section 91(1) above applies."

References   See para 8.10.

69 Reports: monopoly references

In section 83 of the Fair Trading Act 1973—

    (a)   in subsection (1), omit "Subject to subsection (1A) below"; and

    (b)   omit subsection (1A) (reports on monopoly references to be transmitted to certain persons at least twenty-four hours before laying before Parliament).

References   See para 8.9.

PART IV
SUPPLEMENTAL AND TRANSITIONAL

70 Contracts as to patented products etc

Sections 44 and 45 of the Patents Act 1977 shall cease to have effect.

References   See para 10.7.

71 Regulations, orders and rules

(1)   Any power to make regulations or orders which is conferred by this Act is exercisable by statutory instrument.

(2)   The power to make rules which is conferred by section 48 is exercisable by statutory instrument.

(3)   Any statutory instrument made under this Act may—

    (a)   contain such incidental, supplemental, consequential and transitional provision as the Secretary of State considers appropriate; and

    (b)   make different provision for different cases.

(4)   No order is to be made under—

    (a)   section 3,

    (b)   section 19,

    (c)   section 36(8),

    (d)   section 50, or

    (e)   paragraph 6(3) of Schedule 4,

unless a draft of the order has been laid before Parliament and approved by a resolution of each House.

(5)   Any statutory instrument made under this Act, apart from one made—

    (a)   under any of the provisions mentioned in subsection (4), or

    (b)   under section 76(3),

shall be subject to annulment by a resolution of either House of Parliament.

References   See paras 2.92, 10.8, 10.10.

72 Offences by bodies corporate etc

(1)   This section applies to an offence under any of sections 42 to 44, 55(8) or 65.

(2)   If an offence committed by a body corporate is proved—

    (a)   to have been committed with the consent or connivance of an officer, or

    (b)   to be attributable to any neglect on his part,

the officer as well as the body corporate is guilty of the offence and liable to be proceeded against and punished accordingly.

(3)   In subsection (2) "officer", in relation to a body corporate, means a director, manager, secretary or other similar officer of the body, or a person purporting to act in any such capacity.

(4)   If the affairs of a body corporate are managed by its members, subsection (2) applies in relation to the acts and defaults of a member in connection with his functions of management as if he were a director of the body corporate.

(5)   If an offence committed by a partnership in Scotland is proved—

    (a)   to have been committed with the consent or connivance of a partner, or

    (b)   to be attributable to any neglect on his part,

the partner as well as the partnership is guilty of the offence and liable to be proceeded against and punished accordingly.

(6)   In subsection (5) "partner" includes a person purporting to act as a partner.

References   See para 4.24.

73 Crown application

(1)   Any provision made by or under this Act binds the Crown except that—

    (a)   the Crown is not criminally liable as a result of any such provision;

    (b)   the Crown is not liable for any penalty under any such provision; and

    (c)   nothing in this Act affects Her Majesty in her private capacity.

(2)   Subsection (1)(a) does not affect the application of any provision of this Act in relation to persons in the public service of the Crown.

(3)   Subsection (1)(c) is to be interpreted as if section 38(3) of the Crown Proceedings Act 1947 (interpretation of references in that Act to Her Majesty in her private capacity) were contained in this Act.

(4)   If, in respect of a suspected infringement of the Chapter I prohibition or of the Chapter II prohibition otherwise than by the Crown or a person in the public service of the Crown, an investigation is conducted under section 25—

(a)   the power conferred by section 27 may not be exercised in relation to land which is occupied by a government department, or otherwise for purposes of the Crown, without the written consent of the appropriate person; and

(b)   section 28 does not apply in relation to land so occupied.

(5)   In any case in which consent is required under subsection (4), the person who is the appropriate person in relation to that case is to be determined in accordance with regulations made by the Secretary of State.

(6)   Sections 62 and 63 do not apply in relation to land which is occupied by a government department, or otherwise for purposes of the Crown, unless the matter being investigated is a suspected infringement by the Crown or by a person in the public service of the Crown.

(7)   In subsection (6) "infringement" means an infringement of Community law relating to Article 85 or 86 of the Treaty establishing the European Community.

(8)   If the Secretary of State certifies that it appears to him to be in the interests of national security that the powers of entry—

(a)   conferred by section 27, or

(b)   that may be conferred by a warrant under section 28, 62 or 63,

should not be exercisable in relation to premises held or used by or on behalf of the Crown and which are specified in the certificate, those powers are not exercisable in relation to those premises.

(9)   Any amendment, repeal or revocation made by this Act binds the Crown to the extent that the enactment amended, repealed or revoked binds the Crown.

Definitions   For "the Chapter I prohibition", see s 2(8); for "the Chapter II prohibition", see s 18(4).
References   See para 10.9.

74 Amendments, transitional provisions, savings and repeals

(1)   The minor and consequential amendments set out in Schedule 12 are to have effect.

(2)   The transitional provisions and savings set out in Schedule 13 are to have effect.

(3)   The enactments set out in Schedule 14 are repealed.

75 Consequential and supplementary provision

(1)   The Secretary of State may by order make such incidental, consequential, transitional or supplemental provision as he thinks necessary or expedient for the general purposes, or any particular purpose, of this Act or in consequence of any of its provisions or for giving full effect to it.

(2)   An order under subsection (1) may, in particular, make provision—

(a)   for enabling any person by whom any powers will become exercisable, on a date specified by or under this Act, by virtue of any provision made by or under this Act to take before that date any steps which are necessary as a preliminary to the exercise of those powers;

(b)   for making savings, or additional savings, from the effect of any repeal made by or under this Act.

(3)   Amendments made under this section shall be in addition, and without prejudice, to those made by or under any other provision of this Act.

(4)   No other provision of this Act restricts the powers conferred by this section.

References   See paras 10.8, 10.10.

76 Short title, commencement and extent

(1)   This Act may be cited as the Competition Act 1998.

(2)   Sections 71 and 75 and this section and paragraphs 1 to 7 and 35 of Schedule 13 come into force on the passing of this Act.

(3)   The other provisions of this Act come into force on such day as the Secretary of State may by order appoint; and different days may be appointed for different purposes.

(4)   This Act extends to Northern Ireland.

Orders The Competition Act 1998 (Commencement No 1) Order 1998, SI 1998/2750; the Competition Act 1998 (Commencement No 2) Order 1998, SI 1998/3166.

SCHEDULES

SCHEDULE 1

Sections 3(1)(a) and 19(1)(a)

EXCLUSIONS: MERGERS AND CONCENTRATIONS

PART I

MERGERS

Enterprises ceasing to be distinct: the Chapter I prohibition

1.—(1) To the extent to which an agreement (either on its own or when taken together with another agreement) results, or if carried out would result, in any two enterprises ceasing to be distinct enterprises for the purposes of Part V of the Fair Trading Act 1973 ("the 1973 Act"), the Chapter I prohibition does not apply to the agreement.

(2)   The exclusion provided by sub-paragraph (1) extends to any provision directly related and necessary to the implementation of the merger provisions.

(3)   In sub-paragraph (2) "merger provisions" means the provisions of the agreement which cause, or if carried out would cause, the agreement to have the result mentioned in sub-paragraph (1).

(4)   Section 65 of the 1973 Act applies for the purposes of this paragraph as if—
- (a)   in subsection (3) (circumstances in which a person or group of persons may be treated as having control of an enterprise), and
- (b)   in subsection (4) (circumstances in which a person or group of persons may be treated as bringing an enterprise under their control),

for "may" there were substituted "must".

Enterprises ceasing to be distinct: the Chapter II prohibition

2.—(1) To the extent to which conduct (either on its own or when taken together with other conduct)—
- (a)   results in any two enterprises ceasing to be distinct enterprises for the purposes of Part V of the 1973 Act), or
- (b)   is directly related and necessary to the attainment of the result mentioned in paragraph (a),

the Chapter II prohibition does not apply to that conduct.

(2) Section 65 of the 1973 Act applies for the purposes of this paragraph as it applies for the purposes of paragraph 1.

Transfer of a newspaper or of newspaper assets

3.—(1) The Chapter I prohibition does not apply to an agreement to the extent to which it constitutes, or would if carried out constitute, a transfer of a newspaper or of newspaper assets for the purposes of section 57 of the 1973 Act.

(2) The Chapter II prohibition does not apply to conduct (either on its own or when taken together with other conduct) to the extent to which—
  (a) it constitutes such a transfer, or
  (b) it is directly related and necessary to the implementation of the transfer.

(3) The exclusion provided by sub-paragraph (1) extends to any provision directly related and necessary to the implementation of the transfer.

Withdrawal of the paragraph 1 exclusion

4.—(1) The exclusion provided by paragraph 1 does not apply to a particular agreement if the Director gives a direction under this paragraph to that effect.

(2) If the Director is considering whether to give a direction under this paragraph, he may by notice in writing require any party to the agreement in question to give him such information in connection with the agreement as he may require.

(3) The Director may give a direction under this paragraph only as provided in sub-paragraph (4) or (5).

(4) If at the end of such period as may be specified in rules under section 51 a person has failed, without reasonable excuse, to comply with a requirement imposed under sub-paragraph (2), the Director may give a direction under this paragraph.

(5) The Director may also give a direction under this paragraph if—
  (a) he considers—
      (i) that the agreement will, if not excluded, infringe the Chapter I prohibition; and
      (ii) that he is not likely to grant it an unconditional individual exemption; and
  (b) the agreement is not a protected agreement.

(6) For the purposes of sub-paragraph (5), an individual exemption is unconditional if no conditions or obligations are imposed in respect of it under section 4(3)(a).

(7) A direction under this paragraph—
  (a) must be in writing;
  (b) may be made so as to have effect from a date specified in the direction (which may not be earlier than the date on which it is given).

Protected agreements

5. An agreement is a protected agreement for the purposes of paragraph 4 if—
  (a) the Secretary of State has announced his decision not to make a merger reference to the Competition Commission under section 64 of the 1973 Act in connection with the agreement;
  (b) the Secretary of State has made a merger reference to the Competition Commission under section 64 of the 1973 Act in connection with the agreement and the Commission has found that the agreement has given rise to, or would if carried out give rise to, a merger situation qualifying for investigation;
  (c) the agreement does not fall within sub-paragraph (a) or (b) but has given rise to, or would if carried out give rise to, enterprises to which it relates being regarded under section 65 of the 1973 Act as ceasing to be distinct enterprises (otherwise than as the result of subsection (3) or (4)(b) of that section); or
  (d) the Secretary of State has made a merger reference to the Competition Commission under section 32 of the Water Industry Act 1991 in connection with the agreement and the Commission has found that the agreement has given rise to, or would if carried out give rise to, a merger of the kind to which that section applies.

Definitions   For "the Chapter I prohibition", see s 2(8); for "individual exemption", see s 4(2); for "the Chapter II prohibition", see s 18(4); for "the Commission" and "the Director" and as to "information" and "person", see s 59(1).
References   See paras 2.40–2.48, 3.31.

PART II
CONCENTRATIONS SUBJECT TO EC CONTROLS

6.—(1) To the extent to which an agreement (either on its own or when taken together with another agreement) gives rise to, or would if carried out give rise to, a concentration, the Chapter I prohibition does not apply to the agreement if the Merger Regulation gives the Commission exclusive jurisdiction in the matter.

(2) To the extent to which conduct (either on its own or when taken together with other conduct) gives rise to, or would if pursued give rise to, a concentration, the Chapter II prohibition does not apply to the conduct if the Merger Regulation gives the Commission exclusive jurisdiction in the matter.

(3) In this paragraph—
> "concentration" means a concentration with a Community dimension within the meaning of Articles 1 and 3 of the Merger Regulation; and
> "Merger Regulation" means Council Regulation (EEC) No 4064/89 of 21st December 1989 on the control of concentrations between undertakings as amended by Council Regulation (EC) No 1310/97 of 30th June 1997.

Definitions   For "the Chapter I prohibition", see s 2(8); for "the Chapter II prohibition", see s 18(4); for "the Commission", see s 59(1).
References   See paras 2.40, 2.49, 2.50, 3.31.

SCHEDULE 2

Section 3(1)(b)

EXCLUSIONS: OTHER COMPETITION SCRUTINY

PART I
FINANCIAL SERVICES

The Financial Services Act 1986 (c 60)

1.—(1) The Financial Services Act 1986 is amended as follows.

(2) For section 125 (effect of the Restrictive Trade Practices Act 1976), substitute—

"125   The Competition Act 1998: Chapter I prohibition

(1)   The Chapter I prohibition does not apply to an agreement for the constitution of—
> (a)   a recognised self-regulating organisation,
> (b)   a recognised investment exchange, or
> (c)   a recognised clearing house,
to the extent to which the agreement relates to the regulating provisions of the body concerned.

(2)   Subject to subsection (3) below, the Chapter I prohibition does not apply to an agreement for the constitution of—
> (a)   a self-regulating organisation,
> (b)   an investment exchange, or
> (c)   a clearing house,
to the extent to which the agreement relates to the regulating provisions of the body concerned.

(3)   The exclusion provided by subsection (2) above applies only if—
> (a)   the body has applied for a recognition order in accordance with the provisions of this Act; and
> (b)   the application has not been determined.

(4)   The Chapter I prohibition does not apply to a decision made by—
    (a)   a recognised self-regulating organisation,
    (b)   a recognised investment exchange, or
    (c)   a recognised clearing house,
to the extent to which the decision relates to any of that body's regulating provisions or specified practices.

(5)   The Chapter I prohibition does not apply to the specified practices of—
    (a)   a recognised self-regulating organisation, a recognised investment exchange or a recognised clearing house; or
    (b)   a person who is subject to—
        (i)   the rules of one of those bodies, or
        (ii)   the statements of principle, rules, regulations or codes of practice made by a designated agency in the exercise of functions transferred to it by a delegation order.

(6)   The Chapter I prohibition does not apply to any agreement the parties to which consist of or include—
    (a)   a recognised self-regulating organisation, a recognised investment exchange or a recognised clearing house; or
    (b)   a person who is subject to—
        (i)   the rules of one of those bodies, or
        (ii)   the statements of principle, rules, regulations or codes of practice made by a designated agency in the exercise of functions transferred to it by a delegation order,
to the extent to which the agreement consists of provisions the inclusion of which is required or contemplated by any of the body's regulating provisions or specified practices or by the statements of principle, rules, regulations or codes of practice of the agency.

(7)   The Chapter I prohibition does not apply to—
    (a)   any clearing arrangements; or
    (b)   any agreement between a recognised investment exchange and a recognised clearing house, to the extent to which the agreement consists of provisions the inclusion of which in the agreement is required or contemplated by any clearing arrangements.

(8)   If the recognition order in respect of a body of the kind mentioned in subsection (1)(a), (b) or (c) above is revoked, subsections (1) and (4) to (7) above are to have effect as if that body had continued to be recognised until the end of the period of six months beginning with the day on which the revocation took effect.

(9)   In this section—
    "the Chapter I prohibition" means the prohibition imposed by section 2(1) of the Competition Act 1998;
    "regulating provisions" means—
        (a)   in relation to a self-regulating organisation, any rules made, or guidance issued, by the organisation;
        (b)   in relation to an investment exchange, any rules made, or guidance issued, by the exchange;
        (c)   in relation to a clearing house, any rules made, or guidance issued, by the clearing house;
    "specified practices" means—
        (a)   in the case of a recognised self-regulating organisation, the practices mentioned in section 119(2)(a)(ii) and (iii) above (read with section 119(5) and (6)(a));
        (b)   in the case of a recognised investment exchange, the practices mentioned in section 119(2)(b)(ii) and (iii) above (read with section 119(5) and (6)(b));
        (c)   in the case of a recognised clearing house, the practices mentioned in section 119(2)(c)(ii) and (iii) above (read with section 119(5) and (6)(b));
        (d)   in the case of a person who is subject to the statements of principle, rules, regulations or codes of practice issued or made by a designated agency in the exercise of functions transferred to it by a delegation order, the practices mentioned in section 121(2)(c) above (read with section 121(4));

and expressions used in this section which are also used in Part I of the Competition Act 1998 are to be interpreted in the same way as for the purposes of that Part of that Act."

(3) Omit section 126 (certain practices not to constitute anti-competitive practices for the purposes of the Competition Act 1980).

(4) For section 127 (modification of statutory provisions in relation to recognised professional bodies), substitute—

"127 Application of Competition Act 1998 in relation to recognised professional bodies: Chapter I prohibition

(1) This section applies to—
  (a) any agreement for the constitution of a recognised professional body to the extent to which it relates to the rules or guidance of that body relating to the carrying on of investment business by persons certified by it ("investment business rules"); and
  (b) any other agreement, the parties to which consist of or include—
      (i) a recognised professional body,
      (ii) a person certified by such a body, or
      (iii) a member of such a body,
  and which contains a provision required or contemplated by that body's investment business rules.

(2) If it appears to the Treasury, in relation to some or all of the provisions of an agreement to which this section applies—
  (a) that the provisions in question do not have, and are not intended or likely to have, to any significant extent the effect of restricting, distorting or preventing competition; or
  (b) that the effect of restricting, distorting or preventing competition which the provisions in question do have, or are intended or are likely to have, is not greater than is necessary for the protection of investors,
the Treasury may make a declaration to that effect.

(3) If the Treasury make a declaration under this section, the Chapter I prohibition does not apply to the agreement to the extent to which the agreement consists of provisions to which the declaration relates.

(4) If the Treasury are satisfied that there has been a material change of circumstances, they may—
  (a) revoke a declaration made under this section, if they consider that the grounds on which it was made no longer exist;
  (b) vary such a declaration, if they consider that there are grounds for making a different declaration; or
  (c) make a declaration even though they have notified the Director of their intention not to do so.

(5) If the Treasury make, vary or revoke a declaration under this section they must notify the Director of their decision.

(6) If the Director proposes to exercise any Chapter III powers in respect of any provisions of an agreement to which this section applies, he must—
  (a) notify the Treasury of his intention to do so; and
  (b) give the Treasury particulars of the agreement and such other information—
      (i) as he considers will assist the Treasury to decide whether to exercise their powers under this section; or
      (ii) as the Treasury may request.

(7) The Director may not exercise his Chapter III powers in respect of any provisions of an agreement to which this section applies, unless the Treasury—
  (a) have notified him that they have not made a declaration in respect of those provisions under this section and that they do not intend to make such a declaration; or
  (b) have revoked a declaration under this section and a period of six months beginning with the date on which the revocation took effect has expired.

(8)   A declaration under this section ceases to have effect if the agreement to which it relates ceases to be one to which this section applies.

(9)   In this section—

"the Chapter I prohibition" means the prohibition imposed by section 2(1) of the Competition Act 1998,

"Chapter III powers" means the powers given to the Director by Chapter III of Part I of that Act so far as they relate to the Chapter I prohibition, and

expressions used in this section which are also used in Part I of the Competition Act 1998 are to be interpreted in the same way as for the purposes of that Part of that Act.

(10)   In this section references to an agreement are to be read as applying equally to, or in relation to, a decision or concerted practice.

(11)   In the application of this section to decisions and concerted practices, references to provisions of an agreement are to be read as references to elements of a decision or concerted practice."

Definitions   For "investment business", see the Financial Services Act 1986, s 1(2), Sch 1, Pts II, III; for "self-regulating organisation", see s 8(1) of that Act; for "member", "rules" and "guidance" in relation to a professional body, see s 16(2)–(4) of that Act; for "clearing arrangements", see s 38(2) of that Act; for "delegation order" and "designated agency", see s 114(3) of that Act; for "the Director", see s 122(1) of that Act; for "certified", "recognised clearing house", "recognised investment exchange", "recognised professional body", "recognised self-regulating organisation" and "recognition order", see s 207(1) of that Act.
References   See paras 2.52, 2.53.

PART II
COMPANIES

The Companies Act 1989 (c 40)

2.—(1)   The Companies Act 1989 is amended as follows.

(2)   In Schedule 14, for paragraph 9 (exclusion of certain agreements from the Restrictive Trade Practices Act 1976), substitute—

"The Competition Act 1998

9.—(1)   The Chapter I prohibition does not apply to an agreement for the constitution of a recognised supervisory or qualifying body to the extent to which it relates to—

(a)   rules of, or guidance issued by, the body; and

(b)   incidental matters connected with the rules or guidance.

(2)   The Chapter I prohibition does not apply to an agreement the parties to which consist of or include—

(a)   a recognised supervisory or qualifying body, or

(b)   any person mentioned in paragraph 3(5) or (6) above,

to the extent to which the agreement consists of provisions the inclusion of which in the agreement is required or contemplated by the rules or guidance of that body.

(3)   The Chapter I prohibition does not apply to the practices mentioned in paragraph 3(4)(a) and (b) above.

(4)   Where a recognition order is revoked, sub-paragraphs (1) to (3) above are to continue to apply for a period of six months beginning with the day on which the revocation takes effect, as if the order were still in force.

(5)   In this paragraph—

(a)   "the Chapter I prohibition" means the prohibition imposed by section 2(1) of the Competition Act 1998,

(b)   references to an agreement are to be read as applying equally to, or in relation to, a decision or concerted practice,

and expressions used in this paragraph which are also used in Part I of the Competition Act 1998 are to be interpreted in the same way as for the purposes of that Part of that Act.

(6)   In the application of this paragraph to decisions and concerted practices, references to provisions of an agreement are to be read as references to elements of a decision or concerted practice."

The Companies (Northern Ireland) Order 1990 (SI 1990/593 (NI 5))

3.—(1) The Companies (Northern Ireland) Order 1990 is amended as follows.

(2) In Schedule 14, for paragraph 9 (exclusion of certain agreements from the Restrictive Trade Practices Act 1976), substitute—

"The Competition Act 1998

9.—(1)   The Chapter I prohibition does not apply to an agreement for the constitution of a recognised supervisory or qualifying body to the extent to which it relates to—
    (a)   rules of, or guidance issued by, the body; and
    (b)   incidental matters connected with the rules or guidance.

(2)   The Chapter I prohibition does not apply to an agreement the parties to which consist of or include—
    (a)   a recognised supervisory or qualifying body, or
    (b)   any person mentioned in paragraph 3(5) or (6),
to the extent to which the agreement consists of provisions the inclusion of which in the agreement is required or contemplated by the rules or guidance of that body.

(3)   The Chapter I prohibition does not apply to the practices mentioned in paragraph 3(4)(a) and (b).

(4)   Where a recognition order is revoked, sub-paragraphs (1) to (3) are to continue to apply for a period of 6 months beginning with the day on which the revocation takes effect, as if the order were still in force.

(5)   In this paragraph—
    (a)   "the Chapter I prohibition" means the prohibition imposed by section 2(1) of the Competition Act 1998,
    (b)   references to an agreement are to be read as applying equally to, or in relation to, a decision or concerted practice,
and expressions used in this paragraph which are also used in Part I of the Competition Act 1998 are to be interpreted in the same way as for the purposes of that Part of that Act.

(6)   In the application of this paragraph to decisions and concerted practices, references to provisions of an agreement are to be read as references to elements of a decision or concerted practice."

Definitions   For "supervisory body", see the Companies Act 1989, s 30(1); as to "rules" of a supervisory body, see s 30(3) of that Act; as to "guidance" issued by a supervisory body, see s 30(4) of that Act; for "recognised supervisory body", see s 30(5) of, Sch 11 to, that Act; for "qualifying body", see s 32(1) of that Act; as to "rules" of a qualifying body, see s 32(2) of that Act; as to "guidance" issued by a qualifying body, see s 32(3) of that Act; for "recognition order", see Sch 11, para 2(1) or Sch 12, para 2(1) to that Act; for "recognised qualifying body", see Sch 12, para 2(1) to that Act.
References   See paras 2.52, 2.54.

PART III
BROADCASTING

The Broadcasting Act 1990 (c 42)

4.—(1) The Broadcasting Act 1990 is amended as follows.

(2) In section 194A (which modifies the Restrictive Trade Practices Act 1976 in its application to agreements relating to Channel 3 news provision), for subsections (2) to (6), substitute—

"(2)   If, having sought the advice of the Director, it appears to the Secretary of State, in relation to some or all of the provisions of a relevant agreement, that the conditions mentioned in subsection (3) are satisfied, he may make a declaration to that effect.

(3)　The conditions are that—

(a)　the provisions in question do not have, and are not intended or likely to have, to any significant extent the effect of restricting, distorting or preventing competition; or

(b)　the effect of restricting, distorting or preventing competition which the provisions in question do have or are intended or are likely to have, is not greater than is necessary—

(i)　in the case of a relevant agreement falling within subsection (1)(a), for securing the appointment by holders of regional Channel 3 licences of a single body corporate to be the appointed news provider for the purposes of section 31(2), or

(ii)　in the case of a relevant agreement falling within subsection (1)(b), for compliance by them with conditions included in their licences by virtue of section 31(1) and (2).

(4)　If the Secretary of State makes a declaration under this section, the Chapter I prohibition does not apply to the agreement to the extent to which the agreement consists of provisions to which the declaration relates.

(5)　If the Secretary of State is satisfied that there has been a material change of circumstances, he may—

(a)　revoke a declaration made under this section, if he considers that the grounds on which it was made no longer exist;

(b)　vary such a declaration, if he considers that there are grounds for making a different declaration; or

(c)　make a declaration, even though he has notified the Director of his intention not to do so.

(6)　If the Secretary of State makes, varies or revokes a declaration under this section, he must notify the Director of his decision.

(7)　The Director may not exercise any Chapter III powers in respect of a relevant agreement, unless—

(a)　he has notified the Secretary of State of his intention to do so; and

(b)　the Secretary of State—

(i)　has notified the Director that he has not made a declaration in respect of the agreement, or provisions of the agreement, under this section and that he does not intend to make such a declaration; or

(ii)　has revoked a declaration under this section and a period of six months beginning with the date on which the revocation took effect has expired.

(8)　If the Director proposes to exercise any Chapter III powers in respect of a relevant agreement, he must give the Secretary of State particulars of the agreement and such other information—

(a)　as he considers will assist the Secretary of State to decide whether to exercise his powers under this section; or

(b)　as the Secretary of State may request.

(9)　In this section—

"the Chapter I prohibition" means the prohibition imposed by section 2(1) of the Competition Act 1998;

"Chapter III powers" means the powers given to the Director by Chapter III of Part I of that Act so far as they relate to the Chapter I prohibition;

"Director" means the Director General of Fair Trading;

"regional Channel 3 licence" has the same meaning as in Part I;

and expressions used in this section which are also used in Part I of the Competition Act 1998 are to be interpreted in the same way as for the purposes of that Part of that Act.

(10)　In this section references to an agreement are to be read as applying equally to, or in relation to, a decision or concerted practice.

(11)　In the application of this section to decisions and concerted practices, references to provisions of an agreement are to be read as references to elements of a decision or concerted practice."

Networking arrangements under the Broadcasting Act 1990 (c 42)

5.—(1) The Chapter I prohibition does not apply in respect of any networking arrangements to the extent to which they—

    (a)   are subject to Schedule 4 to the Broadcasting Act 1990 (competition references with respect to networking arrangements); or

    (b)   contain provisions which have been considered under that Schedule.

(2) The Independent Television Commission ("ITC") must publish a list of the networking arrangements which in their opinion are excluded from the Chapter I prohibition by virtue of sub-paragraph (1).

(3) The ITC must—

    (a)   consult the Director before publishing the list, and

    (b)   publish the list in such a way as they think most suitable for bringing it to the attention of persons who, in their opinion, would be affected by, or likely to have an interest in, it.

(4) In this paragraph "networking arrangements" means—

    (a)   any arrangements entered into as mentioned in section 39(4) or (7)(b) of the Broadcasting Act 1990, or

    (b)   any agreements—

        (i)   which do not constitute arrangements of the kind mentioned in paragraph (a), but

        (ii)   which are made for the purpose mentioned in section 39(1) of that Act, or

    (c)   any modification of the arrangements or agreements mentioned in paragraph (a) or (b).

Definitions   For "the Chapter I prohibition", see s 2(8); for "the Director" and as to "person", see s 59(1).

References   See paras 2.52, 2.55.

PART IV
ENVIRONMENTAL PROTECTION

Producer responsibility obligations

6.—(1) The Environment Act 1995 is amended as follows.

(2) In section 94(1) (supplementary provisions about regulations imposing producer responsibility obligations on prescribed persons), after paragraph (o), insert—

    "(oa)the exclusion or modification of any provision of Part I of the Competition Act 1998 in relation to exemption schemes or in relation to any agreement, decision or concerted practice at least one of the parties to which is an operator of an exemption scheme;".

(3) After section 94(6), insert—

    "(6A) Expressions used in paragraph (oa) of subsection (1) above which are also used in Part I of the Competition Act 1998 are to be interpreted in the same way as for the purposes of that Part of that Act."

(4) After section 94, insert—

"94A Producer responsibility: competition matters

    (1)   For the purposes of this section, the relevant paragraphs are paragraphs (n), (o), (oa) and (ya) of section 94(1) above.

    (2)   Regulations made by the virtue of any of the relevant paragraphs may include transitional provision in respect of agreements or exemption schemes—

        (a)   in respect of which information has been required for the purposes of competition scrutiny under any regulation made by virtue of paragraph (ya);

        (b)   which are being, or have been, considered for the purposes of competition scrutiny under any regulation made by virtue of paragraph (n) or (ya); or

(c)   in respect of which provisions of the Restrictive Trade Practices Acts 1976 and 1977 have been modified or excluded in accordance with any regulation made by virtue of paragraph (o).

(3)   Subsections (2), (3), (5) to (7) and (10) of section 93 above do not apply to a statutory instrument which contains only regulations made by virtue of any of the relevant paragraphs or subsection (2) above.

(4)   Such a statutory instrument shall be subject to annulment in pursuance of a resolution of either House of Parliament."

Definitions   In the Environment Act 1995, for "exemption scheme" and "operator", see s 94(6) of that Act, and for "modification", see s 124(1) thereof.
References   See paras 2.52, 2.56.

SCHEDULE 3

Sections 3(1)(c) and 19(1)(b)

GENERAL EXCLUSIONS

Planning obligations

1.—(1)   The Chapter I prohibition does not apply to an agreement—
    (a)   to the extent to which it is a planning obligation;
    (b)   which is made under section 75 (agreements regulating development or use of land) or 246 (agreements relating to Crown land) of the Town and Country Planning (Scotland) Act 1997; or
    (c)   which is made under Article 40 of the Planning (Northern Ireland) Order 1991.

(2)   In sub-paragraph (1)(a), "planning obligation" means—
    (a)   a planning obligation for the purposes of section 106 of the Town and Country Planning Act 1990; or
    (b)   a planning obligation for the purposes of section 299A of that Act.

Section 21(2) agreements

2.—(1)   The Chapter I prohibition does not apply to an agreement in respect of which a direction under section 21(2) of the Restrictive Trade Practices Act 1976 is in force immediately before the coming into force of section 2 ("a section 21(2) agreement").

(2)   If a material variation is made to a section 21(2) agreement, sub-paragraph (1) ceases to apply to the agreement on the coming into force of the variation.

(3)   Sub-paragraph (1) does not apply to a particular section 21(2) agreement if the Director gives a direction under this paragraph to that effect.

(4)   If the Director is considering whether to give a direction under this paragraph, he may by notice in writing require any party to the agreement in question to give him such information in connection with the agreement as he may require.

(5)   The Director may give a direction under this paragraph only as provided in sub-paragraph (6) or (7).

(6)   If at the end of such period as may be specified in rules under section 51 a person has failed, without reasonable excuse, to comply with a requirement imposed under sub-paragraph (4), the Director may give a direction under this paragraph.

(7)   The Director may also give a direction under this paragraph if he considers—
    (a)   that the agreement will, if not excluded, infringe the Chapter I prohibition; and
    (b)   that he is not likely to grant it an unconditional individual exemption.

(8)   For the purposes of sub-paragraph (7) an individual exemption is unconditional if no conditions or obligations are imposed in respect of it under section 4(3)(a).

(9) A direction under this paragraph—
    (a)   must be in writing;
    (b)   may be made so as to have effect from a date specified in the direction (which may not be earlier than the date on which it is given).

EEA Regulated Markets

3.—(1) The Chapter I prohibition does not apply to an agreement for the constitution of an EEA regulated market to the extent to which the agreement relates to any of the rules made, or guidance issued, by that market.

(2) The Chapter I prohibition does not apply to a decision made by an EEA regulated market, to the extent to which the decision relates to any of the market's regulating provisions.

(3) The Chapter I prohibition does not apply to—
    (a)   any practices of an EEA regulated market; or
    (b)   any practices which are trading practices in relation to an EEA regulated market.

(4) The Chapter I prohibition does not apply to an agreement the parties to which are or include—
    (a)   an EEA regulated market, or
    (b)   a person who is subject to the rules of that market,
to the extent to which the agreement consists of provisions the inclusion of which is required or contemplated by the regulating provisions of that market.

(5) In this paragraph—
"EEA regulated market" is a market which—
    (a)   is listed by an EEA State other than the United Kingdom pursuant to article 16 of Council Directive No 93/22/EEC of 10th May 1993 on investment services in the securities field; and
    (b)   operates without any requirement that a person dealing on the market should have a physical presence in the EEA State from which any trading facilities are provided or on any trading floor that the market may have;
"EEA State" means a State which is a contracting party to the EEA Agreement;
"regulating provisions", in relation to an EEA regulated market, means—
    (a)   rules made, or guidance issued, by that market,
    (b)   practices of that market, or
    (c)   practices which, in relation to that market, are trading practices;
"trading practices", in relation to an EEA regulated market, means practices of persons who are subject to the rules made by that market, and—
    (a)   which relate to business in respect of which those persons are subject to the rules of that market, and which are required or contemplated by those rules or by guidance issued by that market; or
    (b)   which are otherwise attributable to the conduct of that market as such.

Services of general economic interest etc

4. Neither the Chapter I prohibition nor the Chapter II prohibition applies to an undertaking entrusted with the operation of services of general economic interest or having the character of a revenue-producing monopoly in so far as the prohibition would obstruct the performance, in law or in fact, of the particular tasks assigned to that undertaking.

Compliance with legal requirements

5.—(1) The Chapter I prohibition does not apply to an agreement to the extent to which it is made in order to comply with a legal requirement.

(2) The Chapter II prohibition does not apply to conduct to the extent to which it is engaged in an order to comply with a legal requirement.

(3) In this paragraph "legal requirement" means a requirement—
    (a)   imposed by or under any enactment in force in the United Kingdom;
    (b)   imposed by or under the Treaty or the EEA Agreement and having legal effect in the United Kingdom without further enactment; or
    (c)   imposed by or under the law in force in another Member State and having legal effect in the United Kingdom.

Avoidance of conflict with international obligations

6.—(1) If the Secretary of State is satisfied that, in order to avoid a conflict between provisions of this Part and an international obligation of the United Kingdom, it would be appropriate for the Chapter I prohibition not to apply to—

(a) a particular agreement, or

(b) any agreement of a particular description,

he may by order exclude the agreement, or agreements of that description, from the Chapter I prohibition.

(2) An order under sub-paragraph (1) may make provision for the exclusion of the agreement or agreements to which the order applies, or of such of them as may be specified, only in specified circumstances.

(3) An order under sub-paragraph (1) may also provide that the Chapter I prohibition is to be deemed never to have applied in relation to the agreement or agreements, or in relation to such of them as may be specified.

(4) If the Secretary of State is satisfied that, in order to avoid a conflict between provisions of this Part and an international obligation of the United Kingdom, it would be appropriate for the Chapter II prohibition not to apply in particular circumstances, he may by order provide for it not to apply in such circumstances as may be specified.

(5) An order under sub-paragraph (4) may provide that the Chapter II prohibition is to be deemed never to have applied in relation to specified conduct.

(6) An international arrangement relating to civil aviation and designated by an order-made by the Secretary of State is to be treated as an international obligation for the purposes of this paragraph.

(7) In this paragraph and paragraph 7 "specified" means specified in the order.

Public policy

7.—(1) If the Secretary of State is satisfied that there are exceptional and compelling reasons of public policy why the Chapter I prohibition ought not to apply to—

(a) a particular agreement, or

(b) any agreement of a particular description,

he may by order exclude the agreement, or agreements of that description, from the Chapter I prohibition.

(2) An order under sub-paragraph (1) may make provision for the exclusion of the agreement or agreements to which the order applies, or of such of them as may be specified, only in specified circumstances.

(3) An order under sub-paragraph (1) may also provide that the Chapter I prohibition is to be deemed never to have applied in relation to the agreement or agreements, or in relation to such of them as may be specified.

(4) If the Secretary of State is satisfied that there are exceptional and compelling reasons of public policy why the Chapter II prohibition ought not to apply in particular circumstances, he may by order provide for it not to apply in such circumstances as may be specified.

(5) An order under sub-paragraph (4) may provide that the Chapter II prohibition is to be deemed never to have applied in relation to specified conduct.

Coal and steel

8.—(1) The Chapter I prohibition does not apply to an agreement which relates to a coal or steel product to the extent to which the ECSC Treaty gives the Commission exclusive jurisdiction in the matter.

(2) Sub-paragraph (1) ceases to have effect on the date on which the ECSC Treaty expires ("the expiry date").

(3)   The Chapter II prohibition does not apply to conduct which relates to a coal or steel product to the extent to which the ECSC Treaty gives the Commission exclusive jurisdiction in the matter.

(4)   Sub-paragraph (3) ceases to have effect on the expiry date.

(5)   In this paragraph—

"coal or steel product" means any product of a kind listed in Annex I to the ECSC Treaty; and

"ECSC Treaty" means the Treaty establishing the European Coal and Steel Community.

Agricultural products

9.—(1)   The Chapter I prohibition does not apply to an agreement to the extent to which it relates to production of or trade in an agricultural product and—

(a)   forms an integral part of a national market organisation;

(b)   is necessary for the attainment of the objectives set out in Article 39 of the Treaty; or

(c)   is an agreement of farmers or farmers' associations (or associations of such associations) belonging to a single member State which concerns—

(i)   the production or sale of agricultural products, or

(ii)   the use of joint facilities for the storage, treatment or processing of agricultural products,

and under which there is no obligation to charge identical prices.

(2)   If the Commission determines that an agreement does not fulfil the conditions specified by the provision for agricultural products for exclusion from Article 85(1), the exclusion provided by this paragraph ("the agriculture exclusion") is to be treated as ceasing to apply to the agreement on the date of the decision.

(3)   The agriculture exclusion does not apply to a particular agreement if the Director gives a direction under this paragraph to that effect.

(4)   If the Director is considering whether to give a direction under this paragraph, he may by notice in writing require any party to the agreement in question to give him such information in connection with the agreement as he may require.

(5)   The Director may give a direction under this paragraph only as provided in sub-paragraph (6) or (7).

(6)   If at the end of such period as may be specified in rules under section 51 a person has failed, without reasonable excuse, to comply with a requirement imposed under sub-paragraph (4), the Director may give a direction under this paragraph.

(7)   The Director may also give a direction under this paragraph if he considers that an agreement (whether or not he considers that it infringes the Chapter I prohibition) is likely, or is intended, substantially and unjustifiably to prevent, restrict or distort competition in relation to an agricultural product.

(8)   A direction under this paragraph—

(a)   must be in writing;

(b)   may be made so as to have effect from a date specified in the direction (which may not be earlier than the date on which it is given).

(9)   In this paragraph—

"agricultural product" means any product of a kind listed in Annex II to the Treaty; and

"provision for agricultural products" means Council Regulation (EEC) No 26/62 of 4th April 1962 applying certain rules of competition to production of and trade in agricultural products.

Definitions   For "the Chapter I prohibition", see s 2(8); for "individual exemption", see s 4(2); for "the Chapter II prohibition", see s 18(4); for "Article 85", "the Commission", "the Director", "the EEA Agreement" and "the Treaty" and as to "information" and "person", see s 59(1).
References   See paras 2.58–2.69, 3.32, 7.21.

SCHEDULE 4

Section 3(1)(d)

PROFESSIONAL RULES

PART I
EXCLUSION

General

1.—(1) To the extent to which an agreement (either on its own or when taken together with another agreement)—

(a) constitutes a designated professional rule,

(b) imposes obligations arising from designated professionals, or

(c) constitutes an agreement to act in accordance with such rules,

the Chapter I prohibition does not apply to the agreement.

(2) In this Schedule—

"designated" means designated by the Secretary of State under paragraph 2;

"professional rules" means rules regulating a professional service or the persons providing, or wishing to provide, that service;

"professional service" means any of the services described in Part II of this Schedule; and

"rules" includes regulations, codes of practice and statements of principle.

Designated rules

2.—(1) The Secretary of State must establish and maintain a list designating, for the purposes of this Schedule, rules—

(a) which are notified to him under paragraph 3; and

(b) which, in his opinion, are professional rules.

(2) The list is to be established, and any alteration in the list is to be effected, by an order made by the Secretary of State.

(3) The designation of any rule is to have effect from such date (which may be earlier than the date on which the order listing it is made) as may be specified in that order.

Application for designation

3.—(1) Any body regulating a professional service or the persons who provide, or wish to provide, that service may apply to the Secretary of State for rules of that body to be designated.

(2) An application under this paragraph must—

(a) be accompanied by a copy of the rules to which it relates; and

(b) be made in the prescribed manner.

Alterations

4.—(1) A rule does not cease to be a designated professional rule merely because it is altered.

(2) If such a rule is altered (whether by being modified, revoked or replaced), the body concerned must notify the Secretary of State and the Director of the alteration as soon as is reasonably practicable.

Reviewing the list

5.—(1) The Secretary of State must send to the Director—

(a) a copy of any order made under paragraph 2; and

(b) a copy of the professional rules to which the order relates.

(2) The Director must—

(a) retain any copy of a professional rule which is sent to him under sub-paragraph (1)(b) so long as the rule remains in force;

(b) maintain a copy of the list, as altered from time to time; and

(c) keep the list under review.

(3)   If the Director considers—

    (a)   that, with a view to restricting the exclusion provided by this Schedule, some or all of the rules of a particular body should no longer be designated, or

    (b)   that rules which are not designated should be designated,

he must advise the Secretary of State accordingly.

Removal from the list

6.—(1)   This paragraph applies if the Secretary of State receives advice under paragraph 5(3)(a).

(2)   If it appears to the Secretary of State that another Minister of the Crown has functions in relation to the professional service concerned, he must consult that Minister.

(3)   If it appears to the Secretary of State, having considered the Director's advice and the advice of any other Minister resulting from consultation under sub-paragraph (2), that the rules in question should no longer be designated, he may by order revoke their designation.

(4)   Revocation of a designation is to have effect from such date as the order revoking it may specify.

Inspection

7.—(1)   Any person may inspect, and take a copy of—

    (a)   any entry in the list of designated professional rules as kept by the Director under paragraph 5(2); or

    (b)   any copy of professional rules retained by him under paragraph 5(1).

(2)   The right conferred by sub-paragraph (1) is to be exercised only—

    (a)   at a time which is reasonable;

    (b)   on payment of such fee as the Director may determine; and

    (c)   at such offices of his as the Director may direct.

Definitions   For "the Chapter I prohibition", see s 2(8); for "the Director", "Minister of the Crown" and "prescribed" and as to "person", see s 59(1).
References   See paras 2.71–2.73.

PART II
PROFESSIONAL SERVICES

Legal

8.   The services of barristers, advocates or solicitors.

Medical

9.   The provision of medical or surgical advice or attendance and the performance of surgical operations.

Dental

10.   Any services falling within the practice of dentistry within the meaning of the Dentists Act 1984.

Ophthalmic

11.   The testing of sight.

Veterinary

12.   Any services which constitute veterinary surgery within the meaning of the Veterinary Surgeons Act 1966.

Nursing

13.   The services of nurses.

Midwifery

14.   The services of midwives.

Physiotherapy

15.   The services of physiotherapists.

Chiropody

16. The services of chiropodists.

Architectural

17. The services of architects.

Accounting and auditing

18. The making or preparation of accounts or accounting records and the examination, verification and auditing of financial statements.

Insolvency

19. Insolvency services within the meaning of section 428 of the Insolvency Act 1986.

Patent agency

20. The services of registered patent agents (within the meaning of Part V of the Copyright, Designs and Patents Act 1988).

21. The services of persons carrying on for gain in the United Kingdom the business of acting as agents or other representatives for or obtaining European patents or for the purpose of conducting proceedings in relation to applications for or otherwise in connection with such patents before the European Patent Office or the comptroller and whose names appear on the European list (within the meaning of Part V of the Copyright, Designs and Patents Act 1988).

Parliamentary agency

22. The services of parliamentary agents entered in the register in either House of Parliament as agents entitled to practise both in promoting and in opposing Bills.

Surveying

23. The services of surveyors of land, of quantity surveyors, of surveyors of buildings or other structures and of surveyors of ships.

Engineering and technology etc

24. The services of persons practising or employed as consultants in the field of—
    (a)   civil engineering;
    (b)   mechanical, aeronautical, marine, electrical or electronic engineering;
    (c)   mining, quarrying, soil analysis or other forms of mineralogy or geology;
    (d)   agronomy, forestry, livestock rearing or ecology;
    (e)   metallurgy, chemistry, biochemistry or physics; or
    (f)   any other form of engineering or technology analogous to those mentioned in sub-paragraphs (a) to (e).

Educational

25. The provision of education or training.

Religious

26. The services of ministers of religion.

References   See paras 2.71–2.72.

SCHEDULE 5

Section 12(2)

NOTIFICATION UNDER CHAPTER I: PROCEDURE

Terms used

1. In this Schedule—
    "applicant" means the person making an application to which this Schedule applies;
    "application" means an application under section 13 or an application under section 14;

"application for guidance" means an application under section 13;
"application for a decision" means an application under section 14;
"rules" means rules made by the Director under section 51; and
"specified" means specified in the rules.

General rules about applications

2.—(1) An application must be made in accordance with rules.

(2) A party to an agreement who makes an application must take all reasonable steps to notify all other parties to the agreement of whom he is aware—
 (a) that the application has been made; and
 (b) as to whether it is for guidance or a decision.

(3) Notification under sub-paragraph (2) must be in the specified manner.

Preliminary investigation

3.—(1) If, after a preliminary investigation of an application, the Director considers that it is likely—
 (a) that the agreement concerned will infringe the Chapter I prohibition, and
 (b) that it would not be appropriate to grant the agreement an individual exemption,
he may make a decision ("a provisional decision") under this paragraph.

(2) If the Director makes a provisional decision—
 (a) the Director must notify the applicant in writing of his provisional decision; and
 (b) section 13(4) or (as the case may be) section 14(4) is to be taken as never having applied.

(3) When making a provisional decision, the Director must follow such procedures as may be specified.

(4) A provisional decision does not affect the final determination of an application.

(5) If the Director has given notice to the applicant under sub-paragraph (2) in respect of an application for a decision, he may continue with the application under section 14.

Procedure on application for guidance

4. When determining an application for guidance, the Director must follow such procedure as may be specified.

Procedure on application for a decision

5.—(1) When determining an application for a decision, the Director must follow such procedure as may be specified.

(2) The Director must arrange for the application to be published in such a way as he thinks most suitable for bringing it to the attention of those likely to be affected by it, unless he is satisfied that it will be sufficient for him to seek information from one or more particular persons other than the applicant.

(3) In determining the application, the Director must take into account any representations made to him by persons other than the applicant.

Publication of decisions

6. If the Director determines an application for a decision he must publish his decision, together with his reasons for making it, in such manner as may be specified.

Delay by the Director

7.—(1) This paragraph applies if the court is satisfied, on the application of a person aggrieved by the failure of the Director to determine an application for a decision in accordance with the specified procedure, that there has been undue delay on the part of the Director in determining the application.

(2) The court may give such directions to the Director as it considers appropriate for securing that the application is determined without unnecessary further delay.

Definitions   For "the Chapter I prohibition", see s 2(8); for "individual exemption", see s 4(2); for "the court" and "the Director" and as to "person", see s 59(1).
References   See paras 4.46, 4.52, 4.69.

SCHEDULE 6

Section 20(2)

NOTIFICATION UNDER CHAPTER II: PROCEDURE

Terms used

1. In this Schedule—
   "applicant" means the person making an application to which this Schedule applies;
   "application" means an application under section 21 or an application under section 22;
   "application for guidance" means an application under section 21;
   "application for a decision" means an application under section 22;
   "other party", in relation to conduct of two or more persons, means one of those persons other than the applicant;
   "rules" means rules made by the Director under section 51; and
   "specified" means specified in the rules.

General rules about applications

2.—(1) An application must be made in accordance with rules.

(2) If the conduct to which an application relates is conduct of two or more persons, the applicant must take all reasonable steps to notify all of the other parties of whom he is aware—
   (a)   that the application has been made; and
   (b)   as to whether it is for guidance or a decision.

(3) Notification under sub-paragraph (2) must be in the specified manner.

Preliminary investigation

3.—(1) If, after a preliminary investigation of an application, the Director considers that it is likely that the conduct concerned will infringe the Chapter II prohibition, he may make a decision ("a provisional decision") under this paragraph.

(2) If the Director makes a provisional decision, he must notify the applicant in writing of that decision.

(3) When making a provisional decision, the Director must follow such procedure as may be specified.

(4) A provisional decision does not affect the final determination of an application.

(5) If the Director has given notice to the applicant under sub-paragraph (2) in respect of an application for a decision, he may continue with the application under section 22.

Procedure on application for guidance

4.   When determining an application for guidance, the Director must follow such procedure as may be specified.

Procedure on application for a decision

5.—(1) When determining an application for a decision, the Director must follow such procedure as may be specified.

(2) The Director must arrange for the application to be published in such a way as he thinks most suitable for bringing it to the attention of those likely to be affected by it, unless he is satisfied that it will be sufficient for him to seek information from one or more particular persons other than the applicant.

(3) In determining the application, the Director must take into account any representations made to him by persons other than the applicant.

Publication of decisions

6. If the Director determines an application for a decision he must publish his decision, together with his reasons for making it, in such manner as may be specified.

Delay by the Director

7.—(1) This paragraph applies if the court is satisfied, on the application of a person aggrieved by the failure of the Director to determine an application for a decision in accordance with the specified procedure, that there has been undue delay on the part of the Director in determining the application.

(2) The court may give such directions to the Director as it considers appropriate for securing that the application is determined without unnecessary further delay.

Definitions   For "the Chapter II prohibition", see s 18(4); for "the court" and "the Director" and as to "information" and "person", see s 59(1).
References   See paras 4.46, 4.52.

SCHEDULE 7

Section 45(7)

THE COMPETITION COMMISSION

PART I
GENERAL

Interpretation

1. In this Schedule—
   "the 1973 Act" means the Fair Trading Act 1973;
   "appeal panel member" means a member appointed under paragraph 2(1)(a);
   "Chairman" means the chairman of the Commission;
   "the Commission" means the Competition Commission;
   "Council" has the meaning given in paragraph 5;
   "general functions" means any functions of the Commission other than functions—
   (a)   in connection with appeals under this Act; or
   (b)   which are to be discharged by the Council;
   "member" means a member of the Commission;
   "newspaper merger reference" means a newspaper merger reference under section 59 of the 1973 Act;
   "President" has the meaning given by paragraph 4(2);
   "reporting panel member" means a member appointed under paragraph 2(1)(b);
   "secretary" means the secretary of the Commission appointed under paragraph 9; and
   "specialist panel member" means a member appointed under any of the provisions mentioned in paragraph 2(1)(d).

Membership of the Commission

2.—(1) The Commission is to consist of—
   (a)   members appointed by the Secretary of State to form a panel for the purposes of the Commission's functions in relation to appeals;
   (b)   members appointed by the Secretary of State to form a panel for the purposes of the Commission's general functions;
   (c)   members appointed (in accordance with paragraph 15(5)) from the panel maintained under paragraph 22;
   (d)   members appointed by the Secretary of State under or by virtue of—
        (i)   section 12(4) or 14(8) of the Water Industry Act 1991;
        (ii)   section 12(9) of the Electricity Act 1989;
        (iii)   section 13(10) of the Telecommunications Act 1984;
        (iv)   Article 15(9) of the Electricity (Northern Ireland) Order 1992.

(2) A person who is appointed as a member of a kind mentioned in one of paragraphs (a) to (c) of sub-paragraph (3) may also be appointed as a member of either or both of the other kinds mentioned in those paragraphs.

(3) The kinds of member are—
    (a) an appeal panel member;
    (b) a reporting panel member;
    (c) a specialist panel member.

(4) Before appointing a person who is qualified for appointment to the panel of chairmen (see paragraph 26(2)), the Secretary of State must consult the Lord Chancellor or Lord Advocate, as he considers appropriate.

(5) The validity of the Commission's proceedings is not affected by a defect in the appointment of a member.

Chairman and deputy chairmen

3.—(1) The Commission is to have a chairman appointed by the Secretary of State from among the reporting panel members.

(2) The Secretary of State may appoint one or more of the reporting panel members to act as deputy chairman.

(3) The Chairman, and any deputy chairman, may resign that office at any time by notice in writing addressed to the Secretary of State.

(4) If the Chairman (or a deputy chairman) ceases to be a member he also ceases to be Chairman (or a deputy chairman).

(5) If the Chairman is absent or otherwise unable to act, or there is no chairman, any of his functions may be performed—
    (a) if there is one deputy chairman, by him;
    (b) if there is more than one—
        (i) by the deputy chairman designated by the Secretary of State; or
        (ii) if no such designation has been made, by the deputy chairman designated by the deputy chairmen;
    (c) if there is no deputy chairman able to act—
        (i) by the member designated by the Secretary of State; or
        (ii) if no such designation has been made, by the member designated by the Commission.

President

4.—(1) The Secretary of State must appoint one of the appeal panel members to preside over the discharge of the Commission's functions in relation to appeals.

(2) The member so appointed is to be known as the President of the Competition Commission Appeal Tribunals (but is referred to in this Schedule as "the President").

(3) The Secretary of State may not appoint a person to be the President unless that person—
    (a) has a ten year general qualification within the meaning of section 71 of the Courts and Legal Services Act 1990,
    (b) is an advocate or solicitor in Scotland of at least ten years' standing, or
    (c) is—
        (i) a member of the Bar of Northern Ireland of at least ten years' standing, or
        (ii) a solicitor of the Supreme Court of Northern Ireland of at least ten years' standing,
and appears to the Secretary of State to have appropriate experience and knowledge of competition law and practice.

(4) Before appointing the President, the Secretary of State must consult the Lord Chancellor or Lord Advocate, as he considers appropriate.

(5) If the President ceases to be a member he also ceases to be President.

The Council

5.—(1) The Commission is to have a management board to be known as the Competition Commission Council (but referred to in this Schedule as "the Council").

(2) The Council is to consist of—
    (a)   the Chairman;
    (b)   the President;
    (c)   such other members as the Secretary of State may appoint; and
    (d)   the secretary.

(3) In exercising its functions under paragraphs 3 and 7 to 12 and paragraph 5 of Schedule 8, the Commission is to act through the Council.

(4) The Council may determine its own procedure including, in particular, its quorum.

(5) The Chairman (and any person acting as Chairman) is to have a casting vote on any question being decided by the Council.

Term of office

6.—(1) Subject to the provisions of this Schedule, each member is to hold and vacate office in accordance with the terms of his appointment.

(2) A person is not to be appointed as a member for more than five years at a time.

(3) Any member may at any time resign by notice in writing addressed to the Secretary of State.

(4) The Secretary of State may remove a member on the ground of incapacity or misbehaviour.

(5) No person is to be prevented from being appointed as a member merely because he has previously been a member.

Expenses, remuneration and pensions

7.—(1) The Secretary of State shall pay to the Commission such sums as he considers appropriate to enable it to perform its functions.

(2) The Commission may pay, or make provision for paying, to or in respect of each member such salaries or other remuneration and such pensions, allowances, fees, expenses or gratuities as the Secretary of State may determine.

(3) If a person ceases to be a member otherwise than on the expiry of his term of office and it appears to the Secretary of State that there are special circumstances which make it right for him to receive compensation, the Commission may make a payment to him of such amount as the Secretary of State may determine.

(4) The approval of the Treasury is required for—
    (a)   any payment under sub-paragraph (1);
    (b)   any determination of the Secretary of State under sub-paragraph (2) or (3).

The Commission's powers

8. Subject to the provisions of this Schedule, the Commission has power to do anything (except borrow money)—
    (a)   calculated to facilitate the discharge of its functions; or
    (b)   incidental or conducive to the discharge of its functions.

Staff

9.—(1) The Commission is to have a secretary, appointed by the Secretary of State on such terms and conditions of service as he considers appropriate.

(2) The approval of the Treasury is required as to those terms and conditions.

(3) Before appointing a person to be secretary, the Secretary of State must consult the Chairman and the President.

(4) Subject to obtaining the approval of—
    (a)   the Secretary of State, as to numbers, and
    (b)   the Secretary of State and Treasury, as to terms and conditions of service,
the Commission may appoint such staff as it thinks appropriate.

Procedure

10. Subject to any provision made by or under this Act, the Commission may regulate its own procedure.

Application of seal and proof of instruments

11.—(1) The application of the seal of the Commission must be authenticated by the signature of the secretary or of some other person authorised for the purpose.

(2) Sub-paragraph (1) does not apply in relation to any document which is or is to be signed in accordance with the law of Scotland.

(3) A document purporting to be duly executed under the seal of the Commission—
    (a)   is to be received in evidence; and
    (b)   is to be taken to have been so executed unless the contrary is proved.

Accounts

12.—(1) The Commission must—
    (a)   keep proper accounts and proper records in relation to its accounts;
    (b)   prepare a statement of accounts in respect of each of its financial years; and
    (c)   send copies of the statement to the Secretary of State and to the Comptroller and Auditor General before the end of the month of August next following the financial year to which the statement relates.

(2) The statement of accounts must comply with any directions given by the Secretary of State with the approval of the Treasury as to—
    (a)   the information to be contained in it,
    (b)   the manner in which the information contained in it is to be presented, or
    (c)   the methods and principles according to which the statement is to be prepared,

and must contain such additional information as the Secretary of State may with the approval of the Treasury require to be provided for informing Parliament.

(3) The Comptroller and Auditor General must—
    (a)   examine, certify and report on each statement received by him as a result of this paragraph; and
    (b)   lay copies of each statement and of his report before each House of Parliament.

(4) In this paragraph "financial year" means the period beginning with the date on which the Commission is established and ending with March 31st next, and each successive period of twelve months.

Status

13.—(1) The Commission is not to be regarded as the servant or agent of the Crown or as enjoying any status, privilege or immunity of the Crown.

(2) The Commission's property is not to be regarded as property of, or held on behalf of, the Crown.

Definitions   As to "document", see s 59(1).
References   See para 5.10.

PART II
PERFORMANCE OF THE COMMISSION'S GENERAL FUNCTIONS

Interpretation

14. In this Part of this Schedule "group" means a group selected under paragraph 15.

Discharge of certain functions by groups

15.—(1) Except where sub-paragraph (7) gives the Chairman power to act on his own, any general function of the Commission must be performed through a group selected for the purpose by the Chairman.

(2) The group must consist of at least three persons one of whom may be the Chairman.

(3) In selecting the members of the group, the Chairman must comply with any requirement as to its constitution imposed by any enactment applying to specialist panel members.

(4) If the functions to be performed through the group relate to a newspaper merger reference, the group must, subject to sub-paragraph (5), consist of such reporting panel members as the Chairman may select.

(5) The Secretary of State may appoint one, two or three persons from the panel maintained under paragraph 22 to be members and, if he does so, the group—
- (a) must include that member or those members; and
- (b) if there are three such members, may (if the Chairman so decides) consist entirely of those members.

(6) Subject to sub-paragraphs (2) to (5), a group must consist of reporting panel members or specialist panel members selected by the Chairman.

(7) While a group is being constituted to perform a particular general function of the Commission, the Chairman may—
- (a) take such steps (falling within that general function) as he considers appropriate to facilitate the work of the group when it has been constituted; or
- (b) exercise the power conferred by section 75(5) of the 1973 Act (setting aside references).

Chairmen of groups

16. The Chairman must appoint one of the members of a group to act as the chairman of the group.

Replacement of member of group

17.—(1) If, during the proceedings of a group—
- (a) a member of the group ceases to be a member of the Commission,
- (b) the Chairman is satisfied that a member of the group will be unable for a substantial period to perform his duties as a member of the group, or
- (c) it appears to the Chairman that because of a particular interest of a member of the group it is inappropriate for him to remain in the group,

the Chairman may appoint a replacement.

(2) The Chairman may also at any time appoint any reporting panel member to be an additional member of a group.

Attendance of other members

18.—(1) At the invitation of the chairman of a group, any reporting panel member who is not a member of the group may attend meetings or otherwise take part in the proceedings of the group.

(2) But any person attending in response to such an invitation may not—
- (a) vote in any proceedings of the group; or
- (b) have a statement of his dissent from a conclusion of the group included in a report made by them.

(3) Nothing in sub-paragraph (1) is to be taken to prevent a group, or a member of a group, from consulting any member of the Commission with respect to any matter or question with which the group is concerned.

Procedure

19.—(1) Subject to any special or general directions given by the Secretary of State, each group may determine its own procedure.

(2) Each group may, in particular, determine its quorum and determine—
- (a) the extent, if any, to which persons interested or claiming to be interested in the subject-matter of the reference are allowed—
  - (i) to be present or to be heard, either by themselves or by their representatives;
  - (ii) to cross-examine witnesses; or
  - (iii) otherwise to take part; and
- (b) the extent, if any, to which sittings of the group are to be held in public.

(3) In determining its procedure a group must have regard to any guidance issued by the Chairman.

(4) Before issuing any guidance for the purposes of this paragraph the Chairman must consult the members of the Commission.

Effect of exercise of functions by group

20.—(1) Subject to sub-paragraph (2), anything done by or in relation to a group in, or in connection with, the performance of functions to be performed by the group is to have the same effect as if done by or in relation to the Commission.

(2) For the purposes of—
    (a)   sections 56 and 73 of the 1973 Act,
    (b)   section 19A of the Agricultural Marketing Act 1958,
    (c)   Articles 23 and 42 of the Agricultural Marketing (Northern Ireland) Order 1982,

a conclusion contained in a report of a group is to be disregarded if the conclusion is not that of at least two-thirds of the members of the group.

Casting votes

21. The chairman of a group is to have a casting vote on any question to be decided by the group.

Newspaper merger references

22. The Secretary of State must maintain a panel of persons whom he regards as suitable for selection as members of a group constituted in connection with a newspaper merger reference.

Definitions   For "the 1973 Act", "the Commission", "Chairman", "general functions", "member", "newspaper merger reference", "reporting panel member" and "specialist panel member", see para 1 of this Schedule.
References   See para 5.10.

PART III
APPEALS

Interpretation

23. In this Part of this Schedule—
    "panel of chairmen" means the panel appointed under paragraph 26; and
    "tribunal" means an appeal tribunal constituted in accordance with paragraph 27.

Training of appeal panel members

24. The President must arrange such training for appeal panel members as he considers appropriate.

Acting President

25. If the President is absent or otherwise unable to act, the Secretary of State may appoint as acting president an appeal panel member who is qualified to act as chairman of a tribunal.

Panel of tribunal chairmen

26.—(1) There is to be a panel of appeal panel members appointed by the Secretary of State for the purposes of providing chairmen of appeal tribunals established under this Part of this Schedule.

(2) A person is qualified for appointment to the panel of chairmen only if—
    (a)   he has a seven year general qualification within the meaning of section 71 of the Courts and Legal Services Act 1990,
    (b)   he is an advocate or solicitor in Scotland of at least seven years' standing, or
    (c)   he is—
        (i)   a member of the Bar of Northern Ireland of at least seven years' standing, or
        (ii)   a solicitor of the Supreme Court of Northern Ireland of at least seven years' standing,

and appears to the Secretary of State to have appropriate experience and knowledge of competition law and practice.

Constitution of tribunals

27.—(1) On receipt of a notice of appeal, the President must constitute an appeal tribunal to deal with the appeal.

(2) An appeal tribunal is to consist of—

    (a) a chairman, who must be either the President or a person appointed by him to be chairman from the panel of chairmen; and

    (b) two other appeal panel members appointed by the President.

Definitions   For "appeal tribunal", see s 59(1); for "appeal panel member", see para 1 of this Schedule; for "the President", see para 4(2) of this Schedule.
References   See para 5.10.

PART IV
MISCELLANEOUS

Disqualification of members for House of Commons

28. In Part II of Schedule 1 to the House of Commons Disqualification Act 1975 (bodies of which all members are disqualified) insert at the appropriate place—

"The Competition Commission".

Disqualification of members for Northern Ireland Assembly

29. In Part II of Schedule 1 to the Northern Ireland Assembly Disqualification Act 1975 (bodies of which all members are disqualified) insert at the appropriate place—

"The Competition Commission".

References   See para 5.10.

PART V
TRANSITIONAL PROVISIONS

Interpretation

30. In this Part of this Schedule—

    "commencement date" means the date on which section 45 comes into force; and

    "MMC" means the Monopolies and Mergers Commission.

Chairman

31.—(1) The person who is Chairman of the MMC immediately before the commencement date is on that date to become both a member of the Commission and its chairman as if he had been duly appointed under paragraphs 2(1)(b) and 3.

(2) He is to hold office as Chairman of the Commission for the remainder of the period for which he was appointed as Chairman of the MMC and on the terms on which he was so appointed.

Deputy chairmen

32. The persons who are deputy chairmen of the MMC immediately before the commencement date are on that date to become deputy chairmen of the Commission as if they had been duly appointed under paragraph 3(2).

Reporting panel members

33.—(1) The persons who are members of the MMC immediately before the commencement date are on that date to become members of the Commission as if they had been duly appointed under paragraph 2(1)(b).

(2) Each of them is to hold office as a member for the remainder of the period for which he was appointed as a member of the MMC and on the terms on which he was so appointed.

Specialist panel members

34.—(1) The persons who are members of the MMC immediately before the commencement date by virtue of appointments made under any of the enactments mentioned in paragraph 2(1)(d) are on that date to become members of the Commission as if they had been duly appointed to the Commission under the enactment in question.

(2) Each of them is to hold office as a member for such period and on such terms as the Secretary of State may determine.

Secretary

35. The person who is the secretary of the MMC immediately before the commencement date is on that date to become the secretary of the Commission as if duly appointed under paragraph 9, on the same terms and conditions.

Council

36.—(1) The members who become deputy chairmen of the Commission under paragraph 32 are also to become members of the Council as if they had been duly appointed under paragraph 5(2)(c).

(2) Each of them is to hold office as a member of the Council for such period as the Secretary of State determines.

Definitions For "the Commission", see para 1 of this Schedule; for "the Council", see para 5(1) of this Schedule.
References See para 5.10.

SCHEDULE 8

Sections 46(5) and 48(4)

APPEALS

PART I
GENERAL

Interpretation

1. In this Schedule—
> "the chairman" means a person appointed as chairman of a tribunal in accordance with paragraph 27(2)(a) of Schedule 7;
> "the President" means the President of the Competition Commission Appeal Tribunals appointed under paragraph 4 of Schedule 7;
> "rules" means rules made by the Secretary of State under section 48;
> "specified" means specified in rules;
> "tribunal" means an appeal tribunal constituted in accordance with paragraph 27 of Schedule 7.

General procedure

2.—(1) An appeal to the Competition Commission must be made by sending a notice of appeal to the Commission within the specified period.

(2) The notice of appeal must set out the grounds of appeal in sufficient detail to indicate—
> (a) under which provision of this Act the appeal is brought;
> (b) to what extent (if any) the appellant contends that the decision against, or with respect to which, the appeal is brought was based on an error of fact or was wrong in law; and
> (c) to what extent (if any) the appellant is appealing against the Director's exercise of his discretion in making the disputed decision.

(3) The tribunal may give an appellant leave to amend the grounds of appeal identified in the notice of appeal.

Decisions of the tribunal

3.—(1) The tribunal must determine the appeal on the merits by reference to the grounds of appeal set out in the notice of appeal.

(2) The tribunal may confirm or set aside the decision which is the subject of the appeal, or any part of it, and may—

    (a)   remit the matter to the Director,

    (b)   impose or revoke, or vary the amount of, a penalty,

    (c)   grant or cancel an individual exemption or vary any conditions or obligations imposed in relation to the exemption by the Director,

    (d)   give such directions, or take such other steps, as the Director could himself have given or taken, or

    (e)   make any other decision which the Director could himself have made.

(3) Any decision of the tribunal on an appeal has the same effect, and may be enforced in the same manner, as a decision of the Director.

(4) If the tribunal confirms the decision which is the subject of the appeal it may nevertheless set aside any finding of fact on which the decision was based.

4.—(1) A decision of the tribunal may be taken by a majority.

(2) The decision must—

    (a)   state whether it was unanimous or taken by a majority; and

    (b)   be recorded in a document which—

        (i)   contains a statement of the reasons for the decision; and

        (ii) is signed and dated by the chairman of the tribunal.

(3) When the tribunal is preparing the document mentioned in sub-paragraph (2)(b), section 56 is to apply to the tribunal as it applies to the Director.

(4) The President must make such arrangements for the publication of the tribunal's decision as he considers appropriate.

Definitions   For "individual exemption", see s 4(2); for "the Director" and as to "document" and "person", see s 59(1).

References   See paras 5.22, 5.24–5.26.

PART II
RULES

Registrar of Appeal Tribunals

5.—(1) Rules may provide for the appointment by the Competition Commission, with the approval of the Secretary of State, of a Registrar of Appeal Tribunals.

(2) The rules may, in particular—

    (a)   specify the qualifications for appointment as Registrar; and

    (b)   provide for specified functions relating to appeals to be exercised by the Registrar in specified circumstances.

Notice of appeal

6. Rules may make provision—

    (a)   as to the period within which appeals must be brought;

    (b)   as to the form of the notice of appeal and as to the information which must be given in the notice;

    (c)   with respect to amendment of a notice of appeal;

    (d)   with respect to acknowledgement of a notice of appeal.

Response to the appeal

7. Rules may provide for the tribunal to reject an appeal if—

    (a)   it considers that the notice of appeal reveals no valid ground of appeal; or

    (b)   it is satisfied that the appellant has habitually and persistently and without any reasonable ground—

> > (i)   instituted vexatious proceedings, whether against the same person or against different persons; or
> > (ii)   made vexatious applications in any proceedings.

Pre-hearing reviews and preliminary matters

8.—(1) Rules may make provision—
> (a)   for the carrying-out by the tribunal of a preliminary consideration of proceedings (a "pre-hearing review"); and
> (b)   for enabling such powers to be exercised in connection with a pre-hearing review as may be specified.

(2)   If rules make provision of the kind mentioned in sub-paragraph (1), they may also include—
> (a)   provision for security; and
> (b)   supplemental provision.

(3)   In sub-paragraph (2) "provision for security" means provision authorising a tribunal carrying out a pre-hearing review under the rules, in specified circumstances, to make an order requiring a party to the proceedings, if he wishes to continue to participate in them, to pay a deposit of an amount not exceeding such sum—
> (a)   as may be specified; or
> (b)   as may be calculated in accordance with specified provisions.

(4)   In sub-paragraph (2) "supplemental provision" means any provision as to—
> (a)   the manner in which the amount of such a deposit is to be determined;
> (b)   the consequences of non-payment of such a deposit; and
> (c)   the circumstances in which any such deposit, or any part of it, may be—
> > (i)   refunded to the person who paid it; or
> > (ii)   paid to another party to the proceedings.

Conduct of the hearing

9.—(1) Rules may make provision—
> (a)   as to the manner in which appeals are to be conducted, including provision for any hearing to be held in private if the tribunal considers it appropriate because it may be considering information of a kind to which section 56 applies;
> (b)   as to the persons entitled to appear on behalf of the parties;
> (c)   for requiring persons to attend to give evidence and produce documents and for authorising the administration of oaths to witnesses;
> (d)   as to the evidence which may be required or admitted in proceedings before the tribunal and the extent to which it should be oral or written;
> (e)   allowing the tribunal to fix time limits with respect to any aspect of the proceedings before it and to extend any time limit (whether or not it has expired);
> (f)   for enabling the tribunal to refer a matter back to the Director if it appears to the tribunal that the matter has not been adequately investigated;
> (g)   for enabling the tribunal, on the application of any party to the proceedings before it or on its own initiative—
> > (i)   in England and Wales or Northern Ireland, to order the disclosure between, or the production by, the parties of documents or classes of documents;
> > (ii)   in Scotland, to order such recovery or inspection of documents as might be ordered by a sheriff;
> (h)   for the appointment of experts for the purposes of any proceedings before the tribunal;
> (i)   for the award of costs or expenses, including any allowances payable to persons in connection with their attendance before the tribunal;
> (j)   for taxing or otherwise settling any costs or expenses directed to be paid by the tribunal and for the enforcement of any such direction.

(2)   A person who without reasonable excuse fails to comply with—
> (a)   any requirement imposed by virtue of sub-paragraph (1)(c), or
> (b)   any requirement with respect to the disclosure, production, recovery or inspection of documents which is imposed by virtue of sub-paragraph (1)(g),

is guilty of an offence and liable on summary conviction to a fine not exceeding level 3 on the standard scale.

Interest

10.—(1) Rules may make provision—
    (a)   as to the circumstances in which the tribunal may order that interest is payable;
    (b)   for the manner in which and the periods by reference to which interest is to be calculated and paid.

(2)   The rules may, in particular, provide that compound interest is to be payable if the tribunal—
    (a)   upholds a decision of the Director to impose a penalty, or
    (b)   does not reduce a penalty so imposed by more than a specified percentage,

but in such a case the rules may not provide that interest is to be payable in respect of any period before the date on which the appeal was brought.

Fees

11.—(1) Rules may provide—
    (a)   for fees to be chargeable in respect of specified costs of proceedings before the tribunal;
    (b)   for the amount of such costs to be determined by the tribunal.

(2)   Any sums received in consequence of rules under this paragraph are to be paid into the Consolidated Fund.

Withdrawing an appeal

12.   Rules may make provision—
    (a)   that a party who has brought an appeal may not withdraw it without the leave of—
        (i)   the tribunal, or
        (ii)   in specified circumstances, the President or the Registrar;
    (b)   for the tribunal to grant leave to withdraw the appeal on such conditions as it considers appropriate;
    (c)   enabling the tribunal to publish any decision which it could have made had the appeal not been withdrawn;
    (d)   as to the effect of withdrawal of an appeal;
    (e)   as to any procedure to be followed if parties to proceedings on an appeal agree to settle.

Interim orders

13.—(1) Rules may provide for the tribunal to make an order ("an interim order") granting, on an interim basis, any remedy which the tribunal would have power to grant in its final decision.

(2)   An interim order may, in particular, suspend the effect of a decision made by the Director or vary the conditions or obligations attached to an exemption.

(3)   Rules may also make provision giving the tribunal powers similar to those given to the Director by section 35.

Miscellaneous

14.   Rules may make provision—
    (a)   for a person who is not a party to proceedings on an appeal to be joined in those proceedings;
    (b)   for appeals to be consolidated on such terms as the tribunal thinks appropriate in such circumstances as may be specified.

Definitions   For "the Director" and as to "document", "information" and "person", see s 59(1).
References   See paras 5.22, 5.23.

SCHEDULE 9

Section 51(2)

DIRECTOR'S RULES

General

1.   In this Schedule—
        "application for guidance" means an application for guidance under section 13 or 21;
        "application for a decision" means an application for a decision under section 14 or 22;

"guidance" means guidance given under section 13 or 21;
"rules" means rules made by the Director under section 51; and
"specified" means specified in rules.

Applications

2. Rules may make provision—
    (a)   as to the form and manner in which an application for guidance or an application for a decision must be made;
    (b)   for the procedure to be followed in dealing with the application;
    (c)   for the application to be dealt with in accordance with a timetable;
    (d)   as to the documents and information which must be given to the Director in connection with the application;
    (e)   requiring the applicant to give such notice of the application, to such other persons, as may be specified;
    (f)   as to the consequences of a failure to comply with any rule made by virtue of sub-paragraph (e);
    (g)   as to the procedure to be followed when the application is subject to the concurrent jurisdiction of the Director and a regulator.

Provisional decisions

3. Rules may make provision as to the procedure to be followed by the Director when making a provisional decision under paragraph 3 of Schedule 5 or paragraph 3 of Schedule 6.

Guidance

4. Rules may make provision as to—
    (a)   the form and manner in which guidance is to be given;
    (b)   the procedure to be followed if—
        (i)   the Director takes further action with respect to an agreement after giving guidance that it is not likely to infringe the Chapter I prohibition; or
        (ii)   the Director takes further action with respect to conduct after giving guidance that it is not likely to infringe the Chapter II prohibition.

Decisions

5.—(1) Rules may make provision as to—
    (a)   the form and manner in which notice of any decision is to be given;
    (b)   the person or persons to whom the notice is to be given;
    (c)   the manner in which the Director is to publish a decision;
    (d)   the procedure to be followed if—
        (i)   the Director takes further action with respect to an agreement after having decided that it does not infringe the Chapter I prohibition; or
        (ii)   the Director takes further action with respect to conduct after having decided that it does not infringe the Chapter II prohibition.

(2) In this paragraph "decision" means a decision of the Director (whether or not made on an application)—
    (a)   as to whether or not an agreement has infringed the Chapter I prohibition, or
    (b)   as to whether or not conduct has infringed the Chapter II prohibition,

and, in the case of an application for a decision under section 14 which includes a request for an individual exemption, includes a decision as to whether or not to grant the exemption.

Individual exemptions

6. Rules may make provision as to—
    (a)   the procedure to be followed by the Director when deciding whether, in accordance with section 5—
        (i)   to cancel an individual exemption that he has granted,
        (ii)   to vary or remove any of its conditions or obligations, or
        (iii)   to impose additional conditions or obligations;
    (b)   the form and manner in which notice of such a decision is to be given.

7. Rules may make provision as to—
    (a)   the form and manner in which an application under section 4(6) for the extension of an individual exemption is to be made;

   (b)   the circumstances in which the Director will consider such an application;

   (c)   the procedure to be followed by the Director when deciding whether to grant such an application;

   (d)   the form and manner in which notice of such a decision is to be given.

Block exemptions

8. Rules may make provision as to—

   (a)   the form and manner in which notice of an agreement is to be given to the Director under subsection (1) of section 7;

   (b)   the procedure to be followed by the Director if he is acting under subsection (2) of that section;

   (c)   as to the procedure to be followed by the Director if he cancels a block exemption.

Parallel exemptions

9. Rules may make provision as to—

   (a)   the circumstances in which the Director may—

      (i)   impose conditions or obligations in relation to a parallel exemption,

      (ii)   vary or remove any such conditions or obligations,

      (iii)   impose additional conditions or obligations, or

      (iv)   cancel the exemption;

   (b)   as to the procedure to be followed by the Director if he is acting under section 10(5);

   (c)   the form and manner in which notice of a decision to take any of the steps in sub-paragraph (a) is to be given;

   (d)   the circumstances in which an exemption may be cancelled with retrospective effect.

Section 11 exemptions

10. Rules may, with respect to any exemption provided by regulations made under section 11, make provision similar to that made with respect to parallel exemptions by section 10 or by rules under paragraph 9.

Directions withdrawing exclusions

11. Rules may make provision as to the factors which the Director may take into account when he is determining the date on which a direction given under paragraph 4(1) of Schedule 1 or paragraph 2(3) or 9(3) of Schedule 3 is to have effect.

Disclosure of information

12.—(1) Rules may make provision as to the circumstances in which the Director is to be required, before disclosing information given to him by a third party in connection with the exercise of any of the Director's functions under Part I, to give notice, and an opportunity to make representations, to the third party.

(2) In relation to the agreement (or conduct) concerned, "third party" means a person who is not a party to the agreement (or who has not engaged in the conduct).

Applications under section 47

13. Rules may make provision as to—

   (a)   the period within which an application under section 47(1) must be made;

   (b)   the procedure to be followed by the Director in dealing with the application;

   (c)   the person or persons to whom notice of the Director's response to the application is to be given.

Enforcement

14. Rules may make provision as to the procedure to be followed when the Director takes action under any of sections 32 to 41 with respect to the enforcement of the provisions of this Part.

Definitions   For "the Chapter I prohibition", see s 2(8); for "individual exemption", see s 4(2); for "block exemption", see s 6(4); for "parallel exemption", see s 10(3); for "section 11 exemption", see s 11(3); for "the Chapter II prohibition", see s 18(4); for "regulator", see s 54(1); for "the Director" and as to "document", "information" and "person", see s 59(1).

SCHEDULE 10

Sections 54 and 66(5)

REGULATORS

PART I
MONOPOLIES

1. The amendments of the Fair Trading Act 1973 made by sections 66 and 67 of this Act are to have effect, not only in relation to the jurisdiction of the Director under the provisions amended, but also in relation to the jurisdiction under those provisions of each of the following—

    (a)   the Director General of Telecommunications;
    (b)   the Director General of Electricity Supply;
    (c)   the Director General of Electricity Supply for Northern Ireland;
    (d)   the Director General of Water Services;
    (e)   the Rail Regulator;
    (f)   the Director General of Gas Supply; and
    (g)   the Director General of Gas for Northern Ireland.

Definitions   For "the Director", see s 59(1).
References   See para 7.3.

PART II
THE PROHIBITIONS

Telecommunications

2.—(1) In consequence of the repeal by this Act of provisions of the Competition Act 1980, the functions transferred by subsection (3) of section 50 of the Telecommunications Act 1984 (functions under 1973 and 1980 Acts) are no longer exercisable by the Director General of Telecommunications.

(2) Accordingly, that Act is amended as follows.

(3) In section 3 (general duties of Secretary of State and Director), in subsection (3)(b), for "section 50" substitute "section 50(1) or (2)".

(4) In section 3, after subsection (3A), insert—

"(3B) Subsections (1) and (2) above do not apply in relation to anything done by the Director in the exercise of functions assigned to him by section 50(3) below ("Competition Act functions").

(3C) The Director may nevertheless, when exercising any Competition Act function, have regard to any matter in respect of which a duty is imposed by subsection (1) or (2) above ("a general matter"), if it is a matter to which the Director General of Fair Trading could have regard when exercising that function; but that is not to be taken as implying that, in relation to any of the matters mentioned in subsection (3) or (3A) above, regard may not be had to any general matter."

(5) Section 50 is amended as follows.

(6) For subsection (3) substitute—

"(3) The Director shall be entitled to exercise, concurrently with the Director General of Fair Trading, the functions of that Director under the provisions of Part I of the Competition Act 1998 (other than sections 38(1) to (6) and 51), so far as relating to—

    (a)   agreements, decisions or concerted practices of the kind mentioned in section 2(1) of that Act, or
    (b)   conduct of the kind mentioned in section 18(1) of that Act,
which relate to commercial activities connected with telecommunications.

(3A) So far as necessary for the purposes of, or in connection with, the provisions of subsection (3) above, references in Part I of the Competition Act 1998 to the Director General of Fair Trading are to be read as including a reference to the Director (except in sections 38(1) to (6), 51, 52(6) and (8) and 54 of that Act and in any other provision of that Act where the context otherwise requires)."

(7) In subsection (4), omit paragraph (c) and the "and" immediately after it.

(8) In subsection (5), omit "or (3)".

(9) In subsection (6), for paragraph (b) substitute—

"(b) Part I of the Competition Act 1998 (other than sections 38(1) to (6) and 51),".

(10) In subsection (7), omit "or the 1980 Act".

Gas

3.—(1) In consequence of the repeal by this Act of provisions of the Competition Act 1980, the functions transferred by subsection (3) of section 36A of the Gas Act 1986 (functions with respect to competition) are no longer exercisable by the Director General of Gas Supply.

(2) Accordingly, that Act is amended as follows.

(3) In section 4 (general duties of Secretary of State and Director), after subsection (3), insert—

"(3A) Subsections (1) to (3) above and section 4A below do not apply in relation to anything done by the Director in the exercise of functions assigned to him by section 36A below ("Competition Act functions").

(3B) The Director may nevertheless, when exercising any Competition Act function, have regard to any matter in respect of which a duty is imposed by any of subsections (1) to (3) above or section 4A below, if it is a matter to which the Director General of Fair Trading could have regard when exercising that function."

(4) Section 36A is amended as follows.

(5) For subsection (3) substitute—

"(3) The Director shall be entitled to exercise, concurrently with the Director General of Fair Trading, the functions of that Director under the provisions of Part I of the Competition Act 1998 (other than sections 38(1) to (6) and 51), so far as relating to—
    (a) agreements, decisions or concerted practices of the kind mentioned in section 2(1) of that Act, or
    (b) conduct of the kind mentioned in section 18(1) of that Act,
which relate to the carrying on of activities to which this subsection applies.

(3A) So far as necessary for the purposes of, or in connection with, the provisions of subsection (3) above, references in Part I of the Competition Act 1998 to the Director General of Fair Trading are to be read as including a reference to the Director (except in sections 38(1) to (6), 51, 52(6) and (8) and 54 of that Act and in any other provision of that Act where the context otherwise requires)."

(6) In subsection (5)—
    (a) for "transferred by", in each place, substitute "mentioned in";
    (b) after paragraph (b), insert "and";
    (c) omit paragraph (d) and the "and" immediately before it.

(7) In subsection (6), omit "or (3)".

(8) In subsection (7), for paragraph (b) substitute—

"(b) Part I of the Competition Act 1998 (other than sections 38(1) to (6) and 51),".

(9) In subsection (8)—
    (a) omit "or under the 1980 Act";
    (b) for "or (3) above" substitute "above and paragraph 1 of Schedule 10 to the Competition Act 1998".

(10) In subsection (9), omit "or the 1980 Act".

(11) In subsection (10), for the words from "transferred" to the end substitute "mentioned in subsection (2) or (3) above."

Electricity

4.—(1) In consequence of the repeal by this Act of provisions of the Competition Act 1980, the functions transferred by subsection (3) of section 43 of the Electricity Act 1989 (functions with respect to competition) are no longer exercisable by the Director General of Electricity Supply.

(2) Accordingly, that Act is amended as follows.

(3) In section 3 (general duties of Secretary of State and Director), after subsection (6), insert—

"(6A) Subsections (1) to (5) above do not apply in relation to anything done by the Director in the exercise of functions assigned to him by section 43(3) below ("Competition Act functions").

(6B) The Director may nevertheless, when exercising any Competition Act function, have regard to any matter in respect of which a duty is imposed by any of subsections (1) to (5) above ("a general matter"), if it is a matter to which the Director General of Fair Trading could have regard when exercising that function; but that is not to be taken as implying that, in the exercise of any function mentioned in subsection (6) above, regard may not be had to any general matter."

(4) Section 43 is amended as follows.

(5) For subsection (3) substitute—

"(3) The Director shall be entitled to exercise, concurrently with the Director General of Fair Trading, the functions of that Director under the provisions of Part I of the Competition Act 1998 (other than sections 38(1) to (6) and 51), so far as relating to—
    (a) agreements, decisions or concerted practices of the kind mentioned in section 2(1) of that Act, or
    (b) conduct of the kind mentioned in section 18(1) of that Act,

which relate to commercial activities connected with the generation, transmission or supply of electricity.

(3A) So far as necessary for the purposes of, or in connection with, the provisions of subsection (3) above, references in Part I of the Competition Act 1998 to the Director General of Fair Trading are to be read as including a reference to the Director (except in sections 38(1) to (6), 51, 52(6) and (8) and 54 of that Act and in any other provision of that Act where the context otherwise requires)."

(6) In subsection (4), omit paragraph (c) and the "and" immediately after it.

(7) In subsection (5), omit "or (3)".

(8) In subsection (6), for paragraph (b) substitute—

"(b) Part I of the Competition Act 1998 (other than sections 38(1) to (6) and 51),".

(9) In subsection (7), omit "or the 1980 Act".

Water

5.—(1) In consequence of the repeal by this Act of provisions of the Competition Act 1980, the functions exercisable by virtue of subsection (3) of section 31 of the Water Industry Act 1991 (functions of Director with respect to competition) are no longer exercisable by the Director General of Water Services.

(2) Accordingly, that Act is amended as follows.

(3) In section 2 (general duties with respect to water industry), in subsection (6)(a), at the beginning, insert "subject to subsection (6A) below".

(4) In section 2, after subsection (6), insert—

"(6A) Subsections (2) to (4) above do not apply in relation to anything done by the Director in the exercise of functions assigned to him by section 31(3) below ("Competition Act functions").

(6B) The Director may nevertheless, when exercising any Competition Act function, have regard to any matter in respect of which a duty is imposed by any of subsections (2) to (4) above, if it is a matter to which the Director General of Fair Trading could have regard when exercising that function."

(5) Section 31 is amended as follows.

(6) For subsection (3) substitute—

"(3) The Director shall be entitled to exercise, concurrently with the Director General of Fair Trading, the functions of that Director under the provisions of Part I of the Competition Act 1998 (other than sections 38(1) to (6) and 51), so far as relating to—
    (a) agreements, decisions or concerted practices of the kind mentioned in section 2(1) of that Act, or
    (b) conduct of the kind mentioned in section 18(1) of that Act,
which relate to commercial activities connected with the supply of water or securing a supply of water or with the provision or securing of sewerage services."

(7) In subsection (4)—
    (a) for "to (3)" substitute "and (2)";
    (b) omit paragraph (c) and the "and" immediately before it.

(8) After subsection (4), insert—

"(4A) So far as necessary for the purposes of, or in connection with, the provisions of subsection (3) above, references in Part I of the Competition Act 1998 to the Director General of Fair Trading are to be read as including a reference to the Director (except in sections 38(1) to (6), 51, 52(6) and (8) and 54 of that Act and in any other provision of that Act where the context otherwise requires)."

(9) In subsection (5), omit "or in subsection (3) above".

(10) In subsection (6), omit "or in subsection (3) above".

(11) In subsection (7), omit "or (3)".

(12) In subsection (8), for paragraph (b) substitute—

"(b) Part I of the Competition Act 1998 (other than sections 38(1) to (6) and 51),".

(13) In subsection (9), omit "or the 1980 Act".

Railways

6.—(1) In consequence of the repeal by this Act of provisions of the Competition Act 1980, the functions transferred by subsection (3) of section 67 of the Railways Act 1993 (respective functions of the Regulator and the Director etc) are no longer exercisable by the Rail Regulator.

(2) Accordingly, that Act is amended as follows.

(3) In section 4 (general duties of the Secretary of State and the Regulator), after subsection (7), insert—

"(7A) Subsections (1) to (6) above do not apply in relation to anything done by the Regulator in the exercise of functions assigned to him by section 67(3) below ("Competition Act functions").

(7B) The Regulator may nevertheless, when exercising any Competition Act function, have regard to any matter in respect of which a duty is imposed by any of subsections (1) to (6) above, if it is a matter to which the Director General of Fair Trading could have regard when exercising that function."

(4) Section 67 is amended as follows.

(5) For subsection (3) substitute—

"(3)   The Regulator shall be entitled to exercise, concurrently with the Director, the functions of the Director under the provisions of Part I of the Competition Act 1998 (other than sections 38(1) to (6) and 51), so far as relating to—

   (a)   agreements, decisions or concerted practices of the kind mentioned in section 2(1) of that Act, or

   (b)   conduct of the kind mentioned in section 18(1) of that Act,

which relate to the supply of railway services.

(3A)   So far as necessary for the purposes of, or in connection with, the provisions of subsection (3) above, references in Part I of the Competition Act 1998 to the Director are to be read as including a reference to the Regulator (except in sections 38(1) to (6), 51, 52(6) and (8) and 54 of that Act and in any other provision of that Act where the context otherwise requires)."

(6)   In subsection (4), omit paragraph (c) and the "and" immediately after it.

(7)   In subsection (6)(a), omit "or (3)".

(8)   In subsection (8), for paragraph (b) substitute—

   "(b)   Part I of the Competition Act 1998 (other than sections 38(1) to (6) and 51),".

(9)   In subsection (9)—

   (a)   omit "or under the 1980 Act";

   (b)   for "or (3) above" substitute "above and paragraph 1 of Schedule 10 to the Competition Act 1998".

Definitions   In the Telecommunications Act 1984, for "the Director", see s 1(1) (and s 106(1)) thereof, and for "commercial activities connected with telecommunications", see s 4(3) thereof.
In the Gas Act 1986, for "the Director", see s 1(1) (and s 66) thereof.
In the Electricity Act 1989, for "the Director", see s 1(1) thereof, as to "supply" and "transmission", see s 4(4) thereof.
In the Water Industry Act 1991, for "the Director", "functions" and "sewerage services", see s 219(1) thereof.
In the Railways Act 1993, for "the Regulator", see s 1 thereof, for "the Director", see s 67(1) thereof, for "railway services", see s 82(1) thereof, and for "functions", see s 151(1) thereof.
References   See paras 7.4, 7.5, 7.9–7.11.

PART III
THE PROHIBITIONS: NORTHERN IRELAND

Electricity

7.—(1)   In consequence of the repeal by this Act of provisions of the Competition Act 1980, the functions transferred by paragraph (3) of Article 46 of the Electricity (Northern Ireland) Order 1992 (functions with respect to competition) are no longer exercisable by the Director General of Electricity Supply for Northern Ireland.

(2)   Accordingly, that Order is amended as follows.

(3)   In Article 6 (general duties of the Director), after paragraph (2), add—

   "(3)   Paragraph (1) does not apply in relation to anything done by the Director in the exercise of functions assigned to him by Article 46(3) ("Competition Act functions").

   (4)   The Director may nevertheless, when exercising any Competition Act function, have regard to any matter in respect of which a duty is imposed by paragraph (1) ("a general matter"), if it is a matter to which the Director General of Fair Trading could have regard when exercising that function; but that is not to be taken as implying that, in the exercise of any function mentioned in Article 4(7) or paragraph (2), regard may not be had to any general matter."

(4)   Article 46 is amended as follows.

(5)   For paragraph (3) substitute—

   "(3)   The Director shall be entitled to exercise, concurrently with the Director General of Fair Trading, the functions of that Director under the provisions of Part I of the Competition Act 1998 (other than sections 38(1) to (6) and 51), so far as relating to—

    (a)   agreements, decisions or concerted practices of the kind mentioned in section 2(1) of that Act, or

    (b)   conduct of the kind mentioned in section 18(1) of that Act,

which relate to commercial activities connected with the generation, transmission or supply of electricity.

    (3A) So far as necessary for the purposes of, or in connection with, the provisions of paragraph (3), references in Part I of the Competition Act 1998 to the Director General of Fair Trading are to be read as including a reference to the Director (except in sections 38(1) to (6), 51, 52(6) and (8) and 54 of that Act and in any other provision of that Act where the context otherwise requires)."

(6)   In paragraph (4), omit sub-paragraph (c) and the "and" immediately after it.

(7)   In paragraph (5), omit "or (3)".

(8)   In paragraph (6), for sub-paragraph (b) substitute—

    "(b) Part I of the Competition Act 1998 (other than sections 38(1) to (6) and 51),".

(9)   In paragraph (7), omit "or the 1980 Act".

Gas

8.—(1) In consequence of the repeal by this Act of provisions of the Competition Act 1980, the functions transferred by paragraph (3) of Article 23 of the Gas (Northern Ireland) Order 1996 (functions with respect to competition) are no longer exercisable by the Director General of Gas for Northern Ireland.

(2)   Accordingly, that Order is amended as follows.

(3)   In Article 5 (general duties of the Department and Director), after paragraph (4), insert—

    "(4A) Paragraphs (2) to (4) do not apply in relation to anything done by the Director in the exercise of functions assigned to him by Article 23(3) ("Competition Act functions").

    (4B) The Director may nevertheless, when exercising any Competition Act function, have regard to any matter in respect of which a duty is imposed by any of paragraphs (2) to (4), if it is a matter to which the Director General of Fair Trading could have regard when exercising that function."

(4)   Article 23 is amended as follows.

(5)   For paragraph (3) substitute—

    "(3) The Director shall be entitled to exercise, concurrently with the Director General of Fair Trading, the functions of that Director under the provisions of Part I of the Competition Act 1998 (other than sections 38(1) to (6) and 51), so far as relating to—

    (a)   agreements, decisions or concerted practices of the kind mentioned in section 2(1) of that Act, or

    (b)   conduct of the kind mentioned in section 18(1) of that Act,

connected with the conveyance, storage or supply of gas.

    (3A) So far as necessary for the purposes of, or in connection with, the provisions of paragraph (3), references in Part I of the Competition Act 1998 to the Director General of Fair Trading are to be read as including a reference to the Director (except in sections 38(1) to (6), 51, 52(6) and (8) and 54 of that Act and in any other provision of that Act where the context otherwise requires)."

(6)   In paragraph (4)—

    (a)   for "transferred by", in each place, substitute "mentioned in";

    (b)   after sub-paragraph (b), insert "and";

    (c)   omit sub-paragraph (d) and the "and" immediately before it.

(7)   In paragraph (5), omit "or (3)".

(8)   In paragraph (6), for sub-paragraph (b) substitute—

    "(b) Part I of the Competition Act 1998 (other than sections 38(1) to (6) and 51),".

(9) In paragraph (7)—
    (a) omit "or under the 1980 Act";
    (b) for "or (3)" substitute "and paragraph 1 of Schedule 10 to the Competition Act 1998".

(10) In paragraph (8), omit "or the 1980 Act".

(11) In paragraph (9), for the words from "transferred" to the end substitute "mentioned in paragraph (2) or (3)."

References   See paras 7.9, 7.10.

PART IV
UTILITIES: MINOR AND CONSEQUENTIAL AMENDMENTS

The Telecommunications Act 1984 (c 12)

9.—(1) The Telecommunications Act 1984 is amended as follows.

(2) In section 13 (licence modification references to Competition Commission), for subsections (9) and (10) substitute—

"(9) The provisions mentioned in subsection (9A) are to apply in relation to references under this section as if—
    (a) the functions of the Competition Commission in relation to those references were functions under the Fair Trading Act 1973 (in this Act referred to as "the 1973 Act");
    (b) the expression "merger reference" included a reference under this section;
    (c) in section 70 of the 1973 Act—
        (i) references to the Secretary of State were references to the Director, and
        (ii) the reference to three months were a reference to six months.

(9A) The provisions are—
    (a) sections 70 (time limit for report on merger) and 85 (attendance of witnesses and production of documents) of the 1973 Act;
    (b) Part II of Schedule 7 to the Competition Act 1998 (performance of the Competition Commission's general functions); and
    (c) section 24 of the Competition Act 1980 (modification of provisions about performance of such functions).

(10) For the purposes of references under this section, the Secretary of State is to appoint not less than three members of the Competition Commission.

(10A) In selecting a group to perform the Commission's functions in relation to any such reference, the chairman of the Commission must select up to three of the members appointed under subsection (10) to be members of the group."

(3) In section 14, omit subsection (2) (which falls with the repeal of the Restrictive Trade Practices Act 1976).

(4) In section 16 (securing compliance with licence conditions), in subsection (5), after paragraph (a), omit "or" and after paragraph (b), insert "or
    (c) that the most appropriate way of proceeding is under the Competition Act 1998."

(5) In section 50 (functions under 1973 and 1980 Acts), after subsection (6), insert—

"(6A) Section 93B of the 1973 Act (offences of supplying false or misleading information) is to have effect so far as relating to functions exercisable by the Director by virtue of—
    (a) subsection (2) above and paragraph 1 of Schedule 10 to the Competition Act 1998, or
    (b) paragraph 1 of Schedule 2 to the Deregulation and Contracting Out Act 1994,
as if the reference in section 93B(1)(a) to the Director General of Fair Trading included a reference to the Director."

(6) In section 95 (modification by orders under other enactments)—
    (a) in subsection (1), omit "or section 10(2)(a) of the 1980 Act";
    (b) in subsection (2)—
        (i) after paragraph (a), insert "or";
        (ii) omit paragraph (c) and the "or" immediately before it;
    (c) in subsection (3), omit "or the 1980 Act".

(7) In section 101(3) (general restrictions on disclosure of information)—
    (a) omit paragraphs (d) and (e) (which refer to the Restrictive Trade Practices Act 1976 and the Resale Prices Act 1976);
    (b) after paragraph (m), insert—

"(n) the Competition Act 1998".

(8) At the end of section 101, insert—

"(6) Information obtained by the Director in the exercise of functions which are exercisable concurrently with the Director General of Fair Trading under Part I of the Competition Act 1998 is subject to sections 55 and 56 of that Act (disclosure) and not to subsections (1) to (5) of this section."

The Gas Act 1986 (c 44)

10.—(1) The Gas Act 1986 is amended as follows.

(2) In section 24 (modification references to the Competition Commission), for subsection (7) substitute—

"(7) The provisions mentioned in subsection (7A) are to apply in relation to references under this section as if—
    (a) the functions of the Competition Commission in relation to those references were functions under the Fair Trading Act 1973;
    (b) the expression "merger reference" included a reference under this section;
    (c) in section 70 of the Fair Trading Act 1973—
        (i) references to the Secretary of State were references to the Director, and
        (ii) the reference to three months were a reference to six months.

(7A) The provisions are—
    (a) sections 70 (time limit for report on merger) and 85 (attendance of witnesses and production of documents) of the Fair Trading Act 1973;
    (b) Part II of Schedule 7 to the Competition Act 1998 (performance of the Competition Commission's general functions); and
    (c) section 24 of the Competition Act 1980 (modification of provisions about performance of such functions)."

(3) In section 25, omit subsection (2) (which falls with the repeal of the Restrictive Trade Practices Act 1976).

(4) In section 27 (modification by order under other enactments)—
    (a) in subsection (1), omit "or section 10(2)(a) of the Competition Act 1980";
    (b) in subsection (3)(a), omit from "or" to "competition reference";
    (c) in subsection (6), omit "or the said Act of 1980".

(5) In section 28 (orders for securing compliance with certain provisions), in subsection (5), after paragraph (aa), omit "or" and after paragraph (b), insert "or
    (c) that the most appropriate way of proceeding is under the Competition Act 1998."

(6) In section 42(3) (general restrictions on disclosure of information)—
    (a) omit paragraphs (e) and (f) (which refer to the Restrictive Trade Practices Act 1976 and the Resale Prices Act 1976);
    (b) after paragraph (n), insert—

"(o) the Competition Act 1998".

(7) At the end of section 42, insert—

"(7) Information obtained by the Director in the exercise of functions which are exercisable concurrently with the Director General of Fair Trading under Part I of the Competition Act 1998 is subject to sections 55 and 56 of that Act (disclosure) and not to subsections (1) to (6) of this section."

The Water Act 1989 (c 15)

11.   In section 174(3) of the Water Act 1989 (general restrictions on disclosure of information)—

    (a)   omit paragraphs (d) and (e) (which refer to the Restrictive Trade Practices Act 1976 and the Resale Prices Act 1976);

    (b)   after paragraph (l), insert—

"(ll) the Competition Act 1998".

The Electricity Act 1989 (c 29)

12.—(1) The Electricity Act 1989 is amended as follows.

(2) In section 12 (modification references to Competition Commission), for subsections (8) and (9) substitute—

"(8)   The provisions mentioned in subsection (8A) are to apply in relation to references under this section as if—

    (a)   the functions of the Competition Commission in relation to those references were functions under the 1973 Act;

    (b)   the expression "merger reference" included a reference under this section;

    (c)   in section 70 of the 1973 Act—

        (i)   references to the Secretary of State were references to the Director, and

        (ii)   the reference to three months were a reference to six months.

(8A)   The provisions are—

    (a)   sections 70 (time limit for report on merger) and 85 (attendance of witnesses and production of documents) of the 1973 Act;

    (b)   Part II of Schedule 7 to the Competition Act 1998 (performance of the Competition Commission's general functions); and

    (c)   section 24 of the 1980 Act (modification of provisions about performance of such functions).

(9)   For the purposes of references under this section, the Secretary of State is to appoint not less than eight members of the Competition Commission.

(9A)   In selecting a group to perform the Commission's functions in relation to any such reference, the chairman of the Commission must select up to three of the members appointed under subsection (9) to be members of the group."

(3) In section 13, omit subsection (2) (which falls with the repeal of the Restrictive Trade Practices Act 1976).

(4) In section 15 (modification by order under other enactments)—

    (a)   in subsection (1), omit paragraph (b) and the "or" immediately before it;

    (b)   in subsection (2)—

        (i)   after paragraph (a), insert "or";

        (ii)   omit paragraph (c) and the "or" immediately before it;

    (c)   in subsection (3), omit "or the 1980 Act".

(5) In section 25 (orders for securing compliance), in subsection (5), after paragraph (b), omit "or" and after paragraph (c), insert "or

    (d)   that the most appropriate way of proceeding is under the Competition Act 1998."

(6) In section 43 (functions with respect to competition), after subsection (6), insert—

"(6A) Section 93B of the 1973 Act (offences of supplying false or misleading information) is to have effect so far as relating to functions exercisable by the Director by virtue of—

    (a)   subsection (2) above and paragraph 1 of Schedule 10 to the Competition Act 1998, or

    (b)   paragraph 4 of Schedule 2 to the Deregulation and Contracting Out Act 1994,

as if the reference in section 93B(1)(a) to the Director General of Fair Trading included a reference to the Director."

(7) In section 57(3) (general restrictions on disclosure of information)—
   (a)   omit paragraphs (d) and (e) (which refer to the Restrictive Trade Practices Act 1976 and the Resale Prices Act 1976);
   (b)   after paragraph (no), insert—
   "(nop) the Competition Act 1998".

(8) At the end of section 57, insert—

"(7) Information obtained by the Director in the exercise of functions which are exercisable concurrently with the Director General of Fair Trading under Part I of the Competition Act 1998 is subject to sections 55 and 56 of that Act (disclosure) and not to subsections (1) to (6) of this section."

The Water Industry Act 1991 (c 56)

13.—(1) The Water Industry Act 1991 is amended as follows.

(2) In section 12(5) (determinations under conditions of appointment)—
   (a)   after "this Act", insert "or";
   (b)   omit "or the 1980 Act".

(3) In section 14 (modification references to Competition Commission), for subsections (7) and (8) substitute—

"(7) The provisions mentioned in subsection (7A) are to apply in relation to references under this section as if—
   (a)   the functions of the Competition Commission in relation to those references were functions under the 1973 Act;
   (b)   the expression "merger reference" included a reference under this section;
   (c)   in section 70 of the 1973 Act—
      (i)   references to the Secretary of State were references to the Director, and
      (ii) the reference to three months were a reference to six months.

(7A) The provisions are—
   (a)   sections 70 (time limit for report on merger) and 85 (attendance of witnesses and production of documents) of the 1973 Act;
   (b)   Part II of Schedule 7 to the Competition Act 1998 performance of the Competition Commission's general functions); and
   (c)   section 24 of the 1980 Act (modification of provisions about performance of such functions).

(8) For the purposes of references under this section, the Secretary of State is to appoint not less than eight members of the Competition Commission.

(8A) In selecting a group to perform the Commission's functions in relation to any such reference, the chairman of the Commission must select one or more of the members appointed under subsection (8) to be members of the group."

(4) In section 15, omit subsection (2) (which falls with the repeal of the Restrictive Trade Practices Act 1976).

(5) In section 17 (modification by order under other enactments)—
   (a)   in subsection (1), omit paragraph (b) and the "or" immediately before it;
   (b)   in subsection (2)—
      (i)   after paragraph (a), insert "or";
      (ii) omit paragraph (c) and the "or" immediately before it;
   (c)   in subsection (4), omit "or the 1980 Act".

(6) In section 19 (exceptions to duty to enforce), after subsection (1), insert—

"(1A) The Director shall not be required to make an enforcement order, or to confirm a provisional enforcement order, if he is satisfied that the most appropriate way of proceeding is under the Competition Act 1998."

(7) In section 19(3), after "subsection (1) above", insert "or, in the case of the Director, is satisfied as mentioned in subsection (1A) above,".

(8) In section 31 (functions of Director with respect to competition), after subsection (8), insert—

"(8A) Section 93B of the 1973 Act (offences of supplying false or misleading information) is to have effect so far as relating to functions exercisable by the Director by virtue of—

    (a)   subsection (2) above and paragraph 1 of Schedule 10 to the Competition Act 1998, or

    (b)   paragraph 8 of Schedule 2 to the Deregulation and Contracting Out Act 1994,

as if the reference in section 93B(1)(a) to the Director General of Fair Trading included a reference to the Director."

(9)   After section 206(9) (restriction on disclosure of information), insert—

"(9A) Information obtained by the Director in the exercise of functions which are exercisable concurrently with the Director General of Fair Trading under Part I of the Competition Act 1998 is subject to sections 55 and 56 of that Act (disclosure) and not to subsections (1) to (9) of this section."

(10)   In Schedule 15 (disclosure of information), in Part II (enactments in respect of which disclosure may be made)—

    (a)   omit the entries relating to the Restrictive Trade Practices Act 1976 and the Resale Prices Act 1976;

    (b)   after the entry relating to the Railways Act 1993, insert the entry—

"The Competition Act 1998".

The Water Resources Act 1991 (c 57)

14.   In Schedule 24 to the Water Resources Act 1991 (disclosure of information), in Part II (enactments in respect of which disclosure may be made)—

    (a)   omit the entries relating to the Restrictive Trade Practices Act 1976 and the Resale Prices Act 1976;

    (b)   after the entry relating to the Coal Industry Act 1994, insert the entry—

"The Competition Act 1998".

The Railways Act 1993 (c 43)

15.—(1) The Railways Act 1993 is amended as follows.

(2)   In section 13 (modification references to the Competition Commission), for subsection (8) substitute—

"(8)   The provisions mentioned in subsection (8A) are to apply in relation to references under this section as if—

    (a)   the functions of the Competition Commission in relation to those references were functions under the 1973 Act;

    (b)   the expression "merger reference" included a reference under this section;

    (c)   in section 70 of the 1973 Act—

        (i)   references to the Secretary of State were references to the Director, and

        (ii)   the reference to three months were a reference to six months.

(8A)   The provisions are—

    (a)   sections 70 (time limit for report on merger) and 85 (attendance of witnesses and production of documents) of the 1973 Act;

    (b)   Part II of Schedule 7 to the Competition Act 1998 (performance of the Competition Commission's general functions); and

    (c)   section 24 of the Competition Act 1980 (in this Part referred to as "the 1980 Act") (modification of provisions about performance of such functions)".

(3)   In section 14, omit subsection (2) (which falls with the repeal of the Restrictive Trade Practices Act 1976).

(4)   In section 16 (modification by order under other enactments)—

    (a)   in subsection (1), omit paragraph (b) and the "or" immediately before it;

    (b)   in subsection (2)—

        (i)   after paragraph (a), insert "or";

        (ii)   omit paragraph (c) and the "or" immediately before it;

    (c)   in subsection (5), omit "or the 1980 Act".

(5) In section 22, after subsection (6), insert—

"(6A) Neither the Director General of Fair Trading nor the Regulator may exercise, in respect of an access agreement, the powers given by section 32 (enforcement directions) or section 35(2) (interim directions) of the Competition Act 1998.

(6B) Subsection (6A) does not apply to the exercise of the powers given by section 35(2) in respect of conduct—
    (a) which is connected with an access agreement; and
    (b) in respect of which section 35(1)(b) of that Act applies."

(6) In section 55 (orders for securing compliance), after subsection (5), insert—

"(5A) The Regulator shall not make a final order, or make or confirm a provisional order, in relation to a licence holder or person under closure restrictions if he is satisfied that the most appropriate way of proceeding is under the Competition Act 1998."

(7) In section 55—
    (a) in subsection (6), after "subsection (5)", insert "or (5A)";
    (b) in subsection (11), for "subsection (10)" substitute "subsections (5A) and (10)".

(8) Omit section 131 (modification of Restrictive Trade Practices Act 1976).

(9) In section 145(3) (general restrictions on disclosure of information)—
    (a) omit paragraphs (d) and (e) (which refer to the Restrictive Trade Practices Act 1976 and the Resale Prices Act 1976);
    (b) after paragraph (q), insert—

    "(qq the Competition Act 1998."

(10) After section 145(6), insert—

"(6A) Information obtained by the Regulator in the exercise of functions which are exercisable concurrently with the Director General of Fair Trading under Part I of the Competition Act 1998 is subject to sections 55 and 56 of that Act (disclosure) and not to subsections (1) to (6) of this section."

The Channel Tunnel Rail Link Act 1996 (c 61)

16.—(1) The Channel Tunnel Rail Link Act 1996 is amended as follows.

(2) In section 21 (duties as to exercise of regulatory functions), in subsection (6), at the end of the paragraph about regulatory functions, insert—

"other than any functions assigned to him by virtue of section 67(3) of that Act ("Competition Act functions").

(7) The Regulator may, when exercising any Competition Act function, have regard to any matter to which he would have regard if—
    (a) he were under the duty imposed by subsection (1) or (2) above in relation to that function; and
    (b) the matter is one to which the Director General of Fair Trading could have regard if he were exercising that function."

(3) In section 22 (restriction of functions in relation to competition etc), for subsection (3) substitute—

"(3) The Rail Regulator shall not be entitled to exercise any functions assigned to him by section 67(3) of the Railways Act 1993 (by virtue of which he exercises concurrently with the Director General of Fair Trading certain functions under Part I of the Competition Act 1998 so far as relating to matters connected with the supply of railway services) in relation to—
    (a) any agreements, decisions or concerted practices of the kind mentioned in section 2(1) of that Act that have been entered into or taken by, or
    (b) any conduct of the kind mentioned in section 18(1) of that Act that has been engaged in by,
a rail link undertaker in connection with the supply of railway services, so far as relating to the rail link."

Definitions   In the Telecommunications Act 1984, for "the Director", see s 1(1) (and s 106(1)) thereof. In the Gas Act 1986, for "the Director", see s 1(1) (and s 66) thereof.
In the Electricity Act 1989, for "the Director", see s 1(1) thereof, and for "the 1973 Act" and "the 1980 Act", see s 64(1) thereof.
In the Water Industry Act 1991, for "enforcement order" and "provisional enforcement order", see s 18(7) thereof, for "the 1973 Act" and "the 1980 Act", see s 36(1) thereof, and for "the Director", see s 219(1) thereof.
In the Railways Act 1993, for "the Regulator", see s 1 thereof, for "final order" and "provisional order", see s 55(10) thereof; for "person under closure restrictions", see s 55(11) thereof (as amended by para 15(1), (7)(b) above), for "the Director", see s 67(1) thereof, for "the 1973 Act", "access agreement" and "licence holder", see s 83(1) thereof, and for "functions", see s 151(1) thereof.
References   See paras 7.9, 7.12, 7.13.

PART V
MINOR AND CONSEQUENTIAL AMENDMENTS: NORTHERN IRELAND

The Electricity (Northern Ireland) Order 1992

17.—(1) The Electricity (Northern Ireland) Order 1992 is amended as follows.

(2) In Article 15 (modification references to Competition Commission), for paragraphs (8) and (9) substitute—

"(8) The provisions mentioned in paragraph (8A) are to apply in relation to references under this Article as if—

    (a)   the functions of the Competition Commission in relation to those references were functions under the 1973 Act;

    (b)   "merger reference" included a reference under this Article;

    (c)   in section 70 of the 1973 Act—

        (i)   references to the Secretary of State were references to the Director, and

        (ii)   the reference to three months were a reference to six months.

(8A)   The provisions are—

    (a)   sections 70 (time limit for report on merger) and 85 (attendance of witnesses and production of documents) of the 1973 Act;

    (b)   Part II of Schedule 7 to the Competition Act 1998 (performance of the Competition Commission's general functions); and

    (c)   section 24 of the 1980 Act (modification of provisions about performance of such functions).

(9)   The Secretary of State may appoint members of the Competition Commission for the purposes of references under this Article.

(9A)   In selecting a group to perform the Commission's functions in relation to any such reference, the chairman of the Commission must select up to three of the members appointed under paragraph (9) to be members of the group."

(3)   In Article 16, omit paragraph (2) (which falls with the repeal of the Restrictive Trade Practices Act 1976).

(4)   In Article 18 (modification by order under other statutory provisions)—

    (a)   in paragraph (1), omit sub-paragraph (b) and the "or" immediately before it;

    (b)   in paragraph (2)—

        (i)   after sub-paragraph (a), insert "or";

        (ii)   omit sub-paragraph (c) and the "or" immediately before it;

    (c)   in paragraph (3), omit "or the 1980 Act".

(5)   In Article 28 (orders for securing compliance), in paragraph (5), after sub-paragraph (b), omit "or" and after sub-paragraph (c), insert

    "or

    (d)   that the most appropriate way of proceeding is under the Competition Act 1998."

(6)   In Article 46 (functions with respect to competition), after paragraph (6), insert—

"(6A)   Section 93B of the 1973 Act (offences of supplying false or misleading information) is to have effect so far as relating to functions exercisable by the Director by virtue of—

(a)   paragraph (2) and paragraph 1 of Schedule 10 to the Competition Act 1998, or

(b)   paragraph 5 of Schedule 2 to the Deregulation and Contracting Out Act 1994,

as if the reference in section 93B(1)(a) to the Director General of Fair Trading included a reference to the Director."

(7)   In Article 61(3) (general restrictions on disclosure of information)—

(a)   omit sub-paragraphs (f) and (g) (which refer to the Restrictive Trade Practices Act 1976 and the Resale Prices Act 1976);

(b)   after sub-paragraph (t), add—

"(u) the Competition Act 1998".

(8)   At the end of Article 61, insert—

"(7)   Information obtained by the Director in the exercise of functions which are exercisable concurrently with the Director General of Fair Trading under Part I of the Competition Act 1998 is subject to sections 55 and 56 of that Act (disclosure) and not to paragraphs (1) to (6)."

(9)   In Schedule 12, omit paragraph 16 (which amends the Restrictive Trade Practices Act 1976).

The Gas (Northern Ireland) Order 1996

18.—(1) The Gas (Northern Ireland) Order 1996 is amended as follows.

(2)   In Article 15 (modification references to the Competition Commission), for paragraph (9) substitute—

"(9)   The provisions mentioned in paragraph (9A) are to apply in relation to references under this Article as if—

(a)   the functions of the Competition Commission in relation to those references were functions under the 1973 Act;

(b)   "merger reference" included a reference under this Article;

(c)   in section 70 of the 1973 Act—

(i)   references to the Secretary of State were references to the Director, and

(ii)   the reference to three months were a reference to six months.

(9A) The provisions are—

(a)   sections 70 (time limit for report on merger) and 85 (attendance of witnesses and production of documents) of the 1973 Act;

(b)   Part II of Schedule 7 to the Competition Act 1998 (performance of the Competition Commission's general functions); and

(c)   section 24 of the 1980 Act (modification of provisions about performance of such functions)."

(3)   In Article 16, omit paragraph (2) (which falls with the repeal of the Restrictive Trade Practices Act 1976).

(4)   In Article 18 (modification by order under other statutory provisions)—

(a)   in paragraph (1), omit sub-paragraph (b) and the "or" immediately before it;

(b)   in paragraph (3)—

(i)   after sub-paragraph (a), insert "or";

(ii)   omit sub-paragraph (c) and the "or" immediately before it;

(c)   in paragraph (5), omit "or the 1980 Act".

(5)   In Article 19 (orders for securing compliance), in paragraph (5), after sub-paragraph (b), omit "or" and after sub-paragraph (c), insert

"or

(d)   that the most appropriate way of proceeding is under the Competition Act 1998."

(6)   In Article 44(4) (general restrictions on disclosure of information)—
  (a)   omit sub-paragraphs (f) and (g) (which refer to the Restrictive Trade Practices Act 1976 and the Resale Prices Act 1976);
  (b)   after sub-paragraph (u), add—

  "(v) the Competition Act 1998".

(7)   At the end of Article 44, insert—

  "(8)   Information obtained by the Director in the exercise of functions which are exercisable concurrently with the Director General of Fair Trading under Part I of the Competition Act 1998 is subject to sections 55 and 56 of that Act (disclosure) and not to paragraphs (1) to (7)."

SCHEDULE 11

Section 55(4)

INTERPRETATION OF SECTION 55

Relevant functions

1.   In section 55(3) "relevant functions" means any function under—
  (a)   Part I or any enactment repealed in consequence of Part I;
  (b)   the Fair Trading Act 1973 (c 41) or the Competition Act 1980 (c 21);
  (c)   the Estate Agents Act 1979 (c 38);
  (d)   the Telecommunications Act 1984 (c 12);
  (e)   the Gas Act 1986 (c 44) or the Gas Act 1995 (c 45);
  (f)   the Gas (Northern Ireland) Order 1996;
  (g)   the Airports Act 1986 (c 31) or Part IV of the Airports (Northern Ireland) Order 1994;
  (h)   the Financial Services Act 1986 (c 60);
  (i)   the Electricity Act 1989 (c 29) or the Electricity (Northern Ireland) Order 1992;
  (j)   the Broadcasting Act 1990 (c 42) or the Broadcasting Act 1996 (c 55);
  (k)   the Courts and Legal Services Act 1990 (c 41);
  (l)   the Water Industry Act 1991 (c 56), the Water Resources Act 1991 (c 57), the Statutory Water Companies Act 1991 (c 58), the Land Drainage Act 1991 (c 59) and the Water Consolidation (Consequential Provisions) Act 1991 (c 60);
  (m)   the Railways Act 1993 (c 43);
  (n)   the Coal Industry Act 1994 (c 21);
  (o)   the EC Competition Law (Articles 88 and 89) Enforcement Regulations 1996;
  (p)   any subordinate legislation made (whether before or after the passing of this Act) for the purpose of implementing Council Directive No 91/440/EEC of 29th July 1991 on the development of the Community's railways, Council Directive No 95/18/EC of 19th June 1995 on the licensing of railway undertakings or Council Directive No 95/19/EC of 19th June 1995 on the allocation of railway infrastructure capacity and the charging of infrastructure fees.

Designated persons

2.   In section 55(3) "designated person" means any of the following—
  (a)   the Director;
  (b)   the Director General of Telecommunications;
  (c)   the Independent Television Commission;
  (d)   the Director General of Gas Supply;
  (e)   the Director General of Gas for Northern Ireland;
  (f)   the Civil Aviation Authority;
  (g)   the Director General of Water Services;
  (h)   the Director General of Electricity Supply;
  (i)   the Director General of Electricity Supply for Northern Ireland;
  (j)   the Rail Regulator;
  (k)   the Director of Passenger Rail Franchising;
  (l)   the International Rail Regulator;
  (m)   the Authorised Conveyancing Practitioners Board;

(n)   the Scottish Conveyancing and Executry Services Board;
(o)   the Coal Authority;
(p)   the Monopolies and Mergers Commission;
(q)   the Competition Commission;
(r)   the Securities and Investments Board;
(s)   any Minister of the Crown or any Northern Ireland department.

Definitions   For "the Director" and "Minister of the Crown", see s 59(1).
References   See paras 4.20, 10.2, 10.3.

SCHEDULE 12

Section 74(1)

MINOR AND CONSEQUENTIAL AMENDMENTS

The Fair Trading Act 1973 (c 41)

1.—(1)   The Fair Trading Act 1973 is amended as follows.

(2)   Omit section 4 and Schedule 3 (which make provision in respect of the Monopolies and Mergers Commission).

(3)   Omit—
(a)   section 10(2),
(b)   section 54(5),
(c)   section 78(3),
(d)   paragraph 3(1) and (2) of Schedule 8,
(which fall with the repeal of the Restrictive Trade Practices Act 1976).

(4)   In section 10 (supplementary provisions about monopoly situations), in subsection (8), for "to (7)" substitute "and (3) to (7)".

(5)   In sections 35 and 37 to 41, for "the Restrictive Practices Court", in each place, substitute "a relevant Court".

(6)   After section 41, insert—

"41A   Meaning of "relevant Court"

In this Part of this Act, "relevant Court", in relation to proceedings in respect of a course of conduct maintained in the course of a business, means any of the following courts in whose jurisdiction that business is carried on—
(a)   in England and Wales or Northern Ireland, the High Court;
(b)   in Scotland, the Court of Session."

(7)   In section 42 (appeals from decisions or orders of courts under Part III)—
(a)   in subsection (1), at the end, add "; but this subsection is subject to subsection (3) of this section";
(b)   in subsection (2)(b), after "Scotland," insert "from the sheriff court"; and
(c)   after subsection (2), add—

"(3)   A decision or order of the Court of Session as the relevant Court may be reviewed, whether on a question of fact or on a question of law, by reclaiming to the Inner House."

(8)   Omit section 45 (power of the Director to require information about complex monopoly situations).

(9)   In section 81 (procedure in carrying out investigations)—
(a)   in subsection (1)—
(i)   in the words before paragraph (a), omit from "and the Commission" to "of this Act)";
(ii)   in paragraph (b), omit "or the Commission, as the case may be," and "or of the Commission";
(b)   in subsection (2), omit "or the Commission" and "or of the Commission"; and
(c)   in subsection (3), omit from "and, in the case," to "85 of this Act" and "or the Commission, as the case may be,".

(10) In section 85 (attendance of witnesses and production of documents on investigations by Competition Commission of references under the Fair Trading Act 1973), in subsection (1)(b)—

    (a)   after "purpose", insert "(i)";

    (b)   after the second "notice", insert

> "or
>
>   (ii)   any document which falls within a category of document which is specified, or described, in the notice,".

(11) In section 85, in subsection (1)(c), after "estimates" (in both places), insert "forecasts".

(12) In section 85, after subsection (1), insert—

> "(1A) For the purposes of subsection (1) above—
>
>   (a)   "document" includes information recorded in any form;
>
>   (b)   the power to require the production of documents includes power to take copies of, or extracts from, any document produced; and
>
>   (c)   in relation to information recorded otherwise than in legible form, the power to require it to be produced includes power to require it to be produced in legible form, so far as the means to do so are within the custody or under the control of the person on whom the requirement is imposed."

(13) In section 85(2), for "any such investigation" substitute "an investigation of the kind mentioned in subsection (1)".

(14) In section 133 (general restrictions on disclosure of information), in subsection (2)(a), after "the Coal Industry Act 1994" insert "or the Competition Act 1998".

(15) In section 135(1) (financial provisions)—

    (a)   in the words before paragraph (a) and in paragraph (b), omit "or the Commission"; and

    (b)   omit paragraph (a).

The Energy Act 1976 (c 76)

2.   In the Energy Act 1976, omit section 5 (temporary relief from restrictive practices law in relation to certain agreements connected with petroleum).

The Estate Agents Act 1979 (c 38)

3.   In section 10(3) of the Estate Agents Act 1979 (restriction on disclosure of information), in paragraph (a)—

    (a)   omit "or the Restrictive Trade Practices Act 1976"; and

    (b)   after "the Coal Industry Act 1994", insert "or the Competition Act 1998".

The Competition Act 1980 (c 21)

4.—(1)   The Competition Act 1980 is amended as follows.

(2)   In section 11(8) (public bodies and other persons referred to the Commission), omit paragraph (b) and the "and" immediately before it.

(3)   For section 11(9) (which makes provision for certain functions of the Competition Commission under the Fair Trading Act 1973 to apply in relation to references under the Competition Act 1980) substitute—

> "(9)   The provisions mentioned in subsection (9A) are to apply in relation to a reference under this section as if—
>
>   (a)   the functions of the Competition Commission under this section were functions under the Fair Trading Act 1973;
>
>   (b)   the expression "merger reference" included a reference to the Commission under this section; and
>
>   (c)   in paragraph 20(2)(a) of Schedule 7 to the Competition Act 1998, the reference to section 56 of the Fair Trading Act 1973 were a reference to section 12 below.

(9A)   The provisions are—
  (a)   sections 70 (time limit for report on merger), 84 (public interest) and 85 (attendance of witnesses and production of documents) of the Fair Trading Act 1973; and
  (b)   Part II of Schedule 7 to the Competition Act 1998 (performance of the Competition Commission's general functions)."

(4)   In section 13 (investigation of prices directed by Secretary of State)—
  (a)   in subsection (1), omit from "but the giving" to the end;
  (b)   for subsection (6) substitute—

"(6)   For the purposes of an investigation under this section the Director may, by notice in writing signed by him—
  (a)   require any person to produce—
      (i)   at a time and a place specified in the notice,
      (ii)   to the Director or to any person appointed by him for the purpose,
    any documents which are specified or described in the notice and which are documents in his custody or under his control and relating to any matter relevant to the investigation; or
  (b)   require any person carrying on any business to—
      (i)   furnish to the Director such estimates, forecasts, returns or other information as may be specified or described in the notice; and
      (ii)   specify the time, manner and form in which any such estimates, forecasts, returns or information are to be furnished.

(7)   No person shall be compelled, for the purpose of any investigation under this section—
  (a)   to produce any document which he could not be compelled to produce in civil proceedings before the High Court or, in Scotland, the Court of Session; or
  (b)   in complying with any requirement for the furnishing of information, to give any information which he could not be compelled to give in evidence in such proceedings.

(8)   Subsections (6) to (8) of section 85 of the Fair Trading Act 1973 (enforcement provisions relating to notices requiring production of documents etc) shall apply in relation to a notice under subsection (6) above as they apply in relation to a notice under section 85(1) but as if, in section 85(7), for the words from "any one" to "the Commission" there were substituted "the Director.""

(5)   In section 15 (special provisions for agricultural schemes) omit subsections (2)(b), (3) and (4).

(6)   In section 16 (reports), omit subsection (3).

(7)   In section 17 (publication etc of reports)—
  (a)   in subsections (1) and (3) to (5), omit "8(1)";
  (b)   in subsection (2), omit "8(1) or"; and
  (c)   in subsection (6), for "sections 9, 10 or" substitute "section".

(8)   In section 19(3) (restriction on disclosure of information), omit paragraphs (d) and (e).

(9)   In section 19(3), after paragraph (q), insert—

  "(r)   the Competition Act 1998".

(10)   In section 19(5)(a), omit "or in anything published under section 4(2)(a) above".

(11)   Omit section 22 (which amends the Fair Trading Act 1973).

(12)   In section 24(1) (modifications of provisions about performance of Commission's functions), for from "Part II" to the first "Commission" substitute "Part II of Schedule 7 to the Competition Act 1998 (performance of the Competition Commission's general functions)".

(13)   Omit sections 25 to 30 (amendments of the Restrictive Trade Practices Act 1976).

(14)   In section 31 (orders and regulations)—
  (a)   omit subsection (2); and
  (b)   in subsection (3), omit "10".

(15)   In section 33 (short title etc)—

      (a)   in subsection (2), for "sections 2 to 24" substitute "sections 11 to 13 and sections 15 to 24";

      (b)   omit subsections (3) and (4).

Magistrates' Courts (Northern Ireland) Order 1981 (SI 1981/1675 (NI 26))

5. In Schedule 6 to the Magistrates' Courts (Northern Ireland) Order 1981, omit paragraphs 42 and 43 (which amend the Restrictive Trade Practices Act 1976).

Agricultural Marketing (Northern Ireland) Order 1982 (SI 1982/1080 (NI 12))

6. In Schedule 8 to the Agricultural Marketing (Northern Ireland) Order 1982—

      (a)   omit the entry relating to paragraph 16(2) of Schedule 3 to the Fair Trading Act 1973; and

      (b)   in the entry relating to the Competition Act 1980—

          (i)   for "sections" substitute "section";

          (ii)   omit "and 15(3)".

The Airports Act 1986 (c 31)

7.—(1) The Airports Act 1986 is amended as follows.

(2) In section 44 (which makes provision about references by the CAA to the Competition Commission), for subsection (3) substitute—

    "(3) The provisions mentioned in subsection (3A) are to apply in relation to references under this section as if—

      (a)   the functions of the Competition Commission in relation to those references were functions under the 1973 Act;

      (b)   the expression "merger reference" included a reference under this section;

      (c)   in section 70 of the 1973 Act—

          (i)   references to the Secretary of State were references to the CAA, and

          (ii)   the reference to three months were a reference to six months.

    (3A) The provisions are—

      (a)   sections 70 (time limit for report on merger) and 85 (attendance of witnesses and production of documents) of the 1973 Act;

      (b)   Part II of Schedule 7 to the Competition Act 1998 (performance of the Competition Commission's general functions); and

      (c)   section 24 of the 1980 Act (modification of provisions about performance of such functions)."

(3) In section 45, omit subsection (3) (which falls with the repeal of the Restrictive Trade Practices Act 1976).

(4) In section 54 (orders under the 1973 Act or 1980 Act modifying or revoking conditions)—

      (a)   in subsection (1), omit "or section 10(2)(a) of the 1980 Act";

      (b)   in subsection (3), omit paragraph (c) and the "or" immediately before it;

      (c)   in subsection (4), omit "or the 1980 Act".

(5) In section 56 (co-ordination of exercise of functions by CAA and Director General of Fair Trading), in paragraph (a)(ii), omit "or the 1980 Act".

The Financial Services Act 1986 (c 60)

8. In Schedule 11 to the Financial Services Act 1986, in paragraph 12—

      (a)   in sub-paragraph (1), omit "126";

      (b)   omit sub-paragraph (2).

The Companies Consolidation (Consequential Provisions) (Northern Ireland) Order 1986 (SI 1986/1035 (NI 9))

9. In Part II of Schedule 1 to the Companies Consolidation (Consequential Provisions)(Northern Ireland) Order 1986, omit the entries relating to the Restrictive Trade Practices Act 1976 and the Resale Prices Act 1976.

The Consumer Protection Act 1987 (c 43)

10. In section 38(3) of the Consumer Protection Act 1987 (restrictions on disclosure of information)—

(a)   omit paragraphs (e) and (f); and
(b)   after paragraph (o), insert—

"(p)   the Competition Act 1998."

The Channel Tunnel Act 1987 (c 53)

11. In section 33 of the Channel Tunnel Act 1987—
(a)   in subsection (2), omit paragraph (c) and the "and" immediately before it;
(b)   in subsection (5), omit paragraphs (b) and (c).

The Road Traffic (Consequential Provisions) Act 1988 (c 54)

12. In Schedule 3 to the Road Traffic (Consequential Provisions) Act 1988 (consequential amendments), omit paragraph 19.

The Companies Act 1989 (c 40)

13. In Schedule 20 to the Companies Act 1989 (amendments about mergers and related matters), omit paragraphs 21 to 24.

The Broadcasting Act 1990 (c 42)

14.—(1) The Broadcasting Act 1990 is amended as follows.

(2) In section 193 (modification of networking arrangements in consequence of reports under competition legislation)—
(a)   in subsection (2), omit paragraph (c) and the "and" immediately before it;
(b)   in subsection (4), omit "or the Competition Act 1980".

(3) In Schedule 4 (which makes provision for references to the Director or the Competition Commission in respect of networking arrangements), in paragraph 4, for sub-paragraph (7) substitute—

"(7)   The provisions mentioned in sub-paragraph (7A) are to apply in relation to references under this paragraph as if—
(a)   the functions of the Competition Commission in relation to those references were functions under the Fair Trading Act 1973;
(b)   the expression "merger reference" included a reference under this paragraph.

(7A)   The provisions are—
(a)   section 85 of the Fair Trading Act 1973 (attendance of witnesses and production of documents);
(b)   Part II of Schedule 7 to the Competition Act 1998 (performance of the Competition Commission's general functions); and
(c)   section 24 of the Competition Act 1980 (modification of provisions about performance of such functions)."

The Tribunals and Inquiries Act 1992 (c 53)

15. In Schedule 1 to the Tribunals and Inquiries Act 1992 (tribunals under the supervision of the Council on Tribunals), after paragraph 9, insert—

"Competition   9A   An appeal tribunal established under section 48 of the Competition Act 1998."

The Osteopaths Act 1993 (c 21)

16. Section 33 of the Osteopaths Act 1993 (competition and anti-competitive practices) is amended as follows—
(a)   in subsection (4), omit paragraph (b) and the "or" immediately before it;
(b)   in subsection (5), omit "or section 10 of the Act of 1980".

The Chiropractors Act 1994 (c 17)

17. Section 33 of the Chiropractors Act 1994 (competition and anti-competitive practices) is amended as follows—
(a)   in subsection (4), omit paragraph (b) and the "or" immediately before it;
(b)   in subsection (5), omit "or section 10 of the Act of 1980".

The Coal Industry Act 1994 (c 21)

18. In section 59(4) of the Coal Industry Act 1994 (information to be kept confidential by the Coal Authority)—
    (a) omit paragraphs (e) and (f); and
    (b) after paragraph (m), insert—

    "(n) the Competition Act 1998."

The Deregulation and Contracting Out Act 1994 (c 40)

19.—(1) The Deregulation and Contracting Out Act 1994 is amended as follows.

(2) Omit—
    (a) section 10 (restrictive trade practices: non-notifiable agreements); and
    (b) section 11 (registration of commercially sensitive information).

(3) In section 12 (anti-competitive practices: competition references), omit subsections (1) to (6).

(4) In Schedule 4, omit paragraph 1.

(5) In Schedule 11 (miscellaneous deregulatory provisions: consequential amendments), in paragraph 4, omit sub-paragraphs (3) to (7).

The Airports (Northern Ireland) Order 1994 (SI 1994/426 (NI 1))

20.—(1) The Airports (Northern Ireland) Order 1994 is amended as follows.

(2) In Article 35 (which makes provision about references by the CAA to the Competition Commission), for paragraph (3) substitute—

    "(3) The provisions mentioned in paragraph (3A) are to apply in relation to references under Article 34 as if—
        (a) the functions of the Competition Commission in relation to those references were functions under the 1973 Act;
        (b) the expression "merger reference" included a reference under that Article;
        (c) in section 70 of the 1973 Act—
            (i) references to the Secretary of State were references to the Director, and
            (ii) the reference to three months were a reference to six months.

    (3A) The provisions are—
        (a) sections 70 (time limit for report on merger) and 85 (attendance of witnesses and production of documents) of the 1973 Act;
        (b) Part II of Schedule 7 to the Competition Act 1998 (performance of the Competition Commission's general functions); and
        (c) section 24 of the 1980 Act (modification of provisions about performance of such functions)."

(3) In Article 36, omit paragraph (3) (which falls with the repeal of the Restrictive Trade Practices Act 1976).

(4) In Article 45 (orders under the 1973 Act or 1980 Act modifying or revoking conditions)—
    (a) in paragraph (1), omit "or section 10(2)(a) of the 1980 Act";
    (b) in paragraph (3), omit sub-paragraph (c) and the "or" immediately before it;
    (c) in paragraph (4), omit "or the 1980 Act".

(5) In Article 47 (co-ordination of exercise of functions by CAA and Director of Fair Trading), in paragraph (a)(ii), omit "or the 1980 Act".

(6) In Schedule 9, omit paragraph 5 (which amends the Restrictive Trade Practices Act 1976).

The Broadcasting Act 1996 (c 55)

21. In section 77 of the Broadcasting Act 1996 (which modifies the Restrictive Trade Practices Act 1976 in its application to agreements relating to Channel 3 news provision), omit subsection (2).

Definitions   In the Fair Trading Act 1973, for "business", see s 137(2) thereof.
In the Competition Act 1980, for "business" and "the Director", see, by virtue of s 33(2) thereof, the Fair Trading Act 1973, s 137(2).
In the Airports Act 1986, for "the 1973 Act" and "the 1980 Act", see s 36(1) thereof, and for "the CAA" and "functions", see s 82(1) thereof.

SCHEDULE 13

Section 74(2)

TRANSITIONAL PROVISIONS AND SAVINGS

PART I
GENERAL

Interpretation

1.—(1)   In this Schedule—

"RPA" means the Resale Prices Act 1976;

"RTPA" means the Restrictive Trade Practices Act 1976;

"continuing proceedings" has the meaning given by paragraph 15;

"the Court" means the Restrictive Practices Court;

"Director" means the Director General of Fair Trading;

"document" includes information recorded in any form;

"enactment date" means the date on which this Act is passed;

"information" includes estimates and forecasts;

"interim period" means the period beginning on the enactment date and ending immediately before the starting date;

"prescribed" means prescribed by an order made by the Secretary of State;

"regulator" means any person mentioned in paragraphs (a) to (g) of paragraph 1 of Schedule 10;

"starting date" means the date on which section 2 comes into force;

"transitional period" means the transitional period provided for in Chapters III and IV of Part IV of this Schedule.

(2)   Sections 30, 44, 51, 53, 55, 56, 57 and 59(3) and (4) and paragraph 12 of Schedule 9 ("the applied provisions") apply for the purposes of this Schedule as they apply for the purposes of Part I of this Act.

(3)   Section 2(5) applies for the purposes of any provisions of this Schedule which are concerned with the operation of the Chapter I prohibition as it applies for the purposes of Part I of this Act.

(4)   In relation to any of the matters in respect of which a regulator may exercise powers as a result of paragraph 35(1), the applied provisions are to have effect as if references to the Director included references to the regulator.

(5)   The fact that to a limited extent the Chapter I prohibition does not apply to an agreement, because a transitional period is provided by virtue of this Schedule, does not require those provisions of the agreement in respect of which there is a transitional period to be disregarded when considering whether the agreement infringes the prohibition for other reasons.

General power to make transitional provision and savings

2.—(1)   Nothing in this Schedule affects the power of the Secretary of State under section 75 to make transitional provisions or savings.

(2)   An order under that section may modify any provision made by this Schedule.

Advice and information

3.—(1)   The Director may publish advice and information explaining provisions of this Schedule to persons who are likely to be affected by them.

(2)   Any advice or information published by the Director under this paragraph is to be published in such form and manner as he considers appropriate.

Definitions   As to "person", see s 59(1).
References   See paras 9.1, 9.2.

PART II

DURING THE INTERIM PERIOD

Block exemptions

4.—(1) The Secretary of State may, at any time during the interim period, make one or more orders for the purpose of providing block exemptions which are effective on the starting date.

(2) An order under this paragraph has effect as if properly made under section 6.

Certain agreements to be non-notifiable agreements

5. An agreement which—
    (a)   is made during the interim period, and
    (b)   satisfies the conditions set out in paragraphs (a), (c) and (d) of section 27A(1) of the RTPA,
is to be treated as a non–notifiable agreement for the purposes of RTPA.

Application of RTPA during the interim period

6. In relation to agreements made during the interim period—
    (a)   the Director is no longer under the duty to take proceedings imposed by section 1(2)(c) of the RTPA but may continue to do so;
    (b)   section 21 of that Act has effect as if subsections (1) and (2) were omitted; and
    (c)   section 35(1) of that Act has effect as if the words "or within such further time as the Director may, upon application made within that time, allow" were omitted.

Guidance

7.—(1) Sub-paragraphs (2) to (4) apply in relation to agreements made during the interim period.

(2) An application may be made to the Director in anticipation of the coming into force of section 13 in accordance with directions given by the Director and such an application is to have effect on and after the starting date as if properly made under section 13.

(3) The Director may, in response to such an application—
    (a)   give guidance in anticipation of the coming into force of section 2; or
    (b)   on and after the starting date, give guidance under section 15 as if the application had been properly made under section 13.

(4) Any guidance so given is to have effect on and after the starting date as if properly given under section 15.

Definitions   For "block exemption", see s 6(4); for "RTPA", "Director", "interim period" and "starting date", see para 1(1) of this Schedule.
References   See paras 9.5, 9.8.

PART III

ON THE STARTING DATE

Applications which fall

8.—(1) Proceedings in respect of an application which is made to the Court under any of the provisions mentioned in sub-paragraph (2), but which is not determined before the starting date, cease on that date.

(2) The provisions are—
    (a)   sections 2(2), 35(3), 37(1) and 40(1) of the RTPA and paragraph 5 of Schedule 4 to that Act;
    (b)   section 4(1) of the RTPA so far as the application relates to an order under section 2(2) of that Act; and
    (c)   section 25(2) of the RPA.

(3) The power of the Court to make an order for costs in relation to any proceedings is not affected by anything in this paragraph or by the repeals made by section 1.

Orders and approvals which fall

9.—(1) An order in force immediately before the starting date under—
  (a) section 2(2), 29(1), 30(1), 33(4), 35(3) or 37(1) of the RTPA; or
  (b) section 25(2) of the RPA,

ceases to have effect on that date.

(2) An approval in force immediately before the starting date under section 32 of the RTPA ceases to have effect on that date.

Definitions For "RPA", "RTPA", "the Court" and "starting date", see para 1(1) of this Schedule.
References See para 9.22.

PART IV
ON AND AFTER THE STARTING DATE

CHAPTER I
GENERAL

Duty of Director to maintain register etc

10.—(1) This paragraph applies even though the relevant provisions of the RTPA are repealed by this Act.

(2) The Director is to continue on and after the starting date to be under the duty imposed by section 1(2)(a) of the RTPA to maintain a register in respect of agreements—
  (a) particulars of which are, on the starting date, entered or filed on the register;
  (b) which fall within sub-paragraph (4);
  (c) which immediately before the starting date are the subject of proceedings under the RTPA which do not cease on that date by virtue of this Schedule; or
  (d) in relation to which a court gives directions to the Director after the starting date in the course of proceedings in which a question arises as to whether an agreement was, before that date—
    (i) one to which the RTPA applied;
    (ii) subject to registration under that Act;
    (iii) a non-notifiable agreement for the purposes of that Act.

(3) The Director is to continue on and after the starting date to be under the duties imposed by section 1(2)(a) and (b) of the RTPA of compiling a register of agreements and entering or filing certain particulars in the register, but only in respect of agreements of a kind referred to in paragraph (b), (c) or (d) of sub-paragraph (2).

(4) An agreement falls within this sub-paragraph if—
  (a) it is subject to registration under the RTPA but—
    (i) is not a non-notifiable agreement within the meaning of section 27A of the RTPA, or
    (ii) is not one to which paragraph 5 applies;
  (b) particulars of the agreement have been provided to the Director before the starting date; and
  (c) as at the starting date no entry or filing has been made in the register in respect of the agreement.

(5) Sections 23 and 27 of the RTPA are to apply after the starting date in respect of the register subject to such modifications, if any, as may be prescribed.

(6) In sub-paragraph (2)(d) "court" means—
  (a) the High Court;
  (b) the Court of Appeal;
  (c) the Court of Session;
  (d) the High Court or Court of Appeal in Northern Ireland; or
  (e) the House of Lords.

RTPA section 3 applications

11.—(1) Even though section 3 of the RTPA is repealed by this Act, its provisions (and so far as necessary that Act) are to continue to apply, with such modifications (if any) as may be prescribed—

    (a)   in relation to a continuing application under that section; or

    (b)   so as to allow an application to be made under that section on or after the starting date in respect of a continuing application under section 1(3) of the RTPA.

(2) "Continuing application" means an application made, but not determined, before the starting date.

RTPA section 26 applications

12.—(1) Even though section 26 of the RTPA is repealed by this Act, its provisions (and so far as necessary that Act) are to continue to apply, with such modifications (if any) as may be prescribed, in relation to an application which is made under that section, but not determined, before the starting date.

(2) If an application under section 26 is determined on or after the starting date, this Schedule has effect in relation to the agreement concerned as if the application had been determined immediately before that date.

Right to bring civil proceedings

13.—(1) Even though section 35 of the RTPA is repealed by this Act, its provisions (and so far as necessary that Act) are to continue to apply in respect of a person who, immediately before the starting date, has a right by virtue of section 27ZA or 35(2) of that Act to bring civil proceedings in respect of an agreement (but only so far as that right relates to any period before the starting date or, where there are continuing proceedings, the determination of the proceedings).

(2) Even though section 25 of the RPA is repealed by this Act, the provisions of that section (and so far as necessary that Act) are to continue to apply in respect of a person who, immediately before the starting date, has a right by virtue of subsection (3) of that section to bring civil proceedings (but only so far as that right relates to any period before the starting date or, where there are continuing proceedings, the determination of the proceedings).

Definitions   For "RPA", "RTPA", "Director", "prescribed" and "starting date", see para 1(1) of this Schedule; for "continuing proceedings, see para 15 of this Schedule; as to "person", see s 59(1).
References   See para 9.19.

CHAPTER II
CONTINUING PROCEEDINGS

The general rule

14.—(1) The Chapter I prohibition does not apply to an agreement at any time when the agreement is the subject of continuing proceedings under the RTPA.

(2) The Chapter I prohibition does not apply to an agreement relating to goods which are the subject of continuing proceedings under section 16 or 17 of the RPA to the extent to which the agreement consists of exempt provisions.

(3) In sub-paragraph (2) "exempt provisions" means those provisions of the agreement which would, disregarding section 14 of the RPA, be—

    (a)   void as a result of section 9(1) of the RPA; or

    (b)   unlawful as a result of section 9(2) or II of the RPA.

(4) If the Chapter I prohibition does not apply to an agreement because of this paragraph, the provisions of, or made under, the RTPA or the RPA are to continue to have effect in relation to the agreement.

(5) The repeals made by section 1 do not affect—

    (a)   continuing proceedings; or

    (b)   proceedings of the kind referred to in paragraph 11 or 12 of this Schedule which are continuing after the starting date.

Meaning of "continuing proceedings"

15.—(1) For the purposes of this Schedule "continuing proceedings" means proceedings in respect of an application made to the Court under the RTPA or the RPA, but not determined, before the starting date.

(2) But proceedings under section 3 or 26 of the RTPA to which paragraph 11 or 12 applies are not continuing proceedings.

(3) The question whether (for the purposes of Part III, or this Part, of this Schedule) an application has been determined is to be decided in accordance with sub-paragraphs (4) and (5).

(4) If an appeal against the decision on the application is brought, the application is not determined until—
    (a)   the appeal is disposed of or withdrawn; or
    (b)   if as a result of the appeal the case is referred back to the Court—
        (i)   the expiry of the period within which an appeal ("the further appeal") in respect of the Court's decision on that reference could have been brought had this Act not been passed; or
        (ii)   if later, the date on which the further appeal is disposed of or withdrawn.

(5) Otherwise, the application is not determined until the expiry of the period within which any party to the application would have been able to bring an appeal against the decision on the application had this Act not been passed.

RTPA section 4 proceedings

16. Proceedings on an application for an order under section 4 of the RTPA are also continuing proceedings if—
    (a)   leave to make the application is applied for before the starting date but the proceedings in respect of that application for leave are not determined before that date; or
    (b)   leave to make an application for an order under that section is granted before the starting date but the application itself is not made before that date.

RPA section 16 or 17 proceedings

17. Proceedings on an application for an order under section 16 or 17 of the RPA are also continuing proceedings if—
    (a)   leave to make the application is applied for before the starting date but the proceedings in respect of that application for leave are not determined before that date; or
    (b)   leave to make an application for an order under section 16 or 17 of the RPA is granted before the starting date, but the application itself is not made before that date.

Continuing proceedings which are discontinued

18.—(1) On an application made jointly to the Court by all the parties to any continuing proceedings, the Court must, if it is satisfied that the parties wish it to do so, discontinue the proceedings.

(2) If, on an application under sub-paragraph (1) or for any other reason, the Court orders the proceedings to be discontinued, this Schedule has effect (subject to paragraphs 21 and 22) from the date on which the proceedings are discontinued as if they had never been instituted.

Definitions   For "the Chapter I prohibition", see s 2(8); for "RPA", "RTPTA", "the Court" and "starting date", see para 1(1) of this Schedule.
References   See paras 9.18, 9.20.

CHAPTER III
THE TRANSITIONAL PERIOD

The general rule

19.—(1) Except where this Chapter or Chapter IV provides otherwise, there is a transitional period, beginning on the starting date and lasting for one year, for any agreement made before the starting date.

(2) The Chapter I prohibition does not apply to an agreement to the extent to which there is a transitional period for the agreement.

(3) The Secretary of State may by regulations provide for sections 13 to 16 and Schedule 5 to apply with such modifications (if any) as may be specified in the regulations, in respect of applications to the Director about agreements for which there is a transitional period.

Cases for which there is no transitional period

20.—(1) There is no transitional period for an agreement to the extent to which, immediately before the starting date, it is—
    (a) void under section 2(1) or 35(1)(a) of the RTPA;
    (b) the subject of an order under section 2(2) or 35(3) of the RTPA; or
    (c) unlawful under section 1, 2 or 11 of the RPA or void under section 9 of that Act.

(2) There is no transitional period for an agreement to the extent to which, before the starting date, a person has acted unlawfully for the purposes of section 27ZA(2) or (3) of the RTPA in respect of the agreement.

(3) There is no transitional period for an agreement to which paragraph 25(4) applies.

(4) There is no transitional period for—
    (a) an agreement in respect of which there are continuing proceedings, or
    (b) an agreement relating to goods in respect of which there are continuing proceedings,
to the extent to which the agreement is, when the proceedings are determined, void or unlawful.

Continuing proceedings under the RTPA

21. In the case of an agreement which is the subject of continuing proceedings under the RTPA, the transitional period begins—
    (a) if the proceedings are discontinued, on the date of discontinuance;
    (b) otherwise, when the proceedings are determined.

Continuing proceedings under the RPA

22.—(1) In the case of an agreement relating to goods which are the subject of continuing proceedings under the RPA, the transitional period for the exempt provisions of the agreement begins—
    (a) if the proceedings are discontinued, on the date of discontinuance;
    (b) otherwise, when the proceedings are determined.

(2) In sub-paragraph (1) "exempt provisions" has the meaning given by paragraph 14(3).

Provisions not contrary to public interest

23.—(1) To the extent to which an agreement contains provisions which, immediately before the starting date, are provisions which the Court has found not to be contrary to the public interest, the transitional period lasts for five years.

(2) Sub-paragraph (1) is subject to paragraph 20(4).

(3) To the extent to which an agreement which on the starting date is the subject of continuing proceedings is, when the proceedings are determined, found by the Court not to be contrary to the public interest, the transitional period lasts for five years.

Goods

24.—(1) In the case of an agreement relating to goods which, immediately before the starting date, are exempt under section 14 of the RPA, there is a transitional period for the agreement to the extent to which it consists of exempt provisions.

(2) Sub-paragraph (1) is subject to paragraph 20(4).

(3) In the case of an agreement relating to goods—
    (a) which on the starting date are the subject of continuing proceedings, and
    (b) which, when the proceedings are determined, are found to be exempt under section 14 of the RPA,
there is a transitional period for the agreement, to the extent to which it consists of exempt provisions.

(4)   In each case, the transitional period lasts for five years.

(5)   In sub-paragraphs (1) and (3) "exempt provisions" means those provisions of the agreement which would, disregarding section 14 of the RPA, be—
- (a)   void as a result of section 9(1) of the RPA; or
- (b)   unlawful as a result of section 9(2) or 11 of the RPA.

Transitional period for certain agreements

25.—(1) This paragraph applies to agreements—
- (a)   which are subject to registration under the RTPA but which—
    - (i)   are not non-notifiable agreements within the meaning of section 27A of the RTPA, or
    - (ii)   are not agreements to which paragraph 5 applies; and
- (b)   in respect of which the time for furnishing relevant particulars as required by or under the RTPA expires on or after the starting date.

(2)   "Relevant particulars" means—
- (a)   particulars which are required to be furnished by virtue of section 24 of the RTPA; or
- (b)   particulars of any variation of an agreement which are required to be furnished by virtue of sections 24 and 27 of the RTPA.

(3)   There is a transitional period of one year for an agreement to which this paragraph applies if—
- (a)   relevant particulars are furnished before the starting date; and
- (b)   no person has acted unlawfully (for the purposes of section 27ZA(2) or (3) of the RTPA) in respect of the agreement.

(4)   If relevant particulars are not furnished by the starting date, section 35(1)(a) of the RTPA does not apply in relation to the agreement (unless sub-paragraph (5) applies).

(5)   This sub-paragraph applies if a person falling within section 27ZA(2) or (3) of the RTPA has acted unlawfully for the purposes of those subsections in respect of the agreement.

Special cases

26.—(1) In the case of an agreement in respect of which—
- (a)   a direction under section 127(2) of the Financial Services Act 1986 ("the 1986 Act") is in force immediately before the starting date, or
- (b)   a direction under section 194A(3) of the Broadcasting Act 1990 ("the 1990 Act") is in force immediately before the starting date,

the transitional period lasts for five years.

(2)   To the extent to which an agreement is the subject of a declaration—
- (a)   made by the Treasury under section 127(3) of the 1986 Act, and
- (b)   in force immediately before the starting date,

the transitional period lasts for five years.

(3)   Sub-paragraphs (1) and (2) do not affect the power of—
- (a)   the Treasury to make a declaration under section 127(2) of the 1986 Act (as amended by Schedule 2 to this Act),
- (b)   the Secretary of State to make a declaration under section 194A of the 1990 Act (as amended by Schedule 2 to this Act),

in respect of an agreement for which there is a transitional period.

Definitions   For "the Chapter I prohibition", see s 2(8); for "RPA", "RTPA", "the Court", "Director" and "starting date", see para 1(1) of this Schedule; for "continuing proceedings", see para 15 of this Schedule; as to "person", see s 59(1).
References   See paras 9.10–9.12, 9.21.

CHAPTER IV
THE UTILITIES

General

27.   In this Chapter "the relevant period" means the period beginning with the starting date and ending immediately before the fifth anniversary of that date.

Electricity

28.—(1) For an agreement to which, immediately before the starting date, the RTPA does not apply by virtue of a section 100 order, there is a transitional period—

    (a)   beginning on the starting date; and

    (b)   ending at the end of the relevant period.

(2) For an agreement which is made at any time after the starting date and to which, had the RTPA not been repealed, that Act would not at the time at which the agreement is made have applied by virtue of a section 100 order, there is a transitional period—

    (a)   beginning on the date on which the agreement is made; and

    (b)   ending at the end of the relevant period.

(3) For an agreement (whether made before or after the starting date) which, during the relevant period, is varied at any time in such a way that it becomes an agreement which, had the RTPA not been repealed, would at that time have been one to which that Act did not apply by virtue of a section 100 order, there is a transitional period—

    (a)   beginning on the date on which the variation is made; and

    (b)   ending at the end of the relevant period.

(4) If an agreement for which there is a transitional period as a result of sub-paragraph (1), (2) or (3) is varied during the relevant period, the transitional period for the agreement continues if, had the RTPA not been repealed, the agreement would have continued to be one to which that Act did not apply by virtue of a section 100 order.

(5) But if an agreement for which there is a transitional period as a result of sub-paragraph (1), (2) or (3) ceases to be one to which, had it not been repealed, the RTPA would not have applied by virtue of a section 100 order, the transitional period ends on the date on which the agreement so ceases.

(6) Sub-paragraph (3) is subject to paragraph 20.

(7) In this paragraph and paragraph 29—

    "section 100 order" means an order made under section 100 of the Electricity Act 1989; and

    expressions which are also used in Part I of the Electricity Act 1989 have the same meaning as in that Part.

Electricity: power to make transitional orders

29.—(1) There is a transitional period for an agreement (whether made before or after the starting date) relating to the generation, transmission or supply of electricity which—

    (a)   is specified, or is of a description specified, in an order ("a transitional order") made by the Secretary of State (whether before or after the making of the agreement but before the end of the relevant period); and

    (b)   satisfies such conditions as may be specified in the order.

(2) A transitional order may make provision as to when the transitional period in respect of such an agreement is to start or to be deemed to have started.

(3) The transitional period for such an agreement ends at the end of the relevant period.

(4) But if the agreement—

    (a)   ceases to be one to which a transitional order applies, or

    (b)   ceases to satisfy one or more of the conditions specified in the transitional order,

the transitional period ends on the date on which the agreement so ceases.

(5) Before making a transitional order, the Secretary of State must consult the Director General of Electricity Supply and the Director.

(6) The conditions specified in a transitional order may include conditions which refer any matter to the Secretary of State for determination after such consultation as may be so specified.

(7) In the application of this paragraph to Northern Ireland, the reference in sub-paragraph (5) to the Director General of Electricity Supply is to be read as a reference to the Director General of Electricity Supply for Northern Ireland.

Gas

30.—(1) For an agreement to which, immediately before the starting date, the RTPA does not apply by virtue of section 62 or a section 62 order, there is a transitional period—

    (a)   beginning on the starting date; and

    (b)   ending at the end of the relevant period.

(2) For an agreement which is made at any time after the starting date and to which, had the RTPA not been repealed, that Act would not at the time at which the agreement is made have applied by virtue of section 62 or a section 62 order, there is a transitional period—

    (a)   beginning on the date on which the agreement is made; and

    (b)   ending at the end of the relevant period.

(3) For an agreement (whether made before or after the starting date) which, during the relevant period, is varied at any time in such a way that it becomes an agreement which, had the RTPA not been repealed, would at that time have been one to which that Act did not apply by virtue of section 62 or a section 62 order, there is a transitional period—

    (a)   beginning on the date on which the variation is made; and

    (b)   ending at the end of the relevant period.

(4) If an agreement for which there is a transitional period as a result of sub-paragraph (1), (2) or (3) is varied during the relevant period, the transitional period for the agreement continues if, had the RTPA not been repealed, the agreement would have continued to be one to which that Act did not apply by virtue of section 62 or a section 62 order.

(5) But if an agreement for which there is a transitional period as a result of sub-paragraph (1), (2) or (3) ceases to be one to which, had it not been repealed, the RTPA would not have applied by virtue of section 62 or a section 62 order, the transitional period ends on the date on which the agreement so ceases.

(6) Sub-paragraph (3) also applies in relation to a modification which is treated as an agreement made on or after 28th November 1985 by virtue of section 62(4).

(7) Sub-paragraph (3) is subject to paragraph 20.

(8) In this paragraph and paragraph 31—

    "section 62" means section 62 of the Gas Act 1986;

    "section 62 order" means an order made under section 62.

Gas: power to make transitional orders

31.—(1) There is a transitional period for an agreement of a description falling within section 62(2)(a) and (b) or section 62(2A)(a) and (b) which—

    (a)   is specified, or is of a description specified, in an order ("a transitional order") made by the Secretary of State (whether before or after the making of the agreement but before the end of the relevant period); and

    (b)   satisfies such conditions as may be specified in the order.

(2) A transitional order may make provision as to when the transitional period in respect of such an agreement is to start or to be deemed to have started.

(3) The transitional period for such an agreement ends at the end of the relevant period.

(4) But if the agreement—

    (a)   ceases to be one to which a transitional order applies, or

    (b)   ceases to satisfy one or more of the conditions specified in the transitional order,

the transitional period ends on the date when the agreement so ceases.

(5) Before making a transitional order, the Secretary of State must consult the Director General of Gas Supply and the Director.

(6) The conditions specified in a transitional order may include—

    (a)   conditions which are to be satisfied in relation to a time before the coming into force of this paragraph;

    (b)   conditions which refer any matter (which may be the general question whether the Chapter I prohibition should apply to a particular agreement) to the

Secretary of State, the Director or the Director General of Gas Supply for determination after such consultation as may be so specified.

Gas: Northern Ireland

32.—(1) For an agreement to which, immediately before the starting date, the RTPA does not apply by virtue of an Article 41 order, there is a transitional period—
  (a)   beginning on the starting date; and
  (b)   ending at the end of the relevant period.

(2)   For an agreement which is made at any time after the starting date and to which, had the RTPA not been repealed, that Act would not at the time at which the agreement is made have applied by virtue of an Article 41 order, there is a transitional period—
  (a)   beginning on the date on which the agreement is made; and
  (b)   ending at the end of the relevant period.

(3)   For an agreement (whether made before or after the starting date) which, during the relevant period, is varied at any time in such a way that it becomes an agreement which, had the RTPA not been repealed, would at that time have been one to which that Act did not apply by virtue of an Article 41 order, there is a transitional period—
  (a)   beginning on the date on which the variation is made; and
  (b)   ending at the end of the relevant period.

(4)   If an agreement for which there is a transitional period as a result of sub-paragraph (1), (2) or (3) is varied during the relevant period, the transitional period for the agreement continues if, had the RTPA not been repealed, the agreement would have continued to be one to which that Act did not apply by virtue of an Article 41 order.

(5)   But if an agreement for which there is a transitional period as a result of sub-paragraph (1), (2) or (3) ceases to be one to which, had it not been repealed, the RTPA would not have applied by virtue of an Article 41 order, the transitional period ends on the date on which the agreement so ceases.

(6)   Sub-paragraph (3) is subject to paragraph 20.

(7)   In this paragraph and paragraph 33—
    "Article 41 order" means an order under Article 41 of the Gas (Northern Ireland) Order 1996;
    "Department" means the Department of Economic Development.

Gas: Northern Ireland — power to make transitional orders

33.—(1) There is a transitional period for an agreement of a description falling within Article 41(1) which—
  (a)   is specified, or is of a description specified, in an order ("a transitional order") made by the Department (whether before or after the making of the agreement but before the end of the relevant period); and
  (b)   satisfies such conditions as may be specified in the order.

(2)   A transitional order may make provision as to when the transitional period in respect of such an agreement is to start or to be deemed to have started.

(3)   The transitional period for such an agreement ends at the end of the relevant period.

(4)   But if the agreement—
  (a)   ceases to be one to which a transitional order applies, or
  (b)   ceases to satisfy one or more of the conditions specified in the transitional order,
the transitional period ends on the date when the agreement so ceases.

(5)   Before making a transitional order, the Department must consult the Director General of Gas for Northern Ireland and the Director.

(6)   The conditions specified in a transitional order may include conditions which refer any matter (which may be the general question whether the Chapter I prohibition should apply to a particular agreement) to the Department for determination after such consultation as may be so specified.

Railways

34.—(1) In this paragraph—

"section 131" means section 131 of the Railways Act 1993 ("the 1993 Act");

"section 131 agreement" means an agreement—

    (a) to which the RTPA does not apply immediately before the starting date by virtue of section 131(1); or

    (b) in respect of which a direction under section 131(3) is in force immediately before that date;

"non-exempt agreement" means an agreement relating to the provision of railway services (whether made before or after the starting date) which is not a section 131 agreement; and

"railway services" has the meaning given by section 82 of the 1993 Act.

(2) For a section 131 agreement there is a transitional period of five years.

(3) There is a transitional period for a non-exempt agreement to the extent to which the agreement is at any time before the end of the relevant period required or approved—

    (a) by the Secretary of State or the Rail Regulator in pursuance of any function assigned or transferred to him under or by virtue of any provision of the 1993 Act;

    (b) by or under any agreement the making of which is required or approved by the Secretary of State or the Rail Regulator in the exercise of any such function; or

    (c) by or under a licence granted under Part I of the 1993 Act.

(4) The transitional period conferred by sub-paragraph (3)—

    (a) is to be taken to have begun on the starting date; and

    (b) ends at the end of the relevant period.

(5) Sub-paragraph (3) is subject to paragraph 20.

(6) Any variation of a section 131 agreement on or after the starting date is to be treated, for the purposes of this paragraph, as a separate non-exempt agreement.

The regulators

35.—(1) Subject to sub-paragraph (3), each of the regulators may exercise, in respect of sectoral matters and concurrently with the Director, the functions of the Director under paragraph 3, 7, 19(3), 36, 37, 38 or 39.

(2) In sub-paragraph (1) "sectoral matters" means—

    (a) in the case of the Director General of Telecommunications, the matters referred to in section 50(3) of the Telecommunications Act 1984;

    (b) in the case of the Director General of Gas Supply, the matters referred to in section 36A(3) and (4) of the Gas Act 1986;

    (c) in the case of the Director General of Electricity Supply, the matters referred to in section 43(3) of the Electricity Act 1989;

    (d) in the case of the Director General of Electricity Supply for Northern Ireland, the matters referred to in Article 46(3) of the Electricity (Northern Ireland) Order 1992;

    (e) in the case of the Director General of Water Services, the matters referred to in section 31(3) of the Water Industry Act 1991;

    (f) in the case of the Rail Regulator, the matters referred to in section 67(3) of the Railways Act 1993;

    (g) in the case of the Director General of Gas for Northern Ireland, the matters referred to in Article 23(3) of the Gas (Northern Ireland) Order 1996.

(3) The power to give directions in paragraph 7(2) is exercisable by the Director only but if the Director is preparing directions which relate to a matter in respect of which a regulator exercises concurrent jurisdiction, he must consult that regulator.

(4) Consultations conducted by the Director before the enactment date, with a view to preparing directions which have effect on or after that date, are to be taken to satisfy sub-paragraph (3).

(5) References to enactments in sub-paragraph (2) are to the enactments as amended by or under this Act.

Definitions   For "the Chapter I prohibition", see s 2(8); for "RTPA", "Director", "enactment date", "regulator" and "starting date", see para 1(1) of this Schedule.
References   See paras 9.31, 9.32.

CHAPTER V
EXTENDING THE TRANSITIONAL PERIOD

36.—(1) A party to an agreement for which there is a transitional period may apply to the Director, not less than three months before the end of the period, for the period to be extended.

(2) The Director may (on his own initiative or on an application under sub-paragraph (1))—
    (a) extend a one-year transitional period by not more than twelve months;
    (b) extend a transitional period of any period other than one year by not more than six months.

(3) An application under sub-paragraph (1) must—
    (a) be in such form as may be specified; and
    (b) include such documents and information as may be specified.

(4) If the Director extends the transitional period under this paragraph, he must give notice in such form, and to such persons, as may be specified.

(5) The Director may not extend a transitional period more than once.

(6) In this paragraph—
    "person" has the same meaning as in Part I; and
    "specified" means specified in rules made by the Director under section 51.

Definitions   For "Director" and as to "document" and "information", see para 1(1) of this Schedule.
References   See para 9.13.

CHAPTER VI
TERMINATING THE TRANSITIONAL PERIOD

General

37.—(1) Subject to sub-paragraph (2), the Director may by a direction in writing terminate the transitional period for an agreement, but only in accordance with paragraph 38.

(2) The Director may not terminate the transitional period, nor exercise any of the powers in paragraph 38, in respect of an agreement which is excluded from the Chapter I prohibition by virtue of any of the provisions of Part I of this Act other than paragraph 1 of Schedule 1 or paragraph 2 or 9 of Schedule 3.

Circumstances in which the Director may terminate the transitional period

38.—(1) If the Director is considering whether to give a direction under paragraph 37 ("a direction"), he may in writing require any party to the agreement concerned to give him such information in connection with that agreement as he may require.

(2) If at the end of such period as may be specified in rules made under section 51, a person has failed, without reasonable excuse, to comply with a requirement imposed under sub-paragraph (1), the Director may give a direction.

(3) The Director may also give a direction if he considers—
    (a) that the agreement would, but for the transitional period or a relevant exclusion, infringe the Chapter I prohibition; and
    (b) that he would not be likely to grant the agreement an unconditional individual exemption.

(4) For the purposes of sub-paragraph (3) an individual exemption is unconditional if no conditions or obligations are imposed in respect of it under section 4(3)(a).

(5) In this paragraph—
    "person" has the same meaning as in Part I;
    "relevant exclusion" means an exclusion under paragraph 1 of Schedule 1 or paragraph 2 or 9 of Schedule 3.

Procedural requirements on giving a paragraph 37 direction

39.—(1) The Director must specify in a direction under paragraph 37 ("a direction") the date on which it is to have effect (which must not be less than 28 days after the direction is given).

(2) Copies of the direction must be given to—
   (a) each of the parties concerned, and
   (b) the Secretary of State,

not less than 28 days before the date on which the direction is to have effect.

(3) In relation to an agreement to which a direction applies, the transitional period (if it has not already ended) ends on the date specified in the direction unless, before that date, the direction is revoked by the Director or the Secretary of State.

(4) If a direction is revoked, the Director may give a further direction in respect of the same agreement only if he is satisfied that there has been a material change of circumstance since the revocation.

(5) If, as a result of paragraph 24(1) or (3), there is a transitional period in respect of provisions of an agreement relating to goods—
   (a) which immediately before the starting date are exempt under section 14 of the RPA, or
   (b) which, when continuing proceedings are determined, are found to be exempt under section 14 of the RPA,

the period is not affected by paragraph 37 or 38.

Definitions   For "the Chapter I prohibition", see s 2(8); for "individual exemption", see s 4(2); for "RPA", "Director" and "starting date" and as to "information", see Sch 1, para 1(1) of this Schedule; for "continuing proceedings", see para 15 of this Schedule.
References   See paras 9.14–9.17, 9.34.

PART V
THE FAIR TRADING ACT 1973

References to the Monopolies and Mergers Commission

40.—(1) If, on the date on which the repeal by this Act of a provision mentioned in sub-paragraph (2) comes into force, the Monopolies and Mergers Commission has not completed a reference which was made to it before that date, continued consideration of the reference may include consideration of a question which could not have been considered if the provision had not been repealed.

(2) The provisions are—
   (a) sections 10(2), 54(5) and 78(3) and paragraph 3(1) and (2) of Schedule 8 to the Fair Trading Act 1973 (c 41);
   (b) section 11(8)(b) of the Competition Act 1980 (c 21);
   (c) section 14(2) of the Telecommunications Act 1984 (c 12);
   (d) section 45(3) of the Airports Act 1986 (c 31);
   (e) section 25(2) of the Gas Act 1986 (c 44);
   (f) section 13(2) of the Electricity Act 1989 (c 29);
   (g) section 15(2) of the Water Industry Act 1991 (c 56);
   (h) article 16(2) of the Electricity (Northern Ireland) Order 1992;
   (i) section 14(2) of the Railways Act 1993 (c 43);
   (j) article 36(3) of the Airports (Northern Ireland) Order 1994;
   (k) article 16(2) of the Gas (Northern Ireland) Order 1996.

Orders under Schedule 8

41.—(1) In this paragraph—
   "the 1973 Act" means the Fair Trading Act 1973;
   "agreement" means an agreement entered into before the date on which the repeal of the limiting provisions comes into force;
   "the order" means an order under section 56 or 73 of the 1973 Act;

"the limiting provisions" means sub-paragraph (1) or (2) of paragraph 3 of Schedule 8 to the 1973 Act (limit on power to make orders under paragraph 1 or 2 of that Schedule) and includes any provision of the order included because of either of those sub-paragraphs; and

"transitional period" means the period which—
(a) begins on the day on which the repeal of the limiting provisions comes into force; and
(b) ends on the first anniversary of the starting date.

(2) Sub-paragraph (3) applies to any agreement to the extent to which it would have been unlawful (in accordance with the provisions of the order) but for the limiting provisions.

(3) As from the end of the transitional period, the order is to have effect in relation to the agreement as if the limiting provisions had never had effect.

Part III of the Act

42.—(1) The repeals made by section 1 do not affect any proceedings in respect of an application which is made to the Court under Part III of the Fair Trading Act 1973, but is not determined, before the starting date.

(2) The question whether (for the purposes of sub-paragraph (1)) an application has been determined is to be decided in accordance with sub-paragraphs (3) and (4).

(3) If an appeal against the decision on the application is brought, the application is not determined until—
(a) the appeal is disposed of or withdrawn; or
(b) if as a result of the appeal the case is referred back to the Court—
(i) the expiry of the period within which an appeal ("the further appeal") in respect of the Court's decision on that reference could have been brought had this Act not been passed; or
(ii) if later, the date on which the further appeal is disposed of or withdrawn.

(4) Otherwise, the application is not determined until the expiry of the period within which any party to the application would have been able to bring an appeal against the decision on the application had this Act not been passed.

(5) Any amendment made by Schedule 12 to this Act which substitutes references to a relevant Court for references to the Court is not to affect proceedings of the kind referred to in sub-paragraph (1).

Definitions   For "the Court" and "starting date", see para 1(1) of this Schedule.
References   See para 9.37.

PART VI
THE COMPETITION ACT 1980

Undertakings

43.—(1) Subject to sub-paragraph (2), an undertaking accepted by the Director under section 4 or 9 of the Competition Act 1980 ceases to have effect on the coming into force of the repeal by this Act of that section.

(2) If the undertaking relates to an agreement which on the starting date is the subject of continuing proceedings, the undertaking continues to have effect for the purposes of section 29 of the Competition Act 1980 until the proceedings are determined.

Application of sections 25 and 26

44. The repeals made by section 1 do not affect—
(a) the operation of section 25 of the Competition Act 1980 in relation to an application under section 1(3) of the RTPA which is made before the starting date;
(b) an application under section 26 of the Competition Act 1980 which is made before the starting date.

Definitions   For "RTPA", "Director" and "starting date", see para 1(1) of this Schedule; for "continuing proceedings", see para 15 of this Schedule.
References   See para 9.38.

PART VII
MISCELLANEOUS

Disclosure of information

45.—(1) Section 55 of this Act applies in relation to information which, immediately before the starting date, is subject to section 41 of the RTPA as it applies in relation to information obtained under or as a result of Part I.

(2) But section 55 does not apply to any disclosure of information of the kind referred to in sub-paragraph (1) if the disclosure is made—

 (a) for the purpose of facilitating the performance of functions of a designated person under the Control of Misleading Advertisements Regulations 1988; or

 (b) for the purposes of any proceedings before the Court or of any other legal proceedings under the RTPA or the Fair Trading Act 1973 or the Control of Misleading Advertisements Regulations 1988.

(3) Section 56 applies in relation to information of the kind referred to in sub-paragraph (1) if particulars containing the information have been entered or filed on the special section of the register maintained by the Director under, or as a result of, section 27 of the RTPA or paragraph 10 of this Schedule.

(4) Section 55 has effect, in relation to the matters as to which section 41(2) of the RTPA had effect, as if it contained a provision similar to section 41(2).

The Court

46. If it appears to the Lord Chancellor that a person who ceases to be a non-judicial member of the Court as a result of this Act should receive compensation for loss of office, he may pay to him out of moneys provided by Parliament such sum as he may with the approval of the Treasury determine.

Definitions   For "RTPA", "the Court", "starting date" and as to "information", see para 1(1) of this Schedule.
References   See para 9.39.

SCHEDULE 14

Section 74(3)

REPEALS AND REVOCATIONS

PART I
REPEALS

Chapter	Short title	Extent of repeal
1973 c 41.	The Fair Trading Act 1973.	Section 4.
		Section 10(2).
		Section 45.
		Section 54(5).
		Section 78(3).
		In section 81(1), in the words before paragraph (a), from "and the Commission" to "of this Act)"; in paragraph (b), "or the Commission, as the case may be" and "or of the Commission"; in subsection (2), "or the Commission" and "or of the Commission" and in subsection (3), from "and, in the case," to "85 of this Act", and "or the Commission, as the case may be,".

Chapter	Short title	Extent of repeal
		In section 83, in subsection (1) "Subject to subsection (1A) below" and subsection (1A).
		In section 135(1), in the words before paragraph (a) and in paragraph (b), "or the Commission", and paragraph (a).
		Schedule 3.
		In Schedule 8, paragraph 3(1) and (2).
1976 c 33.	The Restrictive Practices Court Act 1976.	The whole Act.
1976 c 34.	The Restrictive Trade Practices Act 1976.	The whole Act.
1976 c 53.	The Resale Prices Act 1976.	The whole Act.
1976 c 76.	The Energy Act 1976.	Section 5.
1977 c 19.	The Restrictive Trade Practices Act 1977.	The whole Act.
1977 c 37.	The Patents Act 1977.	Sections 44 and 45.
1979 c 38.	The Estate Agents Act 1979.	In section 10(3), "or the Restrictive Trade Practices Act 1976."
1980 c 21.	The Competition Act 1980.	Sections 2 to 10.
		In section 11(8), paragraph (b) and the "and" immediately before it.
		In section 13(1), from "but the giving" to the end.
		In section 15, subsections (2)(b), (3) and (4).
		Section 16(3).
		In section 17, "8(1)" in subsections (1) and (3) to (5) and in subsection (2) "8(1) or".
		In section 19(3), paragraph (d).
		In section 19(5)(a), "or in anything published under section 4(2)(a) above".
		Section 22.
		Sections 25 to 30.
		In section 31, subsection (2) and "10" in subsection (3).
		Section 33(3) and (4).
1984 c 12.	The Telecommunications Act 1984.	Section 14(2).
		In section 16(5), the "or" immediately after paragraph (a).
		In section 50(4), paragraph (c) and the "and" immediately after it.
		In section 50(5), "or (3)".
		In section 50(7), "or the 1980 Act".
		In section 95(1), "or section 10(2)(a) of the 1980 Act".

Chapter	Short title	Extent of repeal
		In section 95(2), paragraph (c) and the "or" immediately before it.
		In section 95(3), "or the 1980 Act".
		In section 101(3), paragraphs (d) and (e).
1986 c 31.	The Airports Act 1986.	Section 45(3).
		In section 54(1), "or section 10(2)(a) of the 1980 Act".
		In section 54(3), paragraph (c) and the "or" immediately before it.
		In section 54(4), "or the 1980 Act".
		In section 56(a)(ii), "or the 1980 Act".
1986 c 44.	The Gas Act 1986.	Section 25(2).
		In section 27(1), "or section 10(2)(a) of the Competition Act 1980".
		In section 27(3)(a), from "or" to "competition reference".
		In section 27(6), "or the said Act of 1980".
		In section 28(5), the "or" immediately after paragraph (aa).
		In section 36A(5), paragraph (d) and the "and" immediately before it.
		In section 36A(6), "or (3)".
		In section 36A(8), "or under the 1980 Act".
		In section 36A(9), "or the 1980 Act".
		In section 42(3), paragraphs (e) and (f).
1986 c 60.	The Financial Services Act 1986.	Section 126.
1987 c 43.	The Consumer Protection Act 1987.	In section 38(3), paragraphs (e) and (f).
1987 c 53.	The Channel Tunnel Act 1987.	In section 33(2), paragraph (c) and the "and" immediately before it.
		In section 33(5), paragraphs (b) and (c).
1988 c 54.	The Road Traffic (Consequential Provisions) Act 1988.	In Schedule 3, paragraph 19.
1989 c 15.	The Water Act 1989.	In section 174(3), paragraphs (d) and (e).
1989 c 29.	The Electricity Act 1989.	Section 13(2).
		In section 15(1), paragraph (b) and the "or" immediately before it.
		In section 15(2), paragraph (c) and the "or" immediately before it.
		In section 15(3), "or the 1980 Act".
		In section 25(5), the "or" immediately after paragraph (b).
		In section 43(4), paragraph (c) and the "and" immediately after it.
		In section 43(5), "or (3)".

Chapter	Short title	Extent of repeal
		In section 43(7), "or the 1980 Act".
		In section 57(3), paragraphs (d) and (e).
1989 c 40.	The Companies Act 1989.	In Schedule 20, paragraphs 21 to 24.
1990 c 42.	The Broadcasting Act 1990.	In section 193(2), paragraph (c) and the "and" immediately before it.
		In section 193(4), "or the Competition Act 1980".
1991 c 56.	The Water Industry Act 1991.	In section 12(5), "or the 1980 Act".
		Section 15(2).
		In section 17(1), paragraph (b) and the "or" immediately before it.
		In section 17(2), paragraph (c) and the "or" immediately before it.
		In section 17(4), "or the 1980 Act".
		In section 31(4), paragraph (c) and the "and" immediately before it.
		In section 31(5), "or in subsection (3) above".
		In section 31(6), "or in subsection (3) above".
		In section 31(7), "or (3)".
		In section 31(9), "or the 1980 Act".
		In Part II of Schedule 15, the entries relating to the Restrictive Trade Practices Act 1976 and the Resale Prices Act 1976.
1991 c 57.	The Water Resources Act 1991.	In Part II of Schedule 24, the entries relating to the Restrictive Trade Practices Act 1976 and the Resale Prices Act 1976.
1993 c 21.	The Osteopaths Act 1993.	In section 33(4), paragraph (b) and the "or" immediately before it.
		In section 33(5), "or section 10 of the Act of 1980".
1993 c 43.	The Railways Act 1993.	Section 14(2).
		In section 16(1), paragraph (b) and the "or" immediately before it.
		In section 16(2), paragraph (c) and the "or" immediately before it.
		In section 16(5), "or the 1980 Act".
		In section 67(4), paragraph (c) and the "and" immediately after it.
		In section 67(6)(a), "or (3)".
		In section 67(9), "or under the 1980 Act".
		Section 131.
		In section 145(3), paragraphs (d) and (e).
1994 c 17.	The Chiropractors Act 1994.	In section 33(4), paragraph (b) and the "or" immediately before it.
		In section 33(5), "or section 10 of the Act of 1980".

Chapter	Short title	Extent of repeal
1994 c 21.	The Coal Industry Act 1994.	In section 59(4), paragraphs (e) and (f).
1994 c 40.	The Deregulation and Contracting Out Act 1994.	Sections 10 and 11.
		In section 12, subsections (1) to (6).
		In Schedule 4, paragraph 1.
		In Schedule 11, in paragraph 4, sub-paragraphs (3) to (6).
1996 c 55.	The Broadcasting Act 1996.	Section 77(2).

PART II

REVOCATIONS

Reference	Title	Extent of revocation
SI 1981/1675 (NI 26).	The Magistrates' Courts (Northern Ireland) Order 1981.	In Schedule 6, paragraphs 42 and 43.
SI 1982/1080 (NI 12).	The Agricultural Marketing (Northern Ireland) Order 1982.	In Schedule 8, the entry relating to paragraph 16(2) of Schedule 3 to the Fair Trading Act 1973 and in the entry relating to the Competition Act 1980, "and 15(3)".
SI 1986/1035 (NI 9).	The Companies Consolidation (Consequential Provisions) (Northern Ireland) Order 1986.	In Part II of Schedule 1, the entries relating to the Restrictive Trade Practices Act 1976 and the Resale Prices Act 1976.
SI 1992/231 (NI 1).	The Electricity (Northern Ireland) Order 1992.	Article 16(2).
		In Article 18—
		(a) in paragraph (1), sub-paragraph (b) and the "or" immediately before it;
		(b) in paragraph (2), sub-paragraph (c) and the "or" immediately before it;
		(c) in paragraph (3) "or the 1980 Act".
		In Article 28(5), the "or" immediately after sub-paragraph (b).
		In Article 46—
		(a) in paragraph (4), sub-paragraph (c) and the "and" immediately after it;
		(b) in paragraph (5), "or (3)";
		(c) in paragraph (7), "or the 1980 Act".
		Article 61(3)(f) and (g).
		In Schedule 12, paragraph 16.
SI 1994/426 (NI 1).	The Airports (Northern Ireland) Order 1994.	Article 36(3).
		In Article 45—
		(a) in paragraph (1), "or section 10(2)(a) of the 1980 Act";

Reference	Title	Extent of revocation
		(b) in paragraph (3), sub-paragraph (c) and the "or" immediately before it;
		(c) in paragraph (4), "or the 1980 Act".
		In Article 47(a)(ii), "or the 1980 Act".
		In Schedule 9, paragraph 5.
SI 1996/275 (NI 2).	The Gas (Northern Ireland) Order 1996.	Article 16(2).
		In Article 18—
		(a) in paragraph (1), sub-paragraph (b) and the "or" immediately before it;
		(b) in paragraph (3), sub-paragraph (c) and the "or" immediately before it;
		(c) in paragraph (5), "or the 1980 Act".
		In Article 19(5), the "or" immediately after sub-paragraph (b).
		In Article 23—
		(a) in paragraph (4), sub-paragraph (d) and the "and" immediately before it;
		(b) in paragraph (5), "or (3)";
		(c) in paragraph (7), "or under the 1980 Act";
		(d) in paragraph (8), "or the 1980 Act".
		Article 44(4)(f) and (g).

Competition Act 1998 (Commencement No 1) Order 1998

(SI 1998/2750)

Made   9 November 1998
Authority Competition Act 1998, s 76.

1 Citation and interpretation

(1)   This Order may be cited as the Competition Act 1998 (Commencement No 1) Order 1998.

(2)   In this Order references to sections and Schedules are references to sections of and Schedules to the Competition Act 1998.

2 Appointed day

(1)   26th November 1998 is the day appointed for the coming into force of—

    (a)   section 51 and Schedule 9 (Director's rules) and section 52 (advice and information); and

    (b)   section 54(2) and paragraphs 2 to 8 of Schedule 10 (regulators) and section 59 (interpretation) for the purposes of the provisions which are brought into force by paragraph (a) above.

(2)   The enactments and orders to which paragraphs 2 to 8 of Schedule 10 make amendments shall continue in force for all other purposes without the amendments made by those paragraphs.

Competition Act 1998 (Commencement No 2) Order 1998

(SI 1998/3166)

Made: 16 December 1998.
Authority: Competition Act 1998, s 76.

1 Citation

(1)   This Order may be cited as the Competition Act 1998 (Commencement No 2) Order 1998.

(2)   In this Order references to sections and Schedules are references to sections of and Schedules to the Competition Act 1998 ("the Act").

2 Provisions of the Act commenced by this Order

11th January 1999 is the appointed day for the coming into force of the provisions of the Act listed in the first column of the Schedule to this Order for the purposes set out in the second column.

SCHEDULE

Article 2

PROVISIONS OF THE COMPETITION ACT 1998 COMING INTO FORCE ON 11TH JANUARY 1999

Provisions of the Act	Purpose
Section 3(1)(a), (c) and (d) and (2) to (6) (Chapter I prohibition: excluded agreements)	For all purposes
Section 3(1)(b) (excluded agreements)	In so far as it relates to paragraph 6 of Schedule 2 (amendment to the Environment Act 1995)
Section 12(3) (regulations in respect of notification etc)	For all purposes
Section 19 (Chapter II prohibition: excluded cases)	For all purposes
Section 38(1) to (7) (guidance as to penalties)	For all purposes
Section 50 (vertical agreements and land agreements)	For all purposes
Section 53 (Director's fees)	For all purposes
Section 54(3) (minor and consequential amendments)	In so far as relating to the provisions in Schedule 10 brought into force by this Order
Section 54(4) to (7) (regulators)	For all purposes

Provisions of the Act	Purpose
Section 55(6) (disclosure of information)	For all purposes
Section 57 (defamation)	For all purposes
Section 59 (interpretation)	In so far as not already in force
Section 60 (governing principles)	For all purposes
Section 69 (monopoly reports)	For all purposes
Section 74 (minor and consequential amendments, transitional provisions and savings, and repeals)	In so far as it relates to the provisions in Schedules 12, 13 and 14 brought into force by this Order
Schedule 1 (exclusions: mergers and concentrations)	For all purposes
In Schedule 2 paragraph 6 (amendment to the Environment Act 1995)	For all purposes
Schedule 3 (general exclusions)	For all purposes
Schedule 4 (professional rules)	For all purposes
In Schedule 10 paragraphs 9(7)(b), 10(6)(b), 11(b), 12(7)(b), 13(10)(b), 14(b), 15(9)(b), 17(7)(b), 18(6)(b) (amendments to enactments and orders to enable information to be disclosed for the purposes of the Act)	For all purposes
In Schedule 12 paragraphs 1(14), 3(b), 4(9), 10(b), 18(b), (amendments to enactments to enable information to be disclosed for the purposes of the Act)	For all purposes
In Schedule 12 paragraph 4(11) (consequential amendment)	For all purposes
In Schedule 13 paragraphs 10(5), and 19(3) (transitional provisions)	For all purposes
In Schedule 13 paragraphs 11 and 12(1) (transitional provisions)	For the purpose of prescribing modifications to the Restrictive Trade Practices Act 1976
In Schedule 14 the entries relating to section 83 of the Fair Trading Act 1973 and to section 22 of the Competition Act 1980 (consequential amendments)	For all purposes

Appendix 2

Treaty of Rome
Arts 81, 82, 86 and 234

TREATY ESTABLISHING THE EUROPEAN COMMUNITY (TREATY OF ROME)

The Treaty is set out as consolidated by the Treaty of Amsterdam amending the Treaty on European Union, the Treaties establishing the European Communities and certain related acts, signed at Amsterdam, 2 October 1997, OJ C340, 10.11.97, p 1. The Treaty of Amsterdam and its consequential renumbering of, and amendments to, these provisions, will take effect when all Member States have ratified the Treaty. The ratification process is expected to be complete by Spring 1999.

PART THREE
COMMUNITY POLICIES

TITLE VI (EX TITLE V)
COMMON RULES ON COMPETITION, TAXATION AND APPROXIMATION OF LAWS

CHAPTER 1
RULES ON COMPETITION

SECTION 1
RULES APPLYING TO UNDERTAKINGS

Article 81 (ex Article 85)

1.   The following shall be prohibited as incompatible with the common market: all agreements between undertakings, decisions by associations of undertakings and concerted practices which may affect trade between Member States and which have as their object or effect the prevention, restriction or distortion of competition within the common market, and in particular those which—

    (a)   directly or indirectly fix purchase or selling prices or any other trading conditions;

    (b)   limit or control production, markets, technical development, or investment;

    (c)   share markets or sources of supply;

    (d)   apply dissimilar conditions to equivalent transactions with other trading parties, thereby placing them at a competitive disadvantage;

    (e)   make the conclusion of contracts subject to acceptance by the other parties of supplementary obligations which, by their nature or according to commercial usage, have no connection with the subject of such contracts.

2.   Any agreements or decisions prohibited pursuant to this Article shall be automatically void.

3.   The provisions of paragraph 1 may, however, be declared inapplicable in the case of—

    —   any agreement or category of agreements between undertakings;

    —   any decision or category of decisions by associations of undertakings;

    —   any concerted practice or category of concerted practices;

which contributes to improving the production or distribution of goods or to promoting technical or economic progress, while allowing consumers a fair share of the resulting benefit, and which does not—

    (a)   impose on the undertakings concerned restrictions which are not indispensable to the attainment of these objectives;

    (b)   afford such undertakings the possibility of eliminating competition in respect of a substantial part of the products in question.

Article 82 (ex Article 86)

Any abuse by one or more undertakings of a dominant position within the common market or in a substantial part of it shall be prohibited as incompatible with the common market in so far as it may affect trade between Member States.

Such abuse may, in particular, consist in—

    (a)   directly or indirectly imposing unfair purchase or selling prices or other unfair trading conditions;

    (b)   limiting production, markets or technical development to the prejudice of consumers;

    (c)   applying dissimilar conditions to equivalent transactions with other trading parties, thereby placing them at a competitive disadvantage;

    (d)   making the conclusion of contracts subject to acceptance by the other parties of supplementary obligations which, by their nature or according to commercial usage, have no connection with the subject of such contracts.

Article 86 (ex Article 90)

1.   In the case of public undertakings and undertakings to which Member States grant special or exclusive rights, Member States shall neither enact nor maintain in force any measure contrary to the rules contained in this Treaty, in particular to those rules provided for in Article 6 and Articles 81 to 89.

2.   Undertakings entrusted with the operation of services of general economic interest or having the character of a revenue-producing monopoly shall be subject to the rules contained in this Treaty, in particular to the rules on competition, insofar as the application of such rules does not obstruct the performance, in law or in fact, of the particular tasks assigned to them. The development of trade must not be affected to such an extent as would be contrary to the interests of the Community.

3.   The Commission shall ensure the application of the provisions of this Article and shall, where necessary, address appropriate directives or decisions to Member States.

PART FIVE
INSTITUTIONS OF THE COMMUNITY

TITLE I
PROVISIONS GOVERNING THE INSTITUTIONS

CHAPTER 1
THE INSTITUTIONS

SECTION 4
THE COURT OF JUSTICE

Article 234 (ex Article 177)

1.   The Court of Justice shall have jurisdiction to give preliminary rulings concerning—

    (a)   the interpretation of this Treaty;

    (b)   the validity and interpretation of acts of the institutions of the Community and of the ECB;

(c)   the interpretation of the statutes of bodies established by an act of the Council, where those statutes so provide.

Where such a question is raised before any court or tribunal of a Member State, that court or tribunal may, if it considers that a decision on the question is necessary to enable it to give judgment, request the Court of Justice to give a ruling thereon.

Where any such question is raised in a case pending before a court or tribunal of a Member State against whose decisions there is no judicial remedy under national law, that court or tribunal shall bring the matter before the Court of Justice.

Appendix 3

Early guidance: directions given by the Director General of Fair Trading under paragraph 7(2) of Schedule 13 to the Act

Form EG

EARLY GUIDANCE: DIRECTIONS GIVEN BY THE DIRECTOR GENERAL OF FAIR TRADING UNDER PARAGRAPH 7(2) OF SCHEDULE 13 TO THE ACT

NOTES

This guidance and Form EG are reproduced by kind permission of the Office of Fair Trading.

1 Form of application

A person who wishes to apply under paragraph 7(2) of Schedule 13 for guidance in relation to an agreement shall submit Form EG to the Director General of Fair Trading.

2 Joint applications

Where a joint application is made, Form EG shall be submitted to the Director General of Fair Trading by or on behalf of all the applicants, and a joint representative may be nominated in the application as authorised to submit and receive documents on behalf of some or all [of] the applicants.

3 Copies

(1)   Documents submitted as part of Form EG shall be either originals or true copies, and the applicant shall certify that each copy is a true copy of the original.

(2)   Subject to paragraph (3) below, two copies of the information submitted as Form EG, in addition to the original, shall be submitted to the Director General of Fair Trading.

(3)   If in the applicant's opinion, one or more regulators has or may have concurrent jurisdiction with the Director General of Fair Trading under paragraph 7 of Schedule 13, one extra copy of the information submitted as Form EG shall be submitted to the Director General of Fair Trading for each such regulator.

4 Content of applications

(1)   The information submitted as Form EG shall, subject to paragraph (3) below, be correct and complete, and for these purposes information which is false or misleading shall be treated as incorrect or incomplete.

(2)   If the applicant considers that any information contained in the application is confidential, in the sense given to that word by direction 11 below, he shall set out that information in a separate annex to the application marked 'confidential information' and explain why it should be treated as such.

(3)   The Director may dispense with the obligation to submit any particular information, including any document, forming part of Form EG if he considers that such information or document is unnecessary for the examination of the case.

5 Effective date of application

(1)   Except where paragraph (3) below applies, an application shall have effect on the date on which it is received by the Director General of Fair Trading; an application received after 6.00 pm on a working day shall be treated as received on the next working day.

(2)   The Director General of Fair Trading shall acknowledge receipt of an application to the applicant without delay.

(3)   Where the Director finds that the information submitted as Form EG is incomplete in a material respect he shall, without delay, inform the applicant in writing of that fact; in such cases, the application shall have effect on the date on which the complete information is received by the Director, and information received after 6.00 pm on a working day shall be treated as received on the next working day.

(4)   Material changes in the facts contained in an application of which the applicant knows, or ought reasonably to know, shall be communicated voluntarily and without delay—

> (a)   to the Director who is exercising jurisdiction under paragraph 7 of Schedule 13 in relation to the application; or
>
> (b)   where the applicant has not yet been informed of which Director that is, to the Director General of Fair Trading.

(5)   If, on the expiry of a period of one month following the date on which an application has been received by the Director General of Fair Trading, the Director has not informed the applicant that the application is incomplete, under paragraph (3) above, the application shall be deemed to have become effective on the date of its receipt by the Director General of Fair Trading.

6 Notification of application to other parties

(1)   A party to an agreement who makes an application under paragraph 7(2) of Schedule 13 shall take all reasonable steps to—

> (a)   give written notification to all the other parties to the agreement of whom he is aware that the application has been made; and
>
> (b)   give such notification within seven working days of the date on which the applicant receives acknowledgement of receipt of his application by the Director General of Fair Trading.

(2)   The applicant shall provide a copy of such notification as is given under paragraph (1) above to the Director General of Fair Trading.

7 Concurrent jurisdiction

(1)   If the Director General of Fair Trading considers that a regulator has or may have concurrent jurisdiction under paragraph 7 of Schedule 13 to give guidance in response to an application made under paragraph 7(2) of Schedule 13, he shall—

> (a)   as soon as practicable, send a copy of the information submitted as Form EG to the regulator; and
>
> (b)   inform the applicant in writing that he has done so.

(2)   As soon as practicable, the Director General of Fair Trading shall inform the applicant in writing of which Director is to exercise jurisdiction under paragraph 7 of Schedule 13 in relation to the application.

8 Giving of guidance

Where the Director gives guidance to the applicant under sub-paragraph 7(3)(a) of Schedule 13, he shall do so in writing without delay after determining the application, stating the facts on which he bases the guidance and his reasons for it.

9 Withdrawal of guidance

(1)   If, having given guidance under sub-paragraph 7(3)(a) of Schedule 13 to the effect that—

> (a)   the agreement is unlikely to infringe the Chapter I prohibition, regardless of whether or not it is exempt; or
>
> (b)   the agreement is likely to be exempt under—
>
> > (i)   a block exemption;

    (ii)   a parallel exemption; or

    (iii)   a section 11 exemption; or

  (c)   he would be likely to grant the agreement an individual exemption if asked to do so,

the Director proposes to withdraw that guidance before the date on which section 2 comes into force, he shall consult the person to whom he gave the guidance.

(2)   Where the Director withdraws such guidance as is referred to in paragraph (1) above, he shall do so by giving written notice of the withdrawal to the person to whom he gave the guidance, stating his reasons for the withdrawal.

10 Confidential third party information

(1)   If a person who is not a party to the agreement to which an application made under paragraph 7(2) of Schedule 13 relates gives information to the Director in connection with the exercise of the Director's functions under paragraph 7 of Schedule 13 in relation to the agreement and considers that any of the information is confidential, in the sense given to that word by direction 11 below, he shall set out the part of the information which he considers to be confidential in that sense in a separate annex marked 'confidential information' and explain why it should be treated as such.

(2)   The Director shall, if he proposes to disclose any of the information contained in an annex provided in accordance with paragraph (1) above, consult the person who provided the information if it is practicable to do so.

11 Interpretation

(1)   In these directions—

  (a)   'a block exemption' is to be construed by reference to section 6;

  (b)   information is confidential if it is—

    (i)   commercial information the disclosure of which would, or might, significantly harm the legitimate business interests of the undertaking to which it relates; or

    (ii)   information relating to the private affairs of an individual the disclosure of which would, or might, significantly harm his interests;

  (c)   where the Director is required to consult a person, he shall—

    (i)   give written notice to the person in question, stating the action he proposes and his reasons for it; and

    (ii)   inform that person that any written representations made to the Director within the period specified in the notice will be considered;

  (d)   a reference to 'the Director' is to be construed as being a reference to the Director General of Fair Trading or to any regulator;

  (e)   'Form EG' means the information, including any document, required to be provided by such form as is from time to time issued by the Director General of Fair Trading;

  (f)   'an individual exemption' is to be construed by reference to section 4;

  (g)   'a parallel exemption' is to be construed by reference to section 10;

  (h)   'regulator' has the meaning given by section 59;

  (i)   'a section 11 exemption' is to be construed by reference to section 11; and

  (j)   'working day' means any day which is not Saturday, Sunday or an official holiday on which the Office of Fair Trading is closed.

(2)   References in these directions to 'the Act' are to the Competition Act 1998 and references to numbered sections or schedules are to the sections or schedules so numbered in the Act.

EG

FORM FOR APPLICATIONS FOR EARLY GUIDANCE UNDER PARAGRAPH 7 OF SCHEDULE 13 TO THE COMPETITION ACT 1998

PART 1: NOTES

1.1   Guidance in anticipation of the coming into force of Chapter I of the Act ('early guidance') is available for agreements made during the period beginning on 9 November 1998 (enactment date) and ending immediately before 1 March 2000 (the date on which the Chapter I prohibition comes into force). It may be applied for under paragraph 7 of Schedule 13 to the Act. Early guidance is not available in respect of the Chapter II prohibition. **This form cannot be used for notifications made on or after 1 March 2000; Form N must be used for such notifications.**

1.2   Although this document is described as 'a Form', it is essentially a check-list of information which must be supplied to the Director General of Fair Trading to enable him to determine an application for early guidance. Before completing the Form, reference should be made to the Early Guidance Directions of the Director General of Fair Trading issued on 26 November 1998.

1.3   The information must be correct and complete for the application to be effective.

1.4   The Form must be supplied in original version plus two copies, together with either an original or a certified copy, plus two further copies, of the agreement(s) and any relevant Annexes.

1.5   All applications for early guidance should be sent to the Director General of Fair Trading and marked for the attention of the 'Early Guidance Co-ordination Unit'.

1.6   The Act is enforced by the Director General of Fair Trading and, in relation to the regulated utility sectors shown in question 3.5 below, concurrently with the sector regulators; these have concurrent jurisdiction with the Director General to give early guidance. If any positive answer is given [to] question 3.5, provide one further copy of the Form and attachments for each relevant regulator who may have concurrent jurisdiction. A copy of the Form (together with its Annexes and copies of agreements) should also be sent to the relevant regulator(s), if the agreement being notified may fall within their sector(s). In general, the relevant regulator will deal with the application. If the Director General considers that a regulator has, or may have, concurrent jurisdiction in relation to an agreement in respect of which an application for early guidance has been submitted, he will send a copy of the Form EG to the regulator(s) and inform the notifying party that he has done so.

1.7   Indicate clearly to which section of the Form any additional pages relate. The application **must** include the form of receipt at Part 3. **Information which is regarded by the undertaking or undertakings as confidential should be clearly identified as such and placed in a separate identified annex. An explanation of why such information is regarded as confidential should also be provided.** Applications may also be made on disk or using other electronic format: please telephone the enquiry point at the Office of Fair Trading on 0171 211 8989 before using this facility.

1.8   **The Director General or, if the applicant has been informed that a regulator is dealing with the application, that regulator, must be informed of any material changes which occur after application has been made and which may affect any information given in this Form.**

PART 2: INFORMATION TO BE PROVIDED BY THE UNDERTAKING NOTIFYING THE AGREEMENT

*Number sections as below. In some cases, it may be possible to dispense with the requirement to provide information in all categories. This should be discussed with officials before making the application. **Information which is regarded by the undertaking(s) as confidential should be clearly identified as such and placed in a separate identified annex.***

1 THE UNDERTAKING(S) SUBMITTING THE APPLICATION

1.1   The identity of the undertaking submitting the application (full name and address, name of representative, telephone and fax numbers, and brief description of the undertaking or association of undertakings). For a partnership, sole trader or other unincorporated body trading under a business name, give the name(s) and address(es) of the proprietor(s) or partners. Please quote any reference which should be used;

1.2   if acting on behalf of another undertaking, state in what capacity, eg solicitor;

Where the Form is signed by a solicitor or other representative, proof of authority to act on behalf of the undertaking submitting the application must be provided.

1.3   if the application is submitted by or on behalf of more than one undertaking, indicate whether a joint representative has been appointed. If so, give the details as requested in 1.1 above in respect of the joint representative. If not, give the details in respect of any representatives who have been authorised to act on behalf of each, or either, of the parties to the agreement, indicating who they represent;

1.4   the Standard Industrial Classification code for the relevant good(s) or service(s), if known. If the code is not known, describe the goods or services involved as fully and accurately as possible;

The directions issued by the Director General require a party to an agreement who makes an application for early guidance in respect of that agreement to take all reasonable steps to notify all other parties to the agreement of whom he is aware that the application has been made. In exceptional cases, it may not be practicable to inform all non-notifying parties to the notified agreement that it has been notified, if, for example, an agreement is concluded with a large number of undertakings. The notification to such other undertakings must be made (a) in writing; and (b) within seven working days of the applicant receiving the Director General's acknowledgement of receipt of his application. The applicant must send a copy of such notification to the Director General.

1.5   the full names, addresses (by registered office, where appropriate, and principal place of business, if different), telephone and fax numbers, nature of business, and brief description of any other parties to the agreement, decision or concerted practice ('the arrangement') being notified;

1.6   details of the steps to be taken to inform any other such parties that the application has been made and indicate whether the remaining parties have received a copy of the application with confidential information and business secrets deleted. State the reasons, if it is not practicable to inform other parties of the application in accordance with the requirements outlined above.

2 PURPOSE OF THE APPLICATION

*The Chapter I prohibition will not apply unless the arrangement has an 'appreciable effect' on competition, and an application for early guidance will not normally be appropriate when that is not the case. Further information is given in the guideline **The Competition Act 1998: the Chapter I prohibition.***

2.1   whether the arrangement that is the subject of the application is considered to be of a type which would benefit from any exclusion from the Chapter I prohibition.

Specify the exclusion: give reasons why you are unsure whether the arrangement will be covered by the exclusion and why an application for early guidance is considered appropriate;

2.2   specify why it is considered that the Chapter I prohibition is likely to be infringed and whether the arrangement is likely to qualify (or in the case of an individual exemption, is likely to qualify if notified) for an exemption (individual, UK block exemption, parallel, or under section 11 of the Act);

3 JURISDICTION

In general, when an arrangement is also caught by Article 85 of the EC Treaty, the Director General considers that the EC Commission is the more appropriate authority to whom notification should be made (see the guideline **The Competition Act 1998: the Chapter I prohibition***).*

3.1   why the arrangement is considered to be not caught by Article 85(1);

3.2   whether the arrangement is the subject of an application to the European Commission. If so, it would assist consideration of the application if three copies of the completed Form A/B and supporting documents, and one further copy if information has been given in response to question 3.5 below, were attached. It is unnecessary to repeat information given on Form A/B, but information specific to the UK market will be necessary (following the format in question 7.1) to the extent that it has not been given on Form A/B, and should be provided separately. Supply three copies of any 'comfort' letter received from the European Commission;

3.3   whether the arrangement is the subject of an application to any other national competition authority;

3.4   if the arrangement relates to transport by rail, road, inland waterway or to services ancillary to transport and is the subject of an application to the European Commission under Regulation 1017/68, it would similarly assist consideration of the application if three copies of the completed Form II and any supporting documents and one further copy if information has been given in response to question 3.5 below were attached;

3.5   whether the arrangement being notified relates to any one or more of—
    (a)   commercial activities connected with telecommunications;
    (b)   the shipping, conveyance or supply of gas and activities ancillary thereto;
    (c)   commercial activities connected with the generation, transmission or supply of electricity;
    (d)   commercial activities connected with the supply of water or securing a supply of water or with the provision or securing of sewerage services;
    (e)   commercial activities connected with the generation, transmission or supply of electricity in Northern Ireland;
    (f)   the conveyance, storage or supply of gas in Northern Ireland;
    (g)   the supply of railway services.
    Identify the sector regulator or regulators who may have concurrent jurisdiction with the Director General of Fair Trading to deal with the application for early guidance;

3.6   names and addresses, telephone and fax numbers, date and the details, including case references, of any previous contacts with the Office of Fair Trading, a regulator, any other national competition authority, or the EC Commission, and of any proceedings in any national court in the European Community, relating to the arrangement being notified and of any relevant previous arrangements.

4 DETAILS OF THE ARRANGEMENT

4.1   a brief description of the arrangement being notified (nature, content, purpose, date(s) and duration);

4.2   if written, attach either an original or a certified copy, together with two further copies, of the most recent version of the text of the arrangement being notified (technical details contained in know-how agreements, for example, may be omitted but omissions should be indicated); if not written, provide a full description;

4.3   identify any provisions in the arrangement which may restrict the parties in their freedom to take independent commercial decisions or to act on those decisions;

4.4   if the application relates to a standard contract, the number expected to be concluded.

5 INFORMATION ON THE PARTIES TO THE ARRANGEMENT AND THE GROUPS TO WHICH THEY BELONG

5.1   for each undertaking identified in 1.5 above, the name of a contact, together with his or her address, telephone and fax numbers, and position held in the undertaking;

5.2   the corporate groups to which each undertaking belongs and the product and/or services market(s) in which the groups are active (hereafter called 'the relevant product market'); include one copy of the most recent consolidated annual report and accounts (or equivalent for unincorporated bodies) for each undertaking;

5.3   for each of the parties to the arrangement, provide a list of all undertakings belonging to the same group which are active in the same relevant product market(s), and those active in markets neighbouring the relevant product markets—that is, those which are not regarded by the consumer as fully interchangeable or substitutable for products in the defined relevant product market, as defined in question 6.1 below.

6 THE RELEVANT PRODUCT AND GEOGRAPHIC MARKETS

A relevant product market comprises all those products and/or services regarded by the consumer of the product or service as interchangeable or substitutable by reason of their characteristics, prices or intended use. The following factors are among those normally considered when determining the relevant product market and should be taken into account, together with any others considered relevant—

> — *the degree of physical similarity between the products/services in question;*
> — *any differences in end-use to which the goods are or may be put;*
> — *differences in price between the products/services;*
> — *the cost of switching between two potentially competing products/services; and*
> — *established consumer preferences for one type or category of product/service.*

The relevant geographic market is the area in which the undertakings concerned are involved in the supply of products or services in which the conditions of competition are appreciably different from neighbouring areas. The following factors are among those normally considered when determining the relevant geographic market and should be taken into account, together with any others considered relevant—

> — *the nature and characteristics of the products or services concerned;*
> — *the existence of entry barriers or consumer preferences;*
> — *appreciable differences of the undertakings' market share or substantial price differences between neighbouring areas; and*
> — *transport costs.*

6.1   In the light of the relevant factors given above (which are not exhaustive), explain the definitions of the relevant product and geographic markets which should be considered, with full reasons, in particular stating the specific products or services directly or indirectly affected by the application and other goods or services that may be viewed as substitutable, with reasons. If the relevant geographic market is considered to be an area smaller, or larger, than the whole of the United Kingdom, the boundaries considered applicable, with reasons. Give reasons for all assumptions or findings, and explain how the factors outlined above have been taken into account. Further details are in the guideline *The Competition Act 1998: Market Definition;*

6.2   provide a copy of the most recent in-house long-term market studies assessing or analysing the relevant markets (including any commissioned by the undertakings from outside consultants), and give references of any external studies of the relevant product market, and, where possible, include a copy of any such studies.

7 THE POSITION OF THE UNDERTAKINGS IN THE RELEVANT PRODUCT MARKETS

The information required under this section relates to both the relevant geographic market and the relevant product market, for the groups of the parties as a whole. Market shares may be calculated either on the basis of value or volume. Justification for the figures provided must be given by reference to the sales or turnover of each of the undertakings in question. The source or sources of information should be given, and, where possible, a copy of the document from which information has been taken.

7.1   for each of the previous three calendar or financial years, as available, give—
  (a)   details of the market shares of each undertaking in the goods or services in the relevant product and geographic markets, as identified in 6.1 above, and, if different, in the UK, and in the European Community;
  (b)   estimates of market shares in the relevant product and geographic markets for each of the five main competitors of each of the undertakings, giving the undertaking's name, address, telephone and fax number, and, where possible, a contact name;
  (c)   identify the five main customers of each of the undertakings in the relevant product and geographic markets, giving the undertaking's name, address, telephone and fax number, and, where possible, a contact name;
  (d)   details of the undertakings' interests in, and arrangements with, any other companies competing in the relevant product and geographic market, together with details of their market shares, if known.

8 MARKET ENTRY AND POTENTIAL COMPETITION IN THE RELEVANT PRODUCT AND GEOGRAPHIC MARKETS

8.1   For all relevant product and geographic markets—
  (a)   describe the factors influencing entry into the relevant product market(s): that is, the barriers which exist to prevent undertakings not presently manufacturing goods within the relevant product market(s) from entering the market(s), taking account of, in particular but not exclusively, the extent to which—
    — entry is regulated by the requirements of government authorisation or standard-setting, in any form, and any legal or regulatory controls on entry to the market(s);
    — entry is influenced by the availability of raw materials;
    — entry is influenced by the length of existing contracts between suppliers and customers;
    — research and development and licensing patents, know-how and other rights are important;
  (b)   describe the factors influencing entry in geographic terms: that is, the barriers that exist to prevent undertakings already producing and/or

marketing goods within the relevant product market(s) outside the relevant geographic market(s) from extending sales into the relevant geographic market(s), taking account of, in particular but not exclusively, the importance of—

— trade barriers imposed by law, such as tariffs, quotas etc;
— local geographical specifications or technical requirements;
— procurement policies;
— the existence of adequate and available local distribution and retailing facilities;
— transport costs;
— strong consumer preference for local brands or products;

(c)   in respect of new entrants in both product and geographic terms, state whether any new undertakings have entered the product market(s) in geographic areas where the undertakings sell, during the last three years. Identify the undertakings concerned by name, address, telephone and fax numbers and, where possible, a contact name, with best estimates of market shares of each in the relevant product and geographic markets.

9 NEGATIVE CLEARANCE

9.1   state reasons for seeking 'negative clearance' (that is, that the Director General should conclude that the arrangement will not be covered by the Chapter I prohibition). Indicate, for example, which provision or effects of the arrangement may breach the prohibition, and state the reasons why it is considered that the arrangements do not have the object or effect of preventing, restricting or distorting competition within the UK to an appreciable extent.

10 EXEMPTION

The criteria which will be taken into account in considering applications for exemption are set out in section 9 of the Act.

10.1   if guidance on exemption from the Chapter I prohibition is sought, explain how the arrangements contribute to improving production or distribution and/or promoting technical or economic progress, and how consumers will be allowed a fair share of those benefits. Explain how each restrictive provision in the arrangements is indispensable to these objectives, and how the arrangements do not eliminate competition in respect of a substantial part of the relevant product or geographic market concerned.

11 TRANSITIONAL PERIODS

11.1   if the arrangement is considered to benefit from any transitional periods during which the Chapter I prohibition does not apply, indicate the duration of the relevant transitional periods by reference to Schedule 13 to the Act.

12 OTHER INFORMATION

12.1   state—

(a)   whether this application should be considered as urgent. If so, give reasons;

(b)   any other information you consider may be helpful.

The application must conclude with the following declaration which is to be signed by or on behalf of all the applicants or notifying undertakings. Unsigned applications are invalid.

DECLARATION

The undersigned declare that all the information given above and in the . . . . pages annexed hereto is correct to the best of their knowledge and belief, and that all estimates are identified as such and are their best estimates of the underlying facts.

Place and date...

Signatures...

....

Status...

....

.... name(s) in block capitals

PART 3: ACKNOWLEDGMENT OF RECEIPT

This Form will be returned to the address inserted below if the top half is completed by the undertaking lodging it.

to be completed by the undertaking making the application

To: ....   (name and address of applicant)

....

....

Your application dated ....

concerning ....

under reference ....

involving the following undertakings—

1. ....

2. .... [and others]

to be completed by the Office of Fair Trading

was received on...

and registered under reference number

.... **Please quote this number in all correspondence**

In the event that this application is not complete in a material respect, you will be informed within one month of its receipt. If you are not informed within that time that it is considered to be incomplete, it is deemed to be effective on the date of its receipt.

Appendix 4
Draft Procedural Rules
Draft Form N

CONSULTATION ON THE DGFT'S [DRAFT] PROCEDURAL RULES

NOTES

These draft rules and draft Form N are reproduced by kind permission of the Office of Fair Trading.

The following introductory comments are intended to assist with the consultation process. They do not form part of the procedural rules.

1. Section 51(1) of the Competition Act 1998 ('the Act') gives the Director General of Fair Trading the power to propose such rules about procedural and other matters in connection with the carrying into effect of the provisions of Part 1 of the Act as he considers appropriate. Schedule 9 sets out matters that the rules may cover. The Director General of Fair Trading is not limited to preparing rules based on the specific powers set out in Schedule 9.

2. Section 51(3) requires the Director General of Fair Trading in preparing the rules to consult such persons as he considers appropriate. The draft rules were sent out to informal consultation on 10th August, 1998. The draft rules have been amended to reflect the comments received. The draft rules are now being sent out for formal consultation to comply with section 51(3).

3. The Director General of Fair Trading's approach is to set out those draft rules which it appears to him will be of most importance to those affected by the new legislation. He intends to extend the draft rules to cover other matters in due course, such as the payment of fees and penalties.

Effect of Section 60 'Governing Principles'

4. Section 60 of the Act sets out certain principles to provide for the UK authorities to handle cases in such a way as to ensure consistency with EC law. The obligation to ensure consistency only reaches to the extent that this is possible having regard to any relevant differences. Section 60 does not require the UK authorities to follow the procedural practices of the EC Commission. The Director General of Fair Trading's procedural rules therefore do not need to be consistent with the procedural practices of the EC Commission.

Scope of Rules

5. The Director General of Fair Trading's procedural rules set out the procedures to be followed by persons making an application for a decision or guidance and the procedures to be followed by the Director General of Fair Trading when dealing with applications. An application for guidance or a decision must include the information required by Form N, which is a form that will be issued by the Director General of Fair Trading from time to time. Form N is also being sent out for public consultation.

6. The Act will be enforced concurrently with the sector regulators for telecommunications, gas, electricity, water and rail (see the guideline: *Concurrent Application to Regulated Industries*). The procedures set out in the rules must be followed by the Director General of Fair Trading and any regulator that exercises concurrent jurisdiction under Part I of the Act.

Informal hearings

7. The procedure to be followed to determine an application for a decision or guidance will be mainly a written procedure. The rules set out when the applicants and the public will be consulted and given an opportunity to make representations. The Director General of Fair Trading does not consider that it is necessary to prescribe any formal procedures to be followed if oral representations are made. However, in cases where an infringement decision is proposed the parties may make oral representations to elaborate a written response.

Procedural matters already covered in the Act

8. The Act and Schedules to the Act set out some of the procedures to be followed by the Director General of Fair Trading and persons making applications. Procedures set out in the Act and Schedules are not repeated in the Director General of Fair Trading's procedural rules. For example, the Act provides that the Director must give written notice to any person to whom he intends to give an interim measures direction and an opportunity to make comments (section 35). This is not repeated in the Director General of Fair Trading's procedural rules.

Confidentiality

9. The rules contain provisions on the confidentiality of material provided by the parties making a notification and by third parties. A document will not be used to support a claim that an undertaking has committed an infringement unless the undertaking has had an opportunity to make known its views on the document.

Timetables

10. The Director General of Fair Trading's draft procedural rules do not set out any timetables for dealing with applications. During debate in Standing Committee in the House of Commons, the Minister of State said that the rules will include a timetable once the new regime has settled down. It is the intention of the Director General of Fair Trading to publish non-binding administrative timetables for dealing with applications as soon as the prohibitions come into force.

Investigations

11. The Director General of Fair Trading's procedural rules do not set out any rules on the exercise of the investigation powers in the Act, with the exception of a provision on access to a legal representative. The procedures to be followed by the Director General of Fair Trading when exercising the powers of investigation are set out in the Act. They are described in the guideline on *The Powers of Investigation*.

Early Guidance

12. Paragraph 7 of Schedule 13 to the Act allows parties to agreements made between 9th November, 1998 and 29th February, 2000 (both dates inclusive) to apply for guidance as to whether or not, in the Director General of Fair Trading's view, the agreement is likely to infringe the Chapter I prohibition and, if so, whether exemption is likely ('early guidance'). The sector regulators may also give early guidance where they exercise concurrent jurisdiction. In order to ensure that there are appropriate procedures for early guidance applications before the rules are in place, the Director General of Fair Trading issued Early Guidance Directions on 26th November, 1998. Applications for early guidance must be made on or before 29th February, 2000 using Form EG and in accordance with the Early Guidance Directions and the notes attached to Form EG.

13. Applications for a decision cannot be made until 1st March, 2000. Early guidance is not available on the Chapter II prohibition. The Director General of Fair Trading's procedural rules will come into force on 1st March, 2000 after being approved by an order made by the Secretary of State. The Director General of Fair Trading's procedural rules will apply to applications for a decision and applications for guidance made on or after 1st March, 2000. Such applications must be made using Form N.

Fees

14. Clause 53 provides for fees to be charged for notifications to the Director General. It is expected that fees will be charged for notifications for guidance and decisions but the level of fees has not been determined. There are as yet no draft rules providing for the mechanism for charging fees or for the amount payable.

Consultation

15. Comments on the Director General of Fair Trading's procedural rules should be sent to Gover James at the Office of Fair Trading, Field House, 15–25 Bream's Buildings, London EC4A 1PR, by 8th January, 1999. It may be appropriate to make available comments received on the draft rules to the sector regulators and others that have an interest. Unless it is made clear that you do not want your comments to be passed on to the regulators and others that have an interest the Director General of Fair Trading will assume that you agree to your comments being passed on.

DIRECTOR'S [DRAFT] PROCEDURAL RULES

1 Form of application

A person who wishes to apply under section 13 or 14 for an agreement to be examined, or, under section 21 or 22, for conduct to be considered, shall in all cases submit Form N to the Director General of Fair Trading.

2 Joint applications

Where a joint application is made, Form N shall be submitted to the Director General of Fair Trading by or on behalf of all the applicants, and a joint representative may be nominated in the application as authorised to submit and receive documents on behalf of some or all of the applicants.

3 Copies

(1) Documents submitted as part of Form N shall be either originals or true copies, and the applicant shall certify that each copy is a true copy of the original.

(2) Subject to paragraph (3) below, two copies of the information submitted as Form N, in addition to the original, shall be submitted to the Director General of Fair Trading.

(3) If, in the applicant's opinion, one or more regulators has or may have concurrent jurisdiction with the Director General of Fair Trading under Part I, one extra copy of the information submitted as Form N shall be submitted to the Director General of Fair Trading for each such regulator.

4 Content of applications

(1) Where the declaration which is submitted as part of Form N is signed by a solicitor or other representative of an applicant, the information submitted as Form N shall include written proof of that representative's authority to act on that applicant's behalf.

(2) The information submitted as Form N shall, subject to paragraph (4) below, be correct and complete, and for these purposes information which is false or misleading shall be treated as incorrect or incomplete.

(3) If the applicant considers that any information contained in the application is confidential, in the sense given to that word by rule 27 below, he shall set out that information in a separate annex to the application marked 'confidential information' and explain why it should be treated as such.

(4) The Director may dispense with the obligation to submit any particular information, including any document, forming part of Form N if he considers that such information or document is unnecessary for the examination of the case.

5 Effective date of application

(1) Except where paragraph (3) below applies, an application shall have effect on the date on which it is received by the Director General of Fair Trading; an application received after 6.00 pm on a working day shall be treated as received on the next working day.

(2) The Director General of Fair Trading shall acknowledge receipt of an application to the applicant without delay.

(3) Where the Director finds that the information submitted as Form N is incomplete in a material respect he shall, without delay, inform the applicant in

writing of that fact; in such cases, the application, if otherwise made in accordance with these rules, shall have effect on the date on which the complete information is received by that Director, and information received after 6.00 pm on a working day shall be treated as received on the next working day.

(4)   Material changes in the facts contained in an application of which the applicant knows, or ought reasonably to know, shall be communicated voluntarily and without delay—

(a)   to the Director who is exercising jurisdiction under Part I in relation to the application; or

(b)   where the applicant has not yet been informed of which Director that is, to the Director General of Fair Trading.

(5)   If, on the expiry of the period of one month following the date on which an application has been received by the Director General of Fair Trading, the Director has not informed the applicant, under paragraph (3) above, that the application is incomplete in a material respect, the application, if made in accordance with these rules, shall be deemed to have become effective on the date of its receipt by the Director General of Fair Trading.

6 Notification of application to other parties

Such notification of an application to other parties as is given under paragraph 2(2) of each of Schedule 5 and 6 shall be written and given within seven working days of the date on which the applicant receives acknowledgement of receipt of his application by the Director General of Fair Trading; the applicant shall provide a copy of the notification to the Director General of Fair Trading.

7 Public Register

(1)   The Director General of Fair Trading shall maintain a register, on which there shall be entered, in respect of every application for a decision, a summary of the nature and objectives of the agreement or conduct in question and an indication of the outcome of the application.

(2)   The register shall be open to public inspection—

(a)   at the Office of Fair Trading, between 10.00 am and 4.30 pm on every working day; and

(b)   on a website, on the Internet.

8 Concurrent jurisdiction

(1)   If the Director General of Fair Trading considers that a regulator has or may have concurrent jurisdiction under Part I to take action in relation to an agreement, or conduct, in respect of which an application has been submitted, he shall—

(a)   as soon as practicable, send a copy of the information submitted as Form N to the regulator; and

(b)   inform the applicant in writing that he has done so.

(2)   As soon as practicable, the Director General of Fair Trading shall inform the applicant in writing of which Director is to exercise jurisdiction under Part I in relation to the application; if, subsequently, the application is transferred to a different Director who is to exercise such jurisdiction instead, the applicant shall be informed in writing of that fact.

9 Provisional decision

(1)   If the Director proposes to make a provisional decision he shall consult the applicant.

(2)   If the Director makes a provisional decision he shall give, in the written notification of the decision to the applicant, an account of the facts on which he bases the decision and his reasons for it.

10 Giving of guidance

After determining an application for guidance, the Director shall without delay give guidance to the applicant in writing, stating the facts on which he bases the guidance and his reasons for it.

11 Further action after guidance

(1)   If, having given guidance with respect to an agreement, to the effect that—
    (a)   the agreement is unlikely to infringe the Chapter I prohibition, regardless of whether or not it is exempt; or
    (b)   the agreement is likely to be exempt under—
        (i)   a block exemption;
        (ii)   a parallel exemption; or
        (iii)   a section 11 exemption; or
    (c)   he would be likely to grant the agreement an individual exemption if asked to do so,

the Director proposes to take further action under Part I, he shall consult the person to whom he gave the guidance.

(2)   If, having given guidance with respect to conduct to the effect that it is unlikely to infringe the Chapter II prohibition, the Director proposes to take further action under Part I, he shall consult the person to whom he gave the guidance.

12 Consultation following certain applications

(1)   On an application under section 14 for an agreement to be examined—
    (a)   if the Director proposes to grant an exemption subject to conditions or obligations, he shall consult the applicant, specifying the proposed conditions or obligations;
    (b)   if the Director proposes to grant an exemption, whether or not subject to conditions or obligations, he shall consult the public; and
    (c)   if the Director proposes to make a decision that the Chapter I prohibition has not been infringed, he may consult the public.

(2)   If, on an application under section 22 for conduct to be considered, the Director proposes to make a decision that the Chapter II prohibition has not been infringed, he may consult the public.

13 Investigations

(1)   An officer shall grant a request of the occupier of premises entered by the officer ('the occupier') to allow a reasonable time for the occupier's legal adviser to arrive at the premises before the investigation continues, if the officer considers it reasonable in the circumstances to do so and if he is satisfied that such conditions as he considers it appropriate to impose in granting the occupier's request are, or will be, complied with.

(2)   For the purposes of paragraph (1) above, 'a reasonable time' means such period of time as the officer considers is reasonable in the circumstances.

(3)   A person required by the Director under section 26(6)(a)(ii) to provide an explanation of a document may be accompanied by a legal adviser.

14 Infringement decisions

(1)   If the Director proposes to make a decision that the Chapter I prohibition or the Chapter II prohibition has been infringed, he shall—

(a)   give written notice of his proposed action—

(i)   where an application has been made, to the applicant and to any other person who the Director is aware is a party to the agreement or conduct, as the case may be, which the Director considers has led to the infringement; or

(ii)   where no application has been made, to any person who the Director is aware is a party to that agreement or conduct, as the case may be,

stating the matters to which he has taken objection, the action he proposes and his reasons for it;

(b)   inform the person to whom written notice is given under paragraph (a) above that any oral and written representations made to the Director within the period specified in the notice will be considered, and give that person an opportunity to make such representations; and

(c)   subject to paragraph (2) below, if so requested by the person referred to in paragraph (b) above, give that person or his authorised representative an opportunity to inspect the documents in the Director's file relating to the proposed decision.

(2)   The Director may withhold any document—

(a)   to the extent that it contains information which a person has stated to the Director to be, and which the Director has found to be, confidential, in the sense given to that word by rule 27 below, or which is, in the opinion of the Director, otherwise confidential; or

(b)   which is internal to the office of the Director.

15 Notice of decision

If the Director has made a decision as to whether or not an agreement has infringed the Chapter I prohibition, or as to whether or not conduct has infringed the Chapter II prohibition, he shall without delay—

(a)   give written notice of the decision—

(i)   where an application has been made, to the applicant and to any other person who the Director is aware is a party to the agreement or conduct, as the case may be; or

(ii)   where no application has been made, to any person who the Director is aware is a party to the agreement or conduct, as the case may be,

stating the facts on which he bases the decision, and his reasons for it; and

(b)   publish the decision and his reasons for making it.

16 Further action after a decision

(1)   If, after having made a decision that an agreement has not infringed the Chapter I prohibition, or that conduct has not infringed the Chapter II prohibition, the Director proposes to take further action under Part I, he shall consult the person to whom he gave notice of the decision.

(2)   After taking such further action, the Director shall publish a notice of the further action taken.

17 Directions and penalties

(1)   Where the Director—

(a) gives a direction to a person under section 32 or 33, he shall at the same time inform that person in writing of the facts on which he bases the direction and his reasons for it giving it; and

(b) requires a person to pay a penalty under section 36, he shall at the same time inform that person in writing of the facts on which he bases the penalty and his reasons for requiring that person to pay it.

(2) The Director shall publish directions given under section 32, 33 or 35.

18 Interim measures

(1) Subject to paragraph (2) below, if the Director proposes to give directions under section 35, he shall, if so requested by the person to whom the directions are to be given, give that person or his authorised representative an opportunity to inspect the documents in the Director's file relating to the proposed directions.

(2) The Director may withhold any document—

(a) to the extent that it contains information which a person has stated to the Director to be, and which the Director has found to be, confidential, in the sense given to that word by rule 27 below, or which is, in the opinion of the Director, otherwise confidential; or

(b) which is internal to the office of the Director.

19 Application for extension of individual exemption

(1) A person who wishes to apply under section 4(6) for an extension of the period for which an individual exemption has effect shall submit Form N to the Director General of Fair Trading.

(2) Such an application shall be submitted not more than twelve months and not less than three months before the expiry of the exemption.

(3) If the Director proposes to grant the application, he shall consult the public.

(4) If the Director has made a decision as to whether or not to grant the application, he shall—

(a) give written notice of the decision to the applicant; and

(b) publish the decision,

specifying, if appropriate, the period of extension granted.

(5) Rules 2 (joint applications), 3 (copies), 4 (content of applications), 5(1) to (4) (effective date), 7 (public register) and 8 (concurrent jurisdiction) above shall apply to an application under this rule, rule 8 applying as if the words 'or conduct,' in paragraph (1) were omitted.

20 Cancellation etc of individual exemption

(1) If, in accordance with section 5, the Director proposes to—

(a) cancel an individual exemption;

(b) vary or remove any condition or obligation to which the exemption is subject; or

(c) impose one or more additional conditions or obligations,

he shall consult the public and the person to whom notice of the decision to grant the exemption was given.

(2) If the Director decides to take any of the steps mentioned in sub-paragraphs (1)(a) to (c) above, he shall give notice of his decision in writing to the person referred to in paragraph (1) above, stating the facts on which he bases the decision and his reasons for it, and shall publish the decision.

21 Cancellation etc of parallel exemption

(1)   Where the Director finds that an agreement which benefits from a parallel exemption has produced, or may produce, significantly adverse effects on a market in the United Kingdom or part of it, he may—

    (a)   impose conditions or obligations subject to which the exemption is to have effect;

    (b)   vary or remove any such condition or obligation;

    (c)   impose one or more additional conditions or obligations; or

    (d)   cancel the exemption.

(2)   If, in accordance with section 10, the Director proposes to take any of the steps mentioned in sub-paragraphs (1)(a) to (d) above, he shall consult the public and each person who is a party to the agreement in question.

(3)   If the Director decides to take any of the steps mentioned in sub-paragraphs (1)(a) to (d) above, he shall give notice of his decision in writing to each person who is a party to the agreement in question, stating the facts on which he bases the decision and his reasons for it, and shall publish the decision.

(4)   If, in accordance with section 10, the Director takes any of the steps mentioned in sub-paragraphs 1(a) to (d) above, he shall do so by giving notice in writing to each person who is a party to the agreement in question.

(5)   Where the Director cancels a parallel exemption in the circumstances mentioned in paragraph (1) above, the date from which cancellation of the exemption is to take effect may be earlier than the date on which notice of such cancellation is given under paragraph (4) above.

22 Withdrawal of exclusions

(1)   If the Director proposes to give a direction under paragraph 4 of Schedule 1 or paragraph 2 or 9 of Schedule 3 to the effect that an exclusion made by a provision specified in paragraph (2) below does not apply to an agreement, he shall consult the parties to that agreement.

(2)   The provisions specified for the purposes of paragraph (1) above are in paragraphs—

    (a)   1(1) of Schedule 1 (mergers);

    (b)   2(1) of Schedule 3 (section 21(2) agreements); and

    (c)   9(1) of Schedule 3 (agricultural products).

(3)   The period specified for the purposes of paragraph 4(4) of Schedule 1 and paragraphs 2(6) and 9(6) of Schedule 3 is seven working days from the date on which the person in question receives notice in writing requiring him to give information to the Director.

(4)   If the Director proposes to give a direction under article [4] of the Vertical Agreements Order, or article [4] of the Land Agreements Order, to the effect that the disapplication of the Chapter I prohibition provided for by the order does not apply to an agreement, he shall consult the parties to that agreement.

(5)   The period specified for the purposes of article [4(4)] of the Vertical Agreements Order and article [4(3)(a)] of the Land Agreements Order is seven working days from the date on which the person in question receives notice in writing requiring him to give information to the Director.

(6)   If the Director has given a direction referred to in paragraph (1) or (4) above, he shall publish it.

23 Termination of transitional periods

(1)   If the Director proposes to give a direction under paragraph 37 of Schedule 13, he shall consult the parties to the agreement concerned.

(2)   The period specified for the purposes of paragraph 38(2) of Schedule 13 is seven working days from the date on which the person in question is required in writing to give information to the Director.

(3)   The Director shall publish a direction given under paragraph 37 of Schedule 13 after the date on which the direction takes effect; if the direction is revoked, he shall publish a notice of that fact.

24 Extension of transitional periods

(1)   A person who wishes to apply under paragraph 36 of Schedule 13 for the extension of a transitional period shall do so in writing to the Director General of Fair Trading and shall submit the following documents with his application—
  (a)   three copies of the agreement; and
  (b)   three copies of the application; and
  (c)   where the application is signed by a solicitor or other representative of an applicant, written proof of that representative's authority to act on that applicant's behalf.

(2)   The application shall include an explanation of—
  (a)   the purpose of the agreement;
  (b)   the basis for the applicant's belief that there is a transitional period;
  (c)   the need for an extension of the transitional period; and
  (d)   the likely application of the Chapter I prohibition to the agreement at the end of the transitional period, and any grounds for believing that an exemption from that prohibition is likely,

and shall specify the length of the transitional period, the date of its expiry and the period of extension applied for.

(3)   The information submitted under paragraphs (1) and (2) above shall be correct and complete.

(4)   If the Director—
  (a)   refuses the application; or
  (b)   grants the application, or grants an extension which is of shorter duration than that applied for,

he shall give written notice of his decision to the applicant, specifying, if appropriate, the period of extension granted.

(5)   If, on the expiry of the period of two months following the effective date of the application, the Director has not informed the applicant to the contrary, the transitional period shall be treated as extended by either the maximum period permitted by paragraph 36(2) of Schedule 13 or, if shorter, the period of extension applied for.

(6)   If the Director extends a transitional period on his own initiative, he shall give written notice of his decision to the parties to the agreement in question, specifying the period of extension granted.

(7)   Rules 2 (joint applications), 4(3) and (4) (content of applications), 5(1)–(4) (effective date) and 8 (concurrent jurisdiction) above shall apply to an application under this rule as they apply to information submitted as Form N; and rule 8 shall apply as if the references to 'Part I' in paragraphs (1) and (2) were substituted by references to 'paragraph 36 of Schedule 13' and as if the words 'or conduct,' in paragraph (1) were omitted.

(8)   If the Director extends a transitional period, he shall publish a notice of that fact, specifying the period of extension granted.

25 Confidential third party information

(1)   If a person gives information to the Director in connection with the exercise of any of the Director's functions under Part I in relation to an agreement to which that person is not a party, or in relation to conduct in which that person has not engaged, and that person considers that any of the information is confidential, in the sense given to that word by rule 27 below, he shall set out the part of the information which he considers to be confidential in that sense in a separate annex marked 'confidential information' and explain why it should be treated as such.

(2)   The Director shall, if he proposes to disclose any of the information contained in an annex provided in accordance with paragraph (1) above, consult the person who provided the information if it is practicable to do so.

26 Third party appeals

(1)   An application under section 47 asking the Director to withdraw or vary a decision shall be made within one month of the publication of that decision and shall state the applicant's reasons for believing that he has a sufficient interest in that decision.

(2)   If the Director proposes to grant the application, he shall consult the person to whom notice of the decision referred to in paragraph (1) above was given.

(3)   If the Director grants the application, he shall give notice of his decision to the applicant, and to the person to whom notice of the decision referred to in paragraph (1) above was given, and shall publish his decision.

27 Interpretation

(1)   In these rules:—
   (a)   a reference to 'the applicant' is to be construed as being a reference to the applicant or to his duly authorised representative if written proof of the representative's authority to act on the applicant's behalf is included in the application;
   (b)   information is confidential if it is—
      (i)   commercial information the disclosure of which would, or might, significantly harm the legitimate business interests of the undertaking to which it relates; or
      (ii)   information relating to the private affairs of an individual the disclosure of which would, or might, significantly harm his interests;
   (c)   where the Director, if he proposes to take action, is required to consult a person, he shall—
      (i)   give written notice to the person in question, stating the action he proposes and his reasons for it; and
      (ii)   inform that person that any written representations made to the Director within the period specified in the notice will be considered;
   (d)   where the Director, if he proposes to take action—
      (i)   is required to consult the public; or
      (ii)   proposes to consult the public in exercise of his discretion to do so,
   he shall publish his proposal and consult such third party, within the meaning of paragraph 12(2) of Schedule 9, as appears to him likely to be interested;

    (e)   a reference to 'the Director' is to be construed as being a reference to the Director General of Fair Trading or to any regulator;

    (f)   'Form N' means the information, including any document, required to be provided by such form as is from time to time issued by the Director General of Fair Trading;

    (g)   'the Land Agreements Order' means the Land Agreements (Competition Act 1998) (Disapplication) Order 1999 (SI 1999 No [ ]);

    (h)   'an officer' means an investigating officer within the meaning of section 27(1) or a named officer of the Director authorised by a warrant under section 28;

    (i)   where the Director is required to publish a decision, a proposal or any other information, he shall do so by means of entry on the register maintained by the Director General of Fair Trading under rule 7 above;

    (j)   'regulator' means any person mentioned in sub-paragraphs (a) to (g) of paragraph 1 of Schedule 10;

    (k)   'the Vertical Agreements Order' means the Vertical Agreements (Competition Act 1998) (Disapplication) Order [1999] (SI [1999] No [ ]); and

    (l)   'working day' means any day which is not Saturday, Sunday, an official holiday on which the Office of Fair Trading is closed, or any other day on which that office is closed.

(2)   References in these rules to 'the Act' are to the Competition Act 1998 and references to numbered parts, sections, schedules or paragraphs are, unless the contrary intention appears, to the parts, sections, schedules or paragraphs so numbered in the Act.

N

[DRAFT] FORM FOR NOTIFICATIONS FOR GUIDANCE OR DECISION UNDER CHAPTERS I OR II OF THE COMPETITION ACT 1998

PART 1: NOTES

1.1   Although this document is described as 'a Form', it is essentially a check-list of information which must be supplied to the Director General of Fair Trading to enable him to determine a notification. Before completing the Form, reference should be made to the Procedural Rules of the Director General of Fair Trading.

1.2   The information must be correct and complete for the notification to be effective.

1.3   The Form must be supplied in original version plus two copies, together with either an original or a certified copy, plus two further copies, of any relevant agreement and Annexes.

1.4   All notifications for guidance or a decision under Chapter I or Chapter II of the Act should be sent to the Director General of Fair Trading. He will place details of all notifications for decision (although not for guidance) on the public register maintained by him at the Office of Fair Trading and on the Office's Internet website. Details of the notification for decision may subsequently be published in suitable trade and/or national press, where it is considered appropriate to do so.

1.5   The Act is enforced by the Director General of Fair Trading and, in relation to the regulated utility sectors shown in question 3.5 below, concurrently with the sector regulators; if any positive answer is given to that question, provide one further copy of the Form and attachments for each relevant regulator who may have concurrent jurisdiction. A copy of the Form (together with its Annexes and copies of agreements) should also be sent to the relevant regulator(s), if the agreement or conduct being notified may fall within their sector(s). In general, the relevant regulator will deal with the notification. If the Director General considers that a regulator has, or may have, concurrent jurisdiction in relation to an agreement or conduct in respect of which a notification has been submitted, he will send a copy of the Form N to the regulator(s) and inform the notifying party that he has done so.

1.6 Indicate clearly to which section of the Form any additional pages relate. The notification **must** *include the form of receipt at Part 3.* **Information which is regarded by the undertaking or undertakings as confidential should be clearly identified as such and placed in a separate identified annex, explaining why the information should be regarded as confidential.** *Notifications may also be made on disk or using other electronic format: please telephone the enquiry point at the Office of Fair Trading on 0171 211 xxxx before using this facility.*

1.7 **The Director General must be informed of any changes which occur after notification has been made and which may affect any information given in this Form.**

COMPLAINTS

1.8   Complaints may be sent either to the Director General of Fair Trading or direct to the relevant regulator. There is no form to complete to make a complaint; further information on making complaints is contained in the guideline **The Competition Act 1998: the Major Provisions.**

PART 2: INFORMATION TO BE PROVIDED BY THE UNDERTAKING NOTIFYING THE AGREEMENT OR CONDUCT

Number sections as below. In some cases, it may be possible to dispense with the requirement to provide information in all categories. This should be discussed with officials before making the notification. **Information which is regarded by the undertaking(s) as confidential should be clearly identified as such and placed in a separate identified annex.**

1. THE UNDERTAKING(S) SUBMITTING THE NOTIFICATION

1.1   The identity of the undertaking submitting the notification (full name and address, name of representative, telephone and fax numbers, and brief description of the undertaking or association of undertakings). For a partnership, sole trader or other unincorporated body trading under a business name, give the name(s) and address(es) of the proprietor(s) or partners. Please quote any reference which should be used;

1.2   if acting on behalf of another undertaking, state in what capacity, eg solicitor;

Where the Form is signed by a solicitor or other representative, proof of authority to act on behalf of the undertaking submitting the notification must be provided.

1.3   if the notification is submitted by or on behalf of more than one undertaking, give the details of the representative(s) as requested in 1.1. above. Indicate whether the representative has been appointed on a joint basis. If not, give the details in respect of representatives who have been authorised to act on behalf of each or either of the parties to the agreement, indicating who they represent;

1.4   the Standard Industrial Classification code for the relevant good(s) or service(s), if known. If the code is not known, describe the goods or services involved as fully and accurately as possible;

Schedules 5 and 6 to the Act require a party to an agreement or conduct who makes a notification for guidance or a decision in respect of that agreement or conduct to take all reasonable steps to notify all other parties to the agreement or conduct of whom he is aware that the notification has been made and whether it is for guidance or a decision. In exceptional cases, it may not be practicable to inform all non-notifying parties to the notified agreement or conduct that it has been notified, if, for example, an agreement is concluded with a large number of undertakings. The notification to such other undertakings must be made (a) in writing; and (b) within seven working days of the notifying undertaking receiving the Director General's acknowledgment of receipt.

1.5   the full names, addresses (by registered office, where appropriate, and principal place of business, if different), telephone and fax numbers, nature of business, and brief description of any other parties to the agreement, decision or concerted practice ('the arrangement') or conduct being notified;

1.6   details of the steps to be taken to inform any other such parties that the notification has been made and indicate whether the remaining parties have received a copy of the notification with confidential information and business secrets deleted. State the reasons, if it is not practicable to inform other parties of the notification in accordance with the requirements outlined above.

2. PURPOSE OF THE NOTIFICATION

The Chapter I prohibition does not apply unless the arrangement has an 'appreciable effect' on competition, and notification will not normally be appropriate when that is not the case. Further information is given in the guideline **The Competition Act 1998: the Chapter I prohibition***. The concept of appreciability does not apply to the Chapter II prohibition.*

2.1   whether the notification is being made under Chapter I, Chapter II or both;

2.2   whether it is for guidance or a decision;

if for guidance as to whether the Chapter I prohibition has been infringed:	2.3	specify why it is considered that the Chapter I prohibition has been infringed and whether the arrangement qualifies (or in the case of an individual exemption, would qualify if notified) for an exemption (individual, UK block exemption, parallel, or under section 11 of the Act);

or

if for a decision as to whether the Chapter I prohibition has been infringed:	2.4	whether an individual exemption is requested, and, if so, the date from which it is required to have effect, if different from the date of notification, giving reasons;

2.5   if the notification is for an extension of an individual exemption, state the date of expiry of the existing exemption and the reason why an extension is sought. Enclose a copy of the decision letter granting the exemption;

2.6   whether the arrangement or conduct that is the subject of the notification is considered to benefit from any exclusion from the Chapter I or Chapter II prohibitions. Specify the exclusion: give reasons why you are unsure whether the arrangement or conduct is covered by the exclusion and why notification is considered appropriate;

3. JURISDICTION

*In general, when an arrangement is also caught by Article 85 of the EC Treaty, the Director General considers that the EC Commission is the more appropriate authority to whom notification should be made (see the guideline **The Competition Act 1998: the Chapter I prohibition**).*

3.1   why the arrangement is considered to be not caught by Article 85(1);

3.2   whether the arrangement or conduct is the subject of a notification to the European Commission. If so, it would assist consideration of the notification if three copies of the completed Form A/B and supporting documents, and one further copy if information has been given in response to question 3.5 below, were attached. It is unnecessary to repeat information given on Form A/B, but information specific to the UK market will be necessary (following the format in question 7.1) to the extent that it has not been given on Form A/B, and should be provided separately. Supply three copies of any 'comfort' letter received from the European Commission;

3.3   whether the arrangement or conduct is the subject of a notification to any other national competition authority;

3.4   if the arrangement relates to transport by rail, road, inland waterway or to services ancillary to transport and is the subject of a notification to the European Commission under Regulation 1017/68, it would similarly assist consideration of the notification if three copies of the completed Form II and any supporting documents and one further copy if information has been given in response to question 3.5 below were attached;

3.5   whether the arrangement or conduct being notified relates to any one or more of—

- (a)   commercial activities connected with telecommunications;
- (b)   the shipping, conveyance or supply of gas and activities ancillary thereto;
- (c)   commercial activities connected with the generation, transmission or supply of electricity;
- (d)   commercial activities connected with the supply of water or securing a supply of water or with the provision or securing of sewerage services;
- (e)   commercial activities connected with the generation, transmission or supply of electricity in Northern Ireland;
- (f)   the conveyance, storage or supply of gas in Northern Ireland;
- (g)   the supply of railway services.

Identify the sector regulator or regulators who may have concurrent jurisdiction with the Director General of Fair Trading to deal with the notification;

3.6   names and addresses, telephone and fax numbers, date, details and case references of any previous contacts with the Office of Fair Trading, a regulator, any other national competition authority, or the EC Commission, and of any proceedings in any national court in the European Community, relating to the arrangement or conduct being notified and of any relevant previous arrangements or conduct.

4. DETAILS OF THE ARRANGEMENT OR CONDUCT

4.1   a brief description of the arrangement or conduct being notified (nature, content, purpose, date(s) and duration);

4.2   if written, attach either an original or a certified copy, together with two further copies, of the most recent version of the text of the arrangement being notified (technical details contained in know-how agreements, for example, may be omitted but omissions should be indicated); if not written, provide a full description;

4.3   identify any provisions in the arrangement which may restrict the parties in their freedom to take independent commercial decisions or to act on those decisions;

4.4   if the notification relates to a standard contract, the number expected to be concluded.

5. CHAPTER I NOTIFICATIONS: INFORMATION ON THE PARTIES TO THE ARRANGEMENT AND THE GROUPS TO WHICH THEY BELONG

5.1   for each undertaking identified in 1.5 above, the name of a contact, together with his or her address, telephone and fax numbers, and position held in the undertaking;

5.2   the corporate groups to which each undertaking belongs and the product and/or services market(s) in which the groups are active (hereafter called 'the relevant product market'); include one copy of the most recent consolidated annual report and accounts (or equivalent for unincorporated bodies) for each undertaking;

5.3   for each of the parties to the arrangement, provide a list of all undertakings belonging to the same group which are active in the same relevant product market(s), and those active in markets neighbouring the relevant product markets—that is, those which are not regarded by the consumer as fully interchangeable or substitutable for products in the defined relevant product market, as defined in question 6.1 below.

6. THE RELEVANT PRODUCT AND GEOGRAPHIC MARKETS

A relevant product market comprises all those products and/or services regarded by the consumer of the product or service as interchangeable or substitutable by reason of their characteristics, prices or intended use. The following factors are among those normally considered when determining the relevant product market and should be taken into account, together with any others considered relevant—

—   *the degree of physical similarity between the products/services in question;*
—   *any differences in end-use to which the goods are or may be put;*
—   *differences in price between the products/services;*
—   *the cost of switching between two potentially competing products/services; and*
—   *established consumer preferences for one type or category of product/service.*

The relevant geographic market is the area in which the undertakings concerned are involved in the supply of products or services in which the conditions of competition are appreciably different from neighbouring areas. The following factors are among those normally considered when determining the relevant geographic market and should be taken into account, together with any others considered relevant—

   — *the nature and characteristics of the products or services concerned;*

   — *the existence of entry barriers or consumer preferences;*

   — *appreciable differences of the undertakings' market share or substantial price differences between neighbouring areas; and*

   — *transport costs.*

6.1 In the light of the relevant factors given above (which are not exhaustive), explain the definitions of the relevant product and geographic markets which should be considered, with full reasons, in particular stating the specific products or services directly or indirectly affected by the notification and other goods or services that may be viewed as substitutable, with reasons. If the relevant geographic market is considered to be an area smaller, or larger, than the whole of the United Kingdom, the boundaries considered applicable, with reasons. Give reasons for all assumptions or findings, and explain how the factors outlined above have been taken into account. Further details are in the guideline ***The Competition Act 1998: Market Definition***;

6.2 provide a copy of the most recent in-house long-term market studies assessing or analysing the relevant markets (including any commissioned by the undertakings from outside consultants), and give references of any external studies of the relevant product market, and, where possible, include a copy of any such studies.

7. THE POSITION OF THE UNDERTAKINGS IN THE RELEVANT PRODUCT MARKET

The information required under this section relates to both the relevant geographic market and the relevant product market, for the groups of the parties as a whole. Market shares may be calculated either on the basis of value or volume. Justification for the figures provided must be given by reference to the sales or turnover of each of the undertakings in question. The source or sources of information should be given, and, where possible, a copy of the document from which information has been taken.

7.1 for each of the previous three calendar or financial years, as available, give—

  (a) details of the market shares of each undertaking in the goods or services in the relevant product and geographic markets, as identified in 6.1 above, and, if different, in the UK, and in the European Community;

  (b) estimates of market shares in the relevant product and geographic markets for each of the five main competitors of each of the undertakings, giving the undertaking's name, address, telephone and fax number, and, where possible, a contact name;

  (c) identify the five main customers of each of the undertakings in the relevant product and geographic markets, giving the undertaking's name, address, telephone and fax number, and, where possible, a contact name;

  (d) details of the undertakings' interests in, and arrangements with, any other companies competing in the relevant product and geographic market, together with details of their market shares, if known.

8. MARKET ENTRY AND POTENTIAL COMPETITION IN THE RELEVANT PRODUCT AND GEOGRAPHIC MARKETS

8.1 For all relevant product and geographic markets—

  (a) describe the factors influencing entry into the relevant product market(s): that is, the barriers which exist to prevent undertakings not presently manufacturing goods within the relevant product market(s) from entering the market(s), taking account of, in particular but not exclusively, the extent to which—

— entry is regulated by the requirements of government authorisation or standard-setting, in any form, and any legal or regulatory controls on entry to the market(s);

— entry is influenced by the availability of raw materials;

— entry is influenced by the length of existing contracts between suppliers and customers;

— research and development and licensing patents, know-how and other rights are important;

(b) describe the factors influencing entry in geographic terms: that is, the barriers that exist to prevent undertakings already producing and/or marketing goods within the relevant product market(s) outside the relevant geographic market(s) from extending sales into the relevant geographic market(s), taking account of, in particular but not exclusively, the importance of—

— trade barriers imposed by law, such as tariffs, quotas etc;

— local geographical specifications or technical requirements;

— procurement policies;

— the existence of adequate and available local distribution and retailing facilities;

— transport costs;

— strong consumer preference for local brands or products;

(c) in respect of new entrants in both product and geographic terms, state whether any new undertakings have entered the product market(s) in geographic areas where the undertakings sell, during the last three years. Identify the undertakings concerned by name, address, telephone and fax numbers and, where possible, a contact name, with best estimates of market shares of each in the relevant product and geographic markets.

9. NEGATIVE CLEARANCE

9.1   state reasons for seeking 'negative clearance' (that is, that the Director General should conclude that the arrangement or conduct is not covered by either the Chapter I or the Chapter II prohibition). Indicate, for example, which provision or effects of the arrangement or conduct may breach the relevant prohibition, and state the reasons why it is considered that the arrangements do not have the object or effect of preventing, restricting or distorting competition within the UK to an appreciable extent, or why the undertaking does not have, or its behaviour does not abuse, a dominant position.

10. EXEMPTION

The criteria which are taken into account in considering notifications for exemption are set out in section 9 of the Act.

10.1   if exemption from the Chapter I prohibition is sought, explain how the arrangements contribute to improving production or distribution and/or promoting technical or economic progress, and how consumers will be allowed a fair share of those benefits. Explain how each restrictive provision in the arrangements is indispensable to these objectives, and how the arrangements do not eliminate competition in respect of a substantial part of the relevant product or geographic market concerned.

11. TRANSITIONAL PERIODS

11.1   if the arrangement is considered to benefit from any transitional periods during which the Chapter I prohibition does not apply, indicate the duration of the relevant transitional periods by reference to Schedule 13 to the Act.

12. OTHER INFORMATION:

12.1 state—

(a) whether this notification should be considered as urgent. If so, give reasons;

(b) details of trade publications in which advertisements seeking the views of third parties might be placed;

(c) any other information you consider may be helpful.

12.2 [fees payable ....]

> Under section 44 of the Act, it is an offence, punishable by a fine or imprisonment or both, to provide information which is false or misleading in a material particular if the undertaking or person providing it knows that it is false or misleading, or is reckless as to whether it is. If the undertaking is a body corporate, under section 72 of the Act its officers may be guilty of an offence

The notification must conclude with the following declaration which is to be signed by or on behalf of all the applicants or notifying undertakings. Unsigned notifications are invalid.

DECLARATION

The undersigned declare that all the information given above and in the .... pages annexed hereto is correct to the best of their knowledge and belief, and that all estimates are identified as such and are their best estimates of the underlying facts.

Place and date ....

Signatures ....

....

Status ....

....

.... name(s) in block capitals

PART 3: ACKNOWLEDGEMENT OF RECEIPT

This Form will be returned to the address inserted below if the top half is completed by the undertaking lodging it.

to be completed by the undertaking making the notification

To: .... (name and address of applicant)

            ....

            ....

            ....

Your notification dated ....
concerning...
under reference ....
involving the following undertakings:

1. ....

2. .... [and others]

to be completed by the Office of Fair Trading

was received on......................................

and registered under reference number

.... **Please quote this number in all correspondence**

In the event that this notification is not complete in a material respect, you will be informed within one month of its receipt. If you are not informed within that time that it is considered to be incomplete, it is deemed to be effective on the date of its receipt.

PART 4—TO BE COMPLETED BY THE UNDERTAKING MAKING THE NOTIFICATION

Public Register Entry: Decision cases only

Following receipt of a notification for a decision, the Director General will place the details on the public register maintained at:

The Office of Fair Trading
[Field House
Breams Buildings
London EC4A 1PR]

The Director General is required to seek comments from third parties on application for a decision; he may therefore publish a notice inviting comments on the notification. The public register entry and published notice will be made without further reference to the parties. You are therefore asked to provide the information which may be used for this purpose. It is important that the answers to these questions do not contain any business secrets or other confidential information.

1. state the names of the parties to the arrangement(s) or conduct notified, as in questions 1.1 and 1.5 above;
2. give a short summary (no more than 250 words) of the nature and objectives of the arrangement(s);
3. the Standard Industrial Classification code for the relevant good(s) or service(s), if known. If the code is not known, describe the goods or services involved as fully and accurately as possible.

Appendix 5

Draft Vertical Agreements (Competition Act 1998) (Exclusion) Order

Draft Land Agreements (Competition Act 1998) (Exclusion) Order

[Draft] Vertical Agreements (Competition Act 1998) (Exclusion) Order [1999]

NOTES
Authority: Competition Act 1998, ss 50, 71.

1.—(1)   This Order may be cited as the Vertical Agreements (Competition Act 1998) (Exclusion) Order [1999] and shall come into force on [   ].

(2) In this Order—

'rules' mean rules made by the Director under section 51 of the Competition Act 1998

'vertical agreement' means an agreement—

(a)   between two or more undertakings, each operating at a different stage of the economic process for the purposes of that agreement; and

(b)   in respect of the supply or purchase, or both, of goods for resale or processing or in respect of the marketing of services.

2   The Chapter I prohibition shall not apply to an agreement to the extent that it is a vertical agreement.

3   Article 2 shall not apply where—

(a)   the vertical agreement, directly or indirectly, in isolation or in combination with other factors under the control of the parties including the exercise of industrial property rights, has the object or effect of—

(i)   fixing resale prices or minimum resale prices;

(ii)   fixing maximum resale prices or recommended resale prices which have the same effect as fixed resale prices or fixed minimum resale prices.

(b)   the vertical agreement takes effect between the same parties and is to the like object or effect to an obligation or restriction contained in an agreement which has been the subject of a direction under Article 4 and is made after the date of the direction in question.

4.—(1)   Article 2 shall not apply to a particular agreement if the Director gives a direction to that effect.

(2)   If the Director is considering whether to give a direction, he may by notice in writing require any party to the vertical agreement in question to give him such information in connection with the agreement as he may require.

(3)   The Director may only give a direction if—

(a)   at the end of such period as may be specified in the rules a person has failed, without reasonable excuse, to comply with a requirement imposed under paragraph (2); or

(b)   he considers that the vertical agreement will infringe the Chapter I prohibition but for the application of Article 2 and that he is not likely to grant it an unconditional individual exemption;

(4)   For the purposes of paragraph (3)(b) above an individual exemption is unconditional if no conditions or obligations are imposed in respect of it under section 4(3)(a) of the Act.

(5)   A direction under this Article—

(a)   must be in writing;

(b)   may be made so as to have effect from a date specified in the direction (which may not be earlier than the date on which it is given).

[Draft] Land Agreements (Competition Act 1998) (Exclusion) Order 1999

Authority: Competition Act 1998, ss 50, 71.

1—(1)   This Order may be cited as the Land Agreements (Competition Act 1998) (Exclusion) Order 1999 and shall come into force on [   ].

(2)   In this Order—

'land agreement' means an agreement between undertakings which creates, alters, transfers or terminates, an interest in land, or an agreement to enter into such an agreement, together with any obligation and restriction which in accordance with Article 3 is to be treated as part of the agreement;

'relevant land' means the land in respect of which a land agreement creates, alters, transfers or terminates an interest, or in respect of which it constitutes an agreement to do so; and 'other relevant land' means other land in which a party to a land agreement has an interest;

'rules' mean rules made by the Director under section 51 of the Competition Act 1998.

2   The Chapter I prohibition shall not apply to an agreement to the extent that it is a land agreement.

3—(1)   An obligation is to be treated as part of a land agreement if—

(a)   it is accepted by a party to the agreement in his capacity as holder of an interest in the relevant land and is for the benefit of another party to the agreement in his capacity as holder of an interest in that land; or

(b)   it relates to the imposition in respect of other relevant land of restrictions of a kind described in (a) above and which correspond to those accepted by a party to the land agreement in his capacity as holder of an interest in the relevant land;

(2)   A restriction is to be treated as part of a land agreement if it restricts the activity that may be carried out on the relevant land or other relevant land; and

(a)   it is accepted by a party to the agreement in his capacity as holder of an interest in the relevant land and is for the benefit of another party to the agreement in his capacity as holder of an interest in that land; or

(b)   it corresponds to restrictions imposed, or to be imposed, on another person in his capacity as holder of an interest in other relevant land.

(3)   An obligation or restriction is not to be treated as part of a land agreement if it takes effect between two or more undertakings [which are parties to the agreement], each operating at a different stage of the economic process for the purposes of that agreement, and is in respect of the supply or purchase, or both, of goods for resale or processing or in respect of the marketing of services.

(4)   A restriction or obligation is not to be treated as part of a land agreement if it takes effect between the same parties and is to the like object or effect to an obligation or restriction contained in an agreement which has been the subject of a direction under article 4 and is contained in an agreement made after the date of the direction in question.

4—(1)   Article 2 does not apply to an agreement if the Director gives a direction to that effect.

(2)   If the Director is considering whether to give a direction, he may by notice in writing require any party to the land agreement in question to give him such information in connection with the agreement as he may require.

(3)   The Director may only give a direction if—
    (a)   at the end of such period as may be specified in the rules a person has failed, without reasonable excuse, to comply with a requirement imposed under paragraph (2); or
    (b)   he considers that the land agreement will infringe the Chapter I prohibition but for the application of article 2 and that he is not likely to grant it an unconditional individual exemption;

(4)   For the purposes of paragraph (3)(b) above an individual exemption is unconditional if no conditions or obligations are imposed in respect of it under section 4(3)(a) of the Act.

(5)   A direction under this Article—
    (a)   must be in writing;
    (b)   may be made so as to have effect from a date specified in the direction (which may not be earlier than the date on which it is given).

Appendix 6

Structure charts

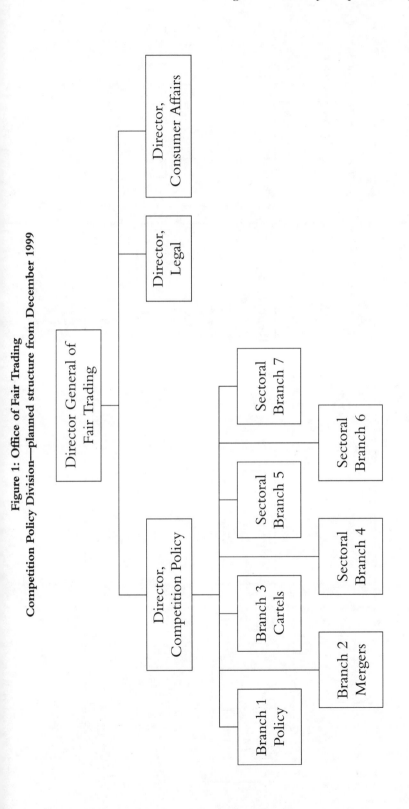

Figure 1: Office of Fair Trading
Competition Policy Division—planned structure from December 1999

Figure 1: Structure of Competition Policy Division

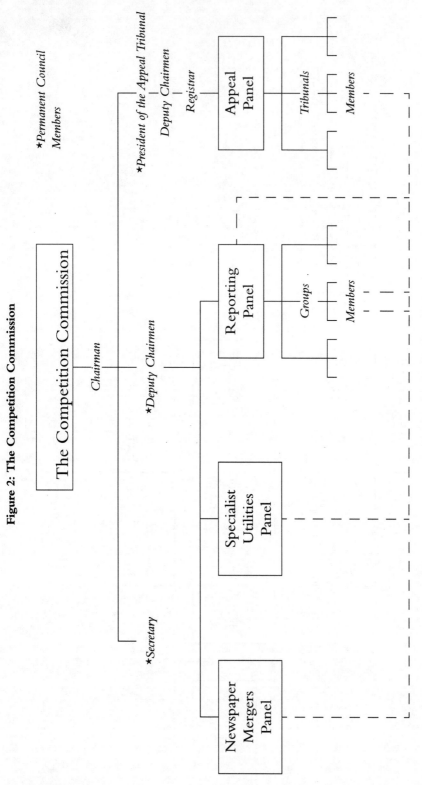

Figure 2: The Competition Commission

Appendix 7

Table of penalties for individuals

Provisions involving liability and penalties for individuals

OFFENCE	PENALTY
Section 42(1) (Failure to comply with a requirement under ss 26, 27 or 28)	Section 42(6) and (7)★
Section 42(5) (Intentional obstruction of an officer acting under s 27)	Section 42(6) and (7)★
Section 43(1) (Destruction etc of documents required to be produced)	Section 43(2)★
Section 44(1) (Knowing or reckless provision to the authorities of false information)	Section 44(3)★
Section 44(2) (Knowing or reckless provision of false information to another person for provision to the authorities)	Section 44(3)★
Section 55(8) (Disclosure in breach of obligation of confidentiality)	Section 55(8)★
Section 65(1) (Obstruction of EC investigations under warrant)	Section 65(2)★
Section 67(3) (Failure to comply with Fair Trading Act investigations)	Section 67(3)
Section 34(1) (Failure to comply with Directions of the DGFT)	Section 34(2) (An award of costs against the responsible officer of the company)
Sch 8, para 9(2) (Failure to give evidence or documents to appeal tribunal)	Sch 8, para 9(2)
Section 72—See generally on the position of officers	

Note
★   includes possibility of imprisonment.

Appendix 8

Table of exclusions from the Chapter I and Chapter II prohibitions

Table of exclusions from the Chapter I and Chapter II prohibitions

Relevant Provision	Exclusion	Exclusion from Chapter I?	Exclusion from Chapter II?
Schedule 1, Pt I, paras 1 and 2	UK mergers	Yes	Yes
Schedule 1, Pt I, para 3	UK newspaper mergers	Yes	Yes
Schedule 1, Pt II	EC mergers	Yes	Yes
Schedule 2, Pt I	Investment business	Yes	[No][1]
Schedule 2, Pt II	Supervision of auditors	Yes	No
Schedule 2, Pt III	Broadcasting: news provision and Networking Arrangements	Yes	No
Schedule 2, Pt IV	Environmental exemption schemes	Yes	No
Schedule 3, para 1	Planning obligations	Yes	No
Schedule 3, para 2	RTPA 1976, s 21(2)	Yes	No
Schedule 3, para 3	EEA regulated markets	Yes	[No][1]
Schedule 3, para 4	Services of general economic interest	Yes	Yes
Schedule 3, para 5	Compliance with legal requirements	Yes	Yes
Schedule 3, para 6	Avoidance of conflict with international obligations	Yes	Yes
Schedule 3, para 7	Public policy	Yes	Yes
Schedule 3, para 8	Coal and steel	Yes	Yes
Schedule 3, para 9	Agricultural products	Yes	No
Schedule 4, Pts I and II	Professional rules	Yes	No
Section 50	Vertical agreements	[Yes][2]	No
Section 50	Land agreements	[Yes][2]	No

NOTES
[1] To be extended to Chapter II by future legislation.
[2] Draft Exclusion Orders circulated for consultation.

Appendix 9

Glossary of terms

Glossary of terms

Term	Meaning
Agreement	Any agreement, whether legally enforceable or not and whether reduced to writing or not, including a so-called 'gentleman's agreement'.
Appeal tribunal	The appeal function of the Competition Commission; headed by a legally qualified and experienced President with a number of panel chairmen (in effect deputy presidents). It is envisaged that tribunals will sit in panels of three, with the chairmen also being suitably legally qualified. The tribunals will hear appeals from decisions by the DGFT and utility regulators and will have the power to review decisions on their merits and substitute their own decision for the contested one. Appeal from the tribunals lies to the Court of Appeal on a point of law or to review the amount of any penalty, and then to the House of Lords. It is envisaged that the tribunals will be able to refer questions to the European Court of Justice under the EC Treaty, Art 234.
Appreciability	Only agreements and conduct which *appreciably* restrict competition are caught by the prohibitions. Assessment of appreciability, or appreciable effect, involves an analysis of the relevant market and of competition within it. The doctrine stems from the jurisprudence of the European Court starting with the case of *Völk v Vervaecke* in 1969.
Block exemption	An exemption granted to a category or 'block' of agreements pursuant to the EC Treaty, Art 81(3) or s 6 of the 1998 Act. Agreements complying with the terms of a block exemption do not need to be individually notified to the authorities. Agreements benefitting from block exemptions under EC law are automatically exempted under UK competition law (cf 'parallel exemptions').
CFI	The Court of First Instance of the European Communities, based in Luxembourg. Established so as to enable the Court of Justice to deal with an ever-increasing workload and to provide a forum where issues of fact and evidence can be properly assessed. The CFI hears appeals, inter alia, from competition decisions of the European Commission. Appeal on points of law lies to the ECJ.
Chapter I prohibition	The prohibition on agreements, concerted practices and decisions of associations of undertakings that restrict competition, similar to the EC Treaty, Art 81.
Chapter II prohibition	The prohibition on conduct that is an abuse of a dominant position by one or more undertakings, similar to the EC Treaty, Art 82.

Community dimension	The jurisdictional test in the European Merger Control Regulation (ECMR) on the basis of which the European Commission acquires the exclusive right to vet concentrations. The test is based on a combination of turnover thresholds of the undertakings concerned in the concentration and, unlike UK merger control, takes no account of assets or market share.
Competition	What the Act is all about—the opposite of collusion, conspiracy or restrictive understanding where undertakings operate independently to maximise their performance, bringing benefits to consumers in terms of lower prices and wider choice. No definition of competition appears in the new legislation.
Competition Commission	The successor body to the Monopolies and Mergers Commission which is established by the 1998 Act. It comprises a 'reporting function' (in effect the old MMC) and an 'appeal function'. The appeal function is described under 'Appeal tribunal' above. The two parts of the Competition Commission will share common facilities and research staff.
Complex monopoly	The situation defined in the Fair Trading Act 1973 by which 25% or more of a given 'market' is held by two or more persons who, without necessarily colluding, conduct their affairs so as to restrict or distort competition. This enables the UK authorities to investigate competition issues affecting an industrial sector where no single company has excessive market power. A complex monopoly finding has no pejorative meaning, it merely enables an investigation by the Competition Commission as to possible adverse effects to take place.
Concentration	The EC law term for mergers and takeovers contained in the ECMR. The term encompasses any structure by which undertakings which were previously independent come under common control or acquire control of each other. The UK definition 'merger situation' is broader.
Concerted practice	Any co-ordination of conduct by unconnected undertakings that replaces or distorts normal competitive activity; sometimes described as an agreement whose existence cannot be proved and similar to an 'arrangement' under the Restrictive Trade Practices Act 1976 ('mutual arousal of expectations as to future conduct').
Dawn raids	The term used to describe on-the-spot investigations by the European Commission, although these rarely commence at such an early hour. It may come to apply to investigations under ss 26 or 27 of the 1998 Act.
Decision by an association of undertakings	A collective act by a group of undertakings (usually in the form of a trade association) liable to be controlled by the Chapter I prohibition; this may be contractually binding or be in the form of a recommendation that members of the group observe voluntarily.

DGFT

The Director General of Fair Trading is the individual charged with applying and enforcing concurrently with regulators most parts of the 1998 Act and in particular the Chapter I and II prohibitions and the rights of investigation and inspection. The DGFT may take decisions, impose penalties and grant exemptions. He is head of the Office of Fair Trading (OFT). He also retains powers in relation to monopolies and mergers under the Fair Trading Act 1973 with extended powers of investigation.

Dominant position

The ability to act independently of competitors, customers or suppliers; often equated with a market share of 40% or more, but lower shares and other factors are equally indicative. A dominant position can be held by one undertaking or jointly by several undertakings where there are close economic or legal links between them.

DTI

The Department of Trade and Industry. Its Competition Policy Division advises the Secretary of State on mergers, monopolies, relations with the EC authorities and policy generally.

European Commission

The administrative arm of the European Union and the guardian of the Treaties. Its correct title is the Commission of the European Communities. 20 Commissioners preside over numerous Directorates General, the relevant DG for competition being DGIV.

ECJ

The Court of Justice of the European Communities, established in Luxembourg. Its role in competition cases is to hear appeals on points of law from the CFI and to give judgments under the EC Treaty, Art 234 on references from national courts and tribunals, including, it is believed, the UK Competition Commission appeal tribunals.

Effect on trade between Member States

The EC law requirement contained in Arts 81 and 82 which acts as a jurisdictional limit to the application of those Articles. Any actual or potential effect is sufficient to bring the Articles in to play and there is no need for the effect to be qualitatively good or bad. It must, however, be 'appreciable'.

Effect on trade in the UK

A criterion in both the Chapter I and II prohibitions, but not of great significance in either context. It is borrowed from the jurisdictional provision in Arts 81 and 82 which refer to effect on 'trade between member states'.

Exclusions

Agreements and conduct excluded from the scope of the Chapter I and II prohibitions by virtue of the 1998 Act, ss 3 and 19. Excluded agreements should be distinguished from exemptions.

Exemptions

A finding of non-applicability of the Chapter I prohibition to particular agreements (on an 'individual', 'block' or 'parallel' basis); to be distinguished from exclusions.

Guidance	An opinion issued by the DGFT or regulators under the 1998 Act, s 13 as to whether or not an agreement is likely to infringe the Chapter I prohibition or under s 23 as to whether conduct is likely to infringe Chapter II. Also in relation to the amount of penalties.
Implemented in the UK	The limit on geographical jurisdiction contained in the Chapter I prohibition, applying to agreements. It is a paraphrase of the European Court's judgement in *Wood Pulp* and is regarded by the UK authorities as negating the so-called 'effects doctrine' espoused by the European Commission and therefore preventing that doctrine from being applied in UK legislation.
Merger situation	The definition given in the Fair Trading Act 1973 as the basis for the merger control system operated by the UK. A broader definition than 'concentration' in an EC context.
OFT	The Office of Fair Trading, which under its head, the DGFT, plays the principal part in applying and enforcing the Chapter I and II prohibitions in conjunction with the regulators exercising concurrent powers. The OFT also examines and advises on merger control and has other consumer protection functions.
Parallel exemption	The exemption under UK competition law which is available to agreements that benefit from an exemption given (either individually or under a block exemption) by the European Commission. This applies even if the agreement in question does not affect trade between member states.
Regulator	The officials appointed to regulate the telecommunications, gas, electricity, water and railways sectors (and their Northern Irish equivalent for gas and electricity), listed in s 54. They are given concurrent powers with the DGFT to apply and enforce the 1998 Act.
Scale monopoly	The situation defined in the Fair Trading Act 1973 whereby 25% or more of a given 'market' is accounted for by a single person, giving rise to the possibility of a reference to the Competition Commission for investigation of any adverse effects.
Secretary of State	The government minister with overall responsibility for competition, being head of the Department of Trade and Industry (DTI). He or she has specific responsibilities under the Fair Trading Act 1973 for mergers and monopolies. The 1998 Act refers generally to the Secretary of State but this term can also mean the corresponding ministers in relation to regulated utilities and parts of the UK (eg Environment, Scotland and Northern Ireland).
Subsidiarity	The principle now set out in the EC Treaty, Art 5, under which, in relation to matters not exclusively within the European Community's competence, and unless the objective can be better achieved by the Community, member states will, whenever possible, take the requisite action themselves.

Supremacy of EC law	The principle under which EC law overrides any prior or subsequent inconsistent or conflicting national law. In the competition context, it prevents national courts and authorities from disregarding EC law or coming to conflicting decisions. The 1998 Act, s 60 is a partial recognition of this principle.
Trade association	A collection of undertakings bound by membership of a body of any legal form for purposes connected with their trade or business; often a focus for competition law issues because of the opportunity they provide for collective action and the fine line that must be drawn between legal and illegal activity.
Void	Restrictive provisions of agreements subject to the Chapter I prohibition are 'automatically void'. In this case, the normal contractual rules of severance govern whether the agreement as a whole survives. Void provisions can be validated retrospectively by exemption, and can cease to be void if, in the economic context, Chapter I ceases to apply.

Index